International Migration and Development in South Asia

In migration studies, the nexus between migration and development in the global South has been meticulously debated. However, a unanimous resolution to this debate has not been found due to the ever-changing nature of international migration. This book advances knowledge on the global debate on the migration–development relationship by documenting experiences in a number of countries in South Asia.

Drawing on the experiences of global South Asians, this book documents the impact of migration on the social, economic and political fields in the broader context of development. It also presents a regional experience by looking into the migration–development nexus in the context of South Asia, and analyses the role South Asian migrants and diaspora communities play in the South Asian society. Contributions from a variety of disciplinary backgrounds, including sociology, anthropology, political science, international relations and economics, document the development implications of South Asian migration. Broad in scope in terms of contents, timeline of migration and geographical coverage, the book presents empirically-based case studies involving India, Bangladesh, Sri Lanka, Pakistan and Nepal and their emigrants living and working in different parts of the world.

Going beyond reporting the impacts of migration on economic development by highlighting the implications of 'social development' on society, this book provides a fascinating contribution to the fields of Asian Development, Migration Studies and South Asian Studies.

Md Mizanur Rahman is Senior Research Fellow at the Institute of South Asian Studies, National University of Singapore. His recent co-edited books include *Diaspora Engagement and Development in South Asia* (2013).

Tan Tai Yong is Professor and Director of the Institute of South Asian Studies, National University of Singapore. He is the author and editor of numerous books, including *The Aftermath of Partition in South Asia* (Routledge, 2002).

Routledge contemporary South Asia series

1 **Pakistan**
Social and cultural transformations in a Muslim nation
Mohammad A. Qadeer

2 **Labor, Democratization and Development in India and Pakistan**
Christopher Candland

3 **China–India Relations**
Contemporary dynamics
Amardeep Athwal

4 **Madrasas in South Asia**
Teaching terror?
Jamal Malik

5 **Labor, Globalization and the State**
Workers, women and migrants confront neoliberalism
Edited by Debdas Banerjee and Michael Goldfield

6 **Indian Literature and Popular Cinema**
Recasting classics
Edited by Heidi R.M. Pauwels

7 **Islamist Militancy in Bangladesh**
A complex web
Ali Riaz

8 **Regionalism in South Asia**
Negotiating cooperation, institutional structures
Kishore C. Dash

9 **Federalism, Nationalism and Development**
India and the Punjab economy
Pritam Singh

10 **Human Development and Social Power**
Perspectives from South Asia
Ananya Mukherjee Reed

11 **The South Asian Diaspora**
Transnational networks and changing identities
Edited by Rajesh Rai and Peter Reeves

12 **Pakistan–Japan Relations**
Continuity and change in economic relations and security interests
Ahmad Rashid Malik

13 **Himalayan Frontiers of India**
Historical, geo-political and strategic perspectives
K. Warikoo

14 **India's Open-Economy Policy**
Globalism, rivalry, continuity
Jalal Alamgir

15 **The Separatist Conflict in Sri Lanka**
Terrorism, ethnicity, political economy
Asoka Bandarage

16 **India's Energy Security**
Edited by Ligia Noronha and Anant Sudarshan

17 **Globalization and the Middle Classes in India**
The social and cultural impact of neoliberal reforms
Ruchira Ganguly-Scrase and Timothy J. Scrase

18 **Water Policy Processes in India**
Discourses of power and resistance
Vandana Asthana

19 **Minority Governments in India**
The puzzle of elusive majorities
Csaba Nikolenyi

20 **The Maoist Insurgency in Nepal**
Revolution in the twenty-first century
Edited by Mahendra Lawoti and Anup K. Pahari

21 **Global Capital and Peripheral Labour**
The history and political economy of plantation workers in India
K. Ravi Raman

22 **Maoism in India**
Reincarnation of ultra-left wing extremism in the twenty-first century
Bidyut Chakrabarty and Rajat Kujur

23 **Economic and Human Development in Contemporary India**
Cronyism and fragility
Debdas Banerjee

24 **Culture and the Environment in the Himalaya**
Arjun Guneratne

25 **The Rise of Ethnic Politics in Nepal**
Democracy in the margins
Susan I. Hangen

26 **The Multiplex in India**
A cultural economy of urban leisure
Adrian Athique and Douglas Hill

27 **Tsunami Recovery in Sri Lanka**
Ethnic and regional dimensions
Dennis B. McGilvray and Michele R. Gamburd

28 **Development, Democracy and the State**
Critiquing the Kerala model of development
K. Ravi Raman

29 **Mohajir Militancy in Pakistan**
Violence and transformation in the Karachi conflict
Nichola Khan

30 **Nationbuilding, Gender and War Crimes in South Asia**
Bina D'Costa

31 **The State in India after Liberalization**
Interdisciplinary perspectives
Edited by Akhil Gupta and K. Sivaramakrishnan

32 **National Identities in Pakistan**
The 1971 war in contemporary Pakistani fiction
Cara Cilano

33 **Political Islam and Governance in Bangladesh**
Edited by Ali Riaz and C. Christine Fair

34 **Bengali Cinema**
'An Other Nation'
Sharmistha Gooptu

35 **NGOs in India**
The challenges of women's empowerment and accountability
Patrick Kilby

36 **The Labour Movement in the Global South**
Trade unions in Sri Lanka
S. Janaka Biyanwila

37 **Building Bangalore**
Architecture and urban transformation in India's Silicon Valley
John C. Stallmeyer

38 **Conflict and Peacebuilding in Sri Lanka**
Caught in the peace trap?
Edited by Jonathan Goodhand, Jonathan Spencer and Benedict Korf

39 **Microcredit and Women's Empowerment**
A case study of Bangladesh
Amunui Faraizi, Jim McAllister and Taskinur Rahman

40 **South Asia in the New World Order**
The role of regional cooperation
Shahid Javed Burki

41 **Explaining Pakistan's Foreign Policy**
Escaping India
Aparna Pande

42 **Development-induced Displacement, Rehabilitation and Resettlement in India**
Current issues and challenges
Edited by Sakarama Somayaji and Smrithi Talwar

43 **The Politics of Belonging in India**
Becoming Adivasi
Edited by Daniel J. Rycroft and Sangeeta Dasgupta

44 **Re-Orientalism and South Asian Identity Politics**
The oriental other within
Edited by Lisa Lau and Ana Cristina Mendes

45 **Islamic Revival in Nepal**
Religion and a new nation
Megan Adamson Sijapati

46 **Education and Inequality in India**
A classroom view
Manabi Majumdar and Jos Mooij

47 **The Culturalization of Caste in India**
Identity and inequality in a multicultural age
Balmurli Natrajan

48 **Corporate Social Responsibility in India**
Bidyut Chakrabarty

49 **Pakistan's Stability Paradox**
Domestic, regional and international dimensions
Edited by Ashutosh Misra and Michael E. Clarke

50 **Transforming Urban Water Supplies in India**
The role of reform and partnerships in globalization
Govind Gopakumar

51 **South Asian Security**
Twenty-first century discourses
Sagarika Dutt and Alok Bansal

52 **Non-discrimination and Equality in India**
Contesting boundaries of social justice
Vidhu Verma

53 **Being Middle-class in India**
A way of life
Henrike Donner

54 **Kashmir's Right to Secede**
A critical examination of contemporary theories of secession
Matthew J. Webb

55 **Bollywood Travels**
Culture, diaspora and border crossings in popular Hindi cinema
Rajinder Dudrah

56 **Nation, Territory, and Globalization in Pakistan**
Traversing the margins
Chad Haines

57 **The Politics of Ethnicity in Pakistan**
The Baloch, Sindhi and Mohajir ethnic movements
Farhan Hanif Siddiqi

58 **Nationalism and Ethnic Conflict**
Identities and mobilization after 1990
Edited by Mahendra Lawoti and Susan Hangen

59 **Islam and Higher Education**
Concepts, challenges and opportunities
Marodsilton Muborakshoeva

60 **Religious Freedom in India**
Sovereignty and (anti) conversion
Goldie Osuri

61 **Everyday Ethnicity in Sri Lanka**
Up-country Tamil identity politics
Daniel Bass

62 **Ritual and Recovery in Post-Conflict Sri Lanka**
Eloquent bodies
Jane Derges

63 **Bollywood and Globalisation**
The global power of popular Hindi cinema
Edited by David J. Schaefer and Kavita Karan

64 **Regional Economic Integration in South Asia**
Trapped in conflict?
Amita Batra

65 **Architecture and Nationalism in Sri Lanka**
The trouser under the cloth
Anoma Pieris

66 Civil Society and Democratization in India
Institutions, ideologies and interests
Sarbeswar Sahoo

67 Contemporary Pakistani Fiction in English
Idea, nation, state
Cara N. Cilano

68 Transitional Justice in South Asia
A study of Afghanistan and Nepal
Tazreena Sajjad

69 Displacement and Resettlement in India
The human cost of development
Hari Mohan Mathur

70 Water, Democracy and Neoliberalism in India
The power to reform
Vicky Walters

71 Capitalist Development in India's Informal Economy
Elisabetta Basile

72 Nation, Constitutionalism and Buddhism in Sri Lanka
Roshan de Silva Wijeyeratne

73 Counterinsurgency, Democracy, and the Politics of Identity in India
From warfare to welfare?
Mona Bhan

74 Enterprise Culture in Neoliberal India
Studies in youth, class, work and media
Edited by Nandini Gooptu

75 The Politics of Economic Restructuring in India
Economic governance and state spatial rescaling
Loraine Kennedy

76 The Other in South Asian Religion, Literature and Film
Perspectives on Otherism and Otherness
Edited by Diana Dimitrova

77 Being Bengali
At home and in the world
Edited by Mridula Nath Chakraborty

78 The Political Economy of Ethnic Conflict in Sri Lanka
Nikolaos Biziouras

79 Indian Arranged Marriages
A social psychological perspective
Tulika Jaiswal

80 Writing the City in British Asian Diasporas
Edited by Seán McLoughlin, William Gould, Ananya Jahanara Kabir and Emma Tomalin

81 Post-9/11 Espionage Fiction in the US and Pakistan
Spies and 'terrorists'
Cara Cilano

82 Left Radicalism in India
Bidyut Chakrabarty

83 'Nation-State' and Minority Rights in India
Comparative perspectives on Muslim and Sikh identities
Tanweer Fazal

84 Pakistan's Nuclear Policy
A minimum credible deterrence
Zafar Khan

85 Imagining Muslims in South Asia and the Diaspora
Secularism, religion, representations
Claire Chambers and Caroline Herbert

86 Indian Foreign Policy in Transition
Relations with South Asia
Arijit Mazumdar

87 Corporate Social Responsibility and Development in Pakistan
Nadeem Malik

88 Indian Capitalism in Development
Barbara Harriss-White and Judith Heyer

89 Bangladesh Cinema and National Identity
In search of the modern?
Zakir Hossain Raju

90 Suicide in Sri Lanka
The anthropology of an epidemic
Tom Widger

91 Epigraphy and Islamic Culture
Arabic and Persian inscriptions of Bengal and their historical and cultural implications
Mohammad Yusuf Siddiq

92 Reshaping City Governance
London, Mumbai, Kolkata, Hyderabad
Nirmala Rao

93 The Indian Partition in Literature and Films
History, politics, and aesthetics
Rini Bhattacharya Mehta and Debali Mookerjea-Leonard

94 Development, Poverty and Power in Pakistan
The impact of state and donor interventions on farmers
Syed Mohammad Ali

95 Ethnic Subnationalist Insurgencies in South Asia
Identities, interests and challenges to state authority
Jugdep S. Chima

96 International Migration and Development in South Asia
Edited by Md Mizanur Rahman and Tan Tai Yong

International Migration and Development in South Asia

Edited by Md Mizanur Rahman and Tan Tai Yong

Routledge
Taylor & Francis Group
LONDON AND NEW YORK

First published 2015 by Routledge

2 Park Square, Milton Park, Abingdon, Oxfordshire OX14 4RN
711 Third Avenue, New York, NY 10017

Routledge is an imprint of the Taylor & Francis Group, an informa business

First issued in paperback 2017

British Library Cataloguing in Publication Data
A catalogue record for this book is available from the British Library

Library of Congress Cataloging in Publication Data
International migration and development in South Asia / edited by
Tan Tai Yong, Md Mizanur Rahman.
pages cm. – (Routledge contemporary South Asia series)
Includes bibliographical references and index.
1. South Asia–Emigration and immigration. 2. South Asia–Economic conditions. I. Tan, Tai Yong. II. Rahman, Md. Mizanur.
JV8752.I57 2015
304.8'54–dc23 2014042836

ISBN: 978-0-415-72423-4 (hbk)
ISBN: 978-0-8153-6801-4 (pbk)

Typeset in Times New Roman
by Wearset Ltd, Boldon, Tyne and Wear

Contents

Figures

Tables

Contributors

Kopalapillai Amirthalingam is a Senior Lecturer attached to the Department of Economics, University of Colombo, Sri Lanka. He works both as a researcher and development consultant with a special interest in public finance, Sri Lankan economy and internally displaced persons (IDPs). He has several publications on taxation and IDP issues in Sri Lanka.

Sanjay Krishno Biswas is Lecturer at the Department of Anthropology, Shahjalal University of Science and Technology, Bangladesh. He has a deep interest in the study of anthropological theories and his area of specialisation includes corporate social responsibility and basic education in Bangladesh and the rural class system in Bangladesh.

Shahid Javed Burki is Visiting Senior Research Fellow at the Institute of South Asian Studies (ISAS), an autonomous research institute at the National University of Singapore. During a professional career spanning over half a century, Mr Burki has held a number of senior positions in Pakistan and at the World Bank. He was the Director of China Operations at the World Bank from 1987 to 1994 and the Vice President of Latin America and the Caribbean Region at the World Bank from 1994 to 1999. On leave of absence from the Bank he was Pakistan's Finance Minister, 1996–97. He is coauthor of *Sustaining Reform with a US-Pakistan Free Trade Agreement* (2006). His other publications include *Pakistan: Development Choices for the Future* (1986, Oxford University Press); *Pakistan: Continuing Search for Nationhood* (1991, Westview Press, Boulder, CO); *Pakistan: Fifty Years of Nationhood* (1999, Westview Press); and *Pakistan: A Historical Dictionary* (1999, Scarecrow Press, London).

Jaswinder Singh Brar is currently Professor of Economics at the Centre for Research in Economic Change, Punjabi University, Patiala. He has been teaching International Economics and Development Economics. His main areas of research include International Trade, Economics of Education, and Micro Development Studies. Dr Brar has authored eight books, published about 50 research papers and handled 11 research projects; nine PhD and six MPhil students completed their degrees under his supervision. He has participated in various national and international conferences in India and abroad.

Marta Bivand Erdal is Senior Researcher at the Peace Research Institute Oslo (PRIO) in Norway. Her research focuses on migrant transnationalism, including remittances and diaspora development engagements, in particular in South Asia. She also works on the implications of migration for identity and citizenship, both conceptually and in lived experience. Her doctoral work focused specifically on remittances in the Norway–Pakistan remittance corridor, exploring sender and receiver perspectives. She has published among other in the *Journal of Ethnic and Migration Studies*, *International Migration Review*, *Population, Space and Place* and *Asian and Pacific Migration Journal*.

Kazi Nurmohammad Hossainul Haque is Senior Research Associate, at the Institute of Governance Studies (IGS), BRAC University. He has an MA in Development Studies from the International Institute of Social Studies (ISS) of the Erasmus University Rotterdam and an MA in Public Policy from the Central European University. He has work experience in research, policy analysis and advocacy. Two of his recent publications are: The Political Economy of Land and Real Estate in Dhaka City, IGS Working Paper No. 03/2012, Dhaka: IGS (2012), and, 'The New Hungary Development Plan: Evaluation of Policy-level Horizontal Goals and Supporting Mechanisms, and the Roma Population of Hungary, Policy Research, Centre for Policy Studies (CPS), Budapest (co-authored) (2010).

Syed Minhaj ul Hassan is Professor of History at the Department of History, University of Peshawar, but is currently deputed as Scholar, Quaid-i-Azam Chair in Pakistan Studies at the Department of Government and International Studies, Hong Kong Baptist University, Hong Kong. He has studied at the University of Peshawar, Pakistan, and Eastern Washington University, Cheney, United States of America. He has been associated with teaching and research for around 25 years. He has to his credit around 27 research publications including a co-edited book titled, *Pakistan-Iran Relations in Historical Perspective*. He has also co-authored a book in Urdu on Pakistan Studies. He has contributed chapters in a number of books written on the history and politics of Pakistan and the Pak-India sub-continent. He has participated and presented papers in more than 33 national and international conferences around the world. He has also delivered special lectures at many universities and institutes on different topics.

Danesh Jayatilaka is a final year PhD student at the Department of Economics, University of Colombo. He is an Executive Committee Officer of the International Association for the Study of Forced Migration (IASFM), co-founder of the Centre for Migration Research and Development (CMRD), and has a number of publications on displacement and other forms of forced and irregular migration.

Mohammad Alamgir Kabir is Assistant Professor at the Department of Applied Statistics, Faculty of Economics and Administration, University of Malaya as well as at the Department of Statistics at Jahangirnagar University, Bangladesh.

Rajith W.D. Lakshman is a research officer at the Institute of Development Studies (IDS), University of Sussex. Previously he was a senior lecturer in Economics attached to the University of Colombo, Sri Lanka. Rajith received his PhD from the University of Melbourne. Though forced migration related topics (conflict, development and disaster induced displacement) had dominated his work, he has also focused on regular forms of migration primarily within the context of Sri Lanka.

Md Mizanur Rahman is Senior Research Fellow at the Institute of South Asian Studies (ISAS), National University of Singapore. He was a postdoctoral fellow at the Asia Research Institute, NUS in 2005–2006 and a research fellow at the Department of Sociology, NUS in 2007–2010. He has worked on a Ford Foundation project on non-traditional security in South Asia, and was a visiting scholar at the Department of Sociology, University of Western Ontario, Canada and the Graduate School of Policy Science, Ritsumeikan University, Kyoto, Japan. He has written a number of reports on international migration issues in Asia for international organisations such as the IOM and UNIFEM – East and Southeast Asia. His work has also appeared in leading migration journals such as *International Migration*, *Population, Space and Place*, *Journal of Ethnic and Migration Studies*, *Journal of International Migration and Integration* and *Asian Population Studies*.

Rakesh Ranjan is Research Scholar, at Centre for the Study of Social Systems, Jawaharlal Nehru University, Delhi. He is part of the editorial team of *Roots and Routes*, Newsletter of the Global Research Forum on Diaspora and Transnationalism (GRFDT), an international think tank based in New Delhi, India. Mr Ranjan has research interest in Diaspora, Entrepreneurship, International Migration, Labour and Development, Gender Studies, Media Studies, etc. In addition, he has worked and participated in various conferences on diaspora, labour and development.

Ajaya Kumar Sahoo is Assistant Professor at the Centre for the Study of Indian Diaspora, University of Hyderabad, India. His areas of research interests comprise international migration, South Asian diaspora, transnationalism, religion and ageing. Some of his recent publications include: *Indian Diaspora and Transnationalism*, co-edited with Michiel Baas and Thomas Faist (Rawat, 2012); *Transnational Migrations: the Indian Diaspora*, co-edited with William Safran and Brij V. Lal (Routledge, 2009); *Tracing an Indian Diaspora: Contexts, Memories, Representations*, co-edited with Parvati Raghuram, Brij Maharaj and Dave Sangha (Sage, 2008); and *Sociology of Diaspora: A Reader*, co-edited with Brij Maharaj (Rawat, 2007).

Thakur Subedi is Assistant Professor at Gyeongju University, South Korea. He holds a Master's degree in English, Rural Development and NGO Studies, and a PhD in Political Science and International Relations. His PhD research focused on 'brain drain' and Nepal's 'diaspora option'. He has worked on contemporary Nepali transnational migration, migrant workers, married immigrants and Nepali diaspora. His current research focuses on the economic activities of returned Nepali migrant workers from South Korea.

Vivek Thakur is Doctoral Scholar at the Centre for Police Administration in Panjab University, Chandigarh, India. He is working on the theme Crime and Non Resident Indians: A Study of NRI Police Stations in Punjab for his Doctoral dissertation. He hold a Master's degree and MPhil in Police Administration. His interests include police reforms, gender related crimes and crime and migrant transnationalism.

V.J. Varghese is Assistant Professor at the Department of History, University of Hyderabad. He was Assistant Professor at the Centre for South and Central Asian Studies, Central University of Punjab, Bathinda prior to this. His areas of interest include modern South Asian history, transnational migrations from South Asia, the making of modern subjectivities and regional modernities in South Asia. He has recently co-authored the book *Dreaming Mobility and Buying Vulnerability: Overseas Recruitment Practices and its Discontents in India* (Routledge, 2011). He is currently co-authoring the book *Rishtidari: Punjabi Transnational Networks*, with Kaveri Harriss for Routledge.

Constantino Xavier is a Fulbright-sponsored PhD candidate in South Asian Studies at the School of Advanced International Studies, Johns Hopkins University, in Washington, DC, where he is also a Special Guest at the Brookings Institution. He has an MA and MPhil in International Politics from Jawaharlal Nehru University, New Delhi, with a dissertation on India's diaspora policy. He previously taught Comparative Politics at the New University of Lisbon, Portugal. His research publications on Indian foreign policy and its diaspora have appeared in *Relações Internacionais* (Lisbon), *Africa Quarterly* and *Seminar* (New Delhi), and *Nationalism and Ethnic Politics* (United Kingdom).

Tan Tai Yong is the Director of the Institute of South Asian Studies (ISAS) and has been an integral part of the institute since its inception. Professor Tan, a historian, is concurrently Vice Provost (Student Life) at the National University of Singapore. Prior to this, he was Dean of the Faculty of Arts and Social Sciences at the National University of Singapore from 2004 to 2009. He has written extensively on South Asian history as well as on Southeast Asia and Singapore. His recent books include *Singapore – A 700-Year History* (2009); *Creating 'Greater Malaysia': Decolonization and the Politics of Merger* (2008); *Partition and Post-Colonial South Asia: A Reader* (co-edited, 2007); *The Garrison State* (2005); *The Aftermath of Partition in South Asia* (co-authored, 2000); and *The Transformation of Southeast Asia: International Perspectives on De-colonization* (co-edited, 2003).

Preface and acknowledgements

With the trend-setting South Asian Diaspora Convention in July 2011, the Institute of South Asian Studies (ISAS) has spearheaded the effort to understand what role South Asian contemporary migrants and settler communities play in South Asian development. This initiative, indeed, reflects the global trend in international migration and development research. The chapters in this book present a South Asian experience, and are contributed by a group of scholars hailing from different disciplinary backgrounds, such as sociology, anthropology, political science, international relations and economics. The contributors of this volume set out to demonstrate the diverse approaches to the study of the linkages between migration and development at a time when the interest in the development potential of migration is at the top and the number of those 'on the move' is increasing at an almost immeasurable rate. By bringing together a range of disciplines, research methods and subject foci, this volume promises to highlight the way in which migration impacts on every facet of life and thus on a multiplicity of disciplines. The interdisciplinary nature of the contributions have, in essence, strengthened the basic theme of this book, which is to promote the understanding of the impact that international migration has on the broader development of South Asia.

We would not have been able to publish this book in a timely manner without the cooperation of a number of people. First of all, we owe many debts to our contributors, who completed chapters of this book. We appreciate these contributors for recognising the importance of the theme of this book and completing excellent chapters in a timely manner. We would like to express our gratitude to Dorothea Schaefter, Jillian Morrison and Rebecca Lawrence from Routledge, the Taylor and Francis Group, for their encouragement and support in the publication process. They were very efficient in communicating with us and processing the manuscript on time. The book proposal was reviewed by two anonymous reviewers. The reviewers' comments and suggestions were of great help in planning how to structure the book and deciding what topics should be included. We would like to express our sincere gratitude to these anonymous reviewers.

Finally, we would like to thank the ISAS's chairman, Ambassador Gopinath Pillai and our colleagues from the institution, Iftekhar Ahmed Chowdhury, Rahul Mukherji, Rajesh Rai, Sukh Deo Muni, Riaz Hassan, S. Narayan,

Amitendu Palit, Ronojoy Sen and Sinderpal Singh for their support and cooperation. A special word of thanks goes to Mr Johnson Paul, senior associate director of ISAS, for his cooperation in the publication process. The administrative and support team members of ISAS, Felicia Ho, Kirby Khoo, Muhammad Yusuf, Kamarunnisa, Sithara Doriasamy, Samuel Neo and Florence Ho, and the administrative team of department of History such as Adeline Loi, Eileen Shen Yanling, Foo Yoke Ling Rona and Lelaytha Chattukutty, also deserve our sincere gratitude for their support.

Yvette Koh assisted us in language editing and formatting the manuscript. Zaara Zain coordinated all the contributors in the publication process. We thank Yvette Koh and Zaara Zain for their sincere support.

All chapters in this book are new research except one chapter (Chapter 7). This chapter, 'Bangladeshi migration to Southern Europe: implications on migrant families' first appeared in *Asia Europe Journal*, 10(4): 251–265. We would like to thank AEJ for granting permission to publish the revised version in this volume.

Md Mizanur Rahman
Tan Tai Yong

Abbreviations

AAPI	American Association of Physicians from India
ABCD workers	Ayahs, bearers, cooks, drivers
AL	Awami League
APSRTC	Andhra Pradesh State Road Transportation Corporation
BDO	Block development officer
BFSI	Banks and financial services institutions
BHRS	Bangladesh Household Remittance Survey
BIA	Bandaranaike International Airport
BISP	Benazir Income Support Programme
BJP	Bharatiya Janata Party
BMET	Bureau of Manpower, Employment and Training
BPL	Below poverty line
BRICS	Brazil, Russia, India, China and South Africa
CME	Compulsory counting medical education
CNS	Centre for Nepal Studies
CNSUK	Centre for Nepal Studies UK
DIPP	Department of Industrial Policy and Promotion
DSP	Deputy superintendent of police
DV	Diversity visa
ECR	Emigration check required
EPS	Employment permit system
FCNRA	Foreign currency non-resident account
FCRA	Foreign Contribution (Regulation) Act
FDA	Federal Democratic Alliance
FDI	Foreign direct investment
FIPB	Foreign Investment Promotion Board
FIR	First Information Report
GATS	General Agreement on Trade in Services
GCC	Gulf Cooperation Council
GDP	Gross domestic product
GFMD	Global Forums on Migration and Development
GNI	Gross national income
GOPIO	Global Organisation of People of Indian Origin

HLCID	High Level Committee on the Indian Diaspora
IDB	India Development Bonds
IDP	Internally displaced persons
IMD	India Millennium Deposit
IMF	International Monetary Fund
IOM	International Organisation for Migration
ISAS	Institute of South Asian Studies
IT	Information technology
LCM	Less concentration of migrants
LPG	Liquefied petroleum gas
MCM	More concentration of migrants
MLA	Member of legislative assembly
MOIA	Ministry of Overseas Indian Affairs
MoU	Memorandum of understanding
MP	Member of Parliament
MPCE	Monthly per capita expenditure
MSM	men who have sex with men
NCAER	National Council of Applied Economic Research
NCR	National capital region
NDVP	Nepalese Diaspora Volunteering Programme
NGO	Non-governmental organisation
NORAD	Norwegian Agency for Development Cooperation
NRE	Non-resident (external) rupee account
NRI	Non-resident Indians
NRN	Non-resident Nepali
NRNA	Non Resident Nepali Association
NSC	Nepal Study Centre
NWC	National Workers Congress
OCAC	Overseas Chinese Affairs Committee
OCAOSC	Overseas Chinese Affairs Office of the State Council
OCI	Overseas Citizenship of India
ODA	Official development assistance
OECD	Organization for Economic Co-operation and Development
OMCAP	Overseas Manpower Company of Andhra Pradesh
PBBY	Pravasi Bharatiya Bima Yojana
PBD	Pravasi Bharatiya Divas
PIO	People of Indian origin
POE	Protector of emigrants
PPP	Public private partnership
PPP	Purchasing power parity
PPS	Probability proportional to size
PRIO	Peace Research Institute in Oslo
RBI	Reserve Bank of India
RDF	Rural Development Foundation
RIB	Resurgent India Bond

RO	Reverse osmosis
SADC	South Asian Diaspora Convention
SC	Scheduled castes
SLBFE	Sri Lanka Bureau of Foreign Employment
SONSIK	Society of Nepalese Students in Korea
TIP	Trafficking in persons
UAE	United Arab Emirates
UGC	University Grants Commission
UNDP	United Nations Development Programme
UNFPA	United Nations Population Fund
UNICEF	United Nations Children's Fund
UP	Union *Parishad*
USINPAC	United States India Political Action Committee
UZP	*Upazila Parishad*
YFN	Youth for Nepal

1 International migration and development in South Asia

An introduction

Md Mizanur Rahman and Tan Tai Yong

In migration studies, one of the more thoroughly investigated research questions raised since the 1950s is whether international migration brings about development in the emigrant countries in the global South. The nexus between migration and development has been meticulously debated over time, producing substantial literature on the topic (for a review, see Papademetriou and Martin 1991; Hammar *et al.* 1997; Sørensen *et al.* 2002; Spaan *et al.* 2005; Omelaniuk 2012; Faist 2000). However, researchers are still grappling to find a unanimous position to this question. This is because migration is a dynamic field, with the patterns, composition, size and nature of international migration constantly changing. This transforms migration into a more difficult research terrain that demands new conceptual approaches and research methods to explicate its complexities in their entirety. What is interesting about the study of this nexus is that with the changes in international migration, new theoretical approaches and research methodologies have also been applied to explain the nature of the relationship between migration and development. The study of this nexus therefore remains a field of continuous academic exercise. It is precisely this dynamic attribute that provides the much-needed rationale for this volume.

People tend to migrate to relatively developed economies, where they generally acquire an economic ascendance that they would be unable to achieve in their home countries. This advantage of access to comparatively developed economies allows the influence of migrants to reach deeper into their origin societies in different ways, affecting the social, economic and political dimensions of the society. Drawing on the experiences of global South Asians, this volume primarily documents the impact of migration on the social, economic and political fields in the broader context of development. This volume also presents a regional experience by looking into the migration–development nexus in the context of South Asia – a region that has over 50 million migrants living outside the region (Tan and Rahman 2013). In addition, this volume also goes beyond reporting the impacts of migration on economic development (remittance-induced), by highlighting the implications of 'social development' on society. Social development relates to the broader development processes that encompass the increase in incomes, accumulation of non-material assets including physical health, education and skills, and institutional aspect of development that allows individuals to translate their economic and human assets into personal welfare (Piper 2011; Van Naerssen *et al.* 2007; Sørensen 2012; Raghuram 2009; Faist 2008; Dannecker 2009; De Haas 2007). Thus, within the broad canvas of the social development approach, there remains room for both economic and social dimensions of development. This volume looks at the impact of international migration as a process, and views migration-led changes at the levels of the household, community and region in terms of a development process.

The power of international migration in inducing development in an origin country or region depends on three main factors: (i) the numbers involved; (ii) the duration of the movement; and (iii) class composition. South Asian countries are particularly relevant for documenting the migration-induced changes in society because the above-mentioned factors are remarkably present in the case of South Asian migrants and diaspora groups. The global South Asian migrants number over 50 million strong. They comprise both earlier settler emigrants and contemporary migrants (skilled/unskilled, temporary/permanent migration), and possess diverse social (caste, religion, lingual, regional and so on) and economic backgrounds (class). In addition to the factors mentioned above, many South Asian emigrants proactively maintain strong social, economic and cultural connections to their countries of origin in South Asia, while others vie for political rights such as dual citizenship and the right to vote. Thus, the effects of international migration are diverse: they often initiate micro-processes of change that affect individuals and their intimate families, meso-processes involving communities and regions, and macro-processes impacting full society. This volume therefore attempts to address migration-induced changes at the micro-, meso- and macro-levels by documenting case studies of various South Asian migrant groups living in different parts of the world, both as settlers and sojourners.

This book takes an interdisciplinary approach by focusing on permanent immigrants and contemporary sojourner migrants of South Asian origin. The chapters are contributed by a group of scholars who hail from different disciplinary backgrounds such as sociology, anthropology, political science, international relations, and economics. This book is therefore broad in scope in terms of contents, the timeline of migration, and its geographical coverage. Another strength of the volume lies in its empirically-based case studies involving India, Bangladesh, Sri Lanka, Pakistan and Nepal, and their emigrants living and working in the different parts of the world. The chapters in this volume not only examine the implications of migration on development, but also critically scrutinise the reliance on migration and migrant remittances as a development strategy in South Asia. Authors also discuss the contradictions that exist in the assumptions made in migration and development policies about structural conditions in South Asia that stand as barriers to development in the region.

By first embracing South Asian migrants who participate in both South–North and South–South migration, and second acknowledging the different human capital they possess and the different time periods these migrations take place in, this book provides us a lens with which we are enabled to take a broader view of international migration. ‘Development’ is approached from the *social development* perspective, which relates it to broader processes of development that encompass a holistic spectrum. This includes the increase in incomes and the accumulation of non-material assets including physical health, education, skill formation and transfers, political participation and female empowerment. The interdisciplinary nature of the contributions have, in essence, strengthened the basic theme of this book, which is to arrive at a holistic understanding of the impact that international migration has on the broader development of South Asia.

The following discussions are divided into four sections. The next section discusses the size of international migration from South Asia and its importance for the origin societies, followed by a theoretical and conceptual section that elaborates the development of migration–development debates. We expand the debate to take into consideration contemporary reality in South Asia. This section thus offers a broader framework that encompasses different types of migrants, directions of migration, forms of migration, and dimensions of development. After setting the conceptual background of the volume, the next section elaborates on the structure of the book, summarising each chapter's key arguments and major findings that revolve around broader themes of this volume. In the conclusion, we provide some final reflections on further research on international migration and development in South Asia.

Significance of international migration for development in South Asia

Broadly, South Asian migration can be divided into two stretches; first the colonial era, and second the post-colonial era (Naujoks 2009; Khatri 2007; Binod 2009; Bronden 2012; Tan and Rahman 2013). Migration during the colonial era started primarily from 1834 after the ban on slavery. Some of the destinations included Suriname, Trinidad and Tobago, Fiji, Mauritius, Guyana, East Africa, Guadeloupe, Martinique, La Reunion, and Natal (South Africa). The second stretch can be understood with the two broader divisions: (i) permanent migration to Europe, Oceania (Australia and New Zealand), and North America (the United States and Canada) that significantly started in the 1950s and 1960 with the liberalisation of immigration policies in these countries, and (ii) temporary labour migration to the Middle East in the 1970s and East and Southeast Asia in the 1980s. The oil-price hike in 1973 changed the directions, composition and volume of international migration from South Asia, where more people started to join the labour markets of the Gulf countries than ever before. With the expanding frame of migrant receiving countries, South Korea, Japan, Malaysia and Singapore have also attracted a large number of skilled and semiskilled migrants from South Asia in the 1980s (Rahman and Ullah 2012).

The outflows of international migrants from South Asia saw a constant increase up to 2008, when the total number of migration from the four countries (Bangladesh, India, Nepal and Sri Lanka) reached over two million. However, the flow was affected in 2008 because of a worldwide economic recession

(Ozaki 2012). Currently, migrant workers going abroad number about two million a year (Table 1.1). Most migrant workers from South Asia are unskilled or semi-skilled and come from a poor background, and worker migration is a male-dominated phenomenon in most South Asian countries. In Bangladesh, India and Nepal, male migrant workers outnumber female migrant workers by a large extent. In Bangladesh, female migration was prohibited until 2003, with a similar case of female migration to the Middle East countries being banned until 2007 in Nepal. Overall, women constitute approximately 15 per cent of the total migrant workers from South Asia (Ozaki 2012).

In South Asia, remittances sent by migrant workers become a significant source of funds for the economic development of the countries (Table 1.1). Most governments in South Asia view worker migration as a facilitator in curtailing unemployment, reducing poverty and earning foreign exchange through remittances. They therefore make worker migration one of the key economic policy priorities. Remittance, one of the direct outcomes of international migration, is the most beneficial private transaction in the global economy. This often stems from relatively developed economies and goes to the migrant households located in the developing economies. The South Asian region draws nearly one-quarter of the global remittance volume that contributes on average to over 11 per cent of the gross domestic product (GDP) of South Asian Countries (Table 1.1).

Among the regions, South Asia was the second largest remittance recipient in 2013, following the East Asia and Pacific (World Bank 2014). The formal remittance inflows to South Asia increased from US$16.13 billion in 2000 to US$111 billion in 2013, where India alone contributed US$70 billion. Among the South Asian countries, India, Pakistan and Bangladesh rank first, seventh and eighth in the world respectively in terms of volume of remittances received in 2013. As a share of GDP, Nepal receives the largest formal remittance inflows (25 per cent) among the South Asian countries and ranks third in the world, followed by Bangladesh (12 per cent), and Sri Lanka (10 per cent). Remittances are also the most important external funding source for South Asian countries (World Bank 2014). The Middle East countries are the largest recipient of South Asian migrant workers and, correspondingly, the amount of remittances originating from the Gulf countries is estimated to account for over 60 per cent of the total remittance inflows to South Asia.

Table 1.1 Outflow of migrants and inflow of remittances in South Asia

Country	*Outflow of migrant workers from South Asia, 2012*	*Remittances US$ million, 2013*	*Remittances % of GDP, 2013*
Bangladesh	607,798	14,228	12
India	747,401	70,000	4
Nepal	384,665	5,210	25
Pakistan	638,587	14,990	6
Sri Lanka	276,639	6,690	10

Source: various sources compiled by author.[1]

The 2009 Human Development report 'Overcoming Barriers: Human Mobility and Development' has noted that 'financial remittances are vital in improving the livelihoods of millions of people in developing countries (UNDP 2009: 71). Many empirical studies have confirmed the positive contribution of international remittances to household welfare, nutrition, food, health and living conditions in places of origin (for details about remittances and their uses in South Asia, see Rahman *et al.* 2014). World Bank's 'Global Economic Prospects' report notes that the remittance inflow has made it possible for Bangladesh to cut poverty by 6 per cent (World Bank 2006: xii). In Nepal, the Nepal Living Standard Survey found that the contribution of remittances in reducing poverty between 1996 and 2003 was 11 per cent. Other contributors included the increase in agricultural wages, an increase in non-farm activities, and some reduction in the dependency ratio. Remittances not only help to reduce poverty, but also reduce the depth and severity of poverty in Nepal and other countries (Khatri 2007). Given the size of the emigrant population and inflows of remittances, international migration has been an avenue for the social uplifting of millions of families in South Asia.

Approaching international migration and development in South Asia

The migration–development nexus – phases and issues

The nexus between migration and development has been predominantly examined from the migrant source country perspective, by debating whether migration triggers development in the source country. The relationship has been traditionally explained from two contrasting theoretical approaches, formulated as early as in the 1960s: the balanced growth approach, or the 'convergence point of view'; and the asymmetrical growth approach, also known as the 'divergence point of view' (for details, see Fischer *et al.* 1997; Papademetriou and Martin 1991; Spaan *et al.* 2005; Hermele 1997; Dewind 2008). The convergence school, rooted in neo-liberal economic theory, states that the sending areas obtain major benefits from out-migration for their development process (Hermele 1997; Lenard and Straehle 2010). This approach primarily posits that emigration leads to an improvement in 'resource availability' and 'income distribution' in origin areas (Spaan *et al.* 2005; Rosewarne 2012). On the other hand, the divergence school argues that out-migration hinders the development of the sending regions because it perpetuates a state of economic dependency that undermines the prospects for development (Hermele 1997). Some scholars describe this situation as a 'syndrome' (Reichert 1981), an 'addiction' (Wiest 1979), and a 'dangerous dependency' (Stuart and Kearney 1981).

In addition to these two perspectives, there exists a third approach, called the 'time perspective'. According to this perspective, negative factors dominate the impact of migration in the short term, while positive factors come to stimulate development in the long term (Hermele 1997). While these studies introduce the debate and its predominant views, they do not reveal much about the development of the debate itself.

Thomas Faist and his colleagues have identified three phases of thinking about the migration–development nexus, and explained how they have enriched our understanding about this nexus: (i) migration and development (the 1950s and 1960s); (ii) underdevelopment and migration (the 1970s and 1980s); and finally (iii) migration and (co)development (since the 1990s) (Faist and Fauser 2011: 2–11; Faist *et al.* 2013). The first phase is dominated by the positive argument, that is, migration has a positive impact on the sending society through remittances and return migration. This phase is marked by the argument that labour migration fills 'labour gaps' in the developed countries and contributes to the development in the developing countries through financial remittances, return migration, and the subsequent transfer of skills and knowledge (Faist and Fauser 2011; Massey *et al.* 1998; Castles 2008). This is based on the neo-classical economic assumption that the mere existence of economic disparities between countries/areas should be sufficient in generating migrant flows. If labour from developing countries move to the developed countries, labour shortage in the developing countries should then attract an inflow of capital from the developed countries and, eventually, lead to economic development in the developing countries (see for details, Faist and Fauser 2011; Castles 2008; Lewis 1954; Todaro 1970, 1976). This is a win–win situation for both the developing and the developed countries. This overwhelmingly positive view in the 1950s and 1960s on the linkages between migration and development is what Stephen Castles called 'a virtuous circle' (Castles 2008). Building on the phases of the virtuous circle pointed out by Castles, we offer a schema of the linkages between migration and development during the first phase (Figure 1.1). However, we see migration and development as a process and therefore prefer to use the term 'virtuous process' over 'virtuous circle'.

In the second phase, we see the emergence of a sociological approach with the historical-institutional approach. This challenged the virtuous process of the linkages between migration and development, and conceptualised the migration of labour as a way of acquiring cheap labour for capital at the core (Castles 2008). The second phase is dominated by the argument that migration leads to underdevelopment in the periphery (developing countries/regions) due to the migration of both low-skilled and high skilled individuals to the core countries. Countries in the periphery invest in the training of human resources, but such trained and skilled individuals spend their working life in the economically developed centres (developed countries), depriving developing countries of the valuable human resources. Migration flows therefore favour the economically developed centres and perpetuate dependency between the peripheral and core regions. The brain drain argument adds a powerful dimension to the migration–development debate in the 1970s and 1980s, and continues to contribute to the debate today (for details, see Cervantes and Guellec 2002).

Having said this, a more comprehensive 'World systems theory' came into being in the 1970s and 1980s. This focused on the way 'peripheral' regions were

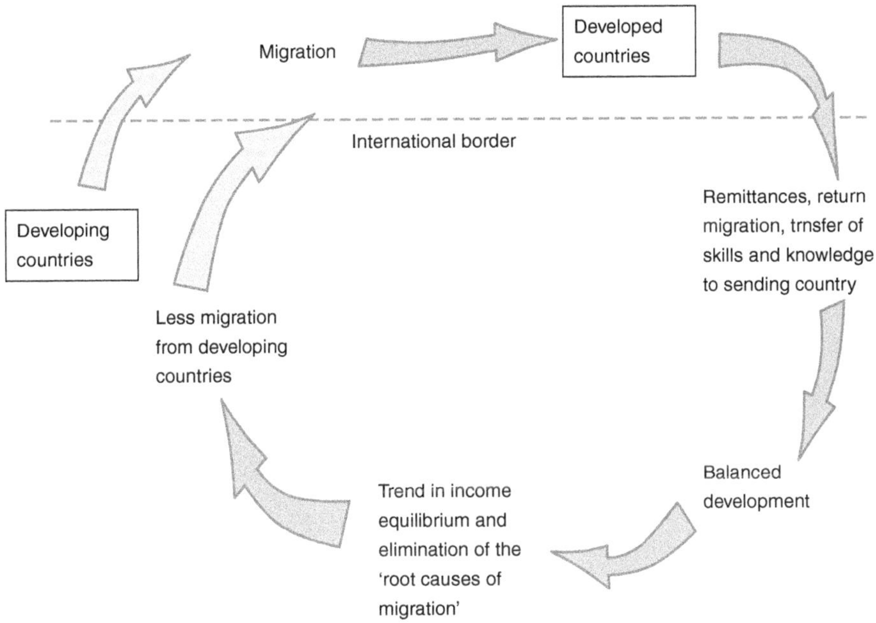

Figure 1.1 Virtuous process of the linkages between migration and development.

incorporated into a world economy (Wallerstein 1974; Portes and Walton 1981). This brought about changes in the rural economy of the peripheral regions, leading to the displacement of agrarian workers, rural poverty, urbanisation, and the growth of the informal economy (for details, see Portes and Walton 1981). The distortion of the peripheral economies created a reserve army of cheap labour that were prone to migrate. Castles conceptualised the pessimistic view of the historical-institutional approach to the linkages between migration and development as a *vicious circle* (Castles 2008). However, we choose to use the term 'vicious process' rather than 'vicious circle' for the same reason mentioned before. Building on the phases noted by Castles, we present a schema of the linkages between migration and development as a 'vicious process' during the second phase (Figure 1.2).

The third phase (approximately since the 1990s) sees the unprecedented rise of migration research and analysis, and is marked by a more optimistic view about the nexus between migration and development, similar to what we noticed in the 1960s. In this phase, the migrant is identified as the development agent par excellence and has been constituted as an element of development cooperation (Faist and Fauser 2011: 7). Today, among the academic and policy circles, the positive relationship of the migration–development nexus for the source country is more prominent (Hugo 2003; De Haas 2007, 2012). It is well accepted that migrants' transnational ties and transfers are seen as carrying enormous potential

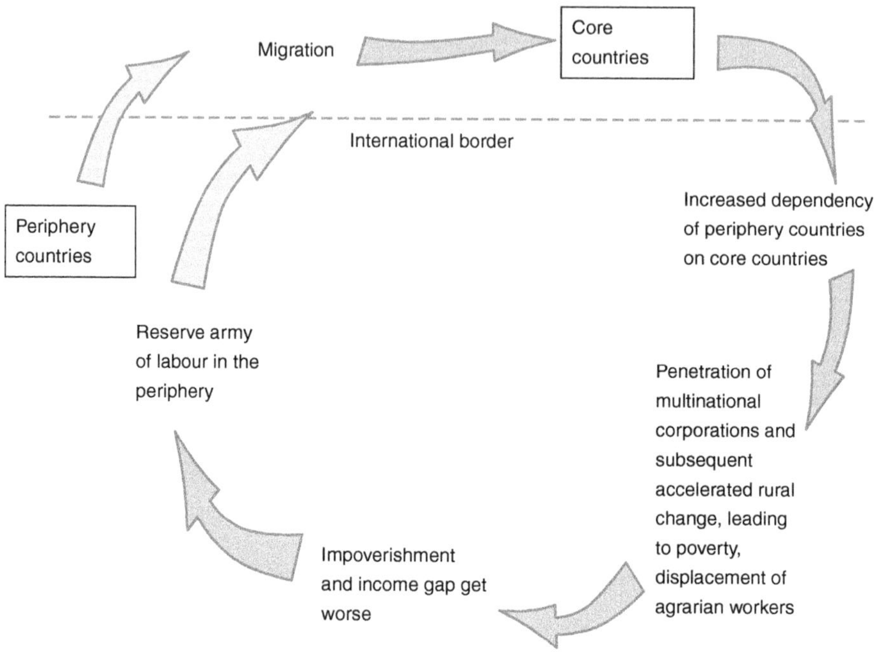

Figure 1.2 Vicious process of the linkages between migration and development.

to overcome underdevelopment in the developing world. Most emphasis is placed on financial, social, individual and collective remittances. Thus, this phase covers a wide range of topics around the circulation of people, money and ideas – what is called the celebration of transnational circulation (for details, see Faist and Fauser 2011: 1–26). New concepts like 'brain gain', 'brain circulation', and 'reverse brain drain' (Zweig 2006) emerged to demonstrate that developing countries are also benefiting from 'brain drain' over time (Saxenian 2005; Boeri *et al.* 2012; Stark 2009).

From the above discussion, it is quite obvious that by far skilled migration, the South–North migration flows, and economic development have dominated the debate. The diversities in the composition and direction of migration and approaches to development have not received adequate attention in the debate. However, all migrants who cross international borders do not necessarily belong to skilled and professional groups, and the movement does not always take place from the global South to the North. Finally, development does not mean economic development alone. In this age of migration in the twenty-first century, we need go beyond these conventional categories in order to come to a more holistic understanding of this nexus.

Beyond skilled migration, South–North migration and economic development

Considering the nature of contemporary migration from South Asia, this section advances that we need to go beyond the fixation on skilled migration, South–North migration, and economic development that has predominated the debates on migration and development. Migrants are not monolithic people moving to a single country with a sole orientation. Broadly speaking, existing studies often tend to analyse the relationship between migration and development without disaggregating migrants across skills, directions and nature of migration. When people migrate to another country, they migrate with different skills, under different social, economic, and political conditions, and for different time periods. Some are skilled migrants with professional qualifications looking for better opportunities in the global labour market, while others are forced to leave the country to seek political refuge. Some migrants move for permanent settlement, while others look for temporary work overseas. Micro factors such as human capital composition, macro factors such as social, economic and political conditions of the global North, and the relatively prosperous economies in the South largely shape the composition of migration and influence the size and direction of global migration.

It is generally assumed that migrants from developing economies migrate to the developed economies in the North through what is often called a 'South–North migration'. The South–North migration has been first and foremost investigated as a case study in the study of the migration and development nexus. However, over time, the direction of migration has changed. This is especially so after events like the oil-price hike in the 1970s, the ensuing emergence of new migration hotspots, the settlement of temporary migrants in Western Europe in the 1970s, the increasing migration control mechanisms in the 1990s, and the securitisation of migration and remittances after 9/11. Now, more and more people migrate within the global South than ever before.

In addition to oil-rich regions, the prosperous and emerging economies of the South have been new destinations for circular forms of migration. In Asia, we find three migration hotspots – oil-rich Gulf countries, Southeast Asia (Singapore, Malaysia, Brunei, Hong Kong Special Administrative Region), and East Asia (South Korea and Japan). Outflows of South Asian migrants to these three regions generate an intra-regional form of circular migration – it is circular in nature because migrants are allowed to work for an extended period with some intervals. While migrants in this South–South migration system may not enjoy similar levels of privileges and economic benefits like their counterparts in the South–North migration system, they mostly enjoy higher economic advantages than those who do not move at all. Given the nature of migration, which is predominantly temporary in nature and where extended family members are not allowed to migrate with individual migrants, these migrants often make significant contributions to the subsistence and social reproduction of family members 'left behind'.

In addition to the nature of contributions to families in the South–South migration, we also need to include the conditions under which most migrants work in host countries, and the migrant support systems in the global South. Migrants in the regional migration systems often encounter hazardous working conditions, non-payment of wages, arbitrary deportation, and become victims of exploitation and human trafficking. For example, Sørensen reports three factors ignored by those who uphold the possibility of development through migration: (i) the rising death tolls and disappearances of migrants en route; (ii) the rising migration costs and the related indebtedness faced by familial networks in home and host countries; and (iii) the risk of losing considerable investments (purchasing air travel and securing job contracts) and savings upon deportation (Sørensen 2012: 62–65). They reveal the heterogeneous contexts that lead to very different results for migrants, their families and their home countries. These losses need to be highlighted when we draw conclusions with the glowing promises of the nexus. Such a realisation will enable us to move beyond mainstream understandings of the debate to a more holistic one.

South Asian skilled and professional migration has received considerable attention in recent years (Kapur 2001, 2010; Saxenian 2005, 2006; Chacko 2007; Nanda and Khanna 2010; Finegold *et al.* 2011; Chanda and Sreenivasan 2006; Tejada *et al.* 2014). These studies report that South Asian professionals and entrepreneurs play an important role in the socio-economic development of the region through the transfer of advanced technical skills and investment capital. There is no doubt that skilled migration offers several beneficial impacts for the economy and society in South Asia (for a review, see Tejada *et al.* 2014; Sahoo and Pattanaik 2014). Given the diversity in human capital compositions, there is a need to look into the relationship between migration and development by also focusing on low-skilled labour migration. Every year, a large number of unskilled and semi-skilled migrants join in the construction of roads, housing and other infrastructural projects, manufacturing, household work, and the service sectors in relatively wealthy countries in Asia. This is because the citizens of many of these prosperous countries in the region are not ready to take up the 4D types of work – demeaning, dangerous, dirty and difficult. This creates a demand for a low-skilled foreign workforce from neighbouring countries that have a labour surplus.

While skilled and professional migrants continue to migrate to these countries, a large number of low-skilled migrants also find solutions for their unemployment in the regional labour markets – a growing phenomenon throughout the labour-sending countries in South Asia and other parts of the world. While skilled and professional migrants are supposed to have higher economic advantages due to their higher salaries and other privileges associated with their positions than unskilled or semi-skilled migrants do, both groups of migrants tend to have considerable impacts on the sending societies due to the circular nature of migration. By highlighting the potential contributions that low-skilled migrants usually make to their sending societies, this volume makes a modest attempt to shed light on this neglected but important group of migrants in the development process.

finds that culture mediates between the individual traits (diaspora entrepreneurs) and the institutional environment back home. The Indian diaspora exhibits clear patterns in the selection and choice of place and sectorial preference. Cultural factors, such as affiliation to a particular region, culture and language, influence the behaviour of the investment and entrepreneurial activities. Unlike the Chinese, the Indian diaspora are latecomers to the field of entrepreneurship. That being said, they are fast growing. This chapter concludes that it is not feasible to expect large-scale entrepreneurial activities from the first generation. The real impact, however, socially or otherwise, can be realised with second-generation entrepreneurs who can potentially be nurtured through entrepreneurial policies back home. This chapter makes policy suggestions in this respect for harnessing the diaspora entrepreneurship through the promotion of entrepreneurial policies, technological transfer, and knowledge dissemination.

The sixth chapter, *A troublesome home? Transnational property and its discontents in Indian Punjab* by V.J. Varghese and Vivek Thakur, addresses the growing ambivalences of migrant/diasporic transnationalism by looking at the properties owned by non-resident Punjabis in their home state of Punjab, India. Drawing from ethnographical research in the Doaba region, the migration belt of Punjab, the chapter argues that the retention and management of properties being owned transnationally is becoming tougher for the non-resident Punjabis, leaving deep fissures in their homeland ties. At the same time, the increasing magnitude of property-related disputes enabled the sub-national state to put in place new infrastructures of governmentality to protect the interests of the non-resident Punjabis. The chapter reveals that such infrastructures in fact act as preconditions for informal practices, and become tools of control and exploitation at multiple levels instead. The problematic negotiations that non-resident Punjabis find themselves caught up in with their home societies call for taking the problematique beyond the discourses of nostalgia and demotic love for motherland, to the spheres of contestations it entails.

The economic relations between migrants and their families are often the centre of discussion in the migration–development debate. The seventh chapter, *Bangladeshi migration to Southern Europe: implications on migrant families* by Md Mizanur Rahman and Mohammad Alamgir Kabir, provide insights into the Bangladeshi migration to Italy and its implications for those families left behind in Bangladesh. Of the Southern European countries, Italy pursued a liberal policy for migrants from non-European countries as early as the 1980s, by introducing the regularisation initiative for unauthorised migrants. The reformation of immigration policy in some Southern European countries has paved the way for the emergence of some non-European emigrant communities in the region. Focusing on the Bangladeshi migration to Southern Europe, this chapter examines the context of immigrant reception, the characteristics of Bangladeshi emigrants, their channels of migration, the role of intermediaries in the migration process, the economic cost of migration, and the inflows of remittances and the implications this has on family dynamics in Bangladesh. This study draws from the Bangladesh Household Remittance Survey conducted by the International

Organisation for Migration (IOM) – Dhaka in 2009. The study reports that opportunities in some Southern European countries, especially the Italian labour market, translate into increased opportunities for the migrant families left behind in Bangladesh.

The oil-rich Gulf countries have been a major destination region for migrants from South Asia. The eighth chapter, *Indian migration to the Gulf and development challenges in India* by Ajaya Kumar Sahoo, examines the trajectories of international migration and the personal experiences of migrant workers in the host society, their reasons for return migration, and their coping patterns after return. This study draws from the experiences of returnees from Gulf countries in the Indian state of Andhra Pradesh and reports that extreme poverty, a lack of employment opportunities, and poor development of the districts had led to large-scale migration to the Gulf countries. However, India has witnessed a significant return migration due to the difficulties that migrants face while working in the Gulf. Since these returnees mostly belong to the semi-skilled and unskilled category, they are commonly treated as 'Gulf victims' in their villages. One of the many socio-economic and psychological consequences of this trajectory is that many of them end up committing suicide. The study calls for a serious need for government intervention, especially to help poor migrant families who are in debt and subsequently commit suicide because of severe economic crisis.

The ninth chapter, *International migration and economic changes in South Asia: the emergence of the middle class* by Shahid Javed Burki, attempts to expand the debate on the impact that South Asian Diaspora groups are having on their countries of origin. It goes beyond the discussion of the quantum and structure of financial resources that flow from the expatriate communities to the countries of their origin. While those financial resources are large – they touched US$100 billion for all South Asia – the story of the impact of the diaspora groups on what were once their homelands should extend beyond matters of finance. We should also look into how the size, structure and pattern of South Asia's middle class, by now nearing one billion people and expanding at a rate three to four times the increase in population, are being influenced by the diaspora groups. The upper end of the South Asian middle class is increasing because of the growth in national incomes in the region. As is now recognised, the well to do segments of South Asian societies are capturing a significant increase in the incomes resulting from economic growth. At the lower end of the income distribution scale, the increasing size of the middle class is largely the consequence of the amount of remittances received by the households in the space between the poor and the not so poor.

The contribution of overseas Indian (Punjabi) emigrants in the transformation of the socio-economic life of the rural Punjab is significant. The tenth chapter, *Punjabi immigrants and rural development in the Doaba region of Indian Punjab* by Jaswinder Singh Brar, addresses various contours, structures and dimensions of diasporic engagement in the rural Doaba region of Indian Punjab. This region constitutes the hub of this diaspora, with about every third household having at least one member settled in a Western country. The study reveals that non-resident Indians (NRIs) have contributed about US$300 million in the 477 villages of this region. The regular flow of remittances constitutes the most fundamental component of this engagement. However, other modes of involvement are also prominent and are becoming catalysts of development. These other modes are: philanthropy, sports and associated infrastructure, buildings for public use, modern crematoria, free health camps, cultural events, sanitation, welcome gates, educational and health institutions, weddings of poor girls, investment in agricultural machinery, holding of religious festivals, old age homes, incentives to village players, special training programmes for village youth, de-addiction camps, etc. There are also cases involving the employment of village labour through work permits on NRI farms abroad.

International migrants of Nepal contribute nearly 25 per cent of the country's GDP by remitting over US$5 billion dollar in a year. The eleventh chapter, *International migration and development: Prospects and challenges for Nepal* by Thakur Subedi, attempts to provide an overview of the prospects and challenges for diaspora-led development practices in Nepal. The chapter argues that a lack of opportunity at home and better prospects abroad push many Nepalese out of the country every year. The volume of remittance that they send is almost a quarter of Nepal's GDP. However, most of this is spent on unproductive sectors. Moreover, remittances aside, the country does not seem to have gained any noticeable benefit, especially in the field of trade, investments, and knowledge and technology transfer. Thus, despite having a strong viability, the study reports that the nexus between 'migration and development' is very weak in Nepal.

The twelfth chapter, *Pakistani migration to the Gulf and development in the Miranzai valley in Pakistan* by Syed Minhaj ul Hassan examines the socio-economic impacts of Gulf migration on the Miranzai valley in Pakistan. The Miranzai valley is located between Kohat and Parachinar, the two southern towns of the Khyber-Pakhtunkhwa province of Pakistan. Economically this valley used to be one of the poorest amongst the territories of Khyber-Pakhtunkhwa. However, the Gulf migration changed its socio-economic gamut, which in turn resulted in a multitude of changes in the overall lives of the people. With increased literacy and economic prosperity, the lives of women also witnessed marked improvement. For example, they used to get up at dawn and go to the mountains to collect firewood. Now, due to the availability of resources, the use of natural gas has replaced firewood. This change not only reduced their hardship, it also had a positive effect on the environment. The forests that used to be cut by these womenfolk for the purpose of cooking and in winters for warmth are now spared. Another important effect is their involvement in the business activities in general.

Finally, the thirteenth chapter, *The other side of the migration and development nexus: human trafficking in Sri Lanka* by Kopalapillai Amirthalingam, Danesh Jayatilaka and Rajith W.D. Lakshman, documents the experiences of those migrants who have been victimised and exploited in the migration process. The chapter embodies the argument that there is a need to include them in the migration–development debate as well. This chapter discusses the risks certain migrants expose themselves to when seeking prosperity overseas. Their findings suggest that the majority of individuals were 'forced to migrate' into the hands of traffickers due to issues related to poverty, disempowerment, and social dislocation.

Future research agendas

International migration and subsequent gains such as skill formation, knowledge transfers, social, political, and financial remittances, have immense potential in impacting society in South Asia. This broad spectrum of migration implications for migrants, their families, regions and countries, constitutes an expanding field of research that needs to be approached from an interdisciplinary perspective. While selective and incomplete, the case studies included in this volume show that international migration has the potential to stimulate development in South Asia. Together, these chapters constitute an initial effort to bring together studies on the nexus between migration and broader development in South Asia. We realise that the role of international migration in education, healthcare, empowerment of women, gendered relations and political emancipation demands independent, in-depth treatment. We suggest this as a field for further study.

In addition to the academic investigation of international migration, there is also a need to closely study the phenomenon from a public policy perspective. Given the development potential of migration and remittances, this is a priority area for policy makers. Some countries in South Asia are showing substantial interest in international migration and the subsequent remittances, and are therefore increasingly adopting emigration policies to facilitate the flows of emigrants and to attract remittance inflows. Further research may identify such policy initiatives regarding emigration governance and remittance mobilisation.

While sending countries are principally concerned about migrants' remittances – these have been a lifeline for some countries in South Asia such as Nepal, Bangladesh and Pakistan – we need to go beyond looking at remittances in order to understand how international migration has changed the life chances of migrants and their families over time. For example, migrants working as unskilled construction workers in Saudi Arabia today may join construction firms in Singapore or other countries with a higher pay and better living conditions. While we have primarily provided case studies highlighting how international migration has impacted on migrant families and societies in South Asia, we could not document the developmental implications of international migration on migrants themselves. The development implication on the life of individual migrants therefore constitutes another area for further research.

Although case studies in this volume largely document the positive role of migration on development, these processes are not without their negative outcomes, and the final chapter documents how labour migrants become victims of human trafficking syndicates, and encounter human and working rights violations in the migration process. However, this phenomenon is not unique to

Sri Lanka; migrants in other countries in South Asia, such as India, Bangladesh, Nepal and Pakistan, also often experience similar experiences. This volume signals that further studies are essential in investigating the negative impacts that international migration may have at the micro and macro levels in South Asia. By documenting such experiences, we will be in a position to reduce, if not eradicate, the adverse consequences of international migration for South Asian countries.

Finally, the chapters in this volume demonstrate that international migration and development can be an exciting field of academic study as well as a vibrant field of policy study. Its multi-disciplinary dimensions enlarge its scope and applicability across several domains. Our hope is that this volume will contribute to the growing field of international migration and development in the academic and policy areas.

Note

1 Migration and Development Brief, 11 April 2014, online, available at: http://siteresources.worldbank.org/INTPROSPECTS/Resources/334934. Bangladesh: Actual Volume: 14,227.94 Million. Central Bank of Bangladesh, online, available at: www.bangladesh-bank.org/econdata/wageremitance.php#. India: Estimated. Migration and Development Brief, 11 April 2014; Nepal: Estimated, International Organization for Migration, online, available at: www.iom.int/cms/nepal; Pakistan: Country Wise Workers' Remittances, Bureau of Emigration and Overseas Employment, Pakistan. Sri Lanka: International Organization for Migration, online, available at: www.iom.int/cms/en/sites/iom/home/where-we-work/asia-and-the-pacific/sri-lanka.html; Central Bank of Bangladesh, online, available at: www.bangladesh-bank.org/econdata/wageremitance.php#. Estimated. Migration and Development Brief, 11 April 2014, online, available at: http://siteresources.worldbank.org/INTPROSPECTS/Resources/334934; Estimated, International Organization for Migration, online, available at: www.iom.int/cms/nepal; Country Wise Workers' Remittances, Bureau of Emigration and Overseas Employment, Pakistan, online, available at: www.sbp.org.pk/ecodata/Homeremit.pdf; International Organization for Migration, online, available at: www.iom.int/cms/en/sites/iom/home/where-we-work/asia-and-the-pacific/sri-lanka.html; Data and Statistics, Ministry of Expatriates' Welfare and Overseas Employment, online, available at: www.probashi.gov.bd/images/stories/data02.png; Annual Report, Department of Foreign Employment (DoFE), online, available at: www.dofe.gov.np/uploads/document/FA66_67_20120621012840.pdf; Wickramasekara, 2011.

References

Bastia, T. 2013. The Migration–Development Nexus: Current Challenges and Future Research Agenda. *Geography Compass* 7(7): 464–477.

Binod, K. 2009. Adversary Analysis and the Quest for Global Development. *Social Analysis* 53(3): 106–122.

Boeri, T., H. Brucker, F. Docquier and H. Rapoport. 2012. *Brain Drain and Brain Gain: the Global Competition to Attract Highly Skilled Migrants*. Oxford: Oxford University Press.

Bronden, B.M. 2012. Migration and Development: Flavors of the 2000s. *International Migration* 50(3): 2–7.

Castles, S. 2008. Development and Migration – Migration and Development: What Comes First? *SSRC Migration and Development Conference Paper No. 2.* New York: Social Science Research Council.

Cervantes, M. and D. Guellec. 2002. *The Brain Drain: Old Myths, New Realities.* Paris: Directorate for Science, Technology and Industry, Paris: OECD.

Chacko, E. 2007. From Brain Drain to Brain Gain: Reverse Migration to Bangalore and Hyderabad, India's Globalizing High Tech Cities. *Geo Journal* 68(2/3): 131–140.

Chanda, R. and N. Sreenivasan. 2006. India's Experience with Skilled Migration. In C. Kuptsch and E.F. Pang (eds), *Competing for global talent.* Geneva: International Labour Organization, pp. 215–256.

Dannecker, P. 2009. Migrant Visions of Development: a Gendered Approach. *Population, Space and Place* 15: 119–132.

De Haas, H. 2007. Remittances, Migration and Social Development, a Conceptual Review of the Literature. *Social Policy and Development Programme Paper Number 34.* United Nations Research Institute for Social Development.

De Haas, H. 2012. The Migration and Development Pendulum: a Critical View on Research and Policy. *International Migration* 50(3): 8–25.

Dewind, J. 2008. Bridging the Fields of Migration and Development Studies: Seeking Complementarities between Contrasting Approaches. *SSRC Migration and Development Conference Paper No 1.*

Faist, T. 2000. *The Volume and Dynamics of International Migration and Transnational Social Spaces.* Oxford: Clarendon Press.

Faist, T. 2008. Migrants as Transnational Development Agents: an Inquiry into the Newest Round of the Migration–Development Nexus. *Population, Space and Place* 14: 21–42.

Faist, T. and M. Fauser. 2011. The Migration–Development Nexus: Toward a Transnational Perspective. In Thomas Faist and Margit Fauser (eds), *The Migration–Development Nexus: A Transnational Perspective.* Basingstoke: Palgrave Macmillan, pp. 1–28.

Faist, T., M. Fauser and E. Reisenauer. 2013. *Transnational Migration.* Cambridge: Polity Press.

Finegold, D., K. Venkatesh, A. Winkler and V. Argod. 2011. Why They Return? Indian Students in the United States. *Economic and Political Weekly* 46(21): 21–25.

Fischer, P.A., R. Martin and T. Straubhaar. 1997. Interdependencies between Development and Migration. In Thomas Hammar, Grete Brochmann, Kristof Tamas and Thomas Faist (eds) *International Migration, Immobility and Development: Multidisciplinary Perspective.* Oxford: Berg, pp. 91–132.

Global Economic Prospects. 2006. *Economic Implications of Remittances and Migration.* Washington, DC: World Bank.

Hammar, T., G. Brochman, K. Tamas and T. Faist. 1997. *International Migration, Immobility and Development.* New York: Berg.

Hermele, K. 1997. The Discourse on Migration and Development. In T. Hammar, G. Brochmann, K. Tamas and T. Faist (eds) *International Migration, Immobility and Development: Multidisciplinary Perspective.* Oxford: Berg.

Hugo, G. 2003. *Migration and Development: A Perspective from Asia.* IOM Migration Research Series, No. 14. Geneva: International Organization for Migration.

Kapur, D. 2001. Diasporas and Technology Transfer. *Journal of Human Development,* 2(2): 265–286.

Kapur, D. 2010. *Diaspora, Development and Democracy: The Domestic impact of international migration from India.* Princeton: Princeton University Press.

Khatri, S.K. 2007. Labor Migration, Employment, and Poverty Alleviation in South Asia. Online, available at: www.saceps.org/upload_file/download_pdf/labor%20migration%20whole%20pdf.pdf (accessed on 20 August 2014).

Lenard, P.T. and C. Straehle. 2010. Temporary Labor Migration: Exploitation, Tool of Development, or Both? *Policy and Society* 29: 283–294.

Lewis, W.A. 1954. Economic Development with Unlimited Supplies of Labour. *Manchester School of Economic and Social Studies* 22: 139–191.

Massey, D.S., J. Arango, G. Hugo, A. Kouaouci, A. Pellegrino and J.E. Taylor. 1998. *Worlds in Motion: Understanding International Migration at the End of the Millennium*. Oxford: Clarendon Press.

Martin, G. and A. Pecoud. 2013. Migration, Development and the Migration Development Nexus. *Population, Space and Place* 19: 369–374.

Nanda, P. and T. Khanna. 2010. Diasporas and Domestic Entrepreneurs: Evidence from the Indian Software Industry. *Journal of Economics and Management Strategy* 19(4): 991–1012.

Naujoks, D. 2009. Emigration, Immigration, and Diaspora Relations in India, Migration Policy Institute. Online, available at: www.migrationinformation.org/Profiles/display.cfm?ID=745 (accessed on 19 August 2014).

Omelaniuk, I. 2012. *Global Perspectives on Migration and Development: GFMD Puerto Vallarta and Beyond, Global Migration Issues*. New York: Springer.

Ozaki, M. 2012. Worker Migration and Remittances in South Asia. South Asia Working Paper Series No. 12 May 2012, Asian Development Bank.

Papademetriou, D.G. and P.L. Martin. 1991. *The Unsettled Relationship: Labor Migration and Economic Development*. London: Greenwood Press.

Parnwell, M.J.G. 2005. Transnational Migration and Development: a Conceptual Overview. *Asian and Pacific Migration Journal* 14(1–2): 11–34.

Piper, N. 2008. Feminization of Migration and the Social Dimensions of Development: the Asian Case. *Third World Quarterly* 29(7): 1287–1303.

Piper, N. 2009. The Complex Interconnections of the Migration–Development Nexus: a Social Perspective. *Population Space and Place* 15(2): 93–101.

Piper, N. 2010. All Quiet on the Eastern Front? Temporary Contract Migration in Asia Revisited from a Development Perspective. *Policy and Society* 29: 399–341.

Piper, N. 2011. *Migration Global Political Economy*. International Political Economy Yearbook. London: Lynne Rienner.

Portes, A. 1976. Determinants of the Brain Drain. *International Migration Review* 10: 489–508.

Portes, A. 2009. Migration and Development: Reconciling Opposite Views. *Ethnic and Racial Studies* 32(1): 5–22.

Portes, A. and J. Walton. 1981. *Labor, Class and the International System*. New York: Academic Press.

Raghuram, P. 2009. Which Migration, what Development? Unsettling the Edifice of Migration and Development. *Population Space and Place* 15: 103–117.

Rahman, M.M and AKM A. Ullah. 2012. *Understanding Asian Migration Policy: South, East and Southeast Asia*. New York: Nova Science Publisher.

Rahman, M.M., T.T. Yong and AKM A. Ullah. 2014. *Migrant Remittance in South Asia: Social, Economic and Political Implications*. London and New York: Palgrave Macmillan.

Reichert, J.S. 1981. The Migrant Syndrome: Seasonal US Wage Labor and Rural Development in Central Mexico. *Human Organization* 40: 56–66.

Rosewarne, S. 2012. Temporary International Labor Migration and Development in South and Southeast Asia. *Feminist Economics* 18(2): 63–90.

Sahoo, S. and B.K. Pattanaik. 2014. *Global Diasporas and Development: Socioeconomic, Cultural and Policy Perspectives*. New Delhi: Springer.

Saxenian, A.L. 2005. From Brain Drain to Brain Circulation: Transnational Communities and Regional Upgrading in India and China. *Studies in Comparative International Development* 40: 35–61.

Saxenian, A.L. 2006. *The New Argonauts: Regional Advantage in a Global Economy*. Cambridge, MA: Harvard University Press.

Sørensen, N.N. 2012. Revisiting the Migration–Development Nexus: from Social Networks and Remittances to Markets for Migration Control. *International Migration* 50(3): 61–76.

Sørensen, N.N., N. Van Hear and P. Engberge-Pedersen. 2002. The Migration–Development Nexus Evidence and Policy Options State of the Art Overview. *International Migration* 40(5): 3–47.

Spaan, E. and T. von Naerssen. 2005. Asia and Europe: Transnationalism, Multiple Linkages and Development. *Asian and Pacific Migration Journal* 14(1–2): 1–9.

Spaan, E., T. von Naerssen and F. Hillmann. 2005. Shifts in the European Discourses on Migration and Development. *Asian and Pacific Migration Journal* 14(1–2): 35–69.

Stark, O. 2009. *Reasons for Remitting*. ZEF Discussion Papers on Development Policy No. 134, Centre for Development Research, Bonn, August, p. 15.

Stuart, J. and M. Kearney. 1981. Causes and Effects of Agricultural Labor Migration from the Mixteca of Oaxaca to California. Working Paper in US–Mexican Studies, 28 La Jolla: Program in United States Mexican Studies, University of California at San Diego.

Tan, T.Y and M.M. Rahman. 2013. *Diaspora Engagement and Development in South Asia*. London: Palgrave Macmillan.

Tejada, G., U. Bhattacharya, B. Khadria and C. Kuptsch. 2014. *Indian Skilled Migration and Development: To Europe and Back*. New York: Springer.

Todaro, M.P. 1970. A Model of Labor Migration and Urban Unemployment in Less Developed Countries. *American Economic Review* 59: 138–148.

Todaro, M.P. 1976. *International Migration in Developing Countries: A Review of Theory, Evidence, Methodology and Research Priorities*. A WEP Study. Geneva: International Labor Office.

UNDP. 2009. *Human Development Report 2009: Overcoming Barriers: Human Mobility and Development*. New York: UNDP.

United Nations. 2013. Making Migration Work. High Level Dialogue on International Migration and Development. Online, available at: www.un.org/en/ga/68/meetings/migration/ (accessed on 19 August 2014).

United Nations Population Fund. 2006. A State of World Population 2006: A Passage to Hope, Women and International Migration. Online, available at: www.unfpa.org/swp/2006/pdf/en_sowp06.pdf (accessed on 20 August 2014).

Van Naerssen, T., E. Spaan and A. Zoomers. 2007. *Globalization, Migration and Development*. New York: Routledge.

Vertovec, S. 2004. Migrant Transnationalism and Modes of Transformation. *International Migration Review* 38: 970–1001.

Wallerstein, I. 1974. *The Modern World System I: Capitalist Agriculture and the Origins of the European World Economy in the Sixteenth Century*. Academic Press: New York.

Wickramasekara, P. 2011. *Labour Migration in South Asia: A Review of Issues, Policies and Practices*. Geneva: International Labour Organization.

Wiest, R.E. 1979. Implications of International Labor Migration for Mexican Rural Development. In F. Camara and R. Van Kemper (eds), *Migration across Frontiers: Mexico and the United States*. Albany: Institute for Mesoamerican Studies, State University of New York, pp. 85–97.

World Bank. 2006. *Global Economic Prospects 2006: Economic Implications of Remittances and Migration*. Washington, DC: World Bank.

World Bank. 2013. *Migration and Development Brief, No. 10*. Washington, DC: World Bank.

World Bank. 2014. *Migration and Development Brief, No. 22*. Washington, DC: World Bank.

Zweig, D. 2006. Learning to Compete: China's Efforts to Encourage a Reverse Brain Drain. *International Labour Review* 145(1/2): 65–90

2 Innovative incorporation

Diasporic representation and political rights in India

Constantino Xavier

India's new diaspora policy, emerging in the early 2000s, exemplified the larger process through which states reach out to their non-resident citizens and former citizens for various objectives – political, economic and cultural. Focusing not only on their expatriate citizens, but also on former nationals and people who have ethnic origins or have maintained a cultural connection with their former homeland, these states nationalised diasporas by incorporating them into their increasingly deterritorialised nations. In particular, they did so by adopting 'diaspora policies', i.e. a public strategy, armed with specific mechanisms, which empowered governments to reach out, target and incorporate extra-territorial populations for a specific purpose. While the nature, scope, and intensity of these policies might vary from country to country, they all aspired to demarcate and designate their overseas population, as well as to reach out and incorporate them in economic, cultural, or political terms. In the broad definition by legal scholar Laurie Brand, this process included:

> Policies and practices of the home state in any arena – legal, political, economic, cultural, religious – that deliberately affect[ed] or target[ed] some aspect of its expatriates' lives. This should also be construed as policies potentially affecting dual citizens, former nationals, and even those of the second or third generation who are [were] not citizens, but remain[ed] of interest to the country of origin.
>
> (Brand 2002: 3–4)

In some cases, diaspora policies were widely institutionalised, therefore attracting large attention from scholars who had set out to investigate them in different geographical and political contexts, as well as from a variety of disciplinary perspectives. In his detailed study, Alan Gamlen observed that such policies were now implemented fairly extensively in at least 15 countries, to varying degrees in almost 60 additional countries spread across all major geopolitical regions of the globe, and in all developmental stages (Gamlen 2006: 23). In most cases however, states were just beginning to develop a consolidated policy, attesting to the novelty of these policies as global migration and mobility intensified. Governments generally started by creating special ministerial or parliamentary committees, or by constituting official bodies and sponsoring research institutions to study their diasporic populations, as well as to evaluate the potential of adopting an institutionalised strategy.

What did these policies consist of, and how did they concretely engage diasporas? Anupam Chander (2006) referred to 'bonding mechanisms' at three different levels. At the political level, they might include dual citizenship, external voting rights, special visa and residence permits, and parliamentary, advisory and other forms of political representation for the diaspora. At the economic level, they included special foreign investment policies, transfer of pensions and bilateral social security agreements, favourable exchange and interest rates, a parallel banking system, and knowledge networks for highly skilled expatriate professionals. Lastly, at the cultural level, these policies often included the organisation of annual festivals or assemblies, financial support for cultural and religious organisations and initiatives, exchange programmes and educational quotas for the youth, and a specialised media or information network.

This idea of the migrant as an economic asset to be tapped reflected an abrupt change of the traditional image of the emigrant as a potential burden. Stephen Castles noted that at the inception of labour migration, emigrants were often seen as either 'deserters' and 'traitors', or as 'surplus population' or 'troublemakers' (Castles 2007: 31). In stark contrast with that past image, Kim Barry noted that they were now increasingly seen as 'heroes of development', who had 'taken up the burden and sacrifice of living abroad to contribute to the national project' (2006: 34), while Johnson and Sedaca described them as 'agents of change … injecting new ideas and resources that [could] catalyse progress in otherwise stagnant economies' (2004: 63). For developing countries engaged in economic state-building in particular, diaspora policies were now increasingly adopted to '(re)incorporate emigrants' by 'extracting material resources from them' (Barry 2006: 28). One such strategy was executed by guaranteeing the continuous inflow of remittances, which facilitated the home country's 'structural insertion in the world economy' (Itzigsohn 2000: 1143). As illustrated by the widely researched case of Mexico, and also by the case of India since 1991, state-led diaspora policies often emerged parallel to neo-liberal economic adjustment and reform processes (Smith 2003: 467–502).

India's evolving state–diaspora nexus

The process of emigration from India spanned several centuries, different regions and socio-economic classes, as well as very diverse migration trajectories and destination countries. A 2001 estimate by the High Level Committee on the Indian Diaspora (HLCID 2002) in more than 100 countries put the total number of overseas Indians at approximately 20 million, six million of which were citizens of India (NRIs) and the remaining being people of Indian origin (PIOs). Despite the global financial recession after 2008, this number continues to rise steadily. The most recent estimate by the Ministry of Overseas Indian

Affairs (MOIA) identified more than ten million NRIs in more than 200 countries worldwide (MOIA 2012).

While India's diaspora policy was formally implemented in the early 2000s, it would be wrong to assume that India had ignored its expatriate and overseas populations prior to this date. Even at the British Imperial Conferences of 1917, 1921 and 1923, Indian representatives systematically raised the issue of discrimination against Indians overseas and, under Tej Bahadur Sapru, reclaimed citizenship rights for those living in the dominions. Mahatma Gandhi, Jawaharlal Nehru and many other independence leaders fostered this connection during the independence struggle, sought both financial and political support from overseas Indians, and underlined the non-territorial nature of their nationalist cause.

However, formal post-Independence measures only emerged in the 1970s when the Reserve Bank of India (RBI) responded to the Gulf oil boom and the consequent rise in Indian migration to the Middle East by tailoring a set of economic and financial mechanisms to attract the inflow of foreign exchange deposits in the form of remittances (Khadria 1991: 65). NRI deposits were first introduced in February 1970 with a non-resident (external) rupee account (NRE), followed in November 1975 by a foreign currency denominated deposit facility, the foreign currency non-resident account (FCNRA). The latter instrument was an unprecedented innovation in India's traditionally protectionist financial structure because it allowed for a repatriable deposit with the RBI assuming the exchange rate risk (Gordon and Gupta 2004: 4166).

Further engagement was observed in 1976, when the Indira Gandhi-led government announced 'steps to encourage investment by non-resident Indians'. In 1982, Manmohan Singh, then a member secretary of the Planning Commission, also noted 'Indian communities abroad ... [had] accumulated large resources of investible funds' (quoted in Prashad 2004: 30). Finally, in 1983 the new Emigration Act came into force, regulating the exit and return of Indian migrants, especially to the Gulf region countries, thus maximising economic benefits.

The way for further incorporation was therefore paved for the period of economic reforms under the leadership of Rajiv Gandhi (1984–1990), which included innovative attempts to link up with temporary workers in the Gulf region and also with skilled professionals in North America. The India Investment Centre was set up, serving as a nodal agency for promoting investment in India by NRIs, PIOs and overseas corporate bodies with NRI holdings, followed by a special diaspora investment cell in the Ministry of Finance.

Following this, the relationship with the diaspora was radically deepened in the 1990s. When foreign investors fled after the country's acute balance of payments crisis in 1990–1991, the government floated India Development Bonds (IDB) to strategically tap NRI funds. From US$290 million in 1990–1991, NRI inflows subsequently surged to almost US$2 billion in 1992–1993 (Rekhi 1998: 59–62). Under the Bharatiya Janata Party (BJP)-led coalition government, starting in 1998, this crisis-driven opportunistic approach to the diaspora continued. After the nuclear tests of May 1998 drew international sanctions, turbulence in the financial markets, and also a decline in the Indian stock markets, the rupee exchange rate, and the sovereign credit rating, the Indian government appealed for a second time to the diaspora's economic support by launching the Resurgent India Bond (RIB). Overseas Indians responded massively and, in only a few weeks, contributed bonds worth US$4.2 billion. This led the government to repeat the initiative in 2000 with a third bond scheme, the India Millennium Deposit (IMD). This fetched an impressive US$5.5 billion in foreign exchange (Chander 2001).

This brief historical background suggests that the new diaspora policy was the institutional face of a transactional relationship between the Indian state and certain sectors of the overseas Indian community. Commenting on its origins and objectives, an MOIA official noted that the policy was meant to 'fulfil the mutual interests [between the diaspora and India]', which he defined as thus:

> For India it [was] its emergence as a developed nation, it wants [wanted] to regain its status and the diaspora is [was] useful for this. For the diaspora the emotional link is [was] most important, especially for the first generation of PIOs. They get [gained] satisfaction for [through] feeling concerned about [India].
>
> (Srivastava 2008)

Government officials, however, rarely acknowledged this candid assertion. Furthermore, the scholarly focus on the cultural and ideological explanations, most notably the Hindu nationalist BJP factor (Lall 2001), have further clouded the economic drivers of the new state–diaspora relation. More recent work by Latha Varadarajan (2010), Devesh Kapur (2010), Srinath Raghavan (2012) and Daniel Naujoks (2013) have contributed to correct this disciplinary bias, but much more research is needed to go beyond the almost exclusively historical, cultural, sociological and literary dimensions of the Indian diaspora.

This chapter argues that one first needs to reframe the India–diaspora relationship as materially contingent, most notably by defining the diaspora policy as a state-initiated effort to reach out to overseas Indians in order to incorporate them economically and extract their resources and value to a redefined national development strategy since the 1980s. Within this context, the BJP's rise to power in 1999 played a catalyst role by exploring the ideational environment composed of forces at the global, diasporic and national levels, and packaged state objectives into a palatable nationalist discourse that addressed diasporic concerns and anxieties (Kanungo 2008).

The process was defined in Arvind Rajagopal's study on television, Hindu nationalism and the diaspora as a 'tacit negotiation', because if overseas Indians had 'financial capital', 'what 'India' could offer in exchange [was] cultural capital, and the reassurance of genuine mutual belonging' (Rajagopal 2001: 242). While possibly balanced and mutually satisfactory, the re-engagement was nevertheless a fragile understanding, which was particularly visible in the case of non-citizen overseas Indians (the PIOs) who were often effectively incorporated in *economic* and *cultural* terms but, contrary to expatriate NRI citizens, remained excluded from *political* India.

Practically integrated: the diaspora's increasingly long political arm

The asymmetry affecting extra-territorial incorporation strategies was magnified by the fact that PIOs already possessed significant leverage in influencing domestic politics and decision-making processes. For example, the Global Organisation of People of Indian Origin (GOPIO) started as early as the late 1980s to lobby the Indian government on domestic issues such as education and economic reforms. PIOs had also made their fundraising for Indian elite higher education institutions like the Indian Institutes of Technology dependent on the restructuring of their curricula along American lines (Lessinger 2003: 163–167). While cases of NRIs advising the government on economic, science and technology matters dated back to the 1980s – the most notable case being that of Sam Pitroda – PIOs were now also being roped into governmental decision-making levels, as exemplified in the 2008 recruitment of two British and US citizens of Indian origin as Officers on Special Duty to the Rajasthan state government (*The Hindu* 2008).

The increasingly effective incorporation of PIOs was also indicated by their growing influence in shaping India's foreign policy, particularly at the bilateral level. For example, in October 2007, a ten-member delegation of the American USINPAC lobby was officially received by several Indian ministers and the opposition Left and BJP parties 'to impress upon them the benefits of the [nuclear cooperation] agreement' between both countries (Press Trust of India 2007), an effort that eventually proved crucial for the success of the landmark deal between two countries that had remained estranged for several decades. The diaspora's influence in foreign capitals had increased dramatically over the last decade. The detailed case studies by Jason Kirk (2008), A. Gandhi (2002) and Ingrid Therwath (2007) attested to their mobilisation power in Washington, and Sanjay Chaturvedi (2007) showed how activist mobilisation abroad led New Delhi to radically revise its assessment of the diaspora's importance in increasing India's international profile and geopolitical stature.

Political events in Uganda, Malaysia and Kenya (in April, November and December 2007 respectively) also illustrated this to be true in the case of less affluent PIOs. In all three cases, the specific security conditions of PIOs (and not only of NRIs) were widely debated in Parliament. Although the government initially refused to interfere in the sovereign matters of other countries, they were eventually forced to make public statements and to take bilateral diplomatic action so as to ensure the protection and rights of PIOs. In the case of the anti-Indian riots in Uganda, for example, the Parliament was assured by the minister of external affairs that 'the Government took up the matter with the Ugandan authorities very strongly and also lodged an immediate request with the Ugandan Government for providing protection to PIOs' (Rajya Sabha Secretariat 2007). In the case of the violent PIO protests in Malaysia, Parliament engaged in a heated debate on the issue (Lok Sabha Secretariat 2007a), with Tamil Nadu Member of Parliament C. Krishnan 'urging' the government 'to take immediate steps – through the diplomatic channel – to protect the ethnic Tamilians living in Malaysia' (Lok Sabha Secretariat 2007b), following a letter that the chief minister of Tamil Nadu had written to the prime minister. In the case of the post-electoral riots in Kenya, the government was pressured by the chief minister of Gujarat to arrange for 'emergency visas' and 'special plane facilities' for PIO Gujaratis who wished 'to come back to India' (*Times of India* 2008).

Finally, even if formally excluded from political participation, PIOs were able to indirectly influence domestic politics, gradually converting their economic clout into political leverage. This was indicated by the specialised cells and representative bodies created by national political parties for overseas Indians, as well as by their expanding initiatives to source the diaspora for electoral campaigns. There were several unconfirmed reports that both national and regional political parties in India had been procuring financial support from NRIs and PIOs. Because such activity is illegal under the Foreign Contribution (Regulation) Act (FCRA) of 1976, the parties used alternative proxy strategies to circumvent the law. For example, a 2001 Congress Party Committee on Party Finances remarked that (emphasis added),

> *theoretically* the Congress Party could (i) establish a Congress Foundation registered, as say a trust under the Indian Trusts Act 1888; and (ii) seek permission from the Central Government *to mobilize funds from NRIs for specified functions that the Foundation would undertake like training, education, publications and conventions.*
>
> (All India Congress Committee 2001)

Beyond official laws and corridors of power, the effective impact of PIOs during electoral periods was witnessed across the country. During the 2002 and 2007 state assembly elections in Punjab, thousands of overseas Indians flew in especially to campaign in their 'home' constituencies, donating billions of Indian rupees. Several had also given up their foreign citizenships in order to be able to contest (Vinayak 2002). According to one candidate, while most were not even legally entitled to vote, they played a highly influential role because 'people in villages listen to them. The village folk here think that NRIs have seen the world and can judge candidates better' (IANS 2007).

In the mid-2000s, PIOs were being incorporated de facto into the political processes of India, and they started to denounce what they perceived to be an asymmetrical incorporation policy that integrated them economically, but denied them political rights and a legal status to operate civically in India. Their dissatisfaction was a typical manifestation of an increasing diasporic assertiveness that followed state-initiated economic incorporation strategies. Kim Barry defined this new state–diaspora tension in the following terms:

> Emigrants who want a thicker version of long-distance membership than the one on offer from the state are advancing counterclaims for the right to participate fully in their home state society beyond the economic sphere....

> Emigrants already participate in the political process by contributing money, time, and support to political parties and candidates. Indeed, they are aggressively solicited for financial support, and even encouraged by politicians of all stripes to try to influence friends and family back home during elections. Emigrants argue that if they are encouraged to play this type of informal role during elections, there is no valid reason for excluding them from formal mechanisms for participation and representation.
>
> (Barry 2006: 52–53)

Overseas Indians demanded a thicker or more symmetric incorporation, which led to subsequent demands for an institutionalisation of their informal political role, most notably via dual citizenship, voting rights, or parliamentary representation. Fuelled by the diaspora policy and its rhetorical emphasis on the overseas Indians as members of the nation, and empowered by their large financial contribution to India's economic development, PIOs also started to assertively demand more than cultural capital and mere symbolic incorporation. Denouncing the Indian diaspora policy as emphasising 'those who hold Dollars, Pounds, Riyals and all those things', a GOPIO office-bearer thus noted that:

> [W]hen Mahendra Chaudhary [Fiji's first prime minister of Indian origin] was held hostage for 28 days [in 2000], India refused to comment. She opened her mouth only when a small country like Mauritius intervened with the United Nations. This cannot continue. *If India is to play her role as a Mother, she must protect her children wherever they are.*
>
> (Bauhadoor 2003, emphasis added)

The same can be observed in the religious and cultural spheres too, as PIOs were increasingly turning towards India to lobby, petition and pressure the government and legal system to protect and defend their interests or rights as cultural and religious minorities in other countries. For example, the French Sikh PIO activists appealed to the Indian government and petitioned India's supreme court to intercede for them with France and the European Union to ensure their rights to publically profess their religious difference. Similarly, the Hindu American Foundation pressured New Delhi to take diplomatic action whenever Hindus were persecuted worldwide. Commenting on the situation of PIOs in the Caribbean during the annual Pravasi Bharatiya Divas convention in 2005, Chandresh Sharma, a member of the Trinidad and Tobago Parliament, and Ramesh Lawrence Maharaj, former attorney general of that country, asked India to 'use its economic and technological clout in support of Indians facing 'persecution and discrimination' and raise the issue at international fora such as the United Nations' (Bhatt 2005).

Naturally, these demands for further incorporation and consequent diasporic dissatisfaction were far from being a coherent trend among PIOs. However, the larger diasporic level of re-engagement with India was marked by ideational factors related to culture, identity, and a transnational quest for cultural preservation and symbolic political association with India. This was acknowledged by governmental sources: a compilation and study of the total 273 'demands and expectations' registered by the High Level Committee on the Indian Diaspora (HLCID) among overseas Indians worldwide showed that more than half were of cultural, political or educational nature, while only a sixth of all expressed concerns were related to business and economic issues (HLCID 2002).[1] The diasporic 'fixation' with citizenship was also reflected in the findings of a MOIA survey, where 72 per cent of all PIO respondents described dual citizenship as an 'important' or 'very important' issue (Bhagavatula and Verma 2006: 77).

Within this context, India's diaspora policy encountered great receptiveness among overseas Indians, because this new expression of governmental interest potentially offered them a desired sense of membership and attachment, as well as access to the symbolic resources necessary to realise their immigrant quest for public recognition and empowerment. Having said this, words were, however, not enough. Institutions had to ensue.

New diaspora institutions

As seen above, India's diaspora engagement process was mostly driven by economic interests. Over time however, increasing pressure from certain segments of the diaspora that started lobbying New Delhi for formal incorporation in the political realm also followed. Many overseas Indians who were PIOs – the non-citizen diaspora in particular – saw this as the expected outcome of a 'mutually beneficial' relationship that they hoped would eventually translate into formal *political* rights and representation in India. As seen in the previous sections, this expectation was reinforced by current practice, given that overseas Indians were often already politically involved and influential in India, at the central, partisan, regional and local levels, albeit not formally recognised. This and the following two sections detail cases in which these tensions and negotiations led to the establishment of new institutions specifically designed to accord new representation and rights to the diaspora in India, both within and beyond the economic realm.

Tables 2.1 and 2.2 list public institutions and initiatives dealing with the diaspora in India at the central and regional levels. There is a long history to these initiatives. While the HLCID was still busy preparing its report, the government had already nominated a special ambassador-at-large for NRIs and PIOs. The assembly-like representative format of the annual Pravasi Bharatiya Divas (PBD), since 2003, was another example, allowing overseas Indians to directly interact with the federal and state governments. The Ministry of Overseas Indians also played an important role in this regard, describing itself as a 'nodal ministry', a 'one-stop-shop' and a 'friend and supporting guide' not only for expatriate citizens, but for all overseas Indians as well (MOIA 2007). More recently, the establishment of the prime minister's Global Advisory Council of People of Indian Origin was announced with the objective of allowing the leader of the executive 'to draw upon the experience, knowledge and wisdom of the best Indian minds wherever they may be based' (Singh 2008).

Table 2.1 Central diaspora institutions in India

Institution (year created)	*Main function*	*Current status*
Ministry of External Affairs, NRI/PIO Division (1977)	Manage consular affairs related to diaspora	Discontinued (merged with MOIA)
Protector General of Emigration (1983)	Regulates (clears) emigration flows of low- and semi-skilled labour	Active
High-level Committee on the Indian Diaspora (2000–2002)	Study the diaspora, offer recommendations for new policy.	Discontinued in 2002
Bharatiya Pravasi Divas (2003)	Interactive event that addresses issues and concerns of the diaspora	Active (annual)
Ministry for Overseas Indian Affairs (2004)	Apex body for diaspora policy	Active. Manages several programs
Overseas Indian Facilitation Centre (2007)	Attract and assist investments from diaspora	Active
India Development Foundation of Overseas Indians (2008)	Attract and assist philanthropy from diaspora	Still being set up
Indian Council of Overseas Employment (2008)	MOIA's think tank on India and international migration	Active
Overseas Workers Resource Centre (2008)	Assists low-skilled Indian migrant workers on legislation, consular and security affairs	Active
Prime Minister's Global Advisory Council of People of Indian Origin (2009)	Advise and inform the prime minister on diaspora affairs	Active. Supposed to meet twice annually

Source: various official sources compiled by author (2012).

Although playing an important role in offering overseas Indians some channels for informal representation and participation, these initiatives fell short of the demand for full-fledged political incorporation. None of them were truly representative: the annual PBD convention, for example, was a conference-like setting in which delegates from the diaspora often voiced their concerns, but were not involved in any type of deliberation. At best, as with the prime minister's Global Advisory Council, a few overseas Indians were invited to participate in meetings with the prime minister to broadly discuss diaspora affairs. Finally, as highlighted in both tables, a majority of these institutions reflected economic concerns, either in terms of attracting foreign investments or philanthropy from the diaspora. This was so even in the case of institutions such as the Indian Council of Overseas Employment and other programmes set up to assist the less-skilled emigrants who were mainly concentrated in the Gulf region.

Table 2.2 Regional diaspora institutions in India

State	*Institution (year created)*	*Attachment*
Andhra Pradesh	NRI Cell (2004)	Principal secretary
Assam	NRI Cell	Department of Industries and Commerce
Bihar	Bihar Foundation (2006)	Chairmanship by deputy chief minister
Goa	Commissioner for NRI Affairs (2006)	Autonomous, cabinet ranked position
Gujarat	NRI Division	General Administration Department
Karnataka	Karnataka Diaspora Cell (2007)	Directorate of Industries and Commerce
Kerala	Non-Resident Keralite Affairs department (1996)	Government secretariat
Madhya Pradesh	NRI Facilitation Cell (2007)	Secretary-level officer nominated by CM
Orissa	NRO Cell (2004)	General Administration Department, special secretary
Punjab	NRI Affairs Department (1990s)	Minister in charge
Rajasthan	Rajasthan Foundation	Chairmanship by chief-minister
Tamil Nadu	NRI Cell (2002)	Guidance Bureau, Industries Department
Uttar Pradesh	NRI Cell	Department of Infrastructure and Industrial Development
West Bengal	NRI Cell (2012)	Announced in 2009 by the chief minister

Source: various sources, compiled by author (2012).

This demonstrated that while innovating on an institutional level to implement the diaspora policy to reach out to overseas Indians, the Indian state always did so with an underlying economic motive as the main focus. First, this was reflected in the objectives and mandates of the two main bodies that masterminded the new policy – the HLCID and the MOIA. As defined by the terms of reference announced in August 2000 by the Ministry of External Affairs, three out of five of the required tasks the commission was expected to take up was related to economic relations between India and its diaspora (HLCID 2022: iii). The trend persisted after the creation of the MOIA, in 2004, whose mandate was extremely vast,[2] but nevertheless privileged an economic focus and the elaboration of mechanisms of economic incorporation. As recognised by Abdul Kalam, then president of India, while announcing its creation in 2004 before Parliament: 'The new Ministry of Non-Resident Indians Affairs, which reflects our recognition of their [overseas Indians] values, will tap their potential for contributing to our economic growth' (Kalam 2004). These economic priorities were also reflected in its bureaucratic arrangement, with one of two joint secretaries being exclusively responsible for finances, as well as in the contents of most of its publications that mostly covered economic matters. For example, the *Handbook for Overseas Indians* had four chapters on economic incentives and schemes, and only one that dealt with all 'other important matters'.

Second, the new policy dedicated special attention to the role of Indian states, noting that any initiative for overseas Indians 'must be anchored in one of the states ... [and they] must therefore be encouraged to become natural stakeholder partners in the process of engagement' (MOIA 2007: 4). Several chief-ministers had attended the annual PBD events and all states were invited to attend with promotional stalls. Rather than a naïve central concession to regionalist or decentralisation demands, this should be seen as a strategic measure to engage the large fragmentation of the diaspora along ethnic, linguistic and regional factors. The government has therefore been paradoxically fostering the regionalisation of the diaspora policy, notably by encouraging states to set up their own strategies to woo their respective regional overseas Indian populations. As a result, most states now have at least one informal 'NRI cell', while some have even created specialised ministries and departments (see Table 2.2).

Third, India has been implementing several new mechanisms under the new diaspora policy. These sought to move its unskilled emigrants up the international labour value chain in order to guarantee the continuous inflow of their remittances, investments and, eventually, the benefits of a reverse skills drain. This was because most low-skilled labour tended to return permanently to India. This initiative sought to tackle the tendency for Indian labour in the Gulf to gradually lose out to more competitive and trained labour forces from other nationalities, a process that had accelerated over the last decade. This phenomenon might have also been the result of drastic changes in the immigration policies of the host countries, now aimed at controlling and reducing the inflows of foreign workers, the recession in the Gulf economies, and the saturation of labour markets in the unskilled and semi-skilled segments (Zachariah *et al.* 2002). Seeking to lower increasing rates of return migration, India thus embraced the need to develop institutions to regulate recruiters and agencies, prevent trafficking and smuggling, train migrants before departure, and protect them while overseas. This was done by shaping what Castles defined as an adequate policy to 'foster the claimed positive link between emigration and economic growth' (2007: 16).

With this in mind, the government proposed to set up the Central Manpower Export Promotion Council in 2002. Although the amendment eventually lapsed, its proposals were implemented after the formation of the MOIA in 2004. For example, the ministry began offering specialised pre-departure programmes

> to impart orientation training and to upgrade the skills of Indian Workers [who] intended to go abroad to give them [the] competitive edge over the workers from other countries ... and help [them to] retain their jobs and also enable them to earn more wages and return more money as remittance in [to] the country.
>
> (MOIA 2006: 68)

This was complemented by the MOIA's efforts to further amend the Emigration Act and convert it into an 'effective instrument for promotion of employment related migration, prevention of irregular migration and graduation of Indian workers up the wage chain' (MOIA 2007: 9).

Other similar mechanisms include the Council for Promotion of Overseas Employment, a think tank for forecasting future opportunities for overseas employment and making projections and plans for overseas deployment of workers, and the Pravasi Bharatiya Bima Yojana (PBBY), a compulsory insurance scheme for all workers who needed authorisation to emigrate. At the international level, this strategic quest to upgrade the value of Indian emigrant labour was reflected in the government's recent interest in signing bilateral agreements and memoranda of understanding (MoU) to regulate, manage and protect Indian labour abroad. In its new engagement with multilateral migration initiatives, most notably in advocating for the liberalisation of Mode 4 of the General Agreement on Trade in Services (GATS), which stipulated restrictions to the movement of natural persons, is another example.

In addition to these, there were also several non-governmental institutions that had been focusing on researching issues related to India's diaspora, many of which were funded by the MOIA and other public institutions. To cite some examples, such centres or research programmes included:

- Centre for the Study of Indian Diaspora, at Hyderabad University (since 1996).
- Centre for Indian Diaspora and Cultural Studies, at the North Gujarat University (2002).
- Research Unit on International Migration, at the Centre for Developing Societies, Thiruvananthapuram (2006).
- Organisation for Diaspora Initiatives, founded by scholars from the Jawaharlal Nehru University (2006).
- Diaspora Cultural Resource Centre, at the Indira Gandhi National Centre for the Arts (2007), in New Delhi.
- Research Group on Indian Diaspora, at the University of Mumbai (2010).
- Diaspora Chair, funded by the University Grants Commission, attributed to Goa University in 2012–2013.

Not surprisingly, most of these research units were publicly funded and tended to focus on socio-economic issues, neglecting the important *political* dimensions of migration and India's diaspora policy.

The Overseas Citizenship of India (OCI)

While there certainly were considerable sections of the Indian diaspora who were not interested in politicising the links with India, it cannot be disputed that at least for a significant and vocal minority of overseas Indians, the citizenship issue was at the centre of the agenda when lobbying the government in New Delhi. However, this possibility was discussed in detail only in 1992, when it received negative consideration from a committee of secretaries and a group of ministers, and then again in 2001 by the HLCID itself. While India's post-colonial anxieties about 'dual loyalties' and extra-territorial citizenship were certainly moderated by the country's increasing openness and its global economic integration in the prior two decades, the issue remained a hostage of possible 'security implications' (HLCID 2002: 526–531). Echoing Benedict Anderson's denunciation of long-distance and non-citizen participation as being 'inevitably non-responsible' (Anderson 1992: 13) and reflecting the country's still precarious consolidation within an extremely volatile regional security context, the Indian state remained fundamentally opposed to any effort directed at unsettling the strictly territorial basis of Indian citizenship.

Naturally, this posed a dilemma, reflected in the state–diaspora stand-off of the mid-2000s. In the view of many PIOs, nothing could replace the symbolic attractiveness and power of citizenship. Recognising this, the government announced in 2003 that it would take a bold, innovative step to upgrade the existent short-term PIO visa scheme to that of a 'dual citizenship'. Following a bill introduced in Parliament by the BJP-led government in May 2003, the Citizenship Act of 1955 was amended just in time for then prime minister Vajpayee to announce 'dual citizenship' during the PBD 2004, although the provision would only come into force almost a year later under the Congress-led government, which then further amended the Act and its OCI provisions in 2005.

In its present form, the Act enabled the central government to register as an 'overseas citizen of India' any person of full age and capacity who is a citizen of another country now, but was a citizen of India at the time of, or at any time after the commencement of the constitution of India on 26 January 1950; who is a citizen of another country, but was eligible to become a citizen of India at the time of commencement of the constitution; who is a citizen of another country, but belonged to a territory that became a part of India after the 15 August 1947, who is child or a grandchild of such a citizen; or a minor child of a person satisfying any of the first four conditions. Excluded are all those who presently are, or have ever been, citizens of Bangladesh and Pakistan.[3]

Registered OCIs are entitled to a limited set of benefits, such as multiple entry, multi-purpose lifelong visa to visit India, exemption from registration or reporting to police authorities for any length of stay in India, and parity with NRIs in financial, economic and educational fields, except in the acquisition of agricultural or plantation properties. Beyond these general legal specifications, the OCI had been repeatedly referred to as providing for the 'dual citizenship' or 'dual nationality' desired by overseas Indians. However, little has been devoted to study its exact legal foundations and status. This begged a simple, albeit significant question: Was the OCI equivalent to a formal and full-fledged citizenship?

On the surface, this appeared to be the case. In its statement of object and reasons, the 2003 bill noted that following the HLCID's recommendation, 'the Central Government [had] accordingly decided to *make provisions for the grant of dual citizenship*' (Rajya Sabha Secretariat 2003, emphasis added). Strengthening this position is the fact that OCI provisions were formally introduced by a legislative amendment into the Citizenship Act of 1955, and placed on par with formal citizenship acquisition by birth, descent, registration, naturalisation or incorporation of territory. Section 9 of the 2003 amendment, which included a clause guaranteeing that any citizen of India who voluntarily acquired a foreign citizenship '*shall not cease to be a citizen of India*, if within six months thereof he/she [made] an application for registration as an overseas citizen of India', also seemed to indicate that dual citizenship provisions had effectively been enforced (Rajya Sabha Secretariat 2003, emphasis added). Finally, the provision that only PIOs who were citizens of countries that 'permit[ted] dual citizenship in some form or the other' were eligible to apply for an OCI further strengthened its quality as a full citizenship (Ministry of Home Affairs 2008a: 25A).

Yet, despite all these indications, it was clear that the OCI did *not* qualify as a regular citizenship because the constitutional provisions that explicitly banned Indian citizens from holding more than one nationality remained in force (for example, Article 9). These provisions were, in legal terms, hierarchically superior to the OCI regulations contained in the Citizenship Act. Those holding OCIs were indeed eligible to apply for Indian citizenship, but they could only do so after being registered for five years and having resided in India for one year before making the relevant application. They were also forced to surrender their foreign citizenship once their request was granted (Rajya Sabha Secretariat 2005: 4). From this perspective, the OCI was not a dual citizenship, but only another avenue for naturalisation. Those wishing to retain their foreign citizenship were therefore not entitled to apply for and obtain a '*normal* Indian passport', which was 'given only to Indian citizens' (MHA 2008b: 8, emphasis added). Therefore, in practice, the OCI was nothing but 'a registration certificate in the form of a booklet' and 'a multiple entry, multi-purpose lifelong 'U'-visa sticker on the foreign passport of the applicant' (MHA 2008a: 5).

The fact that the OCI was not a conventional citizenship was further highlighted in its limited set of civic rights. While regulations extended to its holder parity with Indian citizens in almost every regard, they nevertheless denied an OCI holder access to any formal political participation, and the possibility to register as a voter, and stipulated his or her ineligibility for the posts of president, vice president, judge of the supreme court and high courts, as well as for legislative representative posts in all federal, state and local bodies. He or she was also denied the right to equality of opportunity in matters of public employment and, except in cases specified by the central government, was barred from being appointed to public services and posts in connection with the affairs of the union or of any state (Citizenship Act Article 7B).

Unlike Indian citizens, an OCI was also banned from travelling to the 'security sensitive' protected and restricted areas without the relevant permission (MHA 2008a: 6). This further attested to his condition as a foreign citizen under Indian public law. In the same regard, on grounds of a set of different motives, the OCI registration could simply be 'cancelled' by an order of the government, contrasted with the much more complex process regulating the deprivation of citizenship for Indian citizens.[4]

Finally, other states such as the United States also underlined that the OCI had been 'mischaracterized as "dual nationality" or "dual citizenship" while being only a "special visa"' (US Embassy New Delhi 2007), describing it as being 'similar to a US "green card"' (US Department of State 2007). The OCI represented neither a travel visa nor a residence permit conventionally attributed to foreign citizens. Despite being often referred to as a 'variant of Indian citizenship' or an 'overseas citizen card', it was clear that the OCI did not represent a conventional citizenship. This attested to its novel character, somewhere in between full citizenship rights as traditionally conferred by states, and a precarious visa for a short period of stay.

Non-resident voting rights

This section provides a final case study on how India considered revising its laws innovatively in order to appease the political demands of the diaspora and to formalise overseas Indians' de facto political influence in India. This was related to voting rights for NRIs, i.e. citizens of India that resided abroad and were not entitled to hold any form of dual nationality or citizenship. As per the Constituent Assembly's decision, NRIs were explicitly refused the right of dual citizenship in the new basic law, as well as voting rights if they were not 'ordinarily residents' in his/her home constituency. Effectively, this meant that for almost 60 years (until the adoption of a recent amendment discussed below) NRIs were disenfranchised if they lived more than six months per year outside of India. This indirect disenfranchisement of millions of Indian citizens was denounced by the Parliamentary Standing Committee on External Affairs in its 2005 report:

> The Committee warns that the Ministry [of Overseas Indian Affairs] must seriously consider and explore the feasibility of extending benefits such as voting rights to Overseas Citizens as India is one of the few democracies that denies the voting rights to its own expatriate citizens. The Committee feels that a Government that seeks the allegiance, support and money of its Diaspora should also be willing to be accountable to it.
>
> (SCEA 2005: 62)

Observing that the 'right to vote as demanded by the non-resident Indians was their legitimate right', the government subsequently introduced the Representation of People (Amendment) Bill in 2006 in Parliament, so as to allow NRIs to cast their votes to the 'Lok Sabha and to the State Legislatures in case they happened to be in their constituencies *at the time of polls*' (Rajya Sabha Secretariat 2006, emphasis added). This was a very conservative move, in that it could hardly expect that many expatriate Indians could afford to travel specially to India to cast their vote.

The reasons for this reluctance can be found in anecdotal evidence suggesting that the BJP would not only greatly benefit from the NRI vote, but also in deeply held anxieties about the political and security implications of a sudden enfranchisement of some ten million citizens that the Indian government was only barely able to monitor. While evaluating the possibility, a parliamentary committee thus stressed eventual 'extreme situations', because this could have 'far reaching consequences and [might] create some problems for a conservative society like India' because

> there [was] a strong feeling from certain sections saying that if you allow a person, who is [was] all along living in a foreign country and coming [came] here only at the time of election to vote, [it] may create some disturbance in the environment of elections.
>
> (Standing Committee on Personnel, Public Grievances, Law and Justice 2006: 19, 20)

Another example of domestic anxieties was found in public reactions to the bill, which repeatedly invoked security and cultural concerns against the extension of voting rights to NRIs. For example, on 25 April 2006, the parliamentary committee placed an official advertisement in newspapers inviting citizens to react to the bill. The responses collected, mostly against the bill, illustrated the primacy of security concerns surrounding the possible political incorporation of NRIs: 'they don't pay taxes in India', the danger of 'instability' provoked by their 'foreign funds', they 'cannot understand the needs of the people of his constituency', they could 'jeopardize the security and sovereignty of the country and [this] may result in catastrophe' (Standing Committee on Personnel, Public Grievances, Law and Justice 2006: 5–6). The memory of separatist insurgencies – such as the Khalistan movement in Punjab during the 1980s, which were often supported and financed by radical sectors of the diaspora – further reinforced this intense hostility against the possibility of extending voting rights even to Indian citizens who just happened to reside temporarily outside India.

Eventually, in 2011, the government succeeded in revising electoral laws and allowed for NRIs to vote as 'overseas voters'. However, this was on the precondition that they actually travelled to their home constituencies to personally cast their votes. There was therefore no provision for absentee (postal, consular or electronic) voting. While this was in some ways an improvement in how for the first time, the active disenfranchisement policy targeting the diaspora for over 60 years was reversed, the requirement for physical presence to vote did seem rather archaic and unfeasible for a large majority of the diaspora, especially in a country with a sophisticated electronic voting system that could easily be extended to consular missions abroad.

Conclusion: the new institutional politics of diaspora policies

Diaspora policies originated in the state and were essentially defined as a governmental initiative to advance national interests and maximise state power. This should not, however, minimise the prior constraining effect of economic globalisation that forced governments to reconsider the role of its expatriates in a reformed and open economy. The Indian case, with its sudden reforms after 1991, reflected this well. Despite assertions that 'states [were] appropriating the [diaspora] as part of their globalising strategies' (Dickinson and Bailey 2007: 765) and that the diaspora policy illustrated how processes of globalisation were being exploited by India to the benefit of its national interest (Chaturvedi 2007), the state could only be considered to be, at best, a constrained prime-mover that was forced to respond to the rapidly globalising and interdependent economy. This was an important finding, in that it highlighted how transnational processes originated a priori at the external level. States were therefore fundamentally limited in their subsequent manoeuvring capacity to address structural changes such as those experienced by India in the 1980s.

However, as this chapter has shown, in the case of India and its state–diaspora nexus, governments retained significant capacity to engage transnational forces and were able to adapt through radical institutional innovation. To realise its new economic interests, the Indian government substantially redefined the idea of national membership, as illustrated with the case of its new OCI. The case of citizenship as an institution was the most symbolic example because it demonstrated how states were able to redefine even their most fundamental constituent forms of legality in order to pursue their external interests in an increasingly interdependent and competitive global economy (Sassen 1996). There was thus an inherently *innovative* nature to this process and, instead of 'maddening states' (Aretxaga 2003) we should perhaps consider the possibility of increasingly 'intelligent states' that find new ways to engage with extra-territorial populations.

Returning to the specific case of the extra-territorial politics of incorporation and the work of Alan Gamlen, this intelligence could be observed in the process through which states were able to engage in an iterated negotiation with transnational forces, such as diasporas:

> states may [might] begin by attempting to assert [extra-territorial] thin sovereignty by extracting obligations without extending rights, but if these attempts are [were] sustained, the extension of reciprocal rights becomes [would become] inevitable. The strength of states' claims to legitimately extract benefits from 'their' diasporas arguably flows [flowed] from their reciprocal provision of benefits.
>
> (Gamlen 2006: 13)

As the consequent 'reciprocal provision of benefits' necessarily assumed the shape of partial citizenships and new institutions, there was therefore also an inherently *productive* dimension to state-managed transnationalism. This did not mean that there was a radical shift and a rupture with existing concepts and practices. The specific term 'management' reflected this, in that it described not only a calculated and strategic, but also essentially gradual, transformative, and continuous process. In actual fact, governments and other intervening actors continued to draw upon, and therefore remained bounded by, the power of the existing conceptual languages and signifiers and, more specifically, economic interests. This was illustrated by the legislative process through which the Indian government instituted its specific diasporic membership title, the OCI, qualifying it as a 'type of citizenship', in order to assuage the diaspora's fixation in acquiring this traditional form of membership as a 'proof' of its formal incorporation.

More importantly, the case of India also showed that diaspora policies were not necessarily the neat outcome of rational policies designed and then implemented by bureaucrats or other state actors. Even when such strategies had a clear strategic nature and objective (such as the economic interests in India's case), they faced important obstacles, reactions and other unexpected forces that were able to renegotiate and transform existing policies and institutions. The Indian case suggested that there was significant variation in the outcome: in some instances, such as the central and regional institutions created by the diaspora policy, political rights and representation of the diaspora were largely neglected. Even after the recent legislative changes to electoral law, the approximate ten million expatriate Indian citizens needed to be physically present in their original home constituencies in order to be able to exercise their voting right. In other instances however, as discussed in this chapter in the form of the OCI, state bureaucracies and political interests *did* compromise, creating a new form of diasporic membership that seemed to have largely fulfilled the diaspora's demands.

One may be tempted to question who emerged 'victorious' out of this interaction: the conservative, materially-focused state, or the transnational diasporic forces that advocated and lobbied their homeland for a stronger attachment and formal membership for so long? On one hand, it seemed that India managed to craft a new diaspora policy that had focused on economic interests and, despite occasional opposition, succeeded in avoiding any type of *political* incorporation. The OCI may be called a citizenship (it even looks like one), but, in the end, it paradoxically excluded the most fundamental dimension of citizenship – civic and political rights and responsibilities. On the other hand, for a state that in the past hardly devoted any resources and attention to its large diaspora, the change in recent decades had been monumental and dozens of new institutions and programmes testified to New Delhi's genuine interest in leveraging overseas Indians as a central force that went beyond just foreign investment, remittances and other economic assets: the diaspora was now seen as a population with specific needs that needed to be protected, ranging from socio-cultural and religious concerns, to consular protection and often also military evacuation.

This dichotomous discussion on who 'wins' the engagement is, however, flawed, and would contribute little towards understanding the complex nuances of state–diaspora engagement processes. By default, diaspora policies were not the outcome, but only the beginning of a new and highly contingent interaction between governmental structures and a diverse, transnational, and mobile population.

Notes

1 Author's compilation based on the following definitions: Logistical demands and expectations include pre-departure information and assistance, consular protection while abroad, protection of rights after return, direct air links, etc. Cultural demands and expectations include support for temple construction, opening of new Indian cultural centres, the promotion and preservation of Indian traditions, access to Indian media, etc. Political demands and expectations focus on the PIO and OCI schemes, dual citizenship, voting rights, representation in India, etc. Economic demands and expectations include foreign investment rights, tax benefits, upgrade of bilateral economic links, preferential exchange rates and remittance transfer channels, etc. Educational demands and expectations include Hindi language courses and materials, recognition of academic degrees, scholarships and course opportunities in India, etc.

2 First instituted in 2003 as the Ministry of Non-Resident Indian Affairs. For the ministry's mandate, see section 22AA of the First Schedule of the Government of India (Allocation of Business) Rules 1961.

3 As defined in Ministry of Home Affairs, Overseas Citizenship of India – Frequently Asked Questions, 28 December 2007, online, available at: http://mha.nic.in/pdfs/FAQs-28.12.07.pdf (accessed 25 June 2008).

4 The cancellation procedure of an OCI registration was established in Article 7D of the Citizenship Act, while the provisions regulating the termination of citizenship for Indian citizens by governmental deprivation could be found in Article 10 of the same text. Interestingly, in both cases cancellation or deprivation could be executed if the OCI, or the citizen 'had shown himself by act or speech to be disloyal or disaffected towards the constitution of India as by law established', a provision that did not apply to other foreigners visiting or residing in India.

References

All India Congress Committee. 2001. Dr Manmohan Singh Committee's Report on Party Finances. Online, available at: www.aicc.org.in/documents-detail.php?id=7 (accessed 11 June 2008).

Anderson, B. 1992. The New World Disorder. *New Left Review* 193: 3–13.

Aretxaga, B. 2003. Maddening States. *Annual Review of Anthropology* 32: 393–410.

Barry, K. 2006. Home and Away: the Construction of Citizenship in an Emigration Context. Public Law and Legal Theory research paper series, Working Paper no. 06–13. New York: New York University School of Law.

Bauhadoor, D. 2003. Speech at Plenary Session with the Minister of External Affairs. New Delhi: First Pravasi Bhartiya Divas, 9 January. Online, available at: http://indiandiaspora.nic.in/ch3.pdf (accessed 11 June 2008).

Bhagavatula, S. and G. Verma. 2006. The Expectations of Indian Diaspora and their Linkages with the Home Country, Survey and report submitted to the MOIA, New Delhi.

Bhatt, A. 2005. Indian Diaspora for Proactive Approach to Settle Problems. *The Hindu*, New Delhi, 9 January. Online, available at: www.hinduonnet.com/2005/01/09/stories/2005010902390900.htm (accessed 13 December 2007).

Brand, L.A. 2002. States and their Expatriates: Explaining the Development of Tunisian and Moroccan Emigration-Related Institutions. Working Paper no. 52. San Diego: Center for Comparative Immigration Studies, University of California.

Castles, S. 2007. Comparing the Experience of Five Major Emigration Countries. Working Paper no. 7. Oxford: International Migration Institute.

Chander, A. 2001. Diaspora Bonds. *New York University Law Review* 76(4): 1005–1099.

Chander, A. 2006. Homeward Bound. UC Davis Legal Studies Research Paper Series, Paper no. 68. Davis: University of California.

Chaturvedi, S. 2007. Diaspora in India's Geopolitical Visions: Linkages, Categories and Contestations. In Robert Wirsing and Rouben Azizian (eds), *Ethnic Diasporas and Great Power Strategies in Asia*. New Delhi: India Research Press.

Dickinson, J. and A.J. Bailey. 2007. (Re)membering Diaspora: Uneven Geographies of Indian Dual Citizenship. *Political Geography* 26 (7): 757–774.

Gamlen, A. 2006. Diaspora Engagement Policies: What are they and What Kind of States use them? Working Paper no. 32. Oxford: Centre on Migration, Policy and Society, Oxford University.

Gandhi, A. 2002. The Indian Diaspora in Global Advocacy. *Global Networks* 2(4): 357–363.

Gordon, J. and P. Gupta. 2004. Non-Resident Deposits in India: In Search of. Return? *Economic and Political Weekly* 39(37): 4165–4174.

High Level Committee on the Indian Diaspora, HLCID. 2002. *Report of the High Level Committee on the Indian Diaspora*. New Delhi: Indian Council for World Affairs.

Hindu, The. 2008. Raje Appoints Two Overseas Indians as OSDs. 8 March. Online, available at: www.thehindu.com/2008/03/08/stories/2008030853830500.htm (accessed 11 June 2008).

IANS. 2007. The Big NRI Hand in Punjab Polls. 9 February. Online, available at: www.dnaindia.com/india/report-the-big-nri-hand-in-punjab-polls-1078901 (accessed 26 January 2015).

Indo-Asian News Service. 2007. NRIs Fly In – Even First Class – for Punjab Polls. 2 September. Online, available at: www.andhracafe.com/index.php?m=show&id=18600 (accessed 5 May 2008).

Itzigsohn, J. 2000. Immigration and the Boundaries of Citizenship: the Institutions of Immigrants' Political Transnationalism. International *Migration Review* 34(4): 1126–1154.

Johnson, B. and S. Sedaca. 2004. *Diasporas, Émigrés and Development: Economic Linkages and Programmatic Responses*. Washington, DC: Carana Corporation.

Kalam, A. 2004. President of India's Address to the Indian Parliament. Online, available at: http://ibef.org/artdisplay.aspx?cat_id=100&art_id=2516 (accessed 2 January 2008).

Kanungo, P. 2008. Globalization, the Diaspora and Hindutva. In Bhupinder Brar, Ashutosh Kumar and Ronki Ram (eds), *Globalization and the Politics of Identity in India*. New Delhi: Pearson Longman.

Kapur, D. 2010. *Diaspora, Development, and Democracy the Domestic Impact of International Migration from India*. Princeton, NJ: Princeton University Press.

Khadria, B. 1991. Contemporary Indian Immigration to the United States – Is the Brain Drain over? *Revue Europeenne des Migrations Internationales* 7(1): 65–96.

Kirk, J.A. 2008. Indian-Americans and the US–India Nuclear Agreement: Consolidation of an Ethnic Lobby? *Foreign Policy Analysis* 4(3): 275–300.

Lall, M.C. 2001. *India's Missed Opportunity: India's Relationship with the Non-Resident Indians*. Aldershot: Ashgate.

Lessinger, J. 2003. Indian Immigrants in the United States: the Emergence of a Transnational Population. In B. Parekh *et al.* (eds), *Culture and economy in the Indian diaspora*. London: Routledge, pp. 165–182.

Lok Sabha Secretariat. 2007a. Alleged Ill-treatment Meted Out to Tamilians in Malaysia. Debate on 29 November. Online, available at: http://164.100.47.134/newls/textofdebate detail.aspx?sdate=11/29/2007 (accessed 29 December 2007).

Lok Sabha Secretariat. 2007b. Problems being Faced by Tamilians in Malaysia. Debate on 3 December. Online, available at: http://164.100.24.208/debate14/debtext.asp?slno=9072 (accessed 29 December 2007).

Ministry of Home Affairs, MHA. 2008a. Extract from the Citizenship Rules, 1956. Online, available at: http://mha.nic.in/pdfs/1956.pdf (accessed 25 March 2007).

Ministry of Home Affairs, MHA. 2008b. Overseas Citizenship of India – Frequently Asked Questions. Online, available at: http://mha.nic.in/pdfs/FAQs-28.12.07.pdf (accessed 25 June 2008).

MOIA. 2006. *Handbook for Overseas Indians*. New Delhi: MOIA.

MOIA. 2007. *Outcome Budget for 2007/2008*. New Delhi: MOIA.

MOIA. 2012. Population of NRIs Worldwide. Online, available at: http://moia.gov.in/writereaddata/pdf/NRISPIOS-Data(15-06-12)new.pdf (accessed 10 October 2013).

Naujoks, D. 2013. *Migration, Citizenship, and Development: Diasporic Membership Policies and Overseas Indians in the United States*. New Delhi: Oxford University Press India.

Prashad, V. 2004. Dusra Hindustan. *Seminar* 538: 27–31.

Press Trust of India. 2007. Nuke Deal: USINPAC-led Delegation to Meet Political Parties. Online, available at: www.hindu.com/thehindu/holnus/000200710222140.htm (accessed 27 May 2008).

Raghavan, S. 2012. The Diaspora and India. *India Review* 11(1): 65–72.

Rajagopal, A. 2001. *Politics after Television: Hindu Nationalism and the Reshaping of the Public in India*. Cambridge: Cambridge University Press.

Rajya Sabha Secretariat. 2003. The Citizenship (Amendment) Bill, 2003. New Delhi. Online, available at: http://rajyasabha.gov.in/legislative/amendbills/XXXIX_2003.pdf (accessed 12 December 2007).

Rajya Sabha Secretariat. 2005. The Citizenship (Amendment) Bill, 2005. Bill no. 75 of 2005, New Delhi. Online, available at: http://rajyasabha.nic.in/bills-ls-rs/2005/LXXV-C_2005.pdf (accessed 12 December 2007).

Rajya Sabha Secretariat. 2006. The Representation of the People (Amendment) Bill, 2006. Bill no. 15 of 2006, New Delhi. Online, available at: www.prsindia.org/docs/bills/1179467379/1179467379_representation_of_people_amendment_bill_2006.pdf (accessed 12 December 2007).

Rajya Sabha Secretariat. 2007. Killing of Indians in Uganda. Starred question no. 520, answered on 10 May 2007. Online, available at: www.meaindia.nic.in/parliament/rs/2007/05/10rs01.htm (accessed 12 December 2007).

Rekhi, S. 1998. Forging a Bond. *India Today*, 03 August: 59–62. New Delhi.

Sassen, S. 1996. *Losing Control? Sovereignty in an Age of Globalization*. New York: Columbia University Press.

Singh, M. 2008. PM's address at the Pravasi Bharatiya Diwas. New Delhi: Sixth Pravasi Bharatiya Diwas. Online, available at: http://pmindia.nic.in/lspeech.asp?id=638 (accessed 11 January 2008).

Smith, M.P. 2003. '*Transnationalism, the State and the Extraterritorial Citizen.*' *Politics and Society* 31(4): 467–502.

Srivastava, D.N. 2008. Interview with author, New Delhi, MOIA, Akbar Bhawan, June 10.

Standing Committee on External Affairs. 2005. *Sixth Report: Ministry Of Overseas Indian Affairs – Demands for Grants*. New Delhi: Lok Sabha Secretariat.

Standing Committee on Personnel, Public Grievances, Law and Justice. 2006. *Sixteenth Report: the Representation of the People (Amendment) Act*. New Delhi: Rajya Sabha Secretariat.

Times of India. 2008. Modi to PM: Help Indians Return. 3 January. Online, available at: http://timesofindia.indiatimes.com/India/Modi_to_PM_Help_Indians_return/rssarticleshow/2670345.cms (accessed 11 June 2008).

Therwath, I. 2007. Working for India or against Islam? Islamophobia in Indian American Lobbies. *South Asia Multidisciplinary Academic Journal*, Fall 2007. Online, available at: http://samaj.revues.org/document105.html (accessed 11 June 2008).

US Department of State. 2007. Travel Advisory. Online, available at: http://travel.state.gov/travel/cis_pa_tw/cis/cis_1139.html (accessed 25 March 2007).

US Embassy New Delhi. 2007. Dual Nationality. Online, available at: http://newdelhi.usembassy.gov/acsdualnation.html (accessed 25 March 2007).

Varadarajan, L. 2010. *The Domestic Abroad: Diasporas in International Relations*. New York: Oxford University Press.

Vinayak, R. 2002. Dollar Gains Currency. *India Today*, 4 February. Online, available at: www.india-today.com/itoday/20020204/state.shtml (accessed 5 January 2008).

Zachariah K.C., B.A. Prakash and S. Irudaya Rajan. 2002. Gulf Migration Study: Employment, Wages and Working Conditions of Kerala Emigrants in the United Arab Emirates. Working Paper no. 326. Trivandrum: Centre for Development Studies.

3 The diaspora meets the development industry

Engaging Norwegian-Pakistanis in development back home

Marta Bivand Erdal

Engaging diasporas in development in their countries of origin has been one of the avenues of the migration–development nexus explored at the Global Forums on Migration and Development (GFMD). While the interactions of migration and development have been discussed with alternating optimism and pessimism over the past four decades or so (De Haas 2010; Skeldon 2009), explicit interest in organised engagements of diaspora in development has been expressed more recently. States in both the Global North and Global South have started to develop policies for engaging diasporas in development 'back home' (Brinkerhoff 2009; Turner and Kleist 2013; Sinatti and Horst 2014) in the twenty-first century.

Literature on migration and development, including diaspora engagements in development, has tended to focus on the potential of migrants' remittances for development (Bailey 2010). Based on the sheer volume of remittances, by now widely acknowledged to be double or more of the amounts contributed by foreign aid or foreign direct investment into many countries, this focus on remittance is hardly surprising (Ratha *et al.* 2010). However, remittances are primarily private money, which means that they cannot be treated in the same way as public funds, such as state foreign aid (Carling 2005; Horst *et al.* 2014). Despite the acknowledgment that remittances are private money, the focus on 'leveraging remittances for development' has been persistent during the past decade, both in academic and in policy circles (Kapur 2005; Ratha 2007).

Critics have questioned the ways in which development is conceptualised in the context of migration and development, and who it is directed towards (Raghuram 2009; Mercer *et al.* 2009). Northern states' involvement with migration and development, with regard to so-called voluntary return programmes being financed over foreign aid budgets (Cassarino 2010) in particular, are indicative of the ambiguities within this field (van Houte and Davids 2008; Sinatti 2011). Migration control measures are also suggested to be a hindrance to the fulfilment of migration–development objectives, and contribute to fragmented policies within the field of migration (Åkesson 2011). Simultaneously, states in the 'Global South' are also adopting policies with the explicit aim of encouraging diaspora engagements in development in their country of origin (see for examples on Argentina, Jamaica and Tanzania respectively Margheritis 2007; Sives 2012; Hansen 2012).

Optimism about migration and development in the early twenty-first century intersected with moves toward more neo-liberal policies on development, and the focus on individual migrants and their remittances dove-tailed with de-politicising key questions with regard to development (Åkesson 2011). On one extreme, the celebratory mode of migration and development could be seen to make migrants responsible for development back home (Bakewell 2008; De Haas 2010). On the other extreme was the suggestion that migration and remittance-sending contributed to dependency and inequality in migrant sending communities, and laid illegitimate burdens on migrants struggling to make ends meet, often in contexts of discrimination or racism (Page and Mercer 2012). Arguably, the middle-ground between these two extreme positions is more common, yet a fundamental premise for any discussion about migration and development remains that states are responsible for addressing the 'structural constraints [necessary to shape][...] favorable general conditions for human development to occur' (De Haas 2010: 258).

This chapter explores the experiences of a diaspora[1]-development engagement scheme launched by Norwegian authorities in 2009, targeting Norwegian-Pakistani communities. This co-development funding scheme was launched as part of the Norwegian government's migration–development efforts. Together with measures to offer cheaper, legal and more competitive remittance services, it was the main way of putting migration–development policies into practice (Erdal and Horst 2010; Carling *et al.* 2007). Co-development funding models have previously been tried out in different contexts, including the case of Mexico with its '*Tres por unos*' programme where every dollar sent by a migrant was added to with a dollar by the federal, regional and local authorities (Delgado Wise and Rodríguez Ramírez 2001). European countries such as France, Spain, the Netherlands and the United Kingdom all had their own particular models of co-development funding for diaspora groups at given points in time (Horst *et al.* 2010).

The focus of this chapter is on diaspora development organisations' experiences while participating in a co-development funding scheme, particularly with their interactions with the development industry – an important player in the diaspora-development field. Through this, the ways in which development was understood and practised is explored. The emphasis on actors' practices means that state policies are largely left aside, though their significance for the structural context is acknowledged (for work focusing on state policies on diaspora-development engagements see e.g. Brinkerhoff 2009). Previous studies on migration and development have often adopted a universalist vision of development that does not allow for alternatives, or by contrast, critiquing the 'development industry' as modernist and Western (Mercer *et al.* 2009; Raghuram 2009). This chapter seeks to move beyond and build on this critique, to discuss, based on analysis of experiences of development practice, the complex ways in which the diaspora and the development industry interacted with one another in the Pakistani context.

Diaspora-development engagements

The substantial literature on migration and development that focuses on remittances tends to take an economic starting point, often measuring remittance inflows against economic development at a macro-level. In the sub-field of diaspora engagements in development, where insights from studies of migrants' transnational ties are included, social dimensions are integrated to a greater extent (see e.g. Rahman 2010; Erdal 2014). However, Nicola Piper's call (2009) for the inclusion of a social perspective on the migration–development nexus is, arguably, still relevant. There are social dimensions to be considered even when studying remittances as monetary transfers with developmental impacts (Rahman and Lian 2012; Erdal 2012; Carling 2014). These social dimensions mean that economic behaviour, such as remittance-sending, is intertwined with familial and other social obligations – for example, with regard to weddings, births, funerals or investment in housing and property. Migrants' transnational ties, while usefully disaggregated into economic, socio-cultural and political levels, are inherently linked, and engagements in development cannot be seen as isolated from these broader transnational practices (Page and Mercer 2012).

The 'transnational social fields' (Levitt and Glick-Schiller 2004) in which migrants engage in, and where transnational practices take place, often span long geographic distances. In the context of much research on diaspora and development, they also span the Global North–South divide, with associated wealth inequalities. While the meaning of 'development' has been scrutinised alongside other post-colonial critique in development studies for several decades, little discussion about what 'development' means in the context of migration and development has happened till recently. Academics have questioned the meaning of 'development' with regard to the migration–development nexus in general (Bakewell 2008), as well as more specifically with regard to the ways in which migrants conceive of development (Dannecker 2009). This would acknowledge both gender differences and changing perceptions over time. The differing views and priorities of migrants versus sending communities are important, as development is often assumed to be based on grass roots ownership – whereas in the diaspora-development setting, ownership might become un-clear (Raghuram 2009). The specific context of migration and development has implications for the ways in which development is conceptualised. This centres on the ways in which transnational migration challenges traditional notions of proximity and distance. While migrants and their non-migrant relatives live a great physical distance apart, there is still a greater extent of proximity than in other international development contexts because of transnational ties. Proximity therefore still matters, but the ways in which distance influences diaspora engagements in development are qualitatively different (Mercer *et al.* 2009).

Beyond the fact that there is a great volume of money flowing from diasporas to their countries of origin, one could question why engaging diasporas in development is so important. One view on this is that diaspora engagements in development can also be important in providing an avenue for challenging the development industry's right of definition of what might or might not count as 'development' (Mercer *et al.* 2009). It is important to trace the ways in which development is practised, and diaspora who have close connections both 'here' and 'there' are uniquely positioned in this regard. Diaspora engagement with development often intersects with politics, perhaps particularly so in conflict and post-conflict settings. In these contexts, diaspora engagements in development are often framed as either positive or negative, and either political or apolitical, in relation to the conflict and actors in question (for examples from Sri Lanka and Somalia see e.g. Orjuela 2008; Erdal and Stokke 2009; Horst 2008). These contexts are often where diaspora engagements are both the strongest, and also the most complicated for states and the development industry to deal with. Simultaneously, the challenges from these contexts are not unique, as questions about the de-politicisation of development into a technocratic issue arise in peaceful contexts too (Mohan and Stokke 2006).

The migration–development nexus in South Asian contexts has been explored with emphasis on remittances in particular (Rahman 2010; Suleri and Savage 2006; Kelegama 2011). The broader field of migration studies in Asia often includes development dimensions in its discussions of the implications of e.g. Filipino, Sri Lankan or Pakistani labour migration, but overall little work focuses specifically on diaspora engagements in South Asia's development as more organised development projects. Exceptions include diaspora engagements in emergency relief (in the context of Pakistani earthquakes see e.g. Rytter 2010b; Rehman and Kalra 2006), and an emergent focus on religion and development, as well as the diaspora's role in Islamic faith based organisations (see e.g. Clarke 2007; De Cordier 2009).

This chapter aims to address the gap in the existing literature with regard to organised diaspora engagements in development in the South Asian context, through an empirically based case-study of Norwegian-Pakistani diaspora engagements in development in Pakistan. The importance of transnational social fields as the context for these engagements from the migrants' and their organisations' point of view, and simultaneously the need for a critical reflection on how 'development' is understood by the involved actors, is acknowledged. This section is followed by a brief account of data and context that presents the co-development model discussed in the chapter. The remainder of the chapter explores the experiences of Norwegian-Pakistani engagements with development projects in Pakistan.

Data and context

This chapter draws on qualitative data collected among Norwegian-Pakistanis and involved actors in Pakistan in the period 2008–2010. The main-data set consists of interviews with Norwegian-Pakistani non-governmental organisations (NGOs) and their partner NGOs in Pakistan, as well as field visits to the project sites in Pakistan. This was supplemented with several group discussions and attendance at meetings, most of which were conducted as part of an evaluation of the NORAD (Norwegian Agency for Development Cooperation) funded 'Pilot project Pakistan' co-development funding scheme.[2] Additionally, the chapter also draws on 30 semi-structured interviews with Norwegian-Pakistani migrants and descendants conducted for a Research Council of Norway funded research project on 'Remittances from Immigrants in Norway' (2007–2012).

The Pakistani diaspora is estimated to be about seven million, meaning that its members represent only about 4 per cent of the total population of Pakistan.[3] Yet, international migration remains an important issue in the country, both financially and socially (Hasan 2010). The Pakistani diaspora is global, and the transnational social field that linked the Pakistani Punjab and the Oslo area stretched to parts of the United Kingdom, Denmark, Spain, Greece and the United States. Many migrants in Norway had relatives in several of these countries, and there were significant parallels between the migrant communities in Norway, the United Kingdom and Denmark (Charsley 2007; Rytter 2010a).

Pakistani migration to Norway started around 1967 with male labour migration (Moen 2009) and continued through chain migration from a number of villages and towns in Pakistani Punjab (Østberg 2003; Døving 2005). The population of individuals of Pakistani origin in Norway now stands at around 32,000 people, of whom nearly half were born in Norway. A majority of Norwegian-Pakistanis originate from Pakistani Punjab, from the areas around the towns of Kharian and Gujrat in Gujrat District. This area is located more or less halfway between Islamabad and Lahore.

As previously mentioned, most labour migration from Pakistan is male short-term labour migration directed to the Gulf States. This is reflected in remittances sent to Pakistan, where flows from the Gulf States are the most significant, followed by flows from the United States, then the EU countries, with relatively small flows coming from countries like Norway. Remittances to Pakistan totalled nearly US$14 billion in the financial year 2013 (July 2012–June 2013), and levels have been increasing steadily over the past decade. This is despite the fact that remittances recorded by the State Bank of Pakistan only include transfers made via formal channels (i.e. within the banking system, including large money transfer operators (MTOs) such as Western Union and Moneygram), and not informal transfers (i.e. through *hundi*, the South Asian variety of *hawala*) or hand-carrying. In 2009, the level of officially recorded remittances was equivalent to 5 per cent of Pakistan's GDP, and was more than three times the amounts received as Official Development Assistance (ODA) and Foreign Direct Investment (FDI). Remittances were therefore of considerable economic significance to the Pakistani authorities, who had launched the Pakistan Remittance Initiative to facilitate and boost remittance inflows. This was a joint effort by the State Bank of Pakistan, the Ministry for Overseas Pakistanis, and the Ministry of Finance.

The 'Pakistan Pilot Project' was launched in August 2008 by Norwegian authorities as one measure to boost diaspora engagements in development. The pilot targeted Norwegian-Pakistani communities because of their long-standing history and relatively large numbers in Norway. Further reasons for the choice of country for the pilot could not be confirmed in official documents, but seemed to be related both to the relative political stability in Pakistan – compared with Somalia or Sri Lanka for instance – and the political exchanges between Norwegian ministers visiting Pakistan and (more specifically) the districts of Pakistani Punjab where many migrants originated from. Concerns about diaspora contributions to development in the region were discussed during these meetings. Speculations aside, the pilot was firmly founded in policy objectives that were established around the same time. Two White Papers on Norwegian foreign policy and development policy were published in 2009, both explicitly referring to the potential for diaspora engagements and the importance of seeing diaspora as resources for Norway.

> These minority groups have resources that have been utilized too little in the Norwegian development policy context. They possess valuable knowledge about culture, language, society, history, religion and politics. Both individuals and organizations have good contact with key milieus in their own or their parents' country of origin. They can provide important information and improve our understanding of ongoing political processes.[4]

The objectives of the 'Pakistan Pilot Project' were: to improve the development impacts of Norwegian-Pakistani projects in Pakistan; to make Norwegian-Pakistani organisations able to compete better for development funding; to make use of the diaspora's expertise and experience; to build competence in Norwegian-Pakistani organisations; to gain experience with diaspora engagements in development.[5] In order to achieve its aims, the 'Pakistan Pilot Project' had a complex organisation as a basis for a co-funding scheme. Figure 3.1 is a

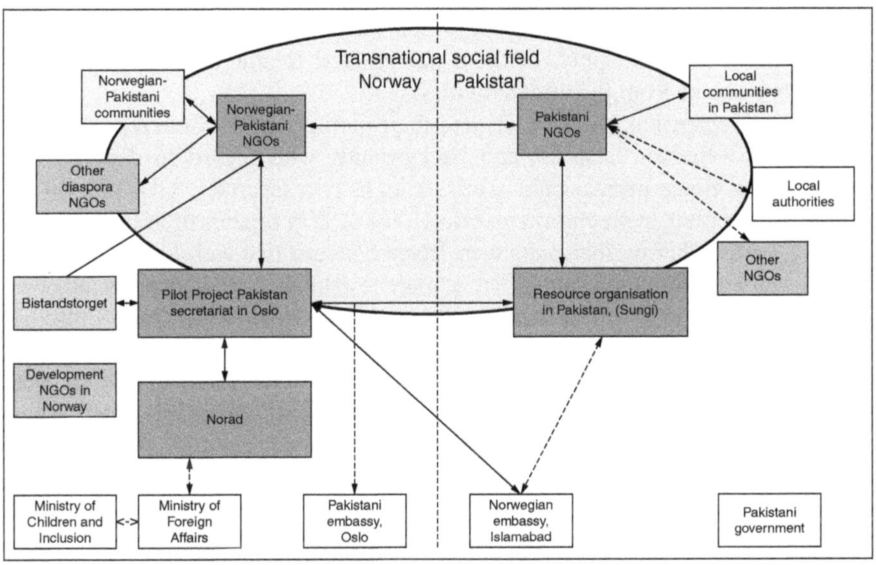

Figure 3.1 The Pakistan pilot project model.

sketch of the different actors involved. The primary actors were the Norwegian-Pakistani NGOs and their partner NGOs in Pakistan, with the support of a Norwegian-based development NGO, which also functioned as a secretariat for the pilot project. A separate but equally important actor was a Pakistani development organisation, which was drawn in for both capacity-building and follow-up action in Pakistan and Norway. The Norwegian funders and owners of the pilot, NORAD, as well as the Ministry of Foreign Affairs, had a very withdrawn role in the course of the pilot. Beyond these main actors, the Norwegian-Pakistani communities, local communities, and the broader socio-political environment that included development NGOs in Norway and Pakistan were also involved, albeit in different ways.

The co-funding scheme meant that Norwegian-Pakistani NGOs could apply for funding – together with their Pakistani partner NGOs – for development projects, and if successful, were granted 50–50 funding from NORAD. The funding was subject to a quality assessment of the application and to a minimum amount of contributions from the Norwegian-Pakistani NGOs that was to be doubled by NORAD. The minimum amount was set at 100,000 Norwegian kroner. This was initially deemed to be a high amount by the NGOs, who had to raise this amount on a voluntary basis within their communities. However, as it turned out, raising this amount was not a great problem for most of the engaged actors, whereas complying with the requirements of NORAD with regard to the nature and quality of development projects in Pakistan proved to be more of a challenge. Furthermore, the requirement of a partnership with Pakistani NGOs was another challenge for some groups. A total of nine Norwegian-Pakistani NGOs succeeded in receiving funding through the pilot in the period from 2008–2010, while several more organisations were able to participate in capacity-building and networking activities. Some groups that were initially interested for various reasons either did not apply, or were not granted funding. These groups distanced themselves from the pilot activities.

The Norwegian-Pakistani NGOs and their partners in Pakistan represented a diversity of experience, focus, and backgrounds with regard to development engagements. Some partner-pairs were set up as two separate NGOs only in the context of the pilot, with enormous efforts invested in organisation building and training, while other partner-pairs were made between two well-established entities in Norway and Pakistan; often a more established development actor in Pakistan, locally or even nationally. The projects, which were funded through the pilot, were by and large within the health and education sectors, with one project focusing more on environmental issues. While some of the projects started up with the pilot launch, most of the Norwegian-Pakistani organisations involved had been involved with development or charity projects of one kind or another prior to the launch of the pilot. The projects funded through the pilot represented a significant proportion of the development and charity engagements among Norwegian-Pakistanis, though not in its entirety.

One of the organisations was explicitly religiously motivated, while several other organisations collected money at one or more mosques in the Oslo-area, illustrating the important intersections between development and Islamic charity in the Pakistani context. A lot of funds for charity and for emergency relief were collected at the many mosques and through their networks, which will be partly covered in the following discussion of Norwegian-Pakistani diaspora engagements in development.[6]

Among those engaged in the diaspora organisations, migrants made up the majority. Having said this, there were also some people who came to Norway as children, or who were born in Norway, contributing to a generational diversity. Finally, most of the involved organisations in Norway had men in primary positions, though a number of them had women on their boards and as active members. Some Norwegian-Pakistani women's organisations exist, but these were more concerned with welfare issues in Norway, and less with transferring funds to Pakistan for developmental purposes.

Engaging the Norwegian-Pakistani diaspora in development back home

When 'Pilot Project Pakistan' was launched as an initiative by the Norwegian authorities, it required gradual progress. Diaspora-development organisations in Norway tried to access development funding through regular channels, but met with only minimal success, (though there were a couple of Norwegian-Pakistani organisations as exceptions). Small-scale development and charity initiatives at the local village level have also been common among Norwegian-Pakistani organisations for decades. The co-development funding scheme meant set requirements, and the diaspora thus met 'the development industry', first in the shape of NORAD, and then through the two support organisations involved in Norway and Pakistan respectively. The review of experiences with the pilot showed that diaspora engagements in development were time consuming, in particular with regard to building trust between the different actors involved. Furthermore, capacity building and networking were extremely important for securing and improving desired development effects.[7]

When the diaspora met the 'development industry', it was uneasy, with obvious trust issues plaguing the relationship. For instance, assumptions about the implications of kinship between diaspora and partner organisations drew the scepticism of the 'development industry' in Norway. Diaspora organisations were also sceptical with regard to the discrepancy between policy and practice, and that the co-development funding model was set to a 50–50 funding, rather than a 10–90 funding split, which was the case in NORAD's main funding schemes.[8] In the following four sections, experiences from this diaspora-development co-funding scheme will be discussed, focusing on types of development, questions on sustainability, and the implications of the transnational social field for diaspora engagements in development.

Service delivery or rights-based empowerment?

The 'development industry' had particular ways of working with and understanding development. This was influenced by international commitments such as the Millennium Development Goals, among other factors. On a general level, the 'development industry' represented a drive for rights-based and empowerment-focused development, including dimensions such as gender mainstreaming and anti-discrimination toward minorities. However, there was a simultaneous need for service delivery, particularly in the context of Pakistan where the state was not capable of providing sufficient services for its population. Resultantly, as a direct consequence of the insufficient state sponsored services that existed, diaspora engagements in development focused on service delivery. In particular, this involved seeking to provide health services closer to where people lived (e.g. in remote villages), and vocational training for women who left school after primary education.

This disjuncture in focus suggested a conflict of ideas in terms of how development was conceptualised between the diaspora actors and the 'development industry' actors, consequently questioning the objectives of development (Bakewell 2008). Of course, many mainstream development actors also sought to address poor service delivery through rights-based programmes together with the 'development industry', with some service-delivery included whenever necessary. However, the actual improvement was not always as substantial as when it was reflected in the policy documents.

Nonetheless, the pressing need that local populations and migrants coming from these populations saw for service was highly understandable – this was a starting point for their development engagements. Interestingly, both diaspora actors and their partners in Pakistan were very open to new insights, as reflected here in the quote from Bilal,[9] a doctor working at a hospital: 'It has been important to learn to think differently about development. I am a trained medical doctor. I only thought about the medical side. It's good to learn about development more broadly'. Bilal worked in a hospital in a very remote village, which now offered health services to inhabitants of villages that had no closer alternative within 8–10 hours of walking; the closest district level hospital was some 2–3 hours' drive away by car, with few options for public transport.

Bilal's reflection was shared among many of the actors involved in Norway and Pakistan. In particular, many like Qamar stressed that

> the capacity-building in Norway [had] been useful, and it [had] been in [conjunction] with the capacity-building in Pakistan, where [the Pakistani resource NGO] [had] been important. We've [had] taken part in courses in Pakistan, and then they [had] been in Norway too.

The significance of the learning experience from taking part in the pilot project was very important. Arguably, this was as much related to new horizons opening up as it was related to a new experience with the 'development industry'.

First, being exposed to different ways of working with and relating to development, both among other Norwegian-Pakistani diaspora NGOs and in the broader 'development' environment, meant possibilities for new approaches to development and external funding of projects. Second, experiencing a professional development NGO from Pakistan, which was very much part of the same 'development industry' as NORAD and other actors in Norway, was an eye-opener for many in the diaspora. Pakistani capacities, experience and knowledge were treated with a high degree of respect in the Norwegian context, encouraging diaspora actors to continue pursuing their development projects in Pakistan.

The empowerment resulting both from capacity building and the interactions with the 'development industry' in Norway and Pakistan were simultaneously made clear through Ali, who said, 'Because of the pilot, people are now more aware that there is a potential for synergies. Those who work on development in Pakistan talk more to each other, exchange experiences and learn from each other'. For Ali and many with him, the networking opportunities offered through the pilot were continued beyond it, and this provided continued opportunities for reflecting on ways to implement and improve diaspora-based development engagements together with partner NGOs in Pakistan, both in terms of service-delivery and rights-based development.

Sustainability of development initiatives

A serious concern both for diaspora-development NGOs as well as for the funders was the question of the sustainability of development initiatives. The fact that a number of hospitals as well as vocational training facilities had been established – including the construction of buildings, purchase of equipment, employment of staff and the ensuing responsibility for their salaries – as well as actual running costs, raised important questions about sustainability. It was hard to imagine how such endeavours could fulfil the requirements for sustainable development, as they were dependent on continued funding from the same diaspora-development NGOs without prospects for sustainability. Nevertheless, these initiatives strived to fill gaps in the service delivery provided to populations, and they often included activities that potentially led to a degree of sustainability. Among these activities was the payment for medical services from the well-off, and the sale of produce from vocational training facilities. While it was questionable whether this would be sufficient to achieve sustainability, it was certainly an important contribution and a signal of the attitudes among both the diaspora and Pakistani organisations with regard to the question of sustainability. Though on the surface, projects seemed impossible from a 'development industry' point of view, differences could well be overcome in practice.

Diaspora engagements, while being 'unsustainable' according to standard measures on the one hand, often overlapped with the stated aims and objectives of the 'development industry' on the other. In this way, the hospital built in the ancestral village (an idea that might be seen as related to maintaining the family's social status) might in fact be a vehicle for strengthening women's opportunities and rights in the Pakistani context. This does not mean that issues related to social status were rendered unimportant. Rather, they illustrated the complexities of the motivations driving diaspora engagements in development. Ahmed's explanation for investing much of his spare time and money in the vocational training facility in his village revealed a clear reflection about the possibility of affecting the status quo, and contributing to development:

> In some communities, the women don't go out. If they can go to a course, they have a reason to leave the house. Then they can take part in the course, and they get a chance to socialize. Maybe they will see what opportunities are there [there are] outside for them, they will get used to go[ing] out, and their families will get used to it.

Ahmed's statement was reflective of an open attitude to the position of women in these communities. He saw that for social and economic reasons, there was a need for greater opportunity for women to leave their homes to benefit themselves and their families. As someone from the area, he was also very much aware of the socio-cultural obstacles that existed in the way of such development. His approach was therefore a careful and slow one. It enabled some women from the village to experience enhanced freedom, and as such was very much in line with the gender equality and empowerment buzzwords that the 'development industry' was so caught up with.

Knowledge transfer in a transnational social field

Peggy Levitt's term 'social remittances' (1998; 2011) was well-known within the field of transnational migration studies. She referred to the broad range of non-monetary transfers of knowledge, ideas and experiences that might flow from a diaspora population to their places of origin through social remittances. The concept acknowledged that these were not unidirectional flows; rather, they were bidirectional, and actors placed in different locations within the transnational social field held agency, and were affected by the structures that existed in different ways.

This back and forth in the context of diaspora engagements in development was significant, as there were equal partners involved, both in Norway and in Pakistan. Development projects were conceived of and implemented jointly through the work of the two-partner NGOs. An enabling factor for many projects was the fact that there was a diaspora NGO involved, as they provided the funding; more often than not, the diaspora NGO was also involved with the nitty-gritty of project planning and implementation. Although the partner NGO in Pakistan held the expertise with regard to development work in Pakistan by employing staff trained in professional development, the interaction between the NGOs was still important to ensure the quality of the projects.

There was one project among the many funded by the Pakistan Pilot Project that seemed to fulfil the ideals of the potential for knowledge transfer in a transnational context of development. This project focused on environmental issues, and started out as a small-scale initiative in a section of a small town, with the aim of clearing garbage in both an environmentally and financially sustainable way. The project was set up much like a business, with the aim that in time it would run as a self-financing non-profit organisation. A respondent, Manzoor, explained the rationale behind this initiative from the Norwegian-Pakistani organisation's side:

> We have learned from our experiences in Norway that it is possible to change people's attitudes. That's why we tried to change people's attitudes to garbage collectors [as they are of different caste and were Christians]. We did not know whether it would work. People said it wouldn't, but now we are seeing that it's possible. The local people are giving the garbage collectors water. Maybe not from glasses from their houses, but they are offering them water in their bottles when they need a drink. This is a huge change from when we started, less than a year ago. Through the pilot we learned how important it is to include the local population, to understand them – and that change is possible.

The environmentally-focused project inspired by garbage collection and sorting in the Oslo area was therefore as much a project about anti-discrimination and changing attitudes in the local target area as it was a development plan. Although it took time, the hard work of challenging long held discriminatory practices provided results because the purpose to this project benefitted the whole community. Not only were Christians provided proper employment with regulated salaries, their experience of interactions with others in the local community changed over time as their work started to be seen as valuable. It can be argued that this change might have been harder to achieve without the combined insider–outsider position of the diaspora actors involved with this project. Simultaneously, it was an example of how goals that were clearly very similar to those of the 'development industry' – prioritising environmental awareness – as well as combating the discrimination of minorities were put centre stage by the diaspora themselves.

At a more practical and concrete level, the reality of these development projects being placed within transnational social fields was illustrated by a local project manager in Rawalpindi, Naisr:

> The project is well placed in terms of people from Norway travelling by, when they are on visits in Pakistan. We sometimes get news from Norwegian-Pakistanis who are individual donors, who visit the project when on holiday in Pakistan. This gives them a chance to check-up on what we're doing.

As Nasir's comment shows, the transnational interconnectedness is important both in order to satisfy donors' curiosity, as well as to serve as a form of control

– they could see for themselves how their donations were being spent. This presented an element of 'social control' for the diaspora-development NGOs too, as individual donors took an interest in the running of projects in Pakistan. Simultaneously, this provided an opportunity for advertisement; when things went according to plan, donors would spread the word in the communities in Norway about the viability and trustworthiness of a particular project. These kinds of exchanges between individual Norwegian-Pakistanis and development professionals in the Pakistani partner organisations also raised the awareness among Norwegian-Pakistanis about the realities of development work in Pakistan, as well as providing them with new knowledge about development processes and societal changes occurring in contemporary Pakistan. Arguably, this also enabled them to be better able to understand the perspectives of the 'development industry' both in Norway and in Pakistan, and to continue their own deliberations about what progress and change in Pakistan should be about.

Conclusion

When the diaspora meets the 'development industry', immediate clashes and conflicts of interests may take place. However, both sides may become strengthened from the exchange, and development outcomes may be enhanced over time. The 'development industry' could be portrayed as the villains, the global and powerful machine against which small-scale voluntary based migrant NGOs did not stand a chance. Likewise, the diaspora-development NGOs with their partners could be seen as victims being overrun. However, the experience from Pakistan showed that this was not true in reality. The 'development industry' may be financed from the global North, but local and indigenous Pakistani development NGOs may well represent some of the finer strands of this 'development industry', thus complicating a binary North–South divide. Furthermore, the ideals of the 'development industry', although phrased in Western buzzwords, were in fact not insensitive to socio-cultural and religious contexts. Rather, in many contexts, combating inequality and poverty may unite the interests of the 'development industry' and diaspora engagements in development.

A risk in the context of diaspora engagements in development and their interactions with the established 'development industry' is what has been termed 'cloning' – where diaspora engagements would replicate what actors had already been doing, while not adding any value.[10] The case of the Pakistan Pilot Project seemed to suggest that reflections on the meaning and practice of development were encouraged (in the form of critical reflection and solid grounding in the transnational social field these development engagements arose in), which prevented cloning. However, there should be an awareness that those seeking funding would always seek to meet the objectives set by the funder. Arguably though, it seemed that objectives were overlapping in this particular context. Diaspora-development actors could therefore benefit from a broadening of horizons on development, without losing the possibility of pursuing the projects they had set out to run in Pakistan.

A question that remains, however, is how the 'development industry' may learn from diaspora engagements in development, not only in terms of future diaspora engagements, but also in terms of how development is understood and practised. While the diaspora-actors investigated in this chapter seemed to be able to – with the support from Norway and Pakistan – find their own voices in the development landscape, there do not seem to be many ways for channelling their reflections and experiences back into the 'development industry' in a systematic and sustainable way. Rather, this is dependent on the goodwill of individuals centrally placed within relevant organisations and structures. In the case of the Pakistan Pilot Project and its follow-up, there has been a beneficial coincidence of individuals in Pakistan and in Norway, which has played an important role in the success of many of the initiatives undertaken as part of this pilot. Depending on individual staff and volunteer efforts is, however, neither a viable nor recommendable strategy for making the most out of diaspora-development contributions in the future.

Notes

1. The term diaspora is used here as a shorthand expression to refer to persons from Pakistan or with Pakistani heritage who are resident outside Pakistan. Theoretical debates regarding the relative benefits of the terms diaspora and transnational communities are not discussed here.
2. Erdal, M.B. and Horst, C., 2010, Engaging Diasporas in Development: A Review of Pilot Project Pakistan. NORAD Report 7. Oslo: NORAD.
3. The following paragraphs are based on text from Erdal 2012 (unpublished) PhD Dissertation, *Transnational Ties and Belonging: Remittances from Pakistani Migrants in Norway*, University of Oslo.
4. White Paper 13: Climate, Conflict and Capital – Norwegian Development Policy Adapting to Change, Report to the Storting, Norwegian Ministry of Foreign Affairs.
5. Erdal and Horst 2010.
6. Research on Islamic charity engagements of the Pakistani diaspora in Norway is currently under work at PRIO (2012–2015).
7. Erdal and Horst 2010.
8. In these instances, the NGOs collected 10 per cent of the funding, and were topped-up with 90 per cent from NORAD.
9. All names are pseudonyms.
10. Horst *et al.* 2010.

References

Åkesson, L. 2011. Making Migrants Responsible for Development: Cape Verdean Returnees and Northern Migration Policies. *Africa Spectrum* 41: 61–83.

Bailey, A. 2010. Population Geographies, Gender and the Migration–Development Nexus. *Progress in Human Geography* 34(3): 375–386.

Bakewell, O. 2008. 'Keeping them in their Place': the Ambivalent Relationship between Migration and Development in Africa. *Third World Quarterly* 29: 1341–1358.

Brinkerhoff, J. 2009. Creating an Enabling Environment for Diaspora's Participation in Homeland Development. *International Migration* 50: 75–95.

Carling, J. 2005. Migrant Remittances and Development Cooperation. In *PRIO Report*. Oslo: Peace Research Institute in Oslo (PRIO).

Carling, J. 2014. Scripting Remittances: Making Sense of Money Transfers in Transnational Relationships. *International Migration Review* 48: 218–262. DOI: 10.1111/imre.12143.

Carling, J., M.B. Erdal, C. Horst and H. Wallacher. 2007. Legal, Rapid and Reasonably Priced? A Survey of Remittance Services in Norway. Oslo: PRIO.

Cassarino, J.-P. 2010. Unbalanced Reciprocities: Cooperation on Readmission in the Euro-Mediterranean Area. In *Viewpoints*. Washington, DC: Middle East Institute.

Charsley, K. 2007. Risk, Trust, Gender and Transnational Cousin Marriage among British Pakistanis. *Ethnic and Racial Studies* 30: 1117–1131.

Clarke, G. 2007. Agents of Transformation? Donors, Faith-based Organisations and International Development. *Third World Quarterly* 28: 77–96.

Dannecker, P. 2009. Migrant Visions of Development: A Gendered Approach. *Population, Space and Place* 15: 119–132.

De Cordier, B. 2009. Faith-based Aid, Globalisation and the Humanitarian Frontline: an Analysis of Western-based Muslim Aid Organisations. *Disasters* 33: 608–628.

De Haas, H. 2010. Migration and Development: A Theoretical Perspective. *International Migration Review* 44: 227–264.

Delgado Wise, R. and H. Rodríguez Ramírez. 2001. The Emergence of Collective Migrants and Their Role in Mexico's Local and Regional Development. *Canadian Journal of Development Studies* 22: 747–764.

Døving, C.A. 2005. Norsk-pakistanske begravelsesritualer: en migrasjonsstudie (PhD thesis). Oslo: Universitetet i Oslo.

Erdal, M. and C. Horst. 2010. Engaging Diasporas in Development. A Review of Pilot Project Pakistan. In *PRIO Chapter*. Oslo: PRIO.

Erdal, M. and K. Stokke. 2009. Contributing to Development? Transnational Activities among Tamils in Norway. *Asian and Pacific Migration Journal* 18: 397–418.

Erdal, M.B. 2012. Who is the Money for? Remittances within and beyond the Household in Pakistan. *Asian and Pacific Migration Journal* 21: 437–457.

Erdal, M.B. 2014. The Social Dynamics of Remittance-receiving in Pakistan: Agency and Opportunity among Non-migrants in a Transnational Social Field. In M. Rahman, Y.T. Tan and A. Ullah (eds), *Migrant Remittances in South: Social, Political and Economic Implications*. Basingstoke, Palgrave Macmillan.

Hansen, P. 2012. Revisiting the Remittance Mantra: A Study of Migration–Development Policy Formation in Tanzania. *International Migration* 50: 77–90.

Hasan, A. 2010. Migration, Small Towns and Social Transformations in Pakistan. *Environment and Urbanization* 22: 33–50.

Horst, C. 2008. The Transnational Political Engagements of Refugees: Remittance Sending Practices amongst Somalis in Norway. *Conflict, Security and Development* 8: 317–339.

Horst, C., V. Saggiomo, A. Warnecke, R. Ezzati, M. Guglielmo, P. Mezzetti, P. Pirkkalainen and G. Sinatti. 2010. Participation of Diasporas in Peacebuilding and Development: a Handbook for Practitioners and Policymakers. In *PRIO Report*. Oslo: PRIO.

Horst, C., M.B. Erdal, J. Carling and K. Afeef. 2014. Private Money, Public Scrutiny? Contrasting Perspectives on Remittances. *Global Networks*. 14: 514–532.

Houte, M. van and T. Davids. 2008. Development and Return Migration: from Policy Panacea to Migrant Perspective Sustainability. *Third World Quarterly* 29: 1411–1429.

Kapur, D. 2005. Remittances: 'The New Development Mantra?' In S.M. Maimbo and D. Ratha (eds), *Remittances: Development Impact and Future Prospects*. Washington, DC: World Bank, pp. 332–360.

Kelegama, S. 2011. *Migration, Remittances and Development in South Asia*. New Delhi: Sage Publications.

Levitt, P. and N. Glick-Schiller. 2004. Conceptualizing Simultaneity: A Transnational Social Field Perspective on Society. *International Migration Review* 38: 595–629.

Margheritis, A. 2007. State-led Transnationalism and Migration: Reaching out to the Argentine Community in Spain. *Global Networks* 7: 87–106.

Mercer, C., B. Page and M. Evans. 2009. Unsettling Connections: Transnational Networks, Development and African Home Town Associations. *Global Networks* 9: 141–161.

Moen, B. 2009. *Tilhørighetens balanse: Norsk-Pakistanske kvinners hverdagsliv i transnasjonale familier*. Oslo: NOVA.

Mohan, G. and K. Stokke. 2006. The Politics of Localization: from Depoliticizing Development to Politicizing Democracy. In K. Cox, J. Robinson and M. Low (eds), *Handbook in Political Geography*. London: Sage.

Orjuela, C. 2008. Distant Warriors, Distant Peace Workers? Multiple Diaspora Roles in Sri Lanka's Violent Conflict. *Global Networks* 8: 436–452.

Østberg, S. 2003. *Muslim i Norge. Religion og hverdagsliv blant unge norsk-pakistanere*. Oslo: Universitetsforlaget.

Page, B. and C. Mercer. 2012. Why Do People Do Stuff? Reconceptualising Remittance Behaviour in Diaspora-development Research Policy. *Progress in Development Studies* 12: 1–18.

Piper, N. 2009. The Complex Interconnections of the Migration–Development Nexus: a Social Perspective. *Population, Space and Place* 15: 93–101.

Raghuram, P. 2009. Which Migration, What Development? Unsettling the Edifice of Migration and Development. *Population, Space and Place* 15: 103–117.

Rahman, M. 2010. Remittances as a Social Process: the Singapore–Bangladesh Remittance Corridor. *Asian and Pacific Migration Journal* 19: 265–294.

Rahman, M. and K.F. Lian. 2012. Towards a Sociology of Migrant Remittances in Asia: Conceptual and Methodological Challenges. *Journal of Ethnic and Migration Studies* 38: 689–706.

Ratha, D. 2007. *Leveraging Remittances for Development*. Washington, DC: Migration Policy Institute.

Ratha, D., S. Mohaptra and A. Silwal. 2010. Migration and Development Brief. In *Brief*. Washington, DC: World Bank.

Rehman, S. and V. Kalra. 2006. Transnationalism from Below: Initial Responses by British Kashmiris to the South Asia Earthquake of 2005. *Contemporary South Asia* 15: 309–323.

Rytter, M. 2010a. A Sunbeam of Hope: Negotiations of Identity and Belonging among Pakistanis in Denmark. *Journal of Ethnic and Migration Studies* 36: 599–617.

Rytter, M. 2010b. Events and Effects: Intensive Transnationalism among Pakistanis in Denmark. *Social Analysis* 54: 90–106.

Sinatti, G. 2011. 'Mobile Transmigrants' or 'Unsettled Returnees'? Myth of Return and Permanent Resettlement among Senegalese Migrants. *Population, Space and Place* 17: 153–166.

Sinatti, G. and C. Horst, 2014. Migrants as Agents of Development: European Diaspora Engagement Discourse and Practice. *Ethnicities*, DOI: 10.1177/1468796814530120.

Sives, A. 2012. Formalizing Diaspora–State Relations: Process and Tensions in the Jamaican Case. *International Migration* 50: 113–128.

Skeldon, R. 2009. Of Skilled Migration, Brain Drains and Policy Responses. *International Migration* 47: 3–29.

Suleri, A.Q. and K. Savage. 2006. Remittances in Crises: a Case Study from Pakistan. In *An Humanitarian Policy Group Background Chapter*. Overseas Development Institute.

Turner, S and N. Kleis. 2013. Agents of Change? Staging and Governing Diasporas and the African State. *African Studies* 72(2): 192–206.

4 British-Bangladeshi immigrants and the local political landscape in Bangladesh

Kazi Nurmohammad Hossainul Haque and Sanjay Krishno Biswas

Bangladesh is one of the major source countries of international migration in the world, with labour migration being the dominant form of international migration from the country. Between 1976 and 2012, an estimated total of 8.3 million people emigrated as short-term contract workers. Annual out-flow of labour migration has followed a general upward trend on a tremendous scale over the decades, from 6,087 in 1976 to 607,798 in 2012 (BMET 2013). According to another estimate, a total of 7.7 million people, or 5.3 per cent of the Bangladesh population, are emigrants at present (IOM – Dhaka 2013). While a majority of the country's emigrant population are migrant workers, a significant portion of them are also diasporic or long-term migrants. Although the Bangladeshi diaspora is not a new phenomenon, there is still no systematic estimate of its stocks and flows. For example, Siddiqui suggests the number of Bangladeshi diaspora in major industrialised countries on the basis of an 'educated guess made by government officials' (2004: 15). These figures showed that the United Kingdom and United States had the largest communities of long-term migrants from Bangladesh followed by Italy, Canada, Japan, Australia and Greece.

Similarly, the diasporic linkages of Bangladesh are manifold but remain largely under researched. What anecdotal evidence and media reports suggest, however, is that the diasporic political linkages have often outpaced diasporic economic linkages in the country. A number of MPs from both the major political parties of Awami League (AL) and the Bangladesh Nationalist Party (BNP) are long-term expatriates, with the leaders of both the parties often making fundraising visits to the key diasporic concentrations of the United Kingdom, United States and Saudi Arabia. Funding from, and participation of, diaspora is most common in local politics (i.e. Union *Parishad*, UP), particularly in the migration prone region of Sylhet. Therefore, a systematic scientific enquiry (even on a small scale) of the country's diasporic political linkage is essential. This is important in mapping the diasporic–development nexus of Bangladesh, since economic development cannot be conceived outside the concerned institutional setting.

The current research therefore analyses the determinants and dynamics of diaspora engagement in the domestic politics of Bangladesh through empirical case studies of local politics. This chapter deals with three research questions: First, it charts the extent and types of diaspora engagement in home country politics; next, it analyses the determinants and associated dynamics of the diaspora engagement; and last, it examines the qualitative shift (if any) that the diaspora engagement is causing to home country politics. By virtue of being a small 'N' empirical investigation, the analytical focus is on local politics, particularly at the UP level, which is the lowest tier of local government. The case study has drawn upon the literature review, semi-structured qualitative interviews, and key informant interviews. Based on anecdotal evidence and media reports that were later verified by key informant interviews, the Jagannathpur *Upazila* of the Sunamganj district in the Sylhet division was selected for our case study[1] because it has become a hub of diaspora engagement in local politics.

Bangladeshi long-term expatriates: diaspora or transnationals?

Faist describes diaspora and transnationalism – the two concepts regarding international migration that refer to cross-border processes – as 'awkward dance partners' (2010: 9). The observation is made in the context of continuous debates in academic and public discourses over their definitions and usage.

Some scholars argue for sharp distinctions between the two phenomena. Bruneau (2010: 35–37) proposes a complete break between diaspora and transnationalism, while addressing the two from a geographical standpoint. Building upon six criteria of diaspora drawn from Cohen (1997) and Sheffer (2003), he defines diaspora as a community that, dispersed into other countries from the country of origin notwithstanding, invokes a common identity through shared social, cultural, religious, economic and political ties, as well as memory of a catastrophe or trauma. The diaspora identity also includes a spatial dimension – a symbolic and iconographic capital manifested in the reproduction of space after the country of origin in the adopted countries. Examples of which include the monasteries reconstructed in Northern Greece by a section of the Greek diaspora originating from Turkey. The transnational communities are a separate phenomenon according to Bruneau (2010: 43–45), despite the involvement of cross-border migration similar to diaspora. Unlike the diaspora, transnational communities are a result of more recent economic migration. Their linkages with their countries of origin have never been severed but are continuously reinforced by periodic returns and localised investments amid a communication revolution. Transnationals acquire the citizenship of their host country and retain that of the country of origin simultaneously, and there is neither any kind of uprooting nor any trauma, as in cases of diaspora.

Dahinden (2010: 51), who is not in favour of contrasting diaspora and transnationalism, concentrates instead on transnationalism, and interprets diaspora as one of its manifestations. She analyses transnational formations as a combination of mobility and locality. (Here, mobility refers to the physical movement of people in transnational spaces and locality means their social, economic or political anchoring in the country of immigration and/or the sending country.) Two of the four mobility–locality combinations developed by Dahinden (2010:

53–59) that are relevant for our discussion are the localised diasporic and localised mobile transnational formations. The former combines low transnational mobility with high local anchorage in the receiving country and low local anchorage in the sending country, while the latter combines high transnational mobility with high local anchorage in both the receiving and sending countries.

If we accept the break between diaspora and transnational community following Bruneau (2010: 35–37), the long-term expatriates from Bangladesh's Jagannathpur present an interesting mix of both elements. Initially, they look more like a transnational community than a diaspora, since their migrations are more recent, economically induced, and no uprooting from homeland or trauma have been involved. It is also true that they acquired the citizenship of their host country without giving up that of their home country.

Simultaneously, some elements of diaspora as described by Bruneau (2010: 35–37) are also visible in the Bangladeshi expatriates. Apart from the existence of a traumatic memory, both the elements of dispersal and shared common identity are vividly present among Bangladeshi long-term expatriates, especially from Jagannathpur. The emigrants from the area have been dispersed across continents from the United Kingdom to the United States, and commonly uphold not only their Bangladeshi identity but also family and village ties. To a smaller extent, the spatial dimension of identity that manifests in the creation of space is also evident. In London and New York – the two cities that have been major destinations for emigrants from the Sylhet region – several Bangladeshi neighbourhoods that are sometimes referred to as Bangla towns have emerged. These areas of Bangladeshi concentrations are characterised by signboards in Bangla. Shops selling *saari* and spices from Bangladesh; groceries selling fruits and vegetables flown in from Bangladesh; mosques and religious seminaries; Bangla schools, newspapers and TV channels; cultural troupes and celebration of Bengali festivals, are all spatial reconstructions of Bangladesh.

However, unlike the regular members of a transnational community as conceived by Bruneau (2010: 35–37), the Bangladeshi expatriates from Jagannathpur do not overemphasise their home country citizenship over their acquired citizenship; it is generally the other way around. Emigration has been a source of economic, social and even political gain for them. A northern country's citizenship is one potent symbol of such success and therefore, even though home country citizenship is retained, the acquired citizenship is more celebrated. The resulting identity assertion is more diasporic than transnational. Whether the expatriates are in their home country or host country, they proclaim a mixed identity, with the host country affiliation being prioritised.

Taking this point into account, the Bangladeshi long-term expatriates, especially from Jagannathpur, start looking more like a diaspora and less like a transnational community. Despite the fact that they combine high transnational mobility with high local anchorage, they are still not a localised mobile transnational formation of Dahinden (2010: 53–59). Instead, according to Bruneau (2010: 35–37), they are almost a diaspora, especially in terms of their geographic dispersal, shared common identity, and the spatial reconstruction of their homeland. We would therefore like to refer to them as diasporic transnationals, because even though they possess both high transnational mobility and high local anchorage, they still assert their diasporic identity over that of their home country.

Migrant political engagement in home country and transnational political practices

The diasporic transnationals of Bangladesh (especially those from Jagannathpur) combine high transnational mobility and high local anchorage while upholding diasporic identity. In other words, they adopt transnationalism as a means for their diasporic existence. Hence, we looked to the transnational political practice literature to offer insights for understanding diasporic political engagement in Jagannathpur.

A pioneering study dealing with a large dataset of immigrant entrepreneurs in the United States has reached two key conclusions about transnational political action connecting immigrants with their countries of origin: of those studied, a small group of immigrants stayed involved with home country politics via electoral and non-electoral means, while a larger number became actively involved during special junctures, like highly contested elections or natural disasters; with respect to determinants, there was no presence of marginalised or poorly educated immigrants (Guarnizo *et al.* 2003: 1238).

While the current research deals with political engagement (defined as active participation in politics including running for public offices), Guarnizo *et al.* (2003) focus on overall political participation. Moreover, our research rests on qualitative information of a single administrative unit as opposed to large quantitative data. However, from the two key conclusions of Guarnizo *et al.* (2003), some inference about the political realities of Jagannathpur can still be drawn. The number of diasporas engaged in the local politics of Jagannathpur is relatively small as compared to the overarching diasporic phenomenon of the area, and they almost exclusively hail from advanced socio-economic classes. Therefore, the diasporic political engagement in Jagannathpur share some traits of the transnational political practice as noted by Guarnizo *et al.* (2003).

Despite their extensive research concerning the level and individual determinants of migrants' transnational political action, Guarnizo *et al.* (2003) did not investigate other aspects like types, contextual factors, causes and outcomes. Migrant politics can be divided into many categories, with immigrant politics and homeland politics being the two main ones. The latter has further subtypes that branch into emigrant politics, diaspora politics, and translocal politics (Østergaard-Nielsen 2003: 762). The type and degree of participation in homeland politics varies according to contextual factors including the history of specific migration and settlement processes and political conditions in the country of residence (Vertovec 2004: 982).

In modern democratic nation-states, opportunity structures for both political participation and engaging in politics have been bounded by contending logics of territoriality and citizenship. With cross-border migration reaching unprecedented proportions, home and host countries alike have had to wake up to the new complexity of political membership. The observation made by Bauböck is succinct in this regard:

> The underlying problem is how to resolve the mismatch between states as territorially bounded jurisdictions and citizenship as an intergenerational status of membership in a political community. Democratic citizenship has a sticky quality: it clings to individuals, and they to it as well when moving across international borders. But democratic states are organized as non-overlapping territorial jurisdictions.
>
> (2010: 297)

While the abovementioned 'mismatch' also exists in the case of long-term expatriates from Bangladesh, it is still not an issue between the home country and the destination countries concerned. For decades, as discussed by Bauböck (2010: 301), the long-term Turkish migrants in Germany have faced the confusing situation of simultaneously retaining their Turkish and German citizenships. On one hand, there have been successive policy insistences from the German government to give up Turkish citizenship as a condition for acquiring German citizenship. On the other, there has been a corresponding side stepping of the German government's policies by the Turkish government in facilitating the retention of Turkish citizenship.

As in the case of Turkish migrants in Germany, retaining home country citizenship by Bangladeshi expatriates does not involve a trade-off with host country citizenships. There is hardly any contention between the home country citizenship and the US, UK, or other host country citizenships for Bangladeshi long-term expatriates. Therefore, while they acquire foreign citizenships, their Bangladesh citizenship automatically continue. Unlike Germany and Turkey, dual citizenship still has not become a thorny issue between Bangladesh and the host countries of its long-term emigrants. The Bangladesh government and leadership neither encourages nor discourages dual or multiple citizenships of its citizens, especially when the acquired citizenship(s) are of affluent northern countries.

For long-term Bangladeshi expatriates whom we refer to as diasporic transnationals, political opportunity structures in both home and host countries has not restrained their political engagement in the former. Therefore, we have a flourishing of diasporic engagement in the local politics of Bangladesh, as is evident in the Jagannathpur *Upazila* in the country's northeastern Sylhet region. While present in Jagannathpur, diasporic political engagement might not be exclusive to that area. Rather, anecdotal evidence suggests that Jagannathpur had been pioneering a trend in the country's politics at both the local and national levels.

A favourable political opportunity structure was, however, not sufficient in explaining an individual diaspora's incentive for political engagement, which is sometimes linked to the identities–borders–orders complex. In this conventional understanding of people's territorial attachment, the sense of identity is presumed to be directly related to a territory demarcated by a border that is underpinned by specific social and political order (Schiffauer *et al.* 2003). Migration contests the identities–borders–orders complex, especially through the migrants' transnational political practices in home countries. Thus, homeland political allegiance and engagement rest on the reconfiguration of the identities–borders–orders complex, since 'increasingly people from one or another particular place regard themselves as legitimate members of the collective identity and social order of that place even though they dwell outside its borders' (Vertovec 2004: 982).

Again, reconfiguration of the identities–borders–orders complex cannot sufficiently account for an individual diaspora's incentive for political engagement, especially in the context of Jagannathpur. For its diasporic transnationals, identity is certainly a motivation, but so are socio-economic imperatives, and in most cases the two are interlinked.

In Bangladesh, the rural political elite stem from the economically dominant classes (Hossain 2005), and traditionally as an agrarian country, big landowners have dominated the country's local politics (Blair 1985). With the expansion of trade and industrialisation, businesspeople have increasingly dominated both national and local politics (Kochanek 2002: 149). Like businesses, migrant remittances have followed an upward trend, especially in the rural areas of migration-prone regions like Sylhet, where richer households have tended to be migrant households, and long-term expatriates have tended to be richest among all migrants. As the economically dominant class, diasporas became a strong contender for the local political elite. With growing wealth, diasporas also invested in the local economy and emerged as new social patrons, thus increasing their stakes and opportunities in local politics.

Research methodology

Goldring (2008: 4–7) gave an extensive review of rcscarch mainly on migrant political participation in development of their homelands. He identified 'a considerable body of scholarship' that covered frequency, intensity, and density of collective and individual claims making, and involvement of migrants in local and national affairs of their home countries. In terms of methodology, there was quantitative survey research as well as qualitative institutional and interpretive analyses. In terms of research orientations, they analysed the frequency, scope and determinants of transnational political practices, identified the institutional and contextual parameters that shape migrant political transnational engagements, focused on cross-border agency, networks and coalition politics, and examined transnational political participation as part of broader processes of social transformation.

Having said this, it is difficult to categorise the current research under any one of the above research orientations proposed by Goldring (2008: 4–7). Our three research questions are more in line with the formulation by Østergaard-Nielsen

(2003: 760), who simultaneously gave attention to the 'why', 'how' and 'what' of migrants' transnational political engagement. We discuss the nature and extent of diasporic political engagement (the 'why' question) in this chapter, along with its determinants (the 'how' question) and whether it has been instrumental in causing any qualitative shift in home country politics (the 'what' question). Thus, elements of at least two of the four research orientations proposed by Goldring (2008: 4–7) have been put together in the current research. However, this research strategy was not methodologically overstretched since the level of analysis was a single *Upazila*, and the unit of analysis was the group of diasporic politicians who had been pursuing public offices.

As a qualitative case-oriented study, the current research could ask more complex questions about diasporic political engagement, rather than the 'why', 'how', and 'what' types. This was, however, a difficult task due to the geographical and (to some extent) analytical novelty of its scope. There was hardly any previous study on the political engagement of Bangladeshi diaspora in their home country. Current literature also pays little attention to diasporic engagement in the local politics of home countries. There were two resulting methodological implications in our research design: One was simplified research questions that were not typical of qualitative studies but went well with the somewhat pioneering nature of our work; The other was pursuing thick description, made convenient by our limited analytical scope.

Our research is based on a case study of the Jagannathpur *Upazila* in the Sunamganj district, Sylhet division. Jagannathpur is a migration prone area where members of many households permanently live abroad, mostly in the United Kingdom, but also in the United States. Some of the prominent members of the Bangladeshi diaspora in the United Kingdom are from Jagannathpur. Two of the most well-known figures are Anwar Chowdhury, the former British high commissioner in Bangladesh, who was the first Asian to achieve senior ambassadorship in the UK foreign office, and Ghulam Murtaza, the mayor of the London Borough of Tower Hamlets. Haji Abdul Matin and Muhammad Gulzar Hossain, two prominent organisers of the Bangladesh liberation war among UK citizens back in 1971, were also from Jagannathpur.

For the purpose of our research, what is more interesting about Jagannathpur is the extent of diaspora engagement in local politics. Chairmen of six out of its eight UPs were citizens of the United Kingdom or United States (these unions are: Kolkolia, Patli, Chilaura Haldipur, Raniganj, Syedpur Shaharpara and Pailgao). Moreover, the candidates they had defeated in the UP elections were also often members of a diaspora. Thus, over the last few years, diasporas have nearly monopolised the UP chairmanships in Jagannathpur. Diasporas were gradually taking interest in other public offices as well, while some were already active in local politics with the ambition of running as *Upazila* chairman and Member of Parliament (MP). The incumbent MP of the parliamentary constituency that Jagannathpur was part of was not from a diaspora, unlike the MP of the neighbouring constituency who had inspired some diasporic politicians of Jagannathpur to emerge as MP hopefuls.

The case study has drawn upon a literature review, semi-structured interviews, and key informant interviews. Based on anecdotal evidence and media reports that were later verified by key informant interviews, Jagannathpur was selected for the case study due to the high intensity of diasporic political engagement in its local politics. Following the selection of the case study area, semi-structured interviews were conducted with diasporic politicians by an open-ended questionnaire. Only diasporic politicians who had been elected to or were running for public offices were interviewed. The reason for not including diasporic politicians who were not exposed to electoral politics was that they would not be able to provide information on the whole gamut of political engagement covered by the research.

Through the in-depth interviews with diasporic politicians, four kinds of information were sought. First, some basic information was gathered about diasporic politicians. This included their age, educational qualification and occupation. The occupational information provided leads for the wider political economy dimension of diasporic political engagement. Second, the nature and extent of diasporic political engagement was looked into. This included types, entry points, duration, modes of political engagement, number of votes received, election expenditure, areas of expenditure, and sources of election funds. The information helped to map diaspora engagement in the local politics of Jagannathpur and was catalytic in deriving its determinants. Third, factors that determined diasporic political engagement in Jagannathpur: political economy, social capital, kinship and history of political and social engagement. Last, whether diasporic political engagement had been able to bring about qualitative change in Jagannathpur's local politics. The four kinds of information also formed the basis of talking points for key informant interviews with long-term observers of local politics. Information collected through the semi-structured interviews was further compared with the findings of the key informant interviews. The case study was thus developed mainly by analysing information from the two sets of interviews mentioned above.

Diaspora engagement in home country politics: a case study of Jagannathpur, Bangladesh

The Jagannathpur *Upazila* is an area of 376.91 sq.km with a population of 225,271. One important physical feature of Jagannathpur is the existence of large water bodies. The area has a river system consisting of 14 rivers that also form part of the famous *haors* or river-like large water bodies of Sunamganj. However, most parts of the *Upazila* can be reached by well paved all-weather rural roads. We travelled through these roads by auto rickshaws while heading to the unions for in-depth interviews and key informant interviews. The *Upazila* has eight unions and one municipality.

In line with the three research objectives, this case study will cover mainly three things about diaspora engagement in the local politics of Jagannathpur: extent and types, determinants, and qualitative shift in local politics, if any, from the diaspora engagement. Before entering into the main discussion, we will share some basic information about the diasporic politicians engaged in local politics.

Diasporic politicians: basic information

The diasporic political engagement in home country politics appears to be an all-male affair from our case study, as all the diasporic politicians we came across in the case of Jagannathpur were men. This might be due to the fact that men have dominated the migration flow from the area, as well as the religiously conservative social structure of the area. The educational qualification of the diasporic politicians was, however, mixed. Most of them had completed school, with fewer of them completing secondary school, and those who received Bachelor or Master's level education even fewer in number. The diasporic politicians we talked to could be divided into two broad age groups: below 40 years old and above 40 years old. Most of them belonged in the latter group. We found three UP chairmen, who were aged 60, 64 and 72 respectively. A few of the diasporic politicians were in their mid or late thirties. Occupation-wise, the diasporic politicians were generally businesspeople and landowners. Their businesses were mainly restaurant and with real estate. We will discuss the political economy of one occupational group's dominance in diasporic political engagement later on in the case study.

Diasporic political engagement: nature and extent

The case study begins with an overall mapping of diasporic political engagement in the local politics of Jagannathpur. It attempts to ascertain the type of political engagement, the entry points and the duration, and also explores the election experience of diasporic politicians if relevant. Information was also sought about their political associates and political mentors. Their modes of political engagement both during their stay in Bangladesh and in their countries of residence are explored.

Types, entry points and duration

The local politics for the scope of this study are bound by the local administrative units that are the sites of the local elected bodies. In the case of Bangladesh, such bodies are UPs in unions, municipalities in recognised townships, and UZPs in *Upazila*s. Parliamentary constituencies, although meant for national representation, are also locally based. Usually, two *Upazila*s constitute one parliamentary constituency. As with the case of Jagannathpur, it is part of the Sunamganj-3 parliamentary constituency along with another *Upazila*, South Sunamganj. Thus, we started by identifying which of the above administrative units the diasporas were politically engaged in, and the subsequent types of political engagement.

In the case of Jagannathpur, diasporic politicians were mostly engaged in union level politics and had their eyes on UP chairmanship – they usually did not run for positions below like UP membership. However, there was a growing tendency to run for municipality mayor and MP. We met one diasporic politician who was the immediate past mayor of Jagannathpur municipality, and another diasporic politician who was a MP hopeful for the next parliamentary election. The incumbent MP of the neighbouring parliamentary constituency was already a diasporic politician. This had become a great source of inspiration for the diasporic politicians of Jagannathpur to aim higher than UP chairmanship and municipal mayorship. The MP hopeful we met was also inspired by the incumbent MP's success. Some observers of local politics told us that several other diasporic politicians were also preparing to bid for MP nomination from both the major parties prior to the upcoming parliamentary election. Their claim seemed more than mere speculation as we came across colourful graphic posters of a number of diasporic politicians who were UK citizens in different parts of Jagannathpur. The posters bore many features of typical election posters of Bangladesh; they had nice photos of the politicians in suits, described them as *shaat* (honest), *jogyo* (qualified), *jonodorodi* (people's friend) and *somaj shebak* (social worker), and sometimes gave their affiliations with the major parties and their leaders. In Bangladesh, such posters are usually the public relations tools of the MP hopefuls.

In the case of most of the diasporic politicians covered in our case study, political engagement did not start with pursuing public office through UP chairmanship. Their political engagement often dated back to an earlier involvement with major political parties in respective unions or *Upazila*s, and sometimes even predated their emigration. This was evident from the duration of the political engagement of the diasporic politicians. In about half of the cases, the duration was 5–7 years, while in the other half, the duration was 10–30 years. Only one diasporic politician reported his duration as just one year. The main reason for reporting such long political engagement was their earlier involvement with student wings or local units of major political parties. However, such claims could be sometimes questioned for the fact that many diasporic politicians, especially the senior ones, had been migrants for 10–20 years. Local political observers also substantiated this. In this way, the duration of their migration and their political engagement coincided. Again, this possibility could not be ruled out altogether in this age of transnationalism. It is possible that the diasporic politicians were in touch with the local units of political parties through phone communication, home visits, and funding contributions. In the following section, we will discuss the history of political engagement of diasporic politicians in detail.

Pursuing political office through election was the ultimate form of political engagement of the diasporic politicians. As seen above in the case of political entry points, getting elected into public offices as UP and UZ chairmen or municipal mayor lies at the centre of a diasporic politician's ambitions; hence local elections to the abovementioned public offices often turned out to be the epitome of diasporic political engagement. The elements of running for an election by diasporic politicians covered in the case study are: number of votes received, election expenditure, areas of expenditure, and sources of election funding.

The votes received by each diasporic politician who ran for election were not overwhelming, even in the cases when they won. The five diasporic UP chairmen of Jagannathpur won elections by the following margin of votes respectively: 440, 399, 900, 211 and 250. The total number of voters in the five UPs ranged from 10,000 to 18,000, and the number of chairman candidates in each union was seven to eight on average. It was apparent that the votes were cast almost equally among most of the candidates, resulting in such marginal election victories of the winning candidates. The diasporic politician who was the former mayor of Jagannathpur municipality won the election with only 4,000 votes in an electorate of 22,000 voters. A similar case happened as in the UP election – there were a total of seven mayoral candidates, and votes cast were divided almost equally among most candidates.

The election expenditure of diasporic politicians was between BDT 500,000 and BDT 5,000,000. However, some observers of local politics suggested that actual election expenditure could be much higher than that reported by the interviewees. The usual contributors to election funds were the candidates themselves, their family members and other kin. The share ratio of different contributors varied among election candidates. The UP chairman of Haldipur union reported that 70 per cent of his election funds came from family members and other kin, while 30 per cent was from himself. This was the opposite for the UP chairman of Patli union, who contributed 80 per cent himself, while the remaining 20 per cent came from his kin. The UP chairman of Raniganj union claimed to have fully financed his election himself. The money for election expenditure mostly came from earnings in the countries of residence, and sometimes from earnings in Bangladesh. The areas of election expenditure as reported by the interviewees were: posters, campaigns, meetings, food, payment for volunteers, and donations. A few observers of local elections alleged in the key informant interviews that a diasporic UP chairman often engaged in 'vote buying' by paying money to individual voters, but this allegation was not widespread and could not be verified within the scope of this research.

Modes of political engagement

Diasporic politicians are at the forefront of transnational existence as they combine their stays in their home countries and their countries of residence through mobile phones, the Internet, and air travel. The duration of stay of the diasporic politicians in our case study in their countries of residence ranged from 1–6 months of every year. Sometimes they stay in their countries of residence for several consecutive months, or sometimes for a number of weeks with an interval of several months. While away from their home country, they stay connected through mobile phones and the Internet, although use of the former was predominant. Depending on their duration of stay in the country of residence, diasporic politicians make 30 to 300 mobile calls per month to their home country. While staying in their home country, their modes of political engagement are mainly meetings, visits, and attending social/cultural events.

Determinants of diasporic political engagement

Østergaard-Nielson (2003) observed that migrants' transnational political practices are as complex as the multi-level processes, structures and actors involved. This research also finds that determinants of diasporic engagement in home country politics are vast and complex. The factors that mainly determine diaspora engagement in the local politics of Jagannathpur are: political economy, social capital, kinship, history of political engagement, and history of associational engagement. These factors are sometimes overlapping and interlinked.

Political economy

Hossain (2005) informed that the rural rich are likely to hold or have held public offices of local government like UP and UZP, while Blair (1985) presented evidence of several decades, spanning the Pakistan period and independent Bangladesh, that large rural landowners tend to control the local government. Their findings suggest that economic affluence is a key determinant for individuals to engage in the local politics of Bangladesh.

As the country traditionally had agriculture as the mainstay of its rural economy, the landowner class was the most economically affluent and therefore influential in local politics. In the last few decades, agriculture's share of the GDP has declined while trade and industry has developed, resulting in the 'growing commercialization of power in the country' (Kochanek 2002: 149). Besides businesses, migrant remittance has become a leading source of national revenue. Business people and migrants are therefore often surpassing traditional landowners in rural Bangladesh as the new rural elites. In the case of many of the diasporic politicians of Jagannathpur, they belong simultaneously to the business, migrant, and landowner groups, and thus hold an unparalleled and unchallenged elite status.

As mentioned earlier, a majority of the diasporic politicians are business people by occupation, and most of them are in the restaurant or real estate business in their countries of residence like the United Kingdom and the United States. Foreign exchange earned abroad is often invested in local businesses such as land development, real estate, hotel, shopping malls, small trading and small manufacturing. Some of the best hotels and shopping malls of Sylhet city are owned by diasporic businesspeople turned local politicians. Diasporas of all sorts, including diasporic politicians, are also interested in land ownership. The monthly income of the diasporic politicians interviewed for this study ranged between BDT 100,000 and BDT 500,000, which is significantly above the national per capita income of the country.

The economic affluence of the diasporic politicians as a class has increasingly shaped the local political economy to their favour, and they are gaining an edge over the non-diasporic politicians in at least two areas: political financing and 'political' philanthropy. Political financing is crucial to bankroll different political activities – mobilisation, organising meetings, maintaining office, election campaigning, and supporting workers. Philanthropy can be 'political' both by design, as voluntary investments in human development to secure political mileage, and by way of outcome as unintended political benefits from such investments.

The stronger political financing of diasporic politicians is evident from the UP election expenditures of diasporic UP chairmen of Jagannathpur. The study shows that the range as reported by the diasporic politicians interviewed is between BDT 500,000 and BDT 5,000,000, leading to an average election expenditure of BDT 1,700,000. However, some observers of local politics suggest that election expenses of diasporic UP chairmen could be much higher. While one UP chairman reported his election expenses as BDT 1,200,000, two business leaders of Jagannathpur contradicted this by claiming that he spent BDT 20,000,000. Although it is difficult to verify the opposing claims within the scope of this study, the UP chairman concerned was capable of spending much more than he reported.

Besides, a diasporic politician's election expenditure should be considered not just in terms of his economic affluence, but also in the context of kinship and social status. It may then become apparent that an UP election is fought not only among the concerned candidates, but also among their respective families and *gushti*, or kinship networks. The UP chairmanship is a status symbol of the candidate, his family, and kin. Additionally, a UP chairman in the family is viewed as an advantageous access to resource allocation through UPs. That is why election expenditures are borne not only by the candidates themselves, but also by family members and kin, both near and distant. Half of the diasporic UP chairmen of Jagannathpur reported family members and kin as funders of election campaigns, with the ratio of their contribution varying from 10 per cent to 70 per cent of the total expenditure. What is also advantageous about funding from family and kin is that many of them are also members of diasporas, who present a better scope of resource mobilisation than non-members.

Diasporic philanthropy predates diasporic political engagement considerably in many of the migrant-prone areas of the Sylhet region, including Jagannathpur. Traditionally, these areas were among the hardest to reach rural fringes of the country, where many public services offered by government agencies were not available. Even when NGOs started providing some of these public services, greater Sylhet still remained outside their programme coverage due to its geographical remoteness. When Katy Gardner was undertaking fieldwork for her *Global Migrants, Local Lives* book in the late 1980s, she wrote the following about the accessibility of one migrant prone village of Sylhet region: 'The nearest metalled road is about six miles away, and the village can only be reached by dirt tracks which link it with the other villages lying around it' (Gardner 1995: 25).

However, when Katy Gardner returned to the village in 1993, she found that the previous dirt path linking the villages to the road had been upgraded and widened, while another road was under construction. This might have been the result of the government's silent revolution in road communication through the introduction of feeder road networks that connected villages to towns. However, she noticed 'many other improvements (a bridge ... a high school ... and an *eid ghar*...) [that] had been paid for by voluntary contributions made by the more prosperous households', who were migrant households in most likelihood (Gardner 1995: 25).

Between 1993 and 2012, diasporic philanthropy in the Sylhet region had expanded in size, scope, and outreach. This had gained further momentum with the political ambitions of the diasporic philanthropists in the backdrop. In our fieldwork, we found numerous examples of diasporic philanthropy that were undertaken by diasporic politicians and their kin. A number of them were initiatives of the diasporas of Jagannathpur (Table 4.1).

The list presented in Table 4.1 sufficiently indicates that diasporic philanthropy in Jagannathpur is considerably large; reaching thousands of people within and outside the *Upazila*, addressing their various social and economic needs, and with an accumulated amount worth millions of BDT. More interesting are the grass roots bases of the philanthropic initiatives, since they are mostly union or village level efforts by respective leading diasporic politicians and/or business persons. Such philanthropic activities have established the credentials of diasporic politicians as patrons of their rural communities, particularly among the weaker sections of society such as the youth, elderly, women, and the poor. In the day-to-day practice of politics in Jagannathpur, philanthropy has become 'politics by other means' either consciously or unconsciously. Hence, almost all the diasporic politicians interviewed identified individual philanthropic and voluntary activities as preparation for political engagement.

Social capital

According to an observer of local politics who was a faculty of the Jagannathpur (Undergraduate) College, members of diasporas who engage in local politics feel that anything less than UP chairmanship does not match up to their higher 'expatriate' (or '*bideshi*' or '*londoni*' in local expression) social status. This observation is also supported by some of the local journalists and business leaders. Such perceptions resonate with current migration literature about the relationship of migration and power, especially in the context of the Sylhet region. Drawing on the migration scholarship's position that migration cannot be fully understood without reference to power relations, Gardner (1995: 77) found that '*bidesh* [had] become a metaphor for power and advancement (in Sylhet)'. While analysing social sources of power in the Talukpur village of Sylhet region (situated in migration prone Nobiganj *Upazila* that is not very far from Jagannathpur), she observed that *bidesh* or foreign lands are associated with strength and prosperity, 'the source of a more materialistic power, upon which the *desh* (or home country) now [depends on]' (Gardner, 1995: 77). Our findings about entry points of diasporic political engagement show that diasporic politicians do not pursue public office lower than UP chairmanship. One reason for this is likely to be

Table 4.1 Diaspora philanthropy in Jagannathpur

Philanthropic initiatives	*Philanthropists involved*	*Sector concerned*	*No. of beneficiaries*	*Resource commitment*
British Bangla Education Trust	Arju Miah, MBE (restaurant businessman in the UK)	Education (scholarship)	Several thousand students (per year)	BDT 2,000,000–2,500,000 (per year)
Eye camp	Rafiq Miah (restaurant businessman in the UK and cousin of chairman, Kolkolia UP, Jagannathpur)	Health (free eye operation and eye care)	1,000	
Road construction	Abdul Hashim, former chairman, Kolkolia UP who led a consortium of 43 diasporic members	Communication	27,239 (population of Kolkolia Union)	BDT 4,300,000 (each of the 43 members contributed BDT 100,000 each)
Sanitary latrine	Abdul Hashim, former chairman, Kolkolia UP who led a consortium of 54 diasporic members	Water, sanitation and hygiene (WASH)	Poor families of the Kolkolia Union	
Individual philanthropy	Md Abul Hasan, UP chairman, Chilaura Haldipur Union	Miscellaneous (financing labour migration and marriage, road repairing and setting up of a college)	Poor families of the Chilaura Haldipur Union	BDT 30,000,000 approx. (consolidated)
Patli Union Welfare Trust	Md Sirajul Haque, UP chairman, Patli Union	Mobilising diaspora contributions to convert Patli Union into a model village	No data	No data
Shafiq-Mahmuda Trust	Mahabubul Haque, unsuccessful candidate, UP chairman election, Mirpur Union	Miscellaneous (clothes, solar power, musical instruments, roads, electric bulbs, tube wells, etc.)	Jagannathpur *Upazila* and other areas of Bangladesh	No data

Source: fieldwork findings.

their higher social status as expatriate or *bideshi.* Since UP chairmanship is the most respected public office at the union level, diasporic politicians find it suitable for their higher social status.

Kinship

Gardner (1995) made an interesting observation about the importance of kinship in the social organisation of rural Sylhet. She observed that *attiyo* or kin is crucial not only for kinship purposes, but also for the principle factors of social, political and economic organisation. What is understood as kinship in social anthropology literature is publicised as family background in the political campaigns of election candidates to local public offices. A candidate's family reputation and the family's political pedigree are often important components of his political capital. With the importance of kinship ties and associated wider lineage, family political background might translate into a number of political assets like the prospective vote bank, pool of political activists, and source of funding. This might be why a number of diasporic politicians are from so-called political families. Such families are often engaged in local politics for many years, and one or more of their members might hold or have held public offices such as UP chairmanship and/or lead/have led local units of major political parties. The diasporic UP chairman of Haldipur Union had several brothers who were involved with the major political parties. The diasporic UP chairman of Raniganj Union had an elder brother who was a four-time UP member. The UP chairman of Kolkolia Union, another diasporic politician, took pride in his long political lineage; both his grandfather and father were village heads during British rule while his uncle was the immediate past UP chairman. A cousin of the MP hopeful diasporic politician was an MP of the neighbouring parliamentary constituency, while two other diasporic politicians claimed that they entered into politics following the footsteps of their fathers who were very active with the local units of a national political party.

History of political engagement

We have already mentioned in the previous section that most diasporic politicians have a history of political engagement. It is not that they start taking an interest in local politics only after becoming a member of diaspora, rather, a background in local politics helps them to re-enter it with the reinforced political identity of a diasporic politician. Due to their previous linkages with local politics, they do not lack familiarity with the constituency; neither do they lack an understanding of the dynamics of politics – two limitations that often constrain new entrants of politics. Although social status and economic affluence and a lack of familiarity is usually not an issue for members of diasporas endowed with good family backgrounds, a lack of understanding of local political dynamics is an issue for them, unless they have had adequate exposure to local politics. That explains why the successful diasporic politicians are mainly from diasporas that already had links with local politics, despite the fact that Jagannathpur *Upazila* had diasporic concentrations in most of its unions.

We found at least two indications of this trend from our case study. One indication was the longer involvement of diasporic politicians with major political parties dating back to the pre-migration period in various forms: voluntary activism, fund contribution, party membership and holding office of local party units. Another indication was the availability of political mentorship to diasporic politicians from the local stalwarts of major political parties.

The diasporic politicians who had family members or kin involved with major political parties often volunteered for their local units. Some of the diasporic politicians first became active in local politics as members and donors of the local units of major political parties before becoming diasporic politicians. Two diasporic politicians – the MP hopeful and *Upazila* chairman hopeful respectively – were active with the student wing of the ruling party prior to emigration, and even held offices of its local units. They also participated in election campaigns of MPs and *Upazila* chairman candidates, and found those experiences and exposures useful for their own public relations. Such previous involvements with major political parties were also instrumental for receiving the mentorship of local political stalwarts. Except for one, all the diasporic politicians interviewed identified one or more local stalwarts of major political parties as their political mentors. These included the immediate past MP of the Jagannathpur-South Sunamganj constituency, who was a renowned national leader from the current ruling party, the presidents of Jagannathpur *Upazila* and district units of the ruling party, other *Upazila* and district leaders of major political parties, and a few MPs.

As mentioned earlier, the diasporic politicians are at the forefront of transnational existence. Their history of political engagement comprises therefore more than just previous involvements with the local units of the major political parties of Bangladesh; they are sometimes also involved with the foreign units of these political parties in their respective countries of residence. Five of the diasporic politicians we interviewed were members of Bangladesh political parties in their countries of residence, and even held or had held leadership positions. These were: former president of the Oxford unit of the AL, secretary of the northeast UK unit of the AL, and the vice president of the UK AL. Their influence as leaders of foreign units of major political parties helped them to win the attention and favour of the national leadership of these parties, which ultimately facilitated the fulfilling of their home country political ambitions. The UK and US units of the country's political parties had become important sources of party finance, and were instrumental for lobbying with governments and political elites of those countries. Many senior leaders of the Bangladeshi political parties often visited the United Kingdom and United States for personal and business purposes. During those visits, the leaderships of the foreign units often provided accommodation and transportation. The diasporic politicians were often also involved with the political parties of their countries of residence. Six of the diasporic politicians we interviewed had such memberships, out of which five of them were UK citizens, four of whom were members of the Labour Party while one was a member of the Liberal Democratic Party. The remaining politician, who was a US citizen, was a member of the Republican Party.

History of associational engagement

Social, cultural and professional associations are often the springboards of political engagement, particularly in democracies. The associational sphere was found to be crucial for the proper functioning of democracy by French political scientist Alexis de Tocqueville, who referred to this as civil society (Tocqueville 1838). In the democratic context of the twentieth century, American political scientist Robert Putnam celebrated associational spaces and activities as essential ingredients of what he termed 'social capital', which according to him drives the democratic civic culture of popular political participation (Putnam 1993). People with political ambitions sometimes use associations as effective stepping stones to political offices. The diasporic politicians of our case study were also found to be active in various associations of expatriate Bangladeshis long before getting into the local politics of their home country.

The UP chairman of Kolkolia union was a member of the Jalalabad Association in New York City. He had been involved with this 20,000-member association of migrants from greater Sylhet for over 20 years, and had even held offices of treasurer and vice president in the association. However, he did not think that membership and holding office in the association helped with his success in local politics. On the contrary, the UP chairman of Patli union who was a leader of Jagannathpur Unnayan Samity, a UK-based association of migrants from Jagannathpur, had a different story to tell. He acknowledged that a leadership role in the association ultimately helped him in pursuing local political leadership. Another diasporic politician who ran for the UP election of Mirpur union but lost was the chairman of the Mirpur Welfare Trust, a charity based in the United Kingdom. He claimed that it was through his involvement with the charitable association that he first started taking an interest in local politics. It was therefore difficult to be conclusive about the link between diasporic political engagement and a history of associational engagement from this case study. However, we saw earlier that there are political returns of diasporic philanthropy, and many of the abovementioned diaspora associations are philanthropy-focused.

Qualitative changes in home country politics

So far, we have discussed the nature and extent of diasporic political engagement in the home country, its determinants, and its associated dynamics. These have more to do with what Østergaard-Nielsen terms as the 'why' and 'how' questions of transnational political engagement process of the diasporas (2003: 765). Within the context of the diaspora and development discourse, we look at whether diasporic political engagement is able to bring about qualitative changes in home country politics. In the words of Østergaard-Nielsen, this is the 'then what' question of the diasporic political engagement process (2003: 774). Diasporic political engagement cannot enhance development unless it can bring about qualitative change in democratic practice. In Bangladesh, the practice of democracy at both national and local levels is still unstable from the undue interventions of abject majoritarianism, corruption and violence. Political outcomes are often alleged to be influenced by the '2 Ms': money and muscle power (coercion). If diasporic political engagement in local politics cannot address such limitations or at least present some alternatives, then it is less likely to have developmental impact.

In order to assess the qualitative changes in the local politics of Jagannathpur due to diaspora engagement, the case study took peoples' expectations of diasporic politicians and the latter's roles in making local politics more transparent and accountable, reducing corruption and the use of force in local politics, and local development into account. It also explored whether diasporic politicians brought over their experiences from their countries of residence to home country politics.

Diasporic politicians were asked about what they thought of people's expectations for them as politicians/public office holders. There were mainly two kinds of understanding: One group of diasporic politicians felt that people expected them to contribute to improving social service provisions. These included the setting up of tube wells, road repairing, improving school buildings, fulfilling basic needs, and providing financial assistance to the poor. Another group felt that people expected them to be honest, non-corrupt and fair. These readings of public expectations were valid when crosschecked with local key informants like journalists, academics and business leaders. The journalists, academics and business leaders felt that people were in favour of individuals in the local leadership who were honest, free of corruption, non-violent, without criminal record and religious; they also expected local leaders to provide them with social and economic support, with or without government resource allocation.

What then are the advantages of the diasporic politicians in fulfilling the abovementioned expectations of the people? They are certainly more resource-endowed than most of their non-diasporic counterparts to be local patrons, a role that people in Jagannathpur often expect from their local leaders. The earlier findings of the research on diasporic philanthropy showed that higher social status by virtue of economic affluence and associated philanthropic contributions to the community might translate into political returns. It would be pertinent to quote one diasporic UP chairman here:

> The resource allocation by the government for our villages is less than required. Additional resource mobilization from private sources is also necessary. I am able to contribute in this regard from my advantageous economic position as a member of diaspora.

Nevertheless, are the diasporic politicians more honest, corruption-free, and non-violent than their non-diasporic counterparts? A number of diasporic politicians interviewed in this research reported how they were trying to promote transparency and accountability to reduce corruption in the UPs. The strategies included setting examples by personal honesty, motivating colleagues against corruption, the free flow of information about resource distribution, and public participation in budgeting. Another group of diasporic politicians revealed their strategies to address the use of force in local politics, which included mobilising the general public, discouraging coercion, promoting peaceful resolution of problems and educating young people.

The public perception shared in Jagannathpur as reflected in the key informant interviews is that diasporic politicians tend to be honest, free of corruption, and non-coercive. Despite the huge amounts of money pumped into the election campaigns of diasporic politicians, there was hardly any use of violence reported. There were some allegations of vote buying against them, though not widespread. They had also shown considerable honesty as holders of public offices of the UP and *Upazila* chairmanships. Although the key informant interviews are not representative, they carry a certain weight since the key informants are long-term observers of local politics. In the context of money and muscle power's (coercion's) alleged domination in Bangladesh politics, the role of diasporic political engagement in invoking any qualitative change was partial. It is commendable that the diasporic politicians avoided using and promoting coercion. However, when it came to financial inputs, diasporic engagement had taken the local politics of Jagannathpur to a new level, where political leadership had gradually gone beyond the reach of anyone other than the rich diasporic businesspeople, and this might not be good for the long-term future of local democracy.

With regards to their role in local development, diasporic politicians in the study provided a long list of achievements, which included mostly infrastructural projects like repairing roads, building culverts and setting up school houses, and also social welfare projects such as the financing of education, marriage and migration, particularly in the poor households. As informed by the interviewees themselves, such projects are mostly funded by the politician's own sources and are unlikely to be from government allocation. These actions reflect an undue merging of their roles as local elected officials and local patrons.

Concluding observations

Diasporic political engagement is significant not just for the countries of residence of migrants but also for their home countries. Amid the transnational existence of today's diaspora who combine living in two different territorial spaces at the same time, there are enough stakes for them to be fully engaged in their home country politics. Members of diasporas are no longer content with voting in home country elections or funding home country political parties. They are increasingly eager to pursue a political career in their home countries and to get elected to public offices. This is already recognised as a global trend in migration literature but there is insufficient knowledge about all parts of world. Despite the fact that Bangladesh has a large diaspora population who often take interest in home country politics, there is no literature on the subject; this chapter is thus a humble attempt towards bridging that knowledge gap. Another specialty of this chapter is with respect to the general state of knowledge on the subject; its analytical focus is on the local politics of the home country instead of national or provincial politics.

The research has uncovered a high level of engagement of diaspora in the local politics of Jagannathpur, one of the sub-districts of Bangladesh most prone to migration. The diasporic political engagement in the area is so high that diasporas have almost monopolised its UP chairmanships, the main category of elected public offices of the rural local government. With the growing clout of diasporic politicians, there is increasing interest to aim higher than UP chairmanship and municipal mayorship. Some diasporic politicians are preparing to seek the nomination of major political parties to contest in the next parliamentary election. Diasporas are also involved in the local units of national political parties.

The main determinants of such widespread diasporic political engagement in local politics are: political economy, social capital, kinship, and histories of political and associational engagements both in Bangladesh and the respective countries of residence. The dynamics of these determinants are overlapping and interlinked. The research findings suggest that an individual diasporic politician's ambition in local politics might only translate into political success through dynamic interactions between the above factors.

With the transition from the predominantly agrarian rural economy to an increasing importance of trade, industry and migrant remittance, businesspeople and rich migrants have replaced big landowners as the rural political elites. Amid the general trend of commercialisation of power, the economic affluence of the diasporas has far surpassed other stakeholders of local political power. A diasporic politician is often a successful businessman and a big landowner, on top of being an affluent migrant. Members of diasporas are outpacing non-members in political financing by amassing resources from their countries of residence to bankroll their political ambitions, and this has led to the 'hyperinflation' of political expenditure that non-diasporic politicians cannot compete with. The political returns from diasporic philanthropy are far more extensive and rewarding. In the patronage-based rural social structure, voluntary investments in human development are sometimes made in order to secure political benefits, while political benefits are sometimes deemed as additional returns from the human development investments.

The economic affluence of diasporas has further reinforced their already elevated social status as migrants. Political offices like the UP chairman and municipal mayor that enjoy wider public respect among the rural and semi-urban populations are often a consolidation of one's social status. Similarly, kinship is another important social factor that shapes diaspora engagement in local politics.

In the rural and semi-urban areas of Jagannathpur where kinship ties and associated wider lineage are important elements of political capital, UP elections are contested not only among individual candidates but also among their respective kith and kin. As election expenses are often borne by family members and kin, the rewards accrued from holding of public offices are also shared with them.

Economic affluence, social status and kinship are insufficient in propelling members of diasporas to political success, unless they have political and associational engagements both in their home country and countries of residence. Previous involvement with local units of major political parties may provide them with an adequate understanding of local political dynamics and the mentorship of local political stalwarts. Involvement with home country political parties' units in countries of residence may earn them unique favour with the national political leadership. Their involvement with expatriate associations in their countries of residence is thus sometimes a stepping-stone for their political career.

Diaspora engagement does not necessarily mean qualitative changes in local politics, as the democratic politics of the country is perennially sickened by two ills: money and muscle power (coercion). Diasporic politicians have thus far been seen to be honest, corruption-free, and non-coercive. While the diasporic politicians are a positive influence to local politics due to their avoidance of coercion, they are a negative influence for their extensive use of money in local politics. Their contribution in local development is also a mixed experience due to the undue merging of their roles as local elected officials and local patrons.

Note

1 A brief introduction to the administrative units of Bangladesh is necessary at this point. The country is a unitary state that is centrally divided into six divisions. There are a total of 64 districts divided among the six divisions. Each district is divided into a number of *Upazilas* or sub-districts. Each *Upazila* has a popularly elected representative body that is the *Upazila Parishad* (UZP), UZPs consist of a chairman, a male vice chairman, a female vice chairman and several members. While direct elections take place for the first three positions, chairmen of the unions under each *Upazila* act as members of the respective UZP. The villages under each *Upazila* are grouped into several unions and the recognised townships under *Upazilas* are municipalities. Each union has a popularly elected representative body that is the Union *Parishad* (UP). UPs consist of a chairman and 12 members (nine male members and three female members) – all elected by direct ballot. The municipalities also have a mayor and several ward councillors all of whom are directly elected.

References

Bauböck, R. 2010. Cold Constellations and Hot Identities: Political Theory Questions About Transnationalism and Diaspora. In R. Bauböck and T. Faist (eds), *Diaspora and Transnationalism: Concepts, Theories and Methods.* Amsterdam: Amsterdam University Press, pp. 295–321.

Blair, H. 1985. Participation, Public Policy, Political Economy and Development in Rural Bangladesh: 1958–85. *World Development* 13(12): 1231–1247.

Bruneau, M. 2010. Diasporas, Transnational Spaces and Communities. In R. Bauböck and T. Faist (eds), *Diaspora and Transnationalism: Concepts, Theories and Methods*. Amsterdam: Amsterdam University Press, pp. 35–50.

Bureau of Manpower Employment and Training (BMET). 2013. Overseas Employment and Remittances from 1976 to 2012. Online, available at: www.bmet.gov.bd/BMET/viewStatReport.action?reportnumber=18 (accessed 24 August 2013).

Cohen, R. 1997. *Global Diasporas: An Introduction*. London: UCL Press.

Faist, T. 2010. Diaspora and Transnationalism: What Kind of Dance Partners? In R. Bauböck and T. Faist (eds), *Diaspora and Transnationalism: Concepts, Theories and Methods*. Amsterdam: Amsterdam University Press.

Gardner, K. 1995. *Global Migrants, Local Lives: Travel and Transformation in Rural Bangladesh*. Oxford: Clarendon Press.

Goldring, L. 2008. Migrant Political Participation and Development: Re-politicizing Development and Re-socializing Politics. Paper presented at the Migration and Development Conference, 28 February–1 March 2008, Social Science Research Council (SSRC), Brooklyn, New York.

Guarnizo, L.E., A. Portes and W. Haller. 2003. Assimilation and Transnationalism: Determinants of Transnational Political Action among Contemporary Migrants. *American Journal of Sociology* 108(6): 1211–1248.

Hossain, N. 2005. *Elite Perceptions of Poverty in Bangladesh*. Dhaka: UPL.

International Organization for Migration (IOM) – Dhaka. 2013. Facts and Figures. Online, available at: www.iom.org.bd/page/facts-and-figures/ (accessed 24 August 2013).

Kochanek, S.A. 2002. The Growing Commercialization of Power. In R. Jahan (ed.), *Bangladesh: Promise and Performance*. Dhaka: UPL.

Østergaard-Nielsen, E. 2003. The Politics of Migrants' Transnational Political Practices. *International Migration Review* 37(3): 760–786.

Putnam, R.D., R. Leonardi and R. Nanetti. 1993. *Making Democracy Work: Civic Traditions in Modern Italy*. Princeton, NJ: Princeton University Press.

Sheffer, G. 2003. *Diaspora Politics: At Home Abroad*. Cambridge: Cambridge University Press.

Schiffauer, W., G. Baumann, R. Kastoryano and S. Vertovec. 2003. *Civil Enculturation: State, School and Ethnic Difference in Four European Countries*. Oxford: Berghahn.

Siddiqui, T. 2004. *Institutionalising Diaspora Linkage: The Emigrant Bangladeshis in UK and USA*. Dhaka: GOB and IOM.

Tocqueville, A. 1838. *Democracy in America*. London: Saunders and Otley.

Vertovec, S. 2004. Migrant Transnationalism and Modes of Transformation. *International Migration Review* 38(3): 970–1001.

5 Indian professional immigrants and the healthcare sector in India

Rakesh Ranjan

Globalisation results in blurred international boundaries and has increased the connectivity and dependence of countries and communities. This has affected the global labour market, particularly in terms of the dependence of developed countries on developing countries for cheap and skilled labour. Globalisation has facilitated mobility, circulation, exchange and income in the form of migration, return migration, employment and remittances. International migration and remittances have engaged the attention of policy makers across the globe as it affects the economic, political, cultural and social life of migrants in the origin and destination countries. The Indian diaspora has contributed significantly towards India's economic development, mostly in the service sector. Overseas Indians estimated at over 30 million are spread across 110 countries. However, the Indian diaspora has not come forward as active investors in the Indian economy in the scale that was expected post-liberalisation, as compared to Chinese investment (Roy and Banarjee 2007). That being said, it has created a reasonable influence towards India's service sector development.

The available information suggests that investments by diaspora in the Indian economy are very low. The total amount of investments by Indian expatriates (NRIs) over the period 1991–2001 was estimated at US$2.6 billion out of the total US$10 billion FDI in India, which was meagre compared to the approximate 70 per cent of the US$196 billion FDI received by China during the late 1980s and 1990s. It should, however, be noted that the Indian government does not keep records of NRI investments separately. According to the World Bank Report 2012 however, India received US$72 billion dollar as remittances, which was the highest among all countries. Similarly, there is an extent of high-level investment from countries with a higher number of diaspora, such as Mauritius (39 per cent) and Singapore (10 per cent) followed by other countries (Department of Industrial Policy and Promotion, Government of India, June 2012). The analysis of the impact of diaspora involvement in the economies of their countries of origin in this chapter is set against the backdrop of the potential for investment possessed by the diaspora and their visible presence in India's healthcare sector.

The lack of systematic data on professional migration in India has made it difficult to estimate the actual magnitude of health worker movement. In the wake of the evolving global and national effort to restructure the migration of professionals – especially that of health professionals – this chapter tries to understand the diaspora entrepreneur approach in the healthcare sector of Delhi-NCR, India. This chapter is divided into four sections. The first section creates a theoretical profile of diaspora entrepreneurship, the growth of diaspora financial instruments, and their gradual usage to fund homeland ventures. The second section looks at the role of the Indian government in diaspora engagement for the healthcare industry, and how the government changes its rules and regulations over time. The third section tries to elaborate on and analyse the diaspora engagement in the healthcare sector through an analysis of four major healthcare institutions of Delhi-NCR. Finally, the fourth section discusses the significance of diaspora engagement in the healthcare sector through findings of the study.

Conceptualising diaspora entrepreneurship through the perspective of homeland engagement

Diaspora entrepreneurship is not a new phenomenon, starting centuries before among ethnic communities such as the Jewish, Greek, Armenian, Japanese and Chinese. Over the last three decades however, diaspora entrepreneurship has gained prominence. Entrepreneurship refers to one of the vital functions in serving the development of a society. A society, through its interactions with other groups or societies and its processes of exchange of goods, is itself a start to an entrepreneurial relationship. Entrepreneurs can be seen as economic functionaries who forecast the wants of the consumers, leading to two kinds of incomes: the contractual income (wage, rent) and residual income (profit) of the entrepreneur (Knight 1921). Schumpeter (1934) defined the entrepreneur with a slightly different perspective as a driver of economic development. Entrepreneurial activities can be seen as the introduction of new goods or new qualities of an existing good, the introduction of a new method of production, the opening of new markets, the utilisation of new sources of raw materials or intermediate goods, and the carrying out of some new organisational form of industry (Schumpeter 1934). Entrepreneurs can be seen as the innovative industrial leaders who assume the risk associated with uncertainty, and organise and coordinate economic activities.

Entrepreneurship, a complex interplay of social, psychological, economic and political factors operates in new dynamics in the globalised environment. Ethnic and social networks have for centuries fostered an important role in promoting transnational trade, by helping to overcome weaknesses in the information and contracting environment faced by buyers and sellers across nations (Curtin 1984; Rauch 2001). There has been growing evidence of diaspora entrepreneurship in India due to the impact of globalisation in recent years. Some of the key changes in society can be observed through three major changes: the market, new technology, and transnational networks, which in turn are interconnected (Jain 2010). With the extension of transnational networks, diaspora are increasingly familiar and better integrated with the regulatory changes in Indian government foreign investment policies. India has started facilitating the investment from foreign players, which also includes her diaspora. Post-1990, liberalisation created an environment for diaspora entrepreneurship, especially in the service sector such as information technology, education, infrastructure and healthcare. There is evidence of an increase of diasporic entrepreneurship in the National Capital Region especially in the healthcare sector since 2000, when the government of India started promoting diasporic relationships through Pravasi Bhartiya Divas, and facilitated diasporic engagement through the MOIA (Agunias and Newland 2012).

During the 1960s, a new concept of the brain drain was introduced to academia with the migration of health professionals, such as doctors and nurses from the United Kingdom to the United States. The vacuum in the supply of health personnel created in the UK health sector was partly filled by the immigration of Asian doctors, and Indians in particular (Khadaria 2004). Accordingly, a large number of skilled health workers, especially doctors and nurses, emigrated in masses from India to the United Kingdom, and later on to different parts of the world. This exodus of Indian health professionals created a huge impact on different parts of the world and fulfilled the healthcare professionals' requirement within English and non-English speaking countries (Report of High Level Committee on Indian Diaspora 2001). However, this notion of diaspora relations, with the help of pre-settled PIOs worldwide, influenced the homeland as well, with three broad levels of participation with the homeland (especially in the healthcare sector): Financial investment by NRIs/PIOs, direct participation by these professionals as knowledge entrepreneurship, and professionals participating in activities through different updated media such as teleconferencing. While it is true that development of entrepreneurship cannot be seen as without risk, innovation, and uncertainty, we cannot ignore the role of culture and homeland interaction in the case of diaspora entrepreneurship.

Diaspora entrepreneurs have ties of religion, language and ethnicity, and usually play a major and remarkable role in many areas of social, cultural, economic and intellectual development (Israel 2005). Diaspora members are often more willing than non-diaspora investors to engage in emerging markets or business activities with high risks. Moreover, their knowledge of the local political, economic and cultural environment, as well as their personal connections and linguistic abilities, usually give diaspora members a 'first mover' advantage and a separate kind of protection while investing in or starting businesses in their countries of origin. Researches (Israel 2005; Jain 2010) have shown that migrants usually use their social networks to find employment as aliens to host countries. A notion of network cultural ties or ethnic enclave economies, as we may call it, can be observed in many cities such as, 'Chinatowns', 'Korea towns', 'Irish towns', 'Little Havanas', 'Little Italies', and 'Little Indias'. This can be seen as a clear reflection of migrant networks in host countries, which is properly facilitated through cultural ties and strong entrepreneurial mentorship.

Diaspora entrepreneurship refers to the development of businesses by immigrants who are in a position to take advantage of diaspora policies and organisations set in place by those countries attempting to promote such entrepreneurship on the part of their citizens living abroad. This kind of economic development relies mostly on organisational ties between migrants and the governments, institutions and agencies that are promoting it (Migration Policy Institute 2012). Diaspora entrepreneurs can serve as a channel for organisational ties between their home countries and countries of immigration. A host of organisations such as the Mexican Talent Network, the Indus Entrepreneurs, the South African Diaspora Network, Global Scot, Armenia 2020, Ethiopia Commodity Exchange, and Foundation Chile promote networking, mentoring, training, investment, and venture capital initiatives for development in the home countries of diaspora members (Newland and Tanaka 2010). Transnational activities can be economic, political, or social, and they depend on both interpersonal and organisational ties. Transnationalism facilitates the development and the transfer of remittances to migrants' home countries, and all transnational activities rely fundamentally on migrant networks and the exchange of goods and resources between social ties.

In the Indian context, we can broadly observe three types of diaspora participating in entrepreneurial activities. The first are voluntary diaspora such as the Gujarati, Sindhi and other entrepreneurs who historically trade from their homeland through different networks. The second are diaspora who went from India on an indenture and later settled there. These emigrants acquired resources in their host land, and subsequently participated in entrepreneurial expansions. The third are skilled migrants who came to India as healthcare or IT professionals after the 1960s. All these distinct categories clearly reflect the influence of culture in diaspora entrepreneurship. Culture cannot be seen as a supplementary factor in the entrepreneurial process; rather, it is an important factor in entrepreneurship and it heavily influences the diaspora entrepreneurs worldwide to participate in the development of their homeland.

This study tries to analyse the role of diaspora entrepreneurship in the healthcare industry of Delhi-NCR. Through the analysis of secondary sources (statistics from various sectors and departments at national and international level) and the survey of different hospitals, this chapter maps out the various patterns of diaspora entrepreneurship in India. Following the objective of the study, the chapter is divided into three sections – the first section discusses the role of diaspora entrepreneurship in India, the second section discusses the role and influence of existing diaspora investment in the healthcare sector especially in Delhi-NCR, and the last section talks about different ways to enhance the diaspora investment.

The broader objectives of this study are: To find out how culture and identity are mediated in entrepreneurial ventures of Indian diaspora through reviewing the extant literature; to highlight the Indian diaspora's entrepreneurial history, especially in post-liberalised India; and to determine the preferred sectors of diaspora entrepreneurship. We also seek to investigate the emergence of the healthcare industry vis-à-vis diaspora engagement and the entrepreneurial inputs of diaspora in healthcare, and to study select ventures of the diaspora in Delhi and the NCR region.

Research methods

Keeping in mind the above objectives, the following methodology has been adopted. The study is exploratory and descriptive, the target population is specific to the hospitals of Delhi-NCR, and the research unit is healthcare professionals. This chapter attempts to draw evidences and cases through an empirical study of selected healthcare ventures. Four major hospitals situated in Delhi-NCR along with one drug agency were selected for the study. The data were broadly collected through different communication channels including emails, phone calls, organisation websites, and frequent visits to hospitals. A total of 424 doctors were approached for the study through different channels, in which 88 doctors responded and were found to be return migrants. Primary data of the study were also collected through the analysis of annual reports, investor relations, and shareholding patterns of each selected healthcare enterprise's website. Four case studies of different hospitals of Delhi were conducted to study the financial contribution and participation of diaspora.

Additionally, the data also include secondary sources drawn from the skilled manpower of Indian diaspora, taken from references and reports from international organisations like the World Bank's *Migration and Remittances Fact Book 2011*, papers of the Migration Policy Institute, the Organization for Economic Co-operation and Development (OECD), websites of Indian government departments, websites of research institutions, press reviews and academic articles. The data on Indian immigration and investment were also collected from the websites of Indian Overseas Affairs, the government of India, and the Reserve Bank of India. We also analysed books, reports and data available through government and non-government sources (including statistics from various sectors), newspaper articles, blogs, and other Internet resources.

Indian diaspora entrepreneurship in post-liberalisation: reflections from the role of government in diaspora engagement

Migration has always been seen as a natural and inevitable process in any human society. The last two centuries have witnessed the mass mobility of people in search of opportunity and livelihood in new places. In the globalisation era, human mobility has taken place all over the world with increasing global competition and different technological advancements. In line with this, more skilled labour was required in the developed countries due to the development of their service sectors.

Developing countries lost a large number of their skilled labour every year. However, the new liberalisation policy that intended to attract more investment also encouraged diaspora participation. The Indian diaspora was encouraged in many ways to engage with the economic development of India. RIBs, PIO cards, special privileges to NRIs, banking, and other forms of financial assistance like streamlining remittances, etc. are some of the initiatives by the government and other institutions that facilitate diaspora engagement.

Parallel to these, development in the information and communication technology helped to unleash the entrepreneurial potential of the diaspora to a great extent. Many countries other than India (Bangladesh, Mexico, Israel, etc.) started their special overseas affairs ministries and departments to facilitate the diaspora relationship, with a special focus on investment. It was a global phenomenon that challenged nation states and led to the birth of multiple networks, transnational or transcontinental, and also regional or local, bringing migration onto the main world stage (Wenden 2009).

India's domestic public debt increased steadily from 1980 to 1991, from 36 per cent to 56 per cent of the GDP, while its external debt more than tripled to US$70 billion (World Bank 2012). Meanwhile, political changes and the Gulf Crisis almost led India to a defaulter situation. In the struggle to overcome this situation, the Indian government accepted the structural adjustment programme and shifted from a closed economy to a relatively open one. Some of the major initiatives of this programme were cuts in public expenditure including subsidies and private investment in social services, relaxation in licensing, and acceptance of foreign direct investment (Klein *et al.* 2001; Tambunan 2005). These changes in the economic structure of India attracted foreign investors as well as diaspora entrepreneurs to invest in their homeland. In order to facilitate diaspora entrepreneurship, the Indian government liberalised many regulations. All these changes in the existing structure and cultural ties created positive impacts on the host country: Diaspora entrepreneurship fosters business development, job creation, and innovation; Diaspora direct investment creates economic, social and political capital through global networks; Diaspora entrepreneurship taps into social capital through cultural and linguistic understanding; All in all, entrepreneurship and economic development are positively linked.

Since the mid-1980s, Indian diaspora communities and the government of India have both altered their stance towards one another. With the salient changes in the regulatory framework, the government of India shifted its policies from 'licence-permit-quota Raj' to the free flow of capital. Such freedom meant being able to marshal financial support from institutions such as the stock exchange and banks with broader entrepreneurial capacity than might be available in India. In the United States, for example, there has been a sudden expansion in the number of organisations that Indian immigrants have launched to foster linkages with India. At the same time, the Indian government created new bank accounts that allowed NRIs to invest money in India under favourable conditions. In 1999, the government launched two new visa status cards for persons of Indian origin and for overseas citizens of India that facilitated Indian emigrants' ability to travel in and out of India, invest in property, and hold Indian rupee bank accounts. In 2000, the Indian government commissioned a high level committee to research and write an extensive report on the Indian diaspora. The Indian government, with prior understanding about the importance of diaspora for development, initiated many programmes, which include the organisation of PBD conventions and Mini-PBDs, the conferment of the Pravasi Bharatiya Samman Award, the dissemination of information concerning the admission of

NRI/PIO students to various educational, technical and cultural institutions in India wherever discretionary quota for NRI/PIO students exists, and programmes dealing with issues related to NRI women.

Indian diaspora relations underwent a huge change after the 2000s, with the new initiatives of the government of India, such as tax relaxation, Pravasi Bhartiya Divas, NRI–PIO scheme, etc. At the same time, India also started a separate ministry for the development of diaspora relations in 2003 – the MOIA. NRIs who intend to permanently reside in India can claim exemption from wealth tax for a period of seven years upon returning to India. NRIs can invest in shares and debentures of Indian companies under the automatic route without obtaining the RBI's or government's approval. There are certain sectors that require the permission of the Foreign Investment Promotion Board (FIPB) for investments by NRIs and OCBs; these investments also enjoy full repatriation benefits. Other investments with repatriation benefits include investment in domestic mutual funds, bonds and shares issued by public sector undertakings and enterprises, government securities, and shares.

Diaspora entrepreneurship in the healthcare industry

The entire concentration of diaspora entrepreneurship in India can be widely observed in five major sectors: education, healthcare, it, infrastructure, and energy and environment. Within all of these, the IT and healthcare sectors can be observed as two of the major focus areas of diaspora entrepreneurship. Both these areas have specific characteristics that separate them from others. Although direct investment in these sectors can be seen as a common feature, there is a specific factor differentiating both these sectors from each other with regards to diaspora entrepreneurship. After the Indian economic liberalisation, the IT industry became widely facilitated in India through overseas networks and trade expansion from developed countries. Although entrepreneurship in the healthcare sector in India entails a similar preposition, cultural ties can be seen in this sector more than in any other industry with the involvement of skilled professionals who directly participate in this entrepreneurship approach either through economic entrepreneurship, knowledge entrepreneurship, or both. Many examples, including the establishment of Apollo Hospitals in different parts of India, the NRI Academy of Sciences, Narayana Hrudayalaya Hospitals in South India, and many others, reflect the involvement of strong cultural ties between health professionals and their homeland.

The Indian healthcare sector is expected to reach US$100 billion in value by 2015 from the current US$65 billion, growing at around 20 per cent a year (OIFC 2012). Some of the major factors driving the growth in the sector include an increasing population, growing lifestyle-related health issues, cheaper costs for treatment, thrust in medical tourism, improving health insurance penetration, increasing disposable income, government initiatives, and focus on public private partnership (PPP) models. According to the latest Department of Industrial Policy and Promotion (DIPP) data, FDI inflow in hospital and diagnostic centres was US$1.3 billion between 2000 and 2012. The sector comprises many segments, including hospitals, medical infrastructure, medical devices, clinical trials, outsourcing, telemedicine and health insurance. The industry has grown at about 13 per cent annually in recent years and is expected to grow at 15 per cent per year over the medium term, driven by rising incomes, a growing propensity to spend on healthcare, and a shift in lifestyle-related diseases and demographics among other factors (IBEF 2011b; Nanda and Khanna 2009). Newland and Tanaka (2010) observed that diaspora entrepreneurship relies substantially on certain sets of known networks through ethnicity, language, religion, or regional preferences, which ultimately leads the diaspora practice of enterprise at culturally familiar places.

Diaspora regional preferences and Delhi

Delhi, as national capital, has certain positive characteristics that have led to it being the preferred destination for entrepreneurs. For example, Delhi does not have specific ethnic sets of people as it is a fusion of migrant populations from different parts of India. It is easy for diaspora entrepreneurs to establish cultural networks in India. Delhi is the capital of the Republic of India, and also the state for administrative purposes. It is one of the largest metropolises in the country. Delhi shares its border with the states of Uttar Pradesh and Haryana, identified as Delhi-NCR, and is also the epicentre of international politics, trade, culture and literature in India. Delhi has emerged as a key state with immense scope for development of the services industry such as banks and financial services institutions (BFSI), IT and ITeS, healthcare, education, infrastructural development, etc. and has one of the best healthcare infrastructures in the country. The state offers among the most sophisticated medical care, with state-of-the-art technology for treatment. As of December 2009, there were 721 medical institutions in Delhi with a total of 38,004 beds. It also has a number of highly specialised hospitals in both the public and private sectors. There has been significant infrastructure and environmental development in Delhi over the last 20 years, while the per capita GDP of the state increased at a compound annual growth rate of 12.3 per cent between 2004–2005 and 2009–2010. Delhi has received cumulative foreign direct investment (FDI) inflows worth US$26.1 billion (including National Capital Territory) during April 2000 to April 2011, according to the Department of Industrial Policy and Promotion (DIPP), and proposes a wide range of fiscal and policy incentives for businesses under the Industrial Policy for Delhi, 2010–2021.

The Indian healthcare industry

Indian doctors and health professionals are the backbone of the National Health Service in the United Kingdom, and also play influential roles in many other countries such as the United States, Canada and Australia. Indian healthcare professionals, particularly nurses, have been integrated into almost all parts of the world, not only developing countries. Indian healthcare professionals as well as other NRIs and PIOs have already made valuable contributions to their homeland by establishing different health institutions. The Indian healthcare sector is predicted to reach US$280 billion in value by 2020. The government of India has permitted 100 per cent FDI inflows into the healthcare sector in India.

Major diaspora-driven organisations in the Indian healthcare industry can be observed in Apollo Hospitals Enterprise Ltd, Fortis Healthcare Ltd, Doctor Z India Healthcare (Pvt.) Ltd, Translational Health Sciences and Technology Institute, Panacea Biotec, and many others. With regards to diaspora activities in the Indian healthcare sector, various roles can be seen, namely: physicians/medical professionals, professional medical organisations, the corporate sector, banks, financial institutions, chambers of commerce and industry, government, the voluntary sector, medical tourism, and the Indian system of medicine, to name but a few. In the Indian healthcare sector, entrepreneurial activities can be facilitated in two ways. The first is through direct investment by different diaspora driven organisations, and the second is through knowledge transfer through different modes of communication such as tele-medicine, tele-consultation, different workshops, trainings, and medical research.

In order to understand the role of diaspora entrepreneurship, we first need to consider different components of the existing diaspora entrepreneurial community, i.e. individual medical professions (knowledge professionals as returnees), professional medical organisations, financial institutions, role of government, and many others. Through the analysis of different industries in Delhi-NCR, which are broadly either run by diaspora entrepreneurship, or getting financial support from NRI communities, we can understand the relationship between cultural factors and diaspora entrepreneurship in the healthcare industry, especially in Delhi-NCR. Indian healthcare professionals (NRIs and PIOs) have made a considerable contribution by establishing many initiatives (return professionals, health camps, establishment of hospitals, training programmes, etc.) towards development of the healthcare sector in India. We can analyse each of them through some grass roots examples.

Return health professionals

The emigration rates for doctors was about 3 per cent during the 1980s. It is 56 per cent for graduates of the All India Institute for Medical Sciences between 1956 and 1980, and 49 per cent in the 1990s. In order to understand the different trends of health professionals in India, we can divide the whole phenomenon into three parts: before the 1990s, after the 1990s and during and after the economic slowdown. The earlier notion of the brain drain gradually shifted to the brain gain through different roles of Individual healthcare professionals. For example, there are some studies stating that Indian health professionals, who join the United Kingdom's National Health Service are likely to return with augmented human capital (Devesh Kapoor 2003). A primary study of four major hospitals in Delhi-NCR reported that it is difficult to generalise that a good number of doctors come from abroad to India, but the trend is fairly good in Delhi-NCR. In the Indraprashta Apollo Hospital of Delhi-NCR, it was observed through a study of 216 doctors that 46 doctors came back to India. Among these 46 doctors, 31 professionals came back after higher education in foreign countries, and 15 came back after working. Data compiled from different hospitals through individual visits and from the web are given in Table 5.1.

In the analysis of return medical professionals in Delhi, it was observed that private sector hospitals attracted more doctors than government hospitals. This phenomenon can be seen as a trickle-down effect created by Dr Prathap C. Reddy's Apollo Hospital, which attracted the majority of health professionals during the 1970s and 1980s (Report of the High Level Committee on Indian Diaspora 2010). Another reason could be that the prospects of acceptance/employment opportunity of these health professionals is higher in private hospitals, as most of the recruitment options in the government sector usually follow standard procedures. In the case of private sector hospitals, appointment is usually conducted through direct consultation, and medical professionals are usually not required to come to India for appointment procedures.

Many health professionals are also engaged in the organisation of health camps and training programmes with the help of different NGOs, self-help groups, and other philanthropic organisations. The voluntary sector has also played a major role in the field of healthcare. Many health professionals including doctors and nurses used to come to India every year to organise free eye camps and render other services, including highly specialised hospitals (Report of the High Level Committee on Indian Diaspora 2001). Many doctors who are not able to personally come participate in activities through different updated mediums, especially through tele-conferencing, which is gradually becoming an important medium of consultation.

A number of professional organisations in the medical field, for example, the American Association of Physicians from India (AAPI), the Association of Indian Neurologists, the Association of Asian Indians in Ophthalmology, etc. in the United States are playing an important role in the transfer of skills.

Table 5.1 Examples from different private and government organisations

S. No.	*Name of hospital (private/government)*	*Total number of doctors*	*Returned professionals*	*Nature of migration (work/education)*	
4	Indraprastha Apollo Hospital (private)	216	46	Work Education	15 31
5	Fortis Healthcare (NOIDA, Gurgaon, Delhi) (private)	166	34	Work Education	15 19
6	AIIMS (government)	42	8	Work Education	0 8

Note
Figures may be incomplete; based on the information revealed by the relevant hospitals.

The AAPI is a forum to facilitate and enable Indian American physicians to excel in patient care, teaching and research, and to pursue their aspirations in professional and community affairs. The AAPI and the AAPI foundation in India have been working with India's health authorities (health ministry officials, ministers, and the Indian Medical Council) to improve the regulation of physicians' education. This includes registering a certain number of hours in continuing medical education (CME) for practicing physicians – a three-year renewal of a practicing license based on completing annual CME of 50 hours, peer reviews in all teaching hospitals and others with a capacity of 100 or more beds, and hospital management. This association currently has more than 10,000 life members. The Association of Indian Neurologists is another association set up to advance patient care, teaching and research of neurological disorders in the United States, India and other countries with neurologists of Indian origin.

Financial participation towards the healthcare industry by NRIs

The corporate sector has been an important institution in facilitating economic as well as cultural orientation towards the home country for diaspora entrepreneurs. Relationships with corporates can help in many ways, such as the manufacture and fabrication of high-tech medical equipment and spare parts, setting up of highly specialised hospitals and diagnostic facilities, spread of corporate hospitals to suburban areas (Report of the High Level Committee on Indian Diaspora 2001) and, more importantly, financial participation for home country hospitals. Although a tradition of financial participation of NRIs/PIOs can be broadly observed after the Indian economic reform, there are other factors that created the atmosphere for healthcare growth.

In the analysis of the hospital network of Delhi-NCR, the Apollo group appears first on the list because of its establishment and spread all over India. The Apollo Hospitals group is a major hospital chain in India. It was founded by Dr Prathap C. Reddy, a return migrant from the United States, on 5 December 1979. Apollo is a private healthcare provider in Asia, with hospitals in India, Sri Lanka, Bangladesh, Ghana, Nigeria, Republic of Mauritius, Qatar, Oman and Kuwait. In 1982, Apollo reserved 500,000 shares for NRIs. Although only 403,450 shares were taken up by NRI investors, it created a huge response towards NRI engagement in Indian industries. The establishment of Apollo healthcare created a huge trickledown effect for other NRI as well as private investors; many healthcare organisations like Max Healthcare, Fortis Healthcare and Medanta hospitals were established along the same lines.

According to the March 2012 shareholding pattern, 1,064 NRIs/PIOs shareholders invested 1,915,405 shares in Apollo Hospitals in India, which is almost 1.42 per cent of the total shareholding (Table 5.2).

The late Dr Parvinder Singh incorporated Fortis Healthcare in 1996. Starting with its first hospital in Mohali, which opened in 2001, Fortis Healthcare Ltd now has a network of 45 hospitals. In 2003–2004, Fortis started operating from

Table 5.2 Year-wise NRI investment in Apollo Healthcare, India

S. No.	*Year*	*Shareholder*	*Shares*	*Percentage in total shares*
6	April 2007–March 2008	953	1,078,250	2.00
7	April 2008–March 2009	980	1,054,883	1.75
8	April 2009–March 2010	964	1,006,501	1.63
9	April 2010–March 2011	1,198	2,055,245	1.65
10	April 2011–March 2012	1,064	1,915,405	1.42

Note
Per share cost of Apollo Healthcare $16 (900 INR) (approx. market value).

the New Okhla Industrial Development Authority, a commercial part of Delhi-NCR. Its hospitals include multi-specialty hospitals as well as highly specialised centres providing comprehensive tertiary and quaternary healthcare to patients across specialties such as cardiac care, orthopaedics, neurosciences, oncology, renal care, gastroenterology, and mother and child care. Out of a total of 405.18 million shares, 22.60 million shares are currently owned by NRI and foreign investors; this excludes promoters' shares and institutional investment. Fortis Healthcare currently has 4,183.48 crore of the total market, in which NRI and Foreign Individual Investment consist almost 22 crore. Although Fortis Healthcare does not reflect separate individual investment by NRIs, it has secured a good amount invested by NRIs and PIOs overall.

Another hospital, Max India, was founded in 1985 by Mr Analjit Singh, a return migrant from the United States. Max India is a public limited company listed on the NSE and BSE of India with over 30,000 shareholders, which include Max Healthcare, Max Bupa, and Max Insurance, etc. The first Max healthcare centre was opened in 2000 as Max Medcentre in Panchsheel Park; New Delhi with OPD facilities and day care surgeries. Total shares held by NRIs and overseas corporate bodies in Max India is 2,863,533, which is almost 1.08 per cent of total shares held by all investors excluding promoters and other institutional investments.

This study also tried to reveal the issues related to healthcare producers and management agencies. Panacea Drugs (P) Ltd, an Indian research based pharmaceutical and health management company formed in 1984, is one of the largest biotech companies in India. Shareholding of individuals includes 64,302 shares held by NRIs in Panacea Biotech of a total of 61,250,746 shares. Although the total number of shares held by NRIs is low in comparison with its total shares, it is still fourth highest in NRI shareholdings in Delhi-NCR in the healthcare sector. While there are many other hospitals involved in financial engagement by diaspora, they would not reveal data about shareholding patterns and return migrants. Overall, especially in the healthcare sector, the role of culture is becoming highly integrative. However, we need to think about different aspects, including India's better economic conditions and better consumption patterns of customers.

Conclusion

Diaspora entrepreneurship needs to be considered as a driver of economic as well as social development in the post-liberalised era. Through certain industries such as education, healthcare, infrastructure and IT, diaspora investment creates a better and more sustained investment than others as there is a large human resource already available and well-networked. Although there are two dynamics of diaspora involvement analysed in this study, i.e. the knowledge and investment contributions of the diaspora, only the healthcare sector involves both these aspects. The role of knowledge transfer from diaspora is also reflected in the IT industry in the form of 'mentorship'. The healthcare sector, however, involves more direct participation of the diaspora. The survey of different hospitals observed that there is a good flow of returned health professionals into many of these corporate hospitals as a result of many factors, including culture. The findings of the case studies interpret incidences of out-migration observed post-independence as a result of a lack of opportunity in India. Medical professionals went abroad mainly to gain better employment opportunity. In addition, higher earnings, better perks and a high quality of life in the host country encouraged them. Although many doctors came back either after education or some work experience, we cannot ignore the role of economic reform in India itself. While it is very difficult to understand the financial contribution of health professionals, it was observed through the study of individual organisations that NRIs were investing huge amounts of money in these healthcare institutions. There were three incidents of engagement of Indian diaspora observed, i.e. direct engagement, consultations, and financial investment.

Among the ways to enhance diaspora direct engagement is to facilitate land acquisition or to provide proper help in overcoming infrastructural constraints, to enhance medical education, and to facilitate the other aspects of private healthcare institutions such as philanthropy, training, free camps, investment in the domestic manufacture of medical equipment and services, and tie-ins with international organisations. These can enhance the capability of health professionals as well as institutions. There is an urgent need to support market firms to attract and retain returned engineers and scientists by improving the social infrastructure and conditions so that returnees find it easier to adjust to life in new places of work.

As entrepreneurship concerns risk and innovation, there should be risk-sharing mechanisms such as loan insurance schemes, credit guarantees, etc. as diaspora entrepreneurship contributes greatly to the process of development of the homeland. However, it is also possible that local entrepreneurship can create problems for diaspora entrepreneurship by presenting the former as threats or competitors; in this scenario the government would need to formulate policies to create better and sustainable diaspora investment and facilitate development. This study has attempted to understand and elaborate on the incidences of Indian diaspora engagement in the healthcare sector of Delhi-NCR. Furthering this research direction, it would be fruitful to analyse the issues with cross-country comparisons or cross-city comparisons, such as comparisons between diaspora engagement of India and China, or how different cities like Mumbai and Delhi deal with this issue. The migration of teachers has also been a visible pattern in recent times, and research can be conducted to understand the nature of homeland engagement of teachers who settle abroad.

References

Agunias, D.R. and N. Kathleen. 2012. *Developing a Road Map for Engaging Diasporas in Development: a Handbook for Policymakers and Practitioners in Home and Host Countries*. Washington, DC: Migration Policy Institute.

Aldrich, H.E., J. Cater, Tr. Jones, D. McEvoy and P. Velleman. 1985. Ethnic Residential Concentration and the Protected Market Hypothesis. *Social Forces* 63(4): 996–1009.

Amrith, S.S. 2011. *Migration and Development*. India: Cambridge University Press.

Apollo Hospitals. 2012a. Shareholding Pattern. April 2007 to March 2012. Online, available at: www.apollohospitals.com/investor_share.php (accessed 11 June 2012).

Apollo Hospitals. 2012b. Super Brands. Online, available at: www.superbrandsindia.com/images/brand_pdf/consumer_3rd_edition/Apollo%20Hospitals.pdf (accessed 17 June 2012).

Azuma, E. 2005. Brief Historical Overview of Japanese Emigration. International Nikkei Research Project. Online, available at: www.janm.org/projects/inrp/english/overview.htm (accessed 12 July 2012).

Balasubramanyam, V.N. and Y.Q. Wei. 2007. The Diaspora and Development. Department of Economics, Lancaster University. Online, available at: www.mse.ac.in/seminar/baloo_seminar%20paper.pdf (accessed 2 April 2012).

BioPlan Associates. 2008. Panacea Biotec Ltd Basic Information. Online, available at: http://top1000bio.com/docs/Sample_Company_Profile_India.pdf (accessed 11 May 2012).

Chanda, R. 2010. Constraints in Foreign Direct Investment in Indian Hospitals. *Journal of International Commerce, Economics and Policy* 1(1): 121–143.

Falzon, M.-A. 2005. *Cosmopolitan Connection: the Sindhi Diaspora 1860–2000*. New Delhi: Oxford University Press.

Foreigners Division. 2012. Overseas Citizenship of India (OCI). Ministry of Home Affairs, Government of India. Online, available at: http://mha1.nic.in/foreigDiv/OCI.html (accessed 17 May 2012).

Harris, N. 2005. Migration and Development. *Economic and Political Weekly*, October 22.

IIFS. 2012. Fortis Healthcare Limited. Online, available at: www.indiainfoline.com/Markets/Company/Fortis-Healthcare-Ltd/532843 (accessed 14 June 2012).

India Brand Equity Foundation. 2011a. Delhi Fact Line. Online, available at: www.ibef.org/states/delhi.aspx (accessed 7 May 2012).

India Brand Equity Foundation. 2011b. Healthcare. Online, available at: www.ibef.org/download/Healthcare50112.pdf (accessed 25 May 2012).

Indiastat. 2013a. Foreign Direct Investment (FDI) Inflows in India (August 1991–March 2000 and 2000–2001 to 2012–2013 up to April 2012). Online, available at: www.indiastat.com (accessed 25 May 2012).

Indiastat. 2013b. Statewise NRI Investment Proposals Approved (January 1998 to September 2001). Online, available at: www.indiastat.com (accessed 25 May 2012).

Israel, J. 2005. Preface: Diasporas Jewish and non-Jewish and the World Maritime Empires. In Ina Baghdiantz McCabe, Gelina Harlaftis and Ioanna Pepelasis Minoglou (eds), *Diaspora Entrepreneurial Networks: Four Centuries of History*. New York: BERG Publication.

Jain, R.K. 2010. *Nation, Diaspora, Trans-nation: Reflections from India*. New Delhi: Routledge.

Kapur, D. 2003. Indian Diaspora as a Strategic Asset. *Economic and Political Weekly*, February 1.

Ketkar, S.L. and D. Ratha. 2007. Development Finance via Diaspora Bonds: Track Record and Potential. In a presentation to the ASSA Annual Meetings in Chicago, IL.

Khadria, B. 2004. Migration of Highly Skilled Indians: Case Studies of IT and Health Professionals. STI Working Paper 2004/6. Paris: OECD.

Klein, M., C. Aaron and B. Hadjimichael. 2001. *Foreign Direct Investment and Poverty Reduction* (Vol. 2613). World Bank Publications.

Knight, F. 1921. *Risk, Uncertainty and Profit*. New York: A.M. Kelley.

LTG Associates Inc. 2012. On the Shoulders of Generations: Philanthropy in the Indian American Community of Silicon Valley. Online, available at: www.siliconvalleycf.org/docs/indian-american-philanthropy-final.pdf (accessed 18 July 2012).

Markovits, C. 2000. *The Global World of Indian Merchant, 1750–1947, Traders of Sind from Bukhara to Panama*. Cambridge, UK: Cambridge University Press.

Max India Website. No date. At a Glance. Online, available at: www.maxindia.com/ (accessed on 12 June 2012).

McCabe I.B., G. Harlaftis and M.I. Pepelasis. 2005. *Diaspora Entrepreneurial Networks: Four Centuries of History*. Oxford New York: BERG Publication.

Menzies, T.V. and G.A. Brenner. 2000. Transnational Entrepreneurship and Bootstrap Capitalism: Social Capital, Networks and Ethnic Minority Entrepreneurs. Working Paper 2000–11, September 2000, ISSN: 0840–853X.

Migration Policy Institute. 2012. Data Hub (All Profiles). Online, available at: www.migrationpolicy.org/programs/data-hub (accessed 11 June 2012).

Ministry of Commerce and Industry, Department of Industrial Policy and Promotion. 2012a. Fact Sheet on Foreign Direct Investment from April 2000 to March 2012. Government of India. Online, available at: http://dipp.nic.in/English/Publications/FDI_Statistics/2012/india_FDI_March2012.pdf (accessed 17 May 2012).

Ministry of Commerce and Industry, Department of Industrial Policy and Promotion. 2012b. Annual Report 2010–11. Government of India.

Ministry of Finance. 2014a. International Taxation Non-Residents. Online, available at: http://law.incometaxindia.gov.in/DIT/intnrcount.aspx (accessed on 17 May 2014).

Ministry of Finance. 2014b. Wealth Tax Act. Online, available at: http://law.incometaxindia.gov.in/DIT/other-income-tax-acts.aspx?page=ODTA&TabId=tab_WTA (accessed on 17 May 2014).

Ministry of Health and Family Welfare. 2012. Annual Report to the People on Health. Government of India.

MOIA. 2001a. Economic Development – Investment, International Trade, Industrial Development and Tourism, Report of the High Level Committee on Indian Diaspora. Online, available at: http://indiandiaspora.nic.in/diasporapdf/chapter29.pdf (accessed 23 July 2014).

MOIA. 2001b. Health, Report of the High Level Committee on Indian Diaspora. Online, available at: http://indiandiaspora.nic.in/diasporapdf/chapter31.pdf (accessed 23 July 2014).

Nanda, R. and T. Khanna. 2009. Diasporas and Domestic Entrepreneurs: Evidence from the Indian Software Industry, Working Paper 08–003, Harvard Business School.

National Council of Applied Economic Research. 2009. FDI in India and its Growth Linkages, National Council of Applied Economic Research Paper. Online, available at: http://dipp.nic.in/english/publications/reports/fdi_ncaer.pdf (accessed 17 May 2014).

Newland, K. 2010. Diaspora Entrepreneurs are People with a Foot in Two Countries. European Urban Knowledge Network. Online, available at: www.eukn.org/Interviews/2010/%E2%80%9CDiaspora_entrepreneurs_are_people_with_a_foot_in_two_countries%E2%80%9D (accessed 19 May 2012).

Newland, K. and H. Tanaka. 2010. Mobilizing Diaspora Entrepreneurship for Development. Migration Policy Institute and United States Agency for International Development, Diasporas and Development Policy Project.

Overseas Indian Facilitation Centre. 2007. Promoting Investments from the Indian Diaspora: A New Beginning. Online, available at: www.oifc.in/Uploads/MediaTypes/Documents/PromotingInvestmentsFromTheIndianDiaspora.pdf (accessed 12 June 2012).

Overseas Indian Facilitation Centre. 2009a. NRI Investment Trends in India. Online, available at: www.oifc.in/Investing-in-India/Investment-Info/Investment-Trends/NRI-Investment-Trends-in-India (accessed 13 April 2012).

Overseas Indian Facilitation Centre. 2009b. Ready Reckoner for NRI. Online, available at: www.oifc.in/Uploads/MediaTypes/Documents/PromotingInvestmentsFromTheIndianDiaspora.pdf (accessed 12 July 2012).

Panacea Biotech. 2012. Share Holding Pattern. March 2012. Online, available at: www.panaceabiotec.com/share_holding.html (accessed 11 May 2012).

Poros, M. 2011. Migrant Social Networks: Vehicles for Migration, Integration, and Development. Migration Policy Institute. March 30. Online, available at: www.migrationinformation.org/Feature/display.cfm?ID=833 (accessed 1 May 2012).

Pravasi Today. 2012a. NRI Helpline. Online, available at: www.pravasitoday.com/nri-helpline/nri-investment (accessed 9 May 2012).

Pravasi Today. 2012b. NRI Investment. Online, available at: www.pravasitoday.com/nri-helpline/nri-investment/ (accessed 11 May 2012).

Pravasi Today. 2012c. Wealth Tax Exemptions. Online, available at: www.pravasitoday.com/wealth-tax-exemptions (accessed 9 May 2012).

Pravasi Today. 2014. Tax Exemptions. Online, available at: www.pravasitoday.com/tax-exemptions (accessed 9 May 2014).

Rai, R. and R. Peter. 2009. *The South Asian Diaspora: Transnational Networks and Changing Identities*. New York: Routledge.

Ratha, D. and A. Silswal. 2012. *Remittance Flows in 2011 – an Update, Migration and Development Brief.* Washington, DC: World Bank.

Rauch, J.E. 2001. Business and Social Networks in International Trade. *Journal of Economic Literature,* 39(4): 1177–1203.

Roy, J. and P. Banarjee. 2007. *Attracting FDI from the Indian Diaspora: the Way Forward.* New Delhi: Confederation of Indian Industry, p. 36.

Sahoo, S. 2007. Brain Drain and Scientific Diaspora: Prospects and Implications Back Home. In Bhabani Shankar Nayak (ed.), *Nationalising Crisis: The Political Economy of Public Policy in Contemporary India.* New Delhi: Atlanta Publication, pp. 171–201.

Securities and Exchange Board of India. 2006. Draft Red Herring Prospectus. Fortis Healthcare Limited. Online, available at: www.sebi.gov.in/dp/fortis.pdf (accessed 17 June 2012).

Shankar, P.B. 2011. Tax Filings by Non Resident Indians. *Economic Times*. 27 May 2011. Online, available at: http://articles.economictimes.indiatimes.com/2011-05-27/news/29589845_1_net-wealth-wealth-tax-income-tax (accessed 12 June 2012).

Tambunan, T. 2005. The Impact of Foreign Direct Investment on Poverty Reduction: a Survey of Literature and a Temporary Finding from Indonesia. Paper presented at consultative meeting on Foreign Direct Investment and Policy Changes: Areas for New Research, United Nations Conference Centre, Bangkok, Thailand.

Wenden, C. de. 2009. Immigration and Globalisation. *Refugee Watch*, 33, June: 48–58.

World Bank. 2011. Remittance Data: Development Prospects Group. Online, available at: http://econ.worldbank.org/ (accessed 4 July 2012).

World Bank. 2012. Independent Evaluation Group Report (IEG). Structural Adjustment in India. Online, available at: http://lnweb90.worldbank.org/oed/oeddoclib.nsf/b57456d58aba40e585256ad400736404/0586cc45a28a2749852567f5005d8c89 (accessed 7 May 2012).

6 A troublesome home?

Transnational property and its discontents in Indian Punjab

V.J. Varghese and Vivek Thakur

The post-nation scholarly literature in English in general celebrates migrant/diasporic transnationalism for its overtly positive positioning as a field despite and beyond the nation states. While transnationalism is seen as a process involving cross-border migrant/diasporic life, the practices and identities of transmigrants provide a counter-narrative to nations with a potential of unsettling the totalising national boundaries (Levitt and Sorenson 2004; Faist 2010; Bhabha 1990; Appadurai 1997). In particular, transnationalism from below, as a field created and maintained by participating people, has been appreciated for exceeding the imposing and restricting structures of the nation state system. It weakens essentialist affinities to a single nation and emphasises multifocality, with oppositional and subversive possibilities instead (Smith and Guarnizo 1998; Portes 1996).[1] Migrant/diasporic transnationalism as a 'social field' is often seen as a site of dense nostalgia, love for homeland, and intense networks that criss-cross the world into innumerable micro-territorialities. This is facilitated by recent developments in communication technologies and advances in modes of travel (Levitt and Schiller 2004; Heath *et al.* 2011). Migration studies has consequently taken a big turn from the paradigms of disjunctures and discontinuities, heading towards 'connectedness', continuities, and reinventions (Smart 2007; Levitt and Schiller 2004; Vertovec 1999). However, the celebrations of supra-national connectedness and social fields of nostalgia overlook some of the prevailing tensions of transnationalism, and some important questions to ask are:

a Are migrant transnational connections essentially demotic?
b Does the prevailing literature privilege migrant homeland ties over their multifarious priorities and considerations?
c Would it be simplistic to paint migrants as eternal benefactors to their home, and home as a treasure house of infinite benevolence and warmth?

The present chapter engages with these questions by looking at the issue of transnational property (owned by Punjabi diaspora/migrants) in Indian Punjab, in an attempt to problematise transnationalism by advancing an argument that transnationalism is essentially a complex cultural field of diverse signifiers.

The investments and financial exchanges that migrants and transnational citizens make also figure in the emergent discourse on migration and development as a new 'development mantra'. These processes have been viewed as an important conduit for the redistribution and convergence of resources, resulting in a call for more migrations and more globalisation (Kapur 2003; Bhagwati 2004). The model has been recommended for developing countries in particular, as the volume of international remittance transfers to the developing world is found to be steadily increasing, reaching the level of US$300 billion in recent times (Guha 2011).

The diaspora philanthropy and charity chain is another channel of migrant transnational resource transfers from the country of settlement to the country of origin (Geithner *et al.* 2004; Dusenbery and Tatla 2010) – migrants are placed at the centre of this discourse as agents of economic exchanges. The barriers to migration, particularly for those people with low skills, considerably limit human choices and chances of even distribution of resources, apart from preventing the advantages of social remittances (Levitt 1998). It is therefore postulated that 'large gains to human development can be achieved by lowering the barriers to movement and improving treatment of movers', even though international migration cannot be seen as a primary national development strategy (UNDP 2009).

India is said to be late in realising the potential of its diasporic resources and recognising Indians abroad as a strategic asset of the nation in its developmental agendas (Kapur 2003; Lall 2001). The shift in position, informed by the contemporary migration–development discourse, has resulted in viewing overseas Indians as a 'vast reservoir of potential investors, entrepreneurs and corporate leaders whose expertise can be deployed in India' (MOIA 2008). Governmental attempts to reinforce overseas Indians' connection with India in a mutually beneficial manner are underwritten by a new nationalist discourse in which the nation seeks its legitimacy through development (Rajan and Varghese 2012). All forms of connections and exchanges between Indians abroad and their motherland are promoted under the new framework, which re-imagines the nation in a transnational space and time.

Punjab is considered as a state that is densely connected with its diaspora through a variety of ways – marrying from Punjab is a preferred measure to reproduce familial values and preserve culture, and many migrants contribute significantly to philanthropic activities in Punjab as well as to the development of their ancestral village and beyond (Dusenbery and Tatla 2010; Thandi 2004). The Non-resident Punjabis are seen to exhibit an enormous amount of love for their motherland, and their cultural and material affiliations to the sub-national state have gone to the extent of a section of Punjabi diaspora supporting the separatist movement in Punjab in the 1980s with both ideology and resources (Chopra 2011; Kapur 1986; Tatla 1999; Fair 2005; Dhillon 2007). Many of the transnational Punjabis, particularly the first generation of migrants, maintain a home in Punjab even when they do not have any plan to return (Varghese and Rajan 2010). The owning of landed property in Punjab, particularly those purchased out of the wealth acquired abroad, is said to be an expression of the love for and attachment towards the migrants' ancestral village. In addition to the considerations of display and mobility, these houses are also perceived by the migrants to be investments that will connect their children to their roots and values (Vinayak 2004). Within such a discourse, Punjab is embodied as a pristine and nostalgic space for those non-resident Punjabis who want to retreat from the hypocrisies and insensitiveness of the mechanical West. This discourse characterises home as quintessentially welcoming and open, and migrants as eternally connected, and hence benevolent towards their home. However, this discourse overlooks the tensions within the migrant/diasporic transnational connection.

For example, it is pointed out that transnationalism creates dependency and lopsided development (Upadhya and Rutten 2012; Kannan 2005; Harilal and Joseph 2003). Existing social hierarchies are reinforced and newer class-caste categories of dominance and competition are created (Taylor *et al.* 2007; Osella and Osella 2000). Transnationalism has also significantly extended patriarchy as the latter assumes newer forms in the transnational space (Varghese and Rajan 2010).

Therefore, as already stated, the present chapter contests existing discourses in an attempt to capture a more nuanced perspective that is in line with a growing set of recent literature. By problematising the overtly positive underpinnings around the discourses on 'transnationalism from below', the migration and development debate has since been broken down into concrete and nuanced realities, recognising also the multifarious locations of affect and spatial-temporal divergences. Such an exercise would significantly add to attempts aimed at reclaiming the migrant transnationalism to a realistic realm, by specifically looking at the issue of non-resident Punjabi-owned properties in Punjab. Although the chapter refers to a few case studies, it largely unfolds itself through a single life history, around which the issues involved are textured into discussion.

Kinship that kills: property as a site of conflict and violence

Kulwinder and his four brothers were born in the United Kingdom. Kulwinder's grandfather first migrated to the United Kingdom in the 1960s, after which his father, Paramjit, followed. In 2007, his father decided to return to his ancestral village in Punjab to construct a house where he would be able to spend time at regular intervals. Though not in favour of the idea, the children sent money to Paramjit, and the house was completed at an approximate cost of Rs.6 million. Kulwinder's paternal cousin, Sukbir, was managing the eight acres of agricultural property and homestead in Punjab. Paramjit supported Sukbir by building him a house, helping to pay for his children's education, as well as financing his daily needs. A tearful call from his father caught Kulwinder by surprise one day, and he found out that his father wanted to return to the United Kingdom after being ill-treated by Sukbir and his family. Two days later, Kulwinder received news from Sukbir that his father had passed away. Sukbir tried to conduct the funeral swiftly, but was stopped by Paramjit's immediate family. During this time, one of Kulwinder's maternal uncles reported cuts and injuries on the dead body. With the help of his maternal uncle and the support of the British High Commission, the body was taken to the United Kingdom after conducting an autopsy. Kulwinder arrived at the village after four months and was confronted by an unfriendly village. When confronted, Sukbir explained that the injuries were a result of the ambulance driver's mishandling on the way to the hospital and the airport, as well as Paramjit's high alcohol consumption. To the villagers, Kulwinder was a complete outsider. Because Kulwinder would eventually return to the United Kingdom while they would have to live with Sukbir, they were fearful of antagonising their neighbour. However, Kulwinder's perseverance eventually drew many of the villagers to his side.

> They are helping now, the village is helping, they are on my side now. It took one and half years to get them on my side. First of all they thought he is going back but now they realize that he will not, he wants justice. That's all I want. The Panchayat is in our favour. My maternal uncles helped me. They spoke to the Panchayat.

With persistence and determination, Kulwinder uncovered the entire story out of the bits of information gathered from different sources. It turned out that Sukbir was helping Paramjit with the construction of the house when Paramjit discovered that Sukbir had been charging him double the price of the building materials. The situation was further aggravated when Paramjit found Sukbir stealing money from him.

The increasing tension gave rise to frequent arguments between Sukbir and Paramjit, and resulted in Paramjit dismissing Sukbir from the construction work. Paramjit also cancelled his payment to Sukbir, which the latter used to fund a bank loan, while Sukbir and his family refused food to Paramjit in retaliation. Paramjit eventually asked Sukbir and his family to vacate his compound, and started constructing a large wall to separate himself from Sukbir's family. This eventually caused him his life.

Upon his arrival, Kulwinder found Sukbir and his family occupying the nearly completed mansion his father had built and had to seek the help of the local police to get them to vacate. However, Sukbir produced a will, supposedly written by Paramjit, stating that all his property – ancestral and the newly acquired – would go to Sukbir and his two brothers. Although this document was eventually found to be unauthentic, Kulwinder's attempt to drive Sukbir out of the house ended with an attempt on Kulwinder's life.

Kulwinder approached the district head of the police, who was on his side; only to be silenced by the intervention of a local politician who supported Sukbir. The superintendent of police of Jalandhar himself suggested that Kulwinder compromise[2] on the matter as the local Akhali MLA had been supporting Sukbir and he was unable to help. Kulwinder remained firm and the police resorted to transferring the case from one officer to another without any concrete results. The case finally reached the fast track NRI court, but Kulwinder was convinced that 'no judge would pronounce a verdict against the will of the politically strong MLA'. Sukbir was able to secure the help of the political elite through one of his cousins in the United Kingdom who had strong networks with the Akhali party. This cousin, too, was interested in Paramjit's property.

Transnational political connections: controlling from overseas

Kulwinder's cousin, Rajinder, was an affluent individual in the UK, owning a successful property business. This made him influential in the political circles of Punjab. According to Kulwinder, he donates three to four million rupees to the political party he supports every election. He, too, is suspected of eyeing Kulwinder's ancestral property: 'My 'bhua' also did some dodgy stuff to get this land before. She never managed to get it. Now I think he is trying to get it. He is not helping Sukbir, he is helping himself'. Under desperate circumstances, Kulwinder turned to the rival political party, the Congress, for support. Kulwinder was firm in his belief to continue the fight for justice and was successful in establishing a link with a congress minister from Punjab. Calling to mind the notion of a network society, Kulwinder was convinced that nothing would work in Punjab without political links. Networks and links have indeed been a resource for mobility and socio-economic engineering among Punjabis within the state and beyond.

> I have been struggling. Once I went to see the SP Dehaati, They turned me away when I said I wanted to see the SP. My driver and I said it was the third or fourth occasion; we want to see the SP. He said come in then. He put us in a room. He went inside. He came back and said SP will see you today, wait here for five minutes. We went inside the room; there was nobody, no nothing. Then the door opened up and I saw a builder therein. I looked inside and asked is SP there? He said no, this room is empty. That's how they treat you, the police. I had a driver with me, who was from Punjab, so they thought he was nothing. NRIs have no say, no chance.

Unfortunately, while the cases about the forged will and the misappropriation of property have reached the court, Paramjit's murder case has yet to reach the stage of even an FIR.

> We lodged complaints with the Lohian police station, DSP Shahkot, SP Headquarters, NRI police station, Internal Vigilance Bureau, they conducted an inquiry, ADCP Crime, he never bothered to call us, we don't even know if a case was registered there or not, then SSP Dehaati, he did nothing either, then SP Dehaati, all these people know our case. When the complaints reach even 4–5 of these, you have to register an FIR, I went to 8 people, high

> ranking officials, DIG [deputy inspector general] Jalandhar Cantt, IG Police [inspector general], he didn't even see me. I have been to DGP Chandigarh [director general of police]. He asked me to speak to his secretary.

Sukbir contended that he had constructed the mansion, to which Kulwinder has responded by producing his father's bank statement that accounted for the money he and his siblings sent from the United Kingdom.

Although the Panchayat's support gives Kulwinder some confidence about the outcome of the cases, it is not all a bed of roses.

> I got threatened, my mother got threatened in England. I am scared of the police. I don't know if they will arrest me or kill me. Now I know the system here, the politics here. I have already been threatened by the police. I am scared one day, and the next day I feel ok. My mother had phone calls saying that your husband is dead; we are going to send your son back in a box as well, tell him to go back.

It is therefore not surprising that Kulwinder stays at his maternal uncle's place while in Punjab, and he also has access to a secret rented house in the city of Jalandhar.

Culture of migration: histories of mobility

Kulwinder's grandfather was part of a robust stream of migrations from Punjab to the United Kingdom in the 1950s and 1960s. Punjab is a state with a dense transnational connection, reinforced by its long history of mobility and consequent culture of migrations. Located on the invasion route into India, the people of Punjab were often made to leave their homes and adapt to newer locations, which arguably made them 'intrinsically' mobile and malleable (Helweg 1979, 1986). Punjabis moved in huge numbers to the West, among which migration to the United Kingdom is longstanding and still vibrant. About 45 per cent of the 1.2 million strong Indian community currently in the United Kingdom are estimated to be Punjabis (RHLCID 2001: 122–124).

Robust mercantile activities, the 'Punjabisation' of the Indian army, as well as the colonial masters' appreciation of Punjabi loyalty facilitated greater amounts of emigrations from Punjab during the colonial times to Britain (Talbot and Thandi 2004; Metcalf 2005; Visram 1986). The Punjabi migrants to Britain in the nineteenth and early twentieth century were mainly personal servants of imperial adventurers and administrators. Others were seamen who worked on British merchant ships as *lascars*, a smaller number were students seeking professional qualifications, and a few members of the erstwhile royal and aristocratic families (Visram 1986). The First World War brought more soldiers and seamen from Punjab to Britain, who slipped quietly away to remain in Britain after the war. This resulted in the migrant Indians in the United Kingdom largely being a community of *ayahs*, *lascars* and *sepoys* (Visram 1986; Ballard 2003;

Singh 2006; Mazumdar 2003; Yong 2005; Lal 2006). Punjabis were a visible presence in Britain's larger ports and industrial cities by the time of independence (Ballard 2003; Ballard and Banks 2007).

Driven by the post-war economic boom and largely facilitated by the existing Punjabi community in Britain, the flows of people from Punjab accelerated so much that it gave an impression of a process of reverse colonisation (Ballard 2003). Making use of the inclusive Commonwealth citizenship regime of the British Nationality Act of 1948 and the family unification clause of the Immigration Bill of 1964, many more emigrated from Punjab to the United Kingdom. This expanded the process of chain migration, virtually sweeping rural Doaba in Punjab with a migration fever (Helweg 1986; Ballard 2003; Harris and Osella 2010).

A significant number of Punjabis also migrated to East African countries like Kenya, Uganda and Tanzania under the colonial indentured regime and on missions of infrastructure development, most of whom re-migrated to the United Kingdom in the 1960s and early 1970s. Even after United Kingdom's tightening of the immigration regime in the 1960s, a good number of Punjabis made their way into the United Kingdom without much trouble. However, this has become increasingly difficult in the aftermath of the Immigration Act of 1971, forcing Punjabis to resort to diverse, informal strategies to migrate to the United Kingdom. It is interesting to note that the first generation of male migrants who entered in the 1950s and 1960s retained strong connections with their home through exchanges of affect and materiality, even after being unified with their wives and children in the United Kingdom.

Objectification and display of transnational success

Most of the early and first generation migrants to the United Kingdom were absorbed into the lower end jobs in factories and foundries. Through hard work and resilience, they were emplaced in their respective new locations and proved to be successful symbols of plenty and cosmopolitanism in their home communities. Most of the early migrants were Jat Sikhs, the land-owning community in Punjab, who shed their feudal/caste pride in their overseas locations to labour, and reinvented their high social position back home through the riches earned overseas. Their social and economic habitus at home was seemingly under threat in the post-colonial political problematic of state interventions on caste discrimination and reservations for lower castes in government jobs, alongside a general agrarian crisis in Punjab. Even today, the community's tendency to migrate is often self-justified by the lack of chances to get into government jobs due to an alleged condition of closure as a result of certain reservation policies and ever dwindling earnings from agriculture. Migrants' representations of their migration, as they remember it, are thick with descriptions of such impossibilities at home and a world of opportunities outside.

Having said this, their hard earned success manifests itself in multiple forms back home, and one of the ways is through the accumulation of landed property.

The early and first generation migrants have been found to be very keen on translating their success into landed property and massive houses. The landholdings have been symbols of status, particularly among the Jat Sikhs, who dominate the Punjabi migration circuits; while the Jat Sikh migrants have been found to use their transnational resources to reinforce their social dominance by accumulating more landed property. Likewise, other groups resort to similar strategies in order to catch up with the dominant mode of gaining social status. Palatial like houses that have been reconfiguring the landscape of rural Punjab are another dominant mode of resource transfer to the state in an attempt for non-resident Punjabis to establish their distinction from the local society and among themselves. The built space of rural Punjab thus becomes significantly reconfigured with money from overseas, and village life becomes resplendent in significant ways with migrant transnationalism.

The objectification of transnationalism also assumes other forms of economic exchanges including the non-resident Punjabis' contributions to rural development, sports, arts, philanthropy and religious charity. Such contributions are also visible in the form of built objects like stadiums, memorial gates, educational institutions, marriage palaces, charitable institutions and religious structures. Festivals, marriages, and styles and richness of clothing are also spheres that have been influenced by transnational objectification and marking.

Alongside the social prestige of owning property in their ancestral village, the decision of buying landed property is also influenced by a rural common feeling shaped by the expectations of friends and family back home. The following conversation with a Punjabi migrant on vacation from the United Kingdom is a fitting example.

Q. When you bought this land, did you ever think that it would turn into a commercial property?

ANS. No, we just bought the land. We saw that villagers who went there, they were buying the land, so we thought we should also buy the land. It was on sale. So my brother and I bought the land. People bought a lot of land here while working there.

Q. How many acres of land did you buy in total?

ANS. We have not divided the land property yet. There are 21 acres. We bought this land at intervals.

Q. This means that apart from your ancestral property of 10 acres, you now have 21 acres?

ANS. Yes.

However, the disputes over such transnationally owned assets – both inherited and acquired – are arguably on the rise. In the wake of reforms and new industrialisation, the real estate boom in India has resulted in a price surge not only in commercial and residential properties, but also in agricultural land (Levien 2011). The flourishing urban real estate sector in India has been open to NRI buyers, as a result of the keenness of the latter to take benefit of the booming market (Varrel 2012). Complementing this boom was the rapid urbanisation of the Punjabi population and the increase in the proportion of middle class (GoA 2013). The resultant price surge made the property owned by the non-resident Punjabis in rural Punjab financially lucrative, with chances of high return and well-paid disposal. Relatives of non-resident Punjabis who often managed such properties had the impression that they would eventually take ownership of the property, as the chances of non-resident Punjabi owners returning or selling off such properties seemed virtually absent. This has subsequently led to an increasing number of disputes over transnationally owned property. It is reported that out of the 3,200 cases registered by non-resident Punjabis with the Punjab police in 2013, 60 per cent were property related cases.[3] The annual NRI *sammelans*, being organised by the government of Punjab, constantly raises concerns over the increasing number of cheating, fraudulence and misappropriation of property owned by non-resident Punjabis.

Though cases similar to Kulwinder's story may fall on the extreme end of the scale, such instances are not isolated. The property disputes between non-resident Punjabis and their relatives, which have led to physical altercations and even murders, are on the rise. Cases in which relatives and neighbours make fictitious claims to usurp property and loot valuables from closed non-resident Punjabi houses are common, as seen from the following case, gathered from a disposed case file at NRI Sabha.

> The petitioner, a resident of UK for the last 44 years, complained that the following articles – AC, Television, big trunk constraining cloths, 5 ceiling fans, 4 double beds, 5/6 coats, gas *chulla*, tables, chairs, sofas, and other valuable articles were stolen from his house at Jallowal village (complaint dated 18.2.2009). The petitioner mentioned the names of 11 persons, some of his relatives included, as the culprits, and demanded action against them. It was also that stated that apart from stealing the above said articles, certain other valuable articles were set ablaze by the perpetuators. There was a counter complaint by the main accused saying that the petitioner's father had taken around 85 lakhs of rupees from him over the years, with a promise of giving him the disputed house. The police enquiry made it clear that the arguments of the accused were fabricated and action was recommended accordingly.
>
> (Case File from NRI Sabha, Jalandhar)

Another common form of violation is the stealing of money sent to relatives or close friends for purchasing landed properties or houses in Punjab. The following case is a typical example, where the accused parties, together with their local political support, attempted to cast the situation in their favour.

> The petitioner and his wife were residents of UK for the last 50 years and kept in touch with their relatives in Punjab. They were quite close with the wife's sister and her son, the accused. In March 2005, when the petitioner

> and his wife visited Jalandhar, they decided to buy a property in the Mohali. The accused made the applicant open an NRI account for which he spent £350. On returning to UK, he deposited £30,000 in the NRI account in Mohali. Between this time and January 2008, the petitioner had transferred Rs.79,16,475 – towards buying the property. In their next visit they found that the land had been registered under the name of the accused. The requests of the petitioner to transfer the property ownership documents to his name and get the accused to return the money had generated no results. The petitioner complained that the accused harassed him and his family through political pressure and illegal force and threatened him with dire consequences in case of a police complaint. The police enquiry confirmed that the complaint of the petitioner was true.
>
> (Case File from NRI Sabha, Jalandhar)

Punjab's transnational space is additionally punctuated with several false cases filed by the locals against the non-resident Punjabis and vice versa. Cases against non-resident Punjabis are expected to prevent them from returning abroad and to compromise their genuine complaints. Expectedly, in most of the non-resident Punjabis' complaints, threats of fake cases lodged by their friends, neighbours, or relatives take centre stage. That being said, some non-resident Punjabis are also guilty of filing fake cases. If police records are to be trusted, as of 2010/2011, of the 303 cases filed by the non-resident Punjabis in the Kapurthala police stations, 52 were found to be false complaints.

State, NGOs and new structures of governmentality

The property related disputes of non-resident Punjabis have consequently become an important focus of concern that has attracted the attention of local governments, political parties, the police, community organisations, and migrant associations, to name a few. A dual process, involving transnational migrant capital being sought for national and sub-national development, as well as the non-resident Punjabis/NRIs pressuring the Punjab government to create structures and institutions to serve and protect their interests, has made migrant transnationalism a compelling economic imperative that manufactures institutional change at multiple levels.

This situation has allowed the sub-national state to governmentalise non-resident Punjabis with the stated intention of supporting their cause and protecting their interests at home. The government of Punjab set up six special NRI police stations in 2008, at Jalandhar, Nawanshrhr, Hoshiarpur, Kapurthala, Ludhiana and Moga. Facing the pressure of an increasing number of cases as well as to extend the infrastructure of governmentality, the government proposes to set up five more police stations dedicated exclusively to NRIs, making a total of 11 NRI police stations.[4] There is a specific NRI cell, headed by an officer in the rank of inspector general of police, dedicated to 'ensure that NRI grievances are received and processed efficiently'. The cell's website facilitates the online registration of complaints, in addition to providing a helpline support for emergency complaints. This is in addition to a separate line dedicated to responding to 'queries of NRIs regarding their problems pertaining to land disputes, fraud and cheating'.[5] In order to expedite the trial duration of cases, a special fast track court exclusively for NRI cases has also been established in Jalandhar. The NRI Sabha – an NGO of non-resident Punjabis with over 15,000 in membership – has been given the authority to intervene on behalf of the non-resident Punjabis and to take up cases with the government agencies to ensure justice to Punjabis overseas. The number of cases registered with NRI Sabha in 2008 and 2009 are listed in Table 6.1.

It was also due to outcries on the part of the non-resident Punjabis that these institutions were established and being significantly expanded to see that the non-resident Punjabis were not exploited by the local society by virtue of their non-resident Punjabi status. In addition, the government of Punjab is also proposing to organise 'NRI Disputes Redressal Sammelan' at regular intervals to dispose the complaints of non-resident Punjabis 'in a transparent and timely manner'.[6] Initiated within the last decade when the state was increasingly looking out for non-resident Punjabi resources, these measures were part of the efforts of the Punjab government to woo non-resident Punjabi resources for its development. It is therefore not surprising that a separate Department of NRI Affairs was established by the government of Punjab only in 2002, despite the many years of emigration history. Likewise, the openness towards diaspora also came significantly late at the national level (Rajan and Varghese 2012).

Controlled informality: pressure for compromise

However, as evidenced by Kulwinder's experience, the NRI police stations often prove to be worse than the local police stations. It was when the local police (Lohian) failed that Kulwinder decided to approach the NRI police station at Jalandhar. Though they called Sukbir and other witnesses to the station for questioning, their progress was inhibited by the intervention of the local Akhali politician. Despite being convinced of the fact that it was a forged will, the inspector himself insisted that Kulwinder arrive at a compromise.

As informed by the respective NRI police stations, in the years 2008, 2009 and 2010 there were 4, 5 and 3 registered cases respectively with First Information Reports (FIRs) with one station, while there were 10, 11 and 7 respectively for the same years in another station.[7] However, as indicated by the number of

Table 6.1 Cases registered in NRI Sabha in 2008 and 2009

Year	*Criminal cases*	*Disposal*	*Civil case*	*Disposal*
2008	460	156	100 (*560*)	25
2009	500	100	311 (*811*)	40

Source: NRI Sabha, Jalandhar.

complaints the NRI police stations are receiving, there seems to be no shortage of complaints. For instance, Nawanshar NRI police station has received as many as 256 complaints between 2 March 2009 and 30 December 2009, whereas Kapurthala station received 424 complaints between 15 April 2008 and 13 April 2009.[8] This gives a clear indication of the number of compromises made – either voluntary or forceful – between making a complaint to the police station, and registering a case with FIR. In the case of Kapurthala NRI police station, out of the 303 petitions received, 102 were recorded as compromised.

It is within such a context that what the Jalandhar NRI police inspector said can be understood: ‘a person earning Rs.200,000 a month should not go to the UK. I will send my children if they are not studying well’.[9] The structures created to protect the interest of the non-resident Punjabis seem to create a situation of controlled informality that allows room for fluidity (Kodoth and Varghese 2012). Controlled informality as a liminal condition neutralises a stricter formal–informal dualism, where infrastructures of governmentality become a precondition for informal practices. The authors witnessed how the inspector of one of the NRI police stations, with a fine balance of counsel and coercion, convinced an NRI couple to arrive at a compromise for a disputed property of theirs. Compromises are deemed to be the best option for non-resident Punjabis. The situation represents a regulatory and policing impasse that promotes the use of ‘informal’ channels. At the same time, it creates a shadow institutional space and a powerful parallel economy in which the police, lawyers, local politicians and property grabbers are partakers. More often than not, non-resident Punjabis are eventually forced to give up their property, and their experiences are said to be able to ‘put any horror film to shame’.[10] Fieldwork in the United Kingdom also confirms how Punjab is increasingly becoming a place of pain and distress for Punjabis overseas.

Kulwinder’s attempt to seek the support of NRI Sabha did not help either. As such, he decided to approach the district superintendent of police and sent complaints to the state DGP, with the former promising the arrest of the accused. However, what followed was three months of inaction, after which Kulwinder was advised to arrive at a compromise. By that time the influential Akhali MLA had already intervened in the case in favour of Sukbir.

> He said they have political connections, it’s better to reach a compromise. I said no, I don’t want to compromise. He said even if I get the land and house, somebody else will just take it away when I go back. He said it’s better for an NRI to just sell everything because there is no worth keeping it. You don’t know about this place, you will have problems, just sell it.

It was then that Kulwinder decided to go to the media to seek redress for his grievances by bringing the issue into the public. However, the political pressure the police faced inhibited them from proceeding any further than passing the case to the Internal Vigilance Bureau and eventually, the fast track NRI court. Kulwinder thought that justice was going to be served in spite of the political pressure and his influential non-resident Punjabi cousin manipulating the progress of the case. However, colluding with the judge, the police cited different reasons to repeatedly postpone the case. Kulwinder is almost convinced now that the judge will not give a judgment against the wishes of the influential Akhali politician.

Conclusion

These experiences certainly run in contradiction to the nostalgia and affirmative linkages between the diaspora and the local society as encapsulated in the concept of transnationalism from below – a field of positive people-to-people ties. The emergent transnational public is a contested terrain with claims and counter-claims, largely dominated by the narratives of relatives and friends of non-resident Punjabis residing in Punjab seeking to take advantage of their relatives' absence and economic affluence.

In these discourses, local Punjabis are figured as villains who are after the non-resident Punjabi's properties. Property grabbing has indeed become an economic activity in Punjab, according to a learned respondent of the authors of this chapter. Several major local players, including the people, the police, politicians and the state, view the non-resident Punjabis as cash cows. This increasing tension faced by the non-resident Punjabis allowed the sub-national state and political society in Punjab to governmentalise the non-resident Punjabis. As one local politician told us, 'they [non-resident Punjabis] cannot antagonise us, they need us for getting their things done'. This is very much in line with the general Punjabi ambivalence towards non-resident Punjabis and migrant transnationalism – on the one hand, non-resident Punjabis are seen as symbols of affluence and cosmopolitanism, and the butt of jokes on the other. In this way, migration is simultaneously a dream and a disdain. Likewise, the non-resident Punjabis view Punjab as simultaneously promising and suffocating – a site of culture, but not of civilisation. It is precisely this shared ambivalence of migrant transnationalism that complicates the discourses of nostalgia.

Acknowledgement

The field research for this chapter has been initiated as part of the research project called Transnationalisation, Migration and Transformation: Multi-level Analysis of Migrant Transnationalism, with special reference to Punjab–UK migrations. The extensive ethnographical field work conducted as part of the project between August 2009 and September 2010 in the Doaba region, has been supplemented by the lead author's frequent forays into the field thereafter. The chapter is also informed by the fieldwork done by him in the Punjabi dominated areas of a few cities in the United Kingdom, such as London, Birmingham and Leicester, during November 2010–January 2011. We are thankful to the project coordinators, Pirkko Pitkanen and S. Irudaya Rajan, for their support and Kaveri Qureshi and Filippo Osella for valuable intellectual inputs.

Notes

1 Transnationalism broadly refers to multiple ties and interactions linking people or institutions across the borders of nation-states, while transnationalism from above on the other hand represents actions across nations by powerful organisations like governments, multinationals and international institutions (Portes *et al.* 1999; Heath *et al.* 2011).

2 A compromise is a channel through which the police collect a bribe from both parties.

3 Statement of IGP, NRI Cell Punjab, Gurpreet Kaur Deo. Reported as 'Property, matrimonial disputes top the list of NRI-related police complaints', online, available at: www.yespunjab.com/punjab/punjabi-diaspora/item/36226-property-matrimonial-disputes-top-the-list-of-nri-related-police-complaints (accessed 14 March 2014).

4 As per the data given by the NRI wing of the Punjab police, 442 cases were pending before the police on NRI complaints of various kinds as of 11 June 2013. See Punjab police website, online, available at: www.punjabpolice.gov.in/nri_cell.aspx (accessed 21 November 2013). This had gone up to 3,200 by the end of the year.

5 Message of Gurpreet Kaur Deo IPS, Inspector General of Police, NRI Affairs; online, available at: www.punjabpolice.gov.in/nri_cell.aspx (accessed 24 February 2014).

6 'Punjab to Organise NRI Disputes Redressal Sammelan', *Daily Post*, 6 February 2014.

7 Reported verbally by the respective NRI police stations to us in late 2010.

8 Figures taken from the respective NRI police station websites in 2011.

9 This was in response to a specific query as to why he was not considering the option of emigrating to the United Kingdom, despite that many of his close relatives are already UK citizens, which includes the parents and siblings of his wife.

10 Kul Bhushan, 'NRI tormented and cheated out of their properties', *Thaindian News,* 26 March 2008.

References

Appadurai, A. 1997. *Modernity at Large: Cultural Dimensions of Globalization*. Oxford: Oxford University Press.

Ballard, R. 2003. The South Asian Presence in Britain and its Transnational Connections. In B. Parekh (ed.), *Culture and Economy in the Indian Diaspora*. London: Routledge, pp. 197–222.

Ballard, R. and M. Banks. 2007. *Desh Pardesh: the South Asian Presence in Britain*. London: C. Hurst & Co. Publishers.

Bernal, V. 2004. Eritrea Goes Global: Reflections on Nationalism in a Transnational Era. *Cultural Anthropology* 19(1): 3–25.

Bhabha, H. 1990. *Nation and Narration*. London New York: Routledge.

Bhagwati, J. 2004. *In Defense of Globalization*. New Delhi: Oxford University Press.

Bryceson, D. and U. Vuorela. 2002. *The Transnational Family: New European Frontiers and Global Networks*. Oxford: Berg.

Chopra, R. 2011. *Militant and Migrant: The Politics and Social History of Punjab*. New Delhi: Routledge.

Dhillon, S. 2007. The Sikh Diaspora and the Quest for Khalistan: a Search for Statehood or for Self-preservation? *IPCS Research Paper No. 12*. New Delhi: Institute of Peace and Conflict Studies.

Dusenbery, V.A. and D.S. Tatla. 2010. *Sikh Diaspora Philanthropy in Punjab: Global Giving for Local Good*. New Delhi: Oxford University Press.

Fair, C. 2005. Diaspora Involvement in Insurgencies: Insights from the Khalistan and Tamil Eelam Movements. *Nationalism and Ethnic Politics* 11(1): 125–156.

Faist, T. 2010. Diaspora and Transnationalism: What Kind of Dance Partners? In R. Baubock and T. Faist (eds), *Diaspora and Transnationalism: Concepts, Theories and Methods*. Amsterdam: Amsterdam University Press, pp. 9–34.

Finch, J. 2007. Displaying Families. *Sociology* 41(1): 65–81.

Geithner, P., C. Lincoln and P. Johnson. 2004. *Diaspora Philanthropy and Equitable Development in China and India.* Cambridge: Harvard University Press.

Government of Australia (GoA). 2013. India: Land Disputes and Moneylenders in Punjab. Issues Paper Series, Migration/Refugee Review Tribunal, March 2013.

Guha, P. 2011. Measuring International Remittances in India: Concepts and Empirics. ProGlo Working Paper No. 1. Bangalore: National Institute of Advanced Studies.

Harilal, K.N. and K.J. Joseph. 2003. International Migration, Remittances and Development: Myths and Facts. *Economic and Political Weekly*, 2 June: 2286–2294.

Harris, K. and F. Osella. 2010. Punjab–UK Migration, Transnationalism and Transformations. Project Report submitted to the European Commission, for the project Transnationalisation, Migration and Transformation: Multi-level Analysis of Migrant Transnationalism. Online, available at: www.uta.fi/edu/tutkimus/transnet/Transnet-UK-Report-final.1.11.pdf (accessed 26 January 2014).

Heath, S., D. McGhee and P. Trevena. 2011. Lost in Transnationalism: Unravelling the Conceptualisation of Families and Personal Life Through a Transnational Gaze. *Sociological Research Online* 16(4): 12. Online, available at: www.socresonline.org.uk/16/4/12.html (accessed 26 January 2014).

Helweg, A.W. 1979. *Sikhs in England: the Development of a Migrant Community.* Oxford: Oxford University Press.

Helweg, A.W. 1986. Indians in England: a Study of the International Relationships of Sending, Receiving and Migrant Societies. In M.S.A. Rao (ed.), *Studies in Migration: Internal and International Migration in India.* New Delhi: Manohar, pp. 363–394.

Kannan, K.P. 2005. Kerala's Turnaround in Growth: Role of Social Development, Remittances and Reform. *Economic and Political Weekly* XL(6): 548–554.

Kapur, D. 2003. Indian Diaspora as a Strategic Asset. *Economic and Political Weekly* February 1: 445–448.

Kapur, R.A. 1986. *Sikh Separatism: the Politics of Faith.* London: Allen & Unwin.

Kodoth, P. and V.J. Varghese. 2012. Protecting Women or Endangering the Emigration Process: Emigrant Women Domestic Workers, Gender and State Policy. *Economic and Political Weekly* 47(43): 56–66.

Lal, B.V. 2006. *The Encyclopedia of the Indian Diaspora.* Singapore: National University of Singapore.

Lall, M.C. 2001. *India's Missed Opportunity: India's Relationship with the Non Resident Indians*. Aldershot: Ashgate.

Levien, M. 2011. Special Economic Zones and Accumulation by Dispossession in India. *Journal of Agrarian Change* 11(4): 454–483.

Levitt, P. 1998. Social Remittances: Migration-Driven Local-Level Forms of Cultural Diffusion. *International Migration Review* 32(4): 926–948.

Levitt, P. and G.N. Schiller. 2004. Conceptualising Simultaneity: a Transnational Social Field Perspective on Society. *International Migration Review* 38 (3): 1001–1039.

Levitt, P. and N.N. Sorensen. 2004. The Transnational Turn in Migration Studies. *Global Migration Perspectives* 6. Geneva: Global Commission on International Migration.

Mazumdar, R.K. 2003. *The Indian Army and the Making of Punjab.* New Delhi: Permanent Black.

Metcalfe, T. 2005. *Forging the Raj: Essays on British India in the Heyday of Empire*. New Delhi: Oxford University Press.

MOIA. 2008. *Annual Report 2007–08*. New Delhi: MOIA, Government of India.

Osella, F and C. Osella. 2000. *Social Mobility in Kerala: Modernity and Identity in Conflict*. London: Pluto Press.

Portes, A. 1996. Transnational Communities: Their Emergence and Significance in the Contemporary World System. In R.P. Korzeniewicz and W.C. Smith (eds), *Latin America in the World Economy*. Westport: Greenwood Press, pp. 151–168.

Portes, A., L. Guarnizo and P. Landoldt. 1999. The Study of Transnationalism: Pitfalls and Promise of an Emergent Research Field. *Ethnic and Racial Studies* 22(2): 242–282.

Rajan, S.I. and V.J. Varghese. 2012. Broadening Exchanges and Changing Institutions: Multiple Sites of Economic Transnationalism. In S.I. Rajan (ed.), *India Migration Report 2012: Global Financial Crisis, Migration and Remittances*. New Delhi: Routledge, pp. 40–41.

RHLCID. 2001. *Report of the High Level Committee on the Indian Diaspora*. New Delhi: Ministry of External Affairs, Government of India.

Singh, G. 2006. The Anatomy of Dissent in the Military of Colonial India during the First and Second World Wars. *Edinburgh Papers in South Asian Studies*, Number 20.

Smart, C. 2007. *Personal Life*. Cambridge: Polity.

Smith, M.P. and L.E. Guarniza. 1998. *Transnationalism from Below: Comparative Urban and Community Research*. New Brunswick, NJ: Transaction Publishers.

Tatla, D.S. 1999. *The Sikh Diaspora: The Search for Statehood*. London: UCL Press.

Taylor, S., M. Singh and B. Deborah. 2007. Migration, Development and Inequality: Eastern Punjabi Transnationalism. *Global Networks* 7(3): 328–347.

Thandi, S.S. 2004. *Vilayati Paisa*: Some Reflections on the Potential of Diaspora Finance in the Socio-Economic Development of Indian Punjab. In S.S. Thandi and I. Talbot (eds), *People on the Move: Punjabi Colonial and Post-Colonial Migration*. Karachi: Oxford University Press, pp. 210–230.

Thandi, S.S. 2006. Punjabi Diaspora and Homeland Relations. Online, available at: www.sikhsineurope.org/index.php?option=com_docman&task=doc_download&gid=11&Itemid=60 (accessed 25 January 2014).

Thandi, S.S. and I. Talbot (eds), *People on the Move: Punjabi Colonial and Post-Colonial Migration*. Karachi: Oxford University Press.

UNODC. 2009. *Smuggling of Migrants from India to Europe and in Particular to the UK*. New Delhi: United Nations Office on Drugs and Crime.

Upadhya, C. and M. Rutten. 2012. Migration, Transnational Flows and Development in India. *Economic and Political Weekly* 47(19): 54–62.

Varghese, V.J and S.I. Rajan. 2010. Sites of Liminality: Punjab–UK Migration, Transnationalism and Ambivalence. Project Report submitted to the European Commission, for the project Transnationalisation, Migration and Transformation: Multi-level Analysis of Migrant Transnationalism. Online, available at: www.uta.fi/edu/tutkimus/transnet/Transnet-India-Report-final.1.11.pdf (accessed 26 January 2014).

Varrel, A. 2012. NRIs in the City: Identifying International Migrants' Investments in the Indian Urban Fabric. *South Asia Multidisciplinary Academic Journal*, 6. Online, available at: http://samaj.revues.org/3425 (accessed 17 December 2013).

Vertovec, S. 1999. Conceiving and Researching Transnationalism. *Ethnic and Racial Studies*, 22(2): 447–462.

Vinayak, R. 2004. Punjabi NRIs Spend Fortune to Recreate Overseas Homes in Ancestral Hometowns. *India* Today, 16 February.

Vishwakarma, V.K. and G.P. Ohannes. 2012. Bubble in the Indian Real Estate Markets: Identification Using Regime-Switching Methodology. *International Journal of Business and Finance Research* 6(3): 27–40.

Visram, R. 1986. *Ayahs, Lascars and Princes: Indians in Britain 17001947*. London: Pluto.

Wimmer, A. and N.G. Schiller. 2002. Methodological Nationalism and Beyond: Nation-state Building, Migration and Social Sciences. *Global Networks* 2(4): 301–334.

Yong, T.T. 2005. *The Garrison State: the Military, Government and Society in Colonial Punjab, 1849 1947*. New Delhi: Sage.

7 Bangladeshi migration to Southern Europe

Implications on migrant families

Md Mizanur Rahman and Mohammad Alamgir Kabir

Southern European countries, especially Italy, Spain, Portugal and Greece, were a major migration destination region for both European and non-European migrants in the late 1970s, soaring through the 1980s (King *et al.* 2000; King 2001; Anthias and Lazaridis 2000; Bonifazi *et al.* 2008). Of these Southern European countries, Italy provides a good case in point. In the period 1990–2000, the stock of immigrants doubled in Italy; increasing from about 650,000 to almost 1,300,000 (Zontini 2010: 3). According to another estimate, between 1986 and 2004, the legally resident foreign population rose from under 300,000 to an estimated 2.6 million, accounting for 4.5 per cent of the total population (Chaloff 2006: 149). The number of immigrants in Italy reached a little over 4.8 million in 2009 (Cesareo 2009: 11). With the fall in employment visas and the rise in family reunion visas in recent years (SOPEMI 2010: 214), Italy has indeed transformed from a country of labour migration to that of family immigration and settlement.

Italy has been one of the major destinations for the Bangladeshi migrants in Southern Europe. For instance, Bangladeshi immigrants living in Italy numbered around 84,000 in 2009 (Blangiardo 2009: 35). The number of (regular) Bangladeshi migrants is projected to reach 118,000 in 2015, 158,000 in 2020, and 232,000 in 2030 (Blangiardo 2009: 49). In addition to regular immigrants, Italy also hosts a large number of irregular immigrants from both European and non-European countries (King 2001). The number of irregular Bangladeshi emigrants was reported to have been 11,000 in 2009 (Blangiardo 2009: 35). However, another source suggests that the number of irregular Bangladeshi emigrants was nearly 74,000 in 2009.[1] This growing presence of Bangladeshi emigrants is indicative that Bangladeshis availed the immigration opportunity in Italy brought about by periodic changes in its immigration laws since the mid-1980s.

Bangladeshi migrants in Italy are predominantly single male migrants living under 'transnationally split' (Yeoh *et al.* 2002) conditions, and are obligated to maintain economic and social relations with their family members back home. The obligation of maintaining sustained economic and social ties with their home stems from the dominance of the family in the social and economic affairs of Bangladeshi society. Migration decisions have been household strategies to diversify risk and to accumulate capital for investment in the developing countries (Stark 1991). An individual migrant is deeply enmeshed in a complex web of household relations and dependencies: he/she moves internationally for work as an envoy of the extended family that places the well-being of the extended family above the individual migrant's interests. Whether it is temporary labour migration such as migration to the Middle East, or more permanent forms of migration such as migration to Italy, maintaining sustained economic relations with left-behind families remains one of the key priorities for migrant members (Ullah 2010). This is increasingly evident in the annual inflow of remittances to Bangladesh, which increased from around US$4.2 billion in 2005 to nearly US$11 billion in 2010.[2]

The economic relations between migrants and their families are often the centre of discussion in the migration–development debate. However, existing studies often tend to highlight the migration–development nexus in the context of selected developed countries such as the United States, Germany, Netherlands and the United Kingdom, or of popular labour migration countries in Asia and Africa (Papademetriou and Martin 1991; Hermele 1997; Piper 2009). Southern European countries, being a new migration destination, are not adequately highlighted in the debate on migration and development. In particular, there is a dearth of research on the linkages between migrants and their families left behind in some new source countries in Asia. This study attempts to close the gap in existing scholarship by highlighting the Bangladeshi migration to Italy and developmental implications on migrant households left behind in Bangladesh.

After decades of pessimism and concern, governments of source countries have put renewed hopes on transnationally-oriented migrants as potential actors of development (Schiller and Faist 2010). Hopes are pinned on transnational migrants sending remittances to their families in origin countries (Faist 2010). Scholars revisiting the debate on the migration–development nexus increasingly see migration as a process and as an integral part of broader transformation processes in society (Faist *et al.* 2011). This research highlights migration as a process and explains remittance-induced changes at the household level in terms of development process. This is in line with Amartya Sen's views on development as a process of increasing the freedoms of the people, or in short, 'development as freedom' (Sen 1999). From an empirical perspective, Sen has proposed three capabilities that are the proximate determinants of the basic freedoms: health, education and income. This study assesses the implication of migration-induced remittances in terms of these three determinants.

In particular, this study attempts to address the following research questions: What is the context of immigrant reception in Italy? What are the socio-demographic profiles of Bangladeshi migrants in Italy? What is the trend of Bangladeshi migration to Italy? What is the trend of remittance flows from Italy to Bangladesh? What are the channels of Bangladeshi migration to Italy? What is the economic cost of migration? How do migrants finance their migration expenses? What are the implications of remittances on family dynamics?

This chapter starts by presenting the data sources for the study. The next section provides the context of immigrant reception in Italy in light of the changes in immigration laws. This is followed by the socio-demographic characteristics of Bangladeshi migrants in Italy. Subsequent sections focus on the channels of Bangladeshi migration to Italy, and implications of remittances for family dynamics. The final section gives a summary of the findings of the study.

Data sources

This study is based on the Bangladesh Household Remittance Survey (BHRS) 2009, conducted by the IOM in Dhaka, with financial support from the Department for International Development – United Kingdom. In addition to survey data, this study also draws from qualitative interviews of migrants, return-migrants, and activists of migrant organisations in Bangladesh between 2010 and 2011. The Bangladesh Migrant Household Survey interviewed migrant households across the country through a nationally representative sample of migrant households from all six administrative divisions of Bangladesh. The districts of the six divisions of the country were divided into two strata, with one stratum consisting of 'more concentration of migrant' (MCM) households and the other stratum consisting of 'less concentration of migrant' (LCM) households'. Following this, clusters were formed with one or more *mauzas* (closely synonymous with a village), depending on the cluster's size as set in terms of the number of general households.

These clusters were selected independently from each stratum using the Probability Proportional to Size (PPS) method of selection. The total sample was made up of 457 clusters (257 from MCM districts and 200 from LCM districts). All households in every selected cluster were listed, identifying only the migrant households. Household listings were done by taking a complete census of the households in each of the clusters. This involved visiting every household in the designated area. A migrant household has been defined as a household that had at least one of its members living/working abroad during the time of the survey. The selection of the migrant households was made independently of their current status (e.g. regular or irregular) in the country of destination. In total, the number of migrants in the survey was 12,893. The survey covered a wide range of migration issues encompassing socio-economic background, processing and economic cost of migration, remittances, and impacts of remittances on households that serve the scope of this paper. Of these 12,893 migrants, 177 migrants were working in Italy. This chapter is based on the experiences of these 177 migrants' households in Bangladesh.

The context of immigrant reception in Italy

Italy was a major emigration country until the early 1970s, when millions of Italians emigrated to North America as well as wealthy Northern Europe. In the late 1970s and 1980s, this migratory pattern changed dramatically, and Italy started to receive foreigners from Eastern Europe, Northern Africa and Asia. Italy was the first country in Mediterranean Europe to acquire a positive migration balance, in 1972 (Knights 1996: 106), and by 1997, the net flow of remittances had reversed (Chaloff 2006: 149). It is often argued that Italy's position in the centre of the Mediterranean, its extensive coastline, and important tourism and pilgrimage industry have made the country relatively accessible for potential migrants from non-European countries (King and Andall 1999; Knights 1996; Chaloff 2004; Triandafyllidou 2007). However, the sharp increase in the immigrant population is also attributed to rapid economic and social transformations in Italy (King and Andall 1999; King 2001).

Italy has passed several sets of immigration legislations since the mid-1980s to control migration flows and to regularise and integrate new immigrants (Chaloff 2004; Cesareo 2009; Blangiardo 2009; Pastore *et al.* 2006). The first attempt was made in 1986 when Italy devised a policy to control the entry of immigrants seeking employment, and regularised those immigrants who were already in Italy and could prove they were employed. This immigration reform facilitated the regularisation of about 105,000 migrants (Cesareo 2007). The second legislation, enacted in 1990 and known as the 'Martelli Law', was broad in scope; it introduced the annual planning of migratory flows (limited admissions of foreigners for work), and certain norms regarding the rights and obligations of foreigners in Italy, stay and work conditions, and other related matters such as family reunion and social integration. The Martelli Law offered immigrants the opportunity to regularise their presence irrespective of their employment status. A total of 217,000 immigrants regularised their status (Knights 1996: 107)

Immigration became a significant issue in the 1990s, leading to the passage of laws in 1995 and 1998. The 1995 law involved the regularisation of 246,000 immigrants (Cesareo 2007) and introduced the possibility of regularisation for family reunification purposes – a sign of transforming single migration to family and settlement migration in Italy. The reform law of 1998, also known as Turco-Napolitano law or Testo Unico, created a three-pillar immigration policy: (i) fighting illegal migration; (ii) regulating legal migration; and (iii) integrating resident foreigners (Chaloff 2006: 153). The first pillar focussed on bilateral agreements and criminal penalties, the second on a quota system, and the third on the integration of new immigrants. New immigration for work was instituted within the national quotas and with either a job offer or 'sponsorship'. The quota system offered work opportunity for non-European migrants from one to three years.

In 2002, Italy passed the immigration law known as the Bossi-Fini Law, paving the way for the regularisation of more than 700,000 immigrants in the country (Cesareo 2007; Chaloff 2006). However, the Bossi-Fini Law imposed restrictions on two domains: entry and conditions of stay. The quota system emerged as a key tool to meet the demand for labour in the country. The quota system was designed to serve both source and host countries, as the sending countries would benefit from remittances and Italy from foreign labour. However, soon after the introduction of the quota system, it became increasingly evident that the quota system was not producing the desired outcome. Two common causes are often cited for this failure: the limited number of visas allowed under this category (an imbalance between demand for labour and supply of labour) and the complicated bureaucratic procedures involved in the quota visa processing (Zanfrini 2003; Chaloff 2006).

The drawback inherent in the quota system created a situation where many potential migrants found their own way to circumvent bureaucratic restrictions: they sneaked into Italy clandestinely and joined the labour market in order to establish a relationship with employers who might be willing to undertake the complicated bureaucratic procedure necessary for legal entry or to support their applications during the regularisation drive. While clandestine entry into the country remains a challenge for potential migrants, the availability of work after entry and the possibility of securing regular immigration status during the frequent regularisation drives remains open to them, providing an adequate incentive for seeking irregular entry into the country. In addition to quota, another important channel for regular migration is the family reunion visa. A family reunion visa is allowed to the dependents of immigrants, especially spouses and children. The current trend in Italy is a fall in employment visas and a rise in family reunion visas. For instance, between 2007 and 2008, the number of visas issued for family reunification rose 39 per cent from 89,000 to 123,000, while entries for employment fell sharply (SOPEMI 2010: 214). This trend suggests that Italy has entered a new phase, from single migration into family immigration and settlement.

Bangladeshi migrants in Italy

Bangladeshi emigration to Italy developed, according to King and Knights, as a 'form of migratory opportunism provoked by the basic push forces back home, and by lax entry controls and regularisation drives in Italy' (1994: 128). Italy's first three sets of legislation for immigration reform (the laws of 1986, 1990 and 1998) played an important role in the emergence of a permanent Bangladeshi migrant community in Italy. Of these legislations, the Martelli Law of 1990 provided a huge impetus for Bangladeshi immigration to Italy. According to Knights, the Martelli Law gave rise to three separate immigration processes for Bangladeshis: (i) opportunistic migration – Bangladeshis from other countries came to Italy to seize the opportunity of becoming regular migrants and subsequently permanent or renewable-status residents in Italy; (ii) recruitment migration (formal and informal recruitment business); and finally, (iii) family or kinship migration (because of the adoption of the family reunion policy) (Knights 1996: 109).

Thus, changes in immigration laws in Italy since the mid-1980s created an opportunity for both authorised and unauthorised Bangladeshi migration to Italy. The Bangladesh government agency in charge of monitoring the outflow of authorised migration for work, the BMET (Bureau of Manpower, Employment, and Training), has been recording the outflow of Bangladeshis to Italy since 2002. As per the BMET source, nearly 33,000 migrants went to Italy through authorised channels between 2002 and 2010 (Figure 7.1). However, the Bangladesh Bank, which is in charge of reporting inflow of remittances into Bangladesh, started reporting the annual inflow of remittances from Italy to Bangladesh in 2000. As per the Bangladesh Bank, Bangladeshi migrants remitted nearly US$1 billion from Italy to Bangladesh between 2000 and 2010 (Figure 7.2). However, before the year 2000, the inflow of remittances from Italy was predominantly through the informal channel called *hundi* – a popular informal channel of remittances used by global Bangladeshis (Rahman and Yeoh 2008). The fear of terrorist-financing after 9/11 has mainly contributed to the increasing use of the formal channel.

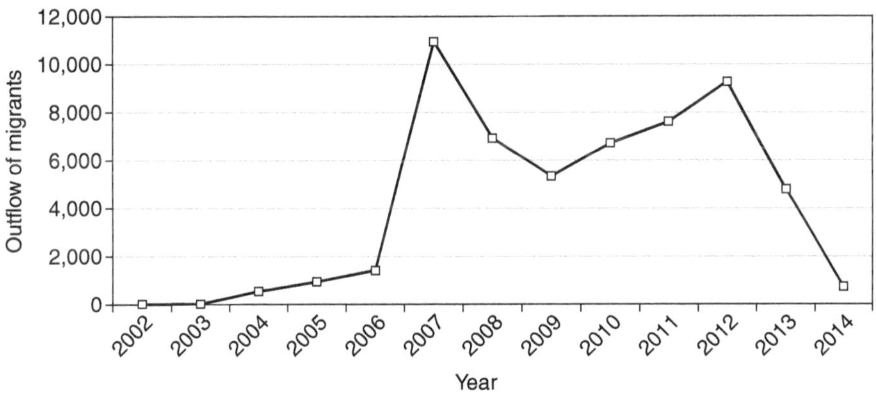

Figure 7.1 Outflow of Bangladeshi migrants to Italy, 2002–2014 (source: Bureau of Manpower, Employment, and Training, Bangladesh (BMET), online, available at: www.bmet.org.bd, accessed 5 August 2014).

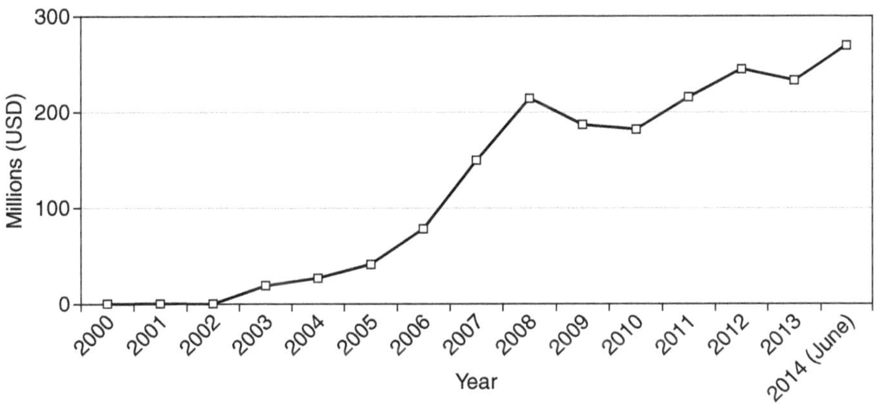

Figure 7.2 Inflows of remittances from Italy to Bangladesh, 2000–2014 (source: Bangladesh Bank, online, available at: www.bangladesh-bank.org/econdata/wagermidtl.php, accessed 5 August 2014).

The Bangladesh Household Remittance Survey (BHRS) covered 172 male migrants and five female migrants in Italy. However, these females were dependent migrants who joined their spouses in Italy, often in the dependent visa category. The mean age of these migrants was 33 years. Although these Bangladeshi migrants in Italy were predominantly single males, not necessarily all were unmarried. In fact, approximately 61 per cent of these migrants were married. With regard to the residence of married migrants' wives, nearly 73 per cent of them were living in Bangladesh. In other words, nearly one-quarter of migrants' wives have so far availed the family reunification programme. However, the rate of family reunification is relatively low because the reunification visa application procedure is complicated and lengthy.

Nearly 30 per cent of these migrants had graduate and post-graduate credentials before their migration to Italy. This educational attainment is exceptionally higher than that of the Bangladeshi migrants who are working in Asian countries, for instance, in Saudi Arabia. Approximately 3 per cent of Bangladeshi migrants had graduate degrees in Saudi Arabia (n=4,427) (Rahman 2011: 10). In another study, Rahman reports that 7 per cent of Bangladeshi migrants working in Singapore were graduates (2010: 270). Thus, it can be safely concluded that Bangladeshis who choose to migrate to European countries have higher educational credentials than those who are seeking temporary employment in the Middle East and Southeast Asia.

In terms of occupational background, 60 per cent of migrants were employed, and the remaining 40 per cent were unemployed before their migration to Italy. After migration to Italy, about 10 per cent could not get jobs in Italy. The major categories of occupations that these migrants were engaged in in Italy include factory work (19 per cent), hotel waiter or cook (14 per cent), general labour (24 per cent), agricultural labour (4 per cent), business (15 per cent), and sales (4 per cent). In total, 45 per cent of the Bangladeshi migrants were living in Italy between one and six years, and the remaining 55 per cent between six and 21 years or more. The duration of stay suggests that both the recent and relatively early migrants, including those who migrated in the late 1980s and 1990s, are netted in the survey. In fact, 70 per cent of migrants in the survey were living in Italy for less than ten years. The average duration of stay of migrants in Italy was eight years, which is likely to be sufficient to offer a clear indication of economic benefits of migration for the migrant households left behind in Bangladesh.

Channels of Bangladeshi migration to Italy

As discussed earlier, there are three main channels of migration to Italy: irregular migration, the quota system, and family reunification. It is important to note that the migrants who eventually ended up in Italy in the 1980s and even the 1990s did not necessarily intend to do so when they first moved to Europe. Many Bangladeshis who were living in other parts of Europe on various statuses such as refugees, students, short term trainees, and irregular migrants chose to settle in Italy because of Italy's liberal immigration policy and periodic regularisation drives. Most Bangladeshi migrants entered Italy clandestinely in the 1980s and 1990s, and a good number of new immigrants still sneak into the country in an unauthorised way through all three routes – air, land, and sea.

Migration through irregular channels usually involves the use of more than one route in the migration process. It is often a combination of air and land or air and sea routes, and sometimes all of the three. In the journey to Italy, potential migrants typically fly to nearby transit countries with a visa first, but later they become irregular in an attempt to enter Italy through land and sea routes. Bangladeshi migrants often use two land routes from the transit country. In the first route, potential migrants fly to Southeastern Europe and then travel over land to Italy. In the second route, potential migrants visit Turkey or Northeastern European countries and use the area of the former Yugoslavia as an entry point to Italy. Some popular transit countries are Poland, Hungary, Albania, Rumania, Russia, Turkey, Libya, Tunisia, Morocco and Algeria.

Irregular migration to Italy through sea borders mainly involves three routes: the crossing of the Otranto channel (Valona-Lecce coast), the Sicily channel (the coast of North Africa to the Sicilian coast); the Eastern Mediterranean channels (Eastern Mediterranean ports – Turkey, Egypt, Syria, Lebanon – to Apulia, Calabria and Sicily route) (for details, see Pastore *et al.* 2006; King and Knights 1994; UNODC 2010; Knights, 1996; Monzini 2007). In the 1980s and 1990s, most Bangladeshis reached Turkey, and a few to Morocco first before continuing to Italy. However, in the last decade, the overwhelming majority of Bangladeshis who used sea routes departed mainly from North African countries, especially Libya. As the UNODC report suggests, the importance of Libya as a country of transit corresponds to the decrease in the importance of routes originating in Albania, Tunisia and Turkey, and to the reduction of flows from the Morocco to Spain migration channel (UNODC 2010: 11).

After the opening-up of Italy's immigration policy in the second half of the 1990s, Bangladeshi migrants are allowed to enter Italy under the quota visa system. Since 2006, 3,000 Bangladeshis could enter Italy for work annually (IOM 2006: 102). In addition to quota visas, family reunification visas are the popular channel for the migration of spouses and children of migrants. Approximately 3,000 family reunification visas are issued from the Italian Embassy in Bangladesh each year (Zeitlyn 2006: 22). It is important to note that potential migrants are offered an 'Italy visa' to land in Italy, but not a 'Schengen visa'; the latter of which would have offered the right to land at any European Union country. As a result, all migrants from Bangladesh need to land in Italy first and claim immigration status as per the visa offered in Dhaka.

The role of *adam baparis* in the migration process

Migration to Italy is considered highly desirable, but is often inaccessible and unaffordable for potential Bangladeshi migrants because of a lack of access to networks of *adam baparis* and the exorbitant fees that a potential migrant is required to pay in the migration process. This section elaborates on the role of *adam baparis*, while the next section addresses the economic cost of migration. The role of *adam baparis*, or intermediaries, is crucial to migration occurrence in the Bangladesh–Italy migration corridor. *Adam bapari* is a Bengali term widely used by Bangladeshi migrants and the local media to describe those people who are familiar with migration procedures and cash in on this familiarity, access, or connection for economic advantage.

The services of *adam baparis* are unavoidable in the migration process, whether it is regular or irregular migration. A prospective regular migrant often requires the services of several *adam baparis* located at both ends of migration – Bangladesh and Italy. In Italy, they provide services to potential dependent visa or quota visa applicants. In Bangladesh, they provide services to both groups of visa applicants in the area of passport application, air ticket booking, visa application, and so on. In addition to serving the formal visa applicants, they also serve irregular migrants by running transnational syndicates of irregular migration to Italy (Monzini 2007; UNODC 2010). More focused research is needed to understand the transnational syndicate of irregular migration in the South Asia–Southern European migration corridor.

However, *adam baparis* usually emerge from the population of early migrants and their relatives and friends, making migration almost a location-specific phenomenon. For instance, there are 64 districts in Bangladesh, but migrants in Italy are predominantly from just a few districts such as Faridpur, Comilla, Dhaka and Noakhali. The survey also reveals how important the network of relatives and friends are in the migration process. In response to a survey question on the people who provided assistance (primarily information and access to networks) in their migration to Italy, nearly 77 per cent of migrants reported receiving assistance from relatives and friends. This overwhelming support from relatives and friends suggests why migration to Italy is a location-specific phenomenon in Bangladesh.

To briefly shed light on the monetary benefits that Bangladeshi migration to Italy generates for *adam baparis*, this study examines areas of expenses for migration to Italy (Figure 7.3). The financial cost of migration to Italy was US$10,000 on average; this is further explained in the next section. For convenience, the study divides the financial cost of migration into the formal service fees, which include government fees, passport fees, travel tax and other fees, and the intermediaries' fees, which include fees for *adam baparis* at different levels and different locations. A detailed investigation on the expenses of migration reveals that formal fees only represent on average 18 per cent of the financial cost of migration, with the intermediaries' fees representing the remaining 82 per cent. In absolute terms, a migrant spends nearly US$1,800 on average for meeting the formal service fees, and nearly US$8,200 for meeting the informal service fees charged by *adam baparis* in the migration process. In the Bangladeshi migration to the Gulf countries, Rahman reports a similar distribution of expenses across formal and informal services (2011: 16). Bangladeshi emigration thus seems to serve a group of intermediaries who enjoy enormous economic rewards from organising and facilitating the migration of labour internationally.

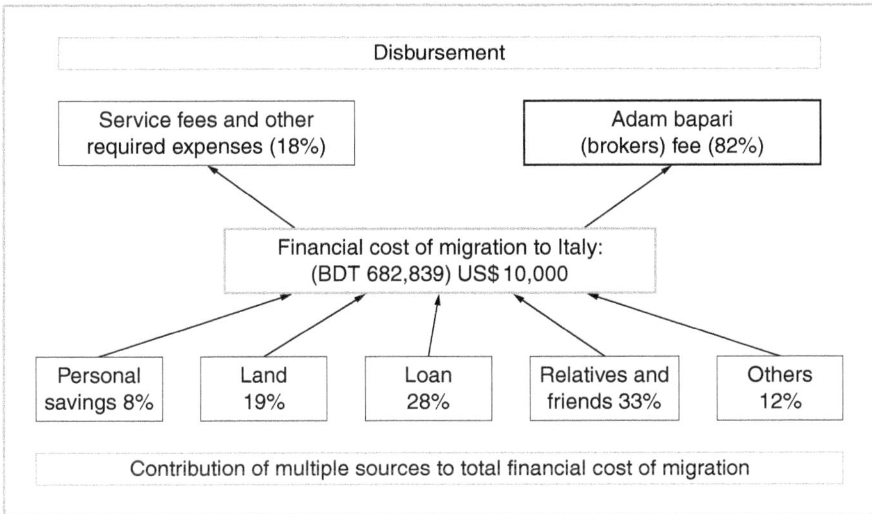

Figure 7.3 Economic cost of migration to Italy.

Financing migration to Italy

The expenses incurred in the migration process are referred to as the financial cost of migration. The financial cost of migration for a Bangladeshi migrant to Italy was BDT 682,839 on average, or approximately US$10,000 (as per the exchange rate of 2009). The expenses for migration varied sharply: the top 27 per cent of migrants paid more than nearly US$15,000 and the bottom 27 per cent paid less than nearly US$4,400 (Table 7.1). The difference in the cost of migration can be attributed to several factors; (i) the relationship with key *adam bapari*, (ii) the nature of migration (irregular or regular migration), (iii) the

Table 7.1 Cost of migration to Italy

Cost of migration (in BDT)	*Percentages*
≤150,000	11.3
150,001–300,000	15.8
300,001–500,000	16.7
500,001–700,000	13.7
700,001–1,000,000	15.7
>1,000,001	26.8
Total	100.0

Source: Bangladesh Household Remittance Survey 2009.

Note
BDT (Bangladesh Taka), Bangladeshi Currency, Exchange Rate US$1 = BDT 68.28 as at late 2013.

nature of the visa (work visa, student visa, sponsored seasonal worker etc.) and the duration of the visa, (iv) the year of migration to Italy, and finally (v) the nature of work and potential wages in Italy. Irregular migration is usually cheaper than regular migration. Early migrants who migrated to Italy in the 1980s and 1990s paid relatively small amounts of cash as compared to new streams of migrants.

Figure 7.3 presents the economic cost of migration to Italy from a family perspective. The figure maps out two important layers that constitute the economic cost of migration, such as contribution of multiple sources to the financial cost of migration, and the disbursement of the financial cost of migration as formal service fees and intermediary fees. The average cost of migration to Italy was virtually beyond the personal and family savings of all migrants. As a result, most migrants had to rely on multiple sources to accumulate the funds for migration, such as personal savings, landed property, loans from money lenders and loans from relatives and friends, personal savings, and other sources such as livestock, gold jewellery and so on. On average, land paid off nearly 19 per cent of the cost of migration and loans from money lenders accounted for 28 per cent. Relatives and friends contributed 33 per cent of the cost, personal savings paid off 8 per cent and other sources accounted for 12 per cent. Emigration undermines family economics in two ways: the outflow of family's income-generating assets hampers family incomes, and the loans from moneylenders put pressure on available family resources and use of remittances, as we will see in the next section.

Family remittances and family dynamics

Remittances are often shown as the most tangible benefit that international migration generates for migrants and their families (Hugo 2003). Financial remittances are commonly categorised as 'family remittances' and 'collective remittances' (Goldring 2004). 'Family remittances' suggests financial flows from individual migrants overseas to their families in source countries, while 'collective remittances' denotes the financial flows raised by a group of migrants in the remittance-sending countries for the welfare of a group or community in the remittance-receiving countries. Although collective remittances in the form of group contribution to the community cause is also noticed in the Italy–Bangladesh remittances corridor, this study is more concerned about family remittances, that is, individual migrants' financial contribution to their families and its implications for family dynamics.

The size and frequency of remittances are important variables for the economic take off of the migrant families, especially when migrant households dispossess family resources and borrow cash from moneylenders to finance their migration ventures. The size of the remittances is contingent on the monthly incomes of the migrants overseas. Therefore, this study investigates the monthly remuneration of migrants from the family perspective. However, this study does not deny the difficulty of investigating individual migrants' remittances to their families in Bangladesh, and stresses the fact that many migrants indeed share their wages with their immediate family members in a traditional society. On average, the monthly remuneration of the migrants was reported to be BDT 70,680 (US$1,050). This amount is several times higher than what a comparable job would have offered in Bangladesh. On average, migrants remitted approximately 3.5 times per year. The average amount of remittances at a time was BDT 36,979, or nearly US$550. If average remittances and frequency of remittances are multiplied, a migrant household would receive approximately US$1,900 on average in a year. In other words, a migrant household with a member in Italy had US$1,900 as remittances for disposal in a year.

Having investigated the annual inflow of remittances, this study moved further to examine the use of remittances at the family level (Table 7.2). The use of remittances is an important indicator for family development dynamics. Migrant families used the funds for a myriad of purposes, starting from family basic expenses (food and clothing mainly) to religious festivals such as *Eid-ul-Fitr* and *Eid-ul-Azha*. The five major areas of use of remittances, as per frequency of uses, are family expenses, followed by medical treatment, education, repayment of debts, and religious festivals. As per frequency, 85 per cent of households used remittances mainly for basic family expenses, 29 per cent for medical treatment, 19 per cent for education, 17 per cent for repayment of debts, and finally 12 per cent for religious festivals.

The reason behind the overwhelming use of remittances for a family's basic necessities is not surprising – migration is a family-funded project and involves the pooling of existing family resources, which curtails the family's ability to finance basic necessities. Remittances increase the ability of households to spend on basic necessities. However, in terms of use of remittances for medical

Table 7.2 Use of remittances at the household

Expenditure of remittance money	*Percentages*
For family's basic expenses	84.89
Purchase of land/property	2.88
Paying of debts	17.27
Savings	8.63
Construction/repairing of house	6.47
Repossession of mortgaged land	0.72
For running a business	0.72
Sending brother abroad	0.72
Marrying off brother/sister	2.16
Education of children	19.42
Medical treatment	29.50
Eid (Muslim religious) festivals	12.23
Others	3.60

Source: Bangladesh Household Remittance Survey 2009.

Note
The percentages are based on multiple responses and therefore do not add to 100.

treatment, the healthcare system in Bangladesh must be highlighted. The public healthcare system in Bangladesh is not adequate to meet the rising demand of the rapidly growing population. Apart from this, the quality of public healthcare is much poorer than that of private healthcare (Andaleeb 2000). This has forced people to seek private healthcare, which usually caters to the needs of the privileged sections of society. Since migrant families had access to disposable resources, many of them sought private healthcare for better treatment.

In a separate set of questions on the impact of the use of remittances on family dynamics, this study discerns that remittances have some visible impacts on migrant families in terms of food consumption, educational attainment, and local income generation. Nearly 72 per cent of families reported having improved food consumption and nearly 59 per cent reported having enhanced educational opportunities. However, the role of remittances in income generation was mixed. Nearly 39 per cent of migrant families reported an increase in incomes through the generation of new sources of incomes. However, given the percentage of recent migrants in the sample, it is not surprising to see the low use of remittances for income generation. Going back to Amartya Sen's argument that development is a process of increasing the freedoms of people, the proximate determinants of the basic freedom that Sen suggests were health, education and income. Looking at the spheres of remittance use, especially health, education and income, it is obvious that migration-induced earnings (remittances) played a substantial role in increasing the opportunities of migrant families in absolute terms.

Conclusion

This chapter has attempted to provide insights into the Bangladeshi migration to Italy, and its implications for families left behind in Bangladesh. Of the Southern European countries, Italy pursued a liberal policy for migrants from non-European countries as early as the 1980s by introducing the regularisation initiative for unauthorised migrants. In the 1990s and 2000s, immigration laws were gradually reformed to meet the demand for foreign labour under the quota system. This invited the dependents of regularised immigrants under family reunion category, and finally to integrate the new immigrants into the Italian society with more rights and privileges. The regularisation drives and subsequent changes in immigration laws paved the way for the emergence of many non-European migrant communities in Italy, including the Bangladeshi community. The size of the Bangladeshi community grew substantially over time through irregular migration, recruitment migration (labour migration), and family reunion migration.

This study has shed light on the routes of immigration for both early and recent Bangladeshi immigrants. In the 1980s and 1990s, Bangladeshi migration was largely irregular, and was a response to the opportunity created by frequent regularisation drives and immigration law reforms in Italy. Migration through irregular channels usually comprised of a combination of air and land routes or air and sea, and sometimes of all three. To put the routes in the order of use, most migrants took the air route and land route in the early 1980s, while land and sea routes emerged as the dominant channels for irregular Bangladeshi migration to Italy in the 1990s and the 2000s. For authorised migration since the late 1990s, the predominant route of travel has been air route. In the immigration process, the key players who facilitate regular and irregular migration are popularly called *adam baparis* (intermediaries) in Bangladesh. They cash in on their familiarity with the routes, their access to Italy's labour market, and their connections with the local bureaucracy. The profit that migration generates for *adam baparis* is around 82 per cent of the financial cost of migration.

The financial cost of migration to Italy is reported to be US$10,000 on average. As international migration is often a family strategy, families use all available resources, including selling and mortgaging of arable land, and borrowing from money lenders and extended family members. The inflow of remittances to migrant families represents the loyalty to and solidarity with those families left behind in Bangladesh. The average amount of remittances was nearly US$550, and the frequency of remittances in a year was 3.5 times. In other words, a migrant household received approximately US$1,900 on average as remittances. Migrant households used this disposable resource for a myriad of purposes, starting from basic consumption to religious and cultural ceremonies. This study reports some visible impacts of the use of remittances on food consumption, education, healthcare and local income generation. Presenting the wide spectrum of use of remittances, this study argues that remittances increase the opportunities of migrant families and contribute to their well-being.

This study should be seen as an early attempt to explicate Bangladeshi migration to Italy, and its implications for migrant families. While this study offers valuable insights into Bangladeshi migration to Italy, more research adopting two-way surveys is required – in Italy as well as in Bangladesh. Ethnographic fieldwork will also facilitate a better understanding of the migration and settlement process in Italy, and their implications for the families left behind in Bangladesh.

Notes

1 'The Number of Bangladeshi Migrants in Italy on the Rise', 30 October 2010, *Amaderdesh*, online, available at: www.amaderdesh.com/desh/italy-on-rise/ (accessed 29 October 2011).

2 BMET, Government Agency in Charge of Monitoring Outflow of Bangladeshi Migrants, Bureau of Manpower, Employment and Training (BMET), online, available at: www.bmet.org.bd/BMET/stattisticalDataAction, accessed 28 October 2011.

References

Andaleeb, S.S. 2000. Service Quality in Public and Private Hospitals in Urban Bangladesh: A Comparative Study. *Health Policy* 53: 25–37.

Anthias, F. and G. Lazaridis. 2000. *Gender and Migration in Southern Europe*. New York: Berg.

Blangiardo, G.C. 2009. Foreigner's Presence in Italy: from a Reference Framework to Future Development Scenarios. In V. Cesareo (ed.), *The Fifteenth Italian Report on Migrations 2009*. Milan: Polimetrica.

Bonifazi, C., M. Okolski, J. Schoorl and P. Simon. 2008. *International Migration in Europe: New Trends and New Methods of Analysis*. Amsterdam: Amsterdam University Press.

Cesareo, V. 2007. *Immigrants Regularization Processes in Italy*. Milan: Polimetrica.

Cesareo, V. 2009. Migrations in 2009: A Comprehensive outlook. In V. Cesareo (ed.), *The Fifteenth Italian Report on Migrations 2009*, Milan: Polimetrica.

Chaloff, J. 2004. From Labour Emigration to Labour Recruitment: the Case Study of Italy. In OECD, *Migration for Employment – Bilateral Agreements at a Crossroads*. Paris: OECD.

Chaloff, J. 2006. Innovating in the Supply of Services to Meet the Needs of Immigrants in Italy. In OCED, *From Immigration to Integration: Local Solutions to a Global Challenge*. Paris: OECD.

Congiano, A. and S. Strozza. 2008. Foreign Immigration in Southern European Receiving Countries: New Evidence from National Data Sources. In Corrado Bonifazi, Marek Okolski, Jeannette School and Patrick Simon (eds), *International Migration in Europe: New trends and new methods of Analysis*. Amsterdam: Amsterdam University Press, pp. 153–178.

Faist, T. 2010. Transnationalization and Development: Toward an Alternative Agenda. In N.G. Schiller and T. Faist (eds), *Migration, Development and Transnationalization: A Critical Stance*. Oxford: Berghahn Books.

Goldring, L. 2004. Family and Collective Remittances to Mexico: A Multi-dimensional Typology. *Development and Change* 35(4): 799–840.

Hermele, K. 1997. The Discourse on Migration and Development. In T. Hammar, G. Brochmann, K. Tamas and T. Faist (eds), *International Migration, Immobility and Development: Multidisciplinary Perspective*. Oxford: Berg.

Hugo, G. 2003. *Migration and Development: a Perspective from Asia*, IOM Migration Research Series, No. 14, International Organization for Migration. IOM: Geneva.

IOM. 2006. *Handbook on Establishing Effective Labour Migration Policies in Countries of Origin and Destination*. Joint publication with Organization for Security and Co-operation in Europe (OSCE). IOM and International Labour Organization: Vienna.

King, R. 1993. Recent Immigration to Italy: Character, Causes, and Consequences. *GeoJournal* 30(3): 283–292.

King, R. 2001. *Mediterranean Passage: Migration and New Cultural Encounters in Southern Europe*. London: Liverpool University Press.

King, R. and J. Andall. 1999. The Geography and Economic Sociology of Recent Immigration to Italy. *Modern Italy* 4(2): 135–158.

King, R. and M. Knights. 1994. Bangladeshis in Rome: a Case of Migratory Opportunism. In W.T.S. Gould and A.M. Findlay (eds), *Population Migration and the Changing World Order*. New York: John Wiley and Sons.

King, R., G. Lazaridis and C. Tsardanidis. 2000. *Eldorado or Fortress?: Migration in Southern Europe*. New York: Macmillan Press Ltd.

Knights, M. 1996. Bangladeshi Immigrants in Italy: from Geopolitics to Micropolitics. *Transactions of the Institute of British Geographers* New Series 21(1): 105–123.

Monzini, P. 2007. Sea-Border Crossings: the Organization of Irregular Migration to Italy. *Mediterranean Politics* 12(2): 163–184.

Papademetriou, D. and P.L. Martin. 1991. *The Unsettled Relationship: Labor Migration and Economic Development*. London: Greenwood Press.

Pastore, F., P. Monzini and G. Sciortino. 2006. Schengen's Soft Underbelly? Irregular Migration and Human Smuggling across Land and Sea Border to Italy. *International Migration* 44(4): 95–119.

Rahman, M.M. 2011. Does Labour Migration bring about Economic Advantage? A Case of Bangladeshi migrants in Saudi Arabia. Institute of South Asian Studies, (Singapore) Working Paper no. 135, September 2011.

Rahman, M.M. and B.S.A. Yeoh. 2008. The Social Organization of Hundi: Channelling Migrant Remittances from East and Southeast Asia to Bangladesh. *Asian Population Studies* 4(1): 5–29.

Schiller, N.G. 2010. A Global Perspective on Migration and Development. In N.G. Schiller and T. Faist (eds), *Migration, Development and Transnationalism: a Critical Stance*. Oxford: Berghahn Books.

Schiller, N.G. and T. Faist. 2010. Introduction: Migration, Development and Social Transformation. In N.G. Schiller and T. Faist (eds), *Migration, Development and Transnationalism: a Critical Stance*. Oxford: Berghahn Books.

Sen, A. 1999. *Development as Freedom*. Oxford: Oxford University Press.

SOPEMI. 2010. *International Migration Outlook*. OECD: Paris.

Stark, O. 1991. *The Migration of Labor*. Oxford: Basil Blackwell.

Triandafyllidou, A. 2007. Mediterranean Migrations: Problems and Prospects for Greece and Italy in the Twenty-first Century. *Mediterranean Politics* 12(1): 77–84.

Ullah, AKM A. 2010. *Rationalizing Migration Decisions: Labour Migrants in East and Southeast Asia*. London: Ashgate.

UNODC (United Nations Office on Drugs and Crime). 2010. Smuggling of Migrants Into, Through and From North Africa. Vienna: UNODC.

Yeoh, B.S.A., E. Graham and P.J. Boyle. 2002. Migrations and Family Relations in the Asia Pacific Region. *Asian and Pacific Migration Journal* 11(1): 117–143.

Zanfrini, L. 2003. Employment Needs of Firms and Planning of Flows. IRES Report.

Zeitlyn, B. 2006. Migration from Bangladesh to Italy and Spain. Occasional Paper 11, Refugee and Migratory Movements Research Unit, University of Dhaka.

Zontini, E. 2010. *Transnational Families, Migration and Gender: Moroccan and Filipino Women in Bologna and Barcelona*. Oxford: Berghahn Books.

8 Indian migration to the Gulf and development challenges in India

Ajaya Kumar Sahoo

International migration is not a new phenomenon for globetrotting Indians who, today, constitute more than 25 million living in different countries around the world. After India's independence, the first wave of migration saw Indians moving to the United States, United Kingdom, Canada and Australia, and with a smaller number to Western Europe. This flow began in the early 1950s and continued until the mid-1970s. During these periods, Indians from other parts of the world – especially from former colonies – also migrated to these countries as 'twice migrants' (Bhachu 1985). The second wave of migration took place when Indians moved to oil-exporting countries in the Middle East spanning the Persian Gulf; the six countries belonging to the Gulf Cooperation Council (GCC) – the United Arab Emirates (UAE), Saudi Arabia, Oman, Kuwait, Bahrain and Qatar.

Although Indian migration to the Persian Gulf started as early as the 1930s after oil was discovered in the region (Khadria 2006; Pradhan 2010), large-scale migration only took place in the early 1970s as a result of the price-hike in oil and the consequent large revenues, which accelerated the process of industrialisation and social change in the GCC states. This period was characterised by massive investment in social and economic infrastructure, which necessitated the service of a large number of foreign workers. As Gardner rightly points out,

> each of the states configured modernization and economic diversification plans to make use of this wealth, and those plans required heavy infrastructural development: cities would grow; highways would be constructed; electricity would be generated; new industries would prosper; universities, mosques, stadiums, hospitals, and federal buildings would be constructed and staffed.
>
> (2011a: 6)

For a brief period during the 1990–1991 Gulf War 'the number of low-skilled Indian workers in the Gulf declined due to Indian government restrictions' (Khadria 2010: 67). However, it later picked up again when the demand for labour in the GCC states increased and diversified across many sectors from construction, services, oil and manufacturing (Breeding 2011).

Although the literature on migration and development focus largely on the positive impacts on the originating country in terms of remittances received, the results of this study show the flip sides of migration. This chapter argues that returnees are unsuccessful in contributing to potential development because they lose substantial resources of family and are often indebted in the migration process. Hence, migration poses challenges to their livelihood in the village, therefore affecting their families negatively.

The context

The fieldwork for this study was carried out between January 2009 and June 2011 among the return migrants[1] from the Gulf countries in the four districts of Andhra Pradesh – the Karimnagar and Nizamabad districts from Telangana region, East Godavari from the Costal Andhra region and Cuddapah (Kadapa) from the Rayalaseema region – from which migration to Gulf countries has been considerable in the recent past.[2] One of the main factors for migration in these districts is landlessness. A majority of respondents in this study reported that they do not have sufficient agricultural land; some of them are even landless. Even those who have agricultural land are unable to cultivate and seek profits due to droughts and lack of irrigation facilities. Natural calamities like famines and floods, shrinking of the cottage industry, and lack of employment opportunities has forced many of them to migrate to urban areas and the Gulf countries.

Migration from Andhra Pradesh started with internal migration especially 'from the rural areas of Telangana districts to the coal fields of Godavarikhani, textile centers of Gujarat and Maharashtra' (Sampath 2006: 6). The male migrants used to migrate to Bombay (present day Mumbai) to work in the industrial and construction sites, where they gathered information about the opportunities available in the Gulf countries. This trend was noticeable during the 1980s and 1990s (Azeez and Begum 2009). Once the migrants have settled in the Gulf countries, they send information to their own children, relatives, and neighbours about the opportunities available there. This is what scholars call the migrant 'network' that facilitates further migration (Gold 2005). As Andrew Gardner stated, 'chain migration through personal contacts, often arranged by other family members or acquaintances already in the Gulf, remains a significant force in the Gulf' (2011a: 9). Several scholars have also discussed the role of personal networks in migration (Vertovec 2002).

Methodology

The study is based on data collected from both primary and secondary sources. The primary data was collected from respondents in the four districts of Andhra Pradesh. Through snowball sampling, 198 respondents were selected for this study. The demographics of the respondents are presented in Table 8.1. For the collection of information from the respondents, a structured questionnaire was used, consisting of nine pages in which the questions were arranged sequentially

Table 8.1 Demographic characteristic of the respondents

Variables	*Frequency* (n = *198*)	*Percentage (%)*
Gender		
Male	161	81.31
Female	37	18.68
Age group		
18–30	69	34.84
31–40	66	33.33
41–50	43	21.71
>51	20	10.10
Marital status		
Married	172	86.86
Unmarried	19	9.59
Divorced/separated	7	3.53
District of origin		
Karimnagar	100	50.50
Nizamabad	44	22.22
East Godavari	27	13.63
Cuddapah	27	13.63

– personal information, migration and living conditions in the Gulf, and coping patterns after return. Besides this primary data, relevant information from the NRI Cell in Karimnagar district and the Overseas Manpower Company of Andhra Pradesh (OMCAP) Limited in Hyderabad was also gathered. These two organisations conduct various programmes for the migrants in Andhra Pradesh. For the secondary sources, published literature in various journals, books, reports, national and local (Telugu) newspapers and the Internet were used.

Out of the total respondents selected for this study, 81 per cent were male and 19 per cent were female. Female migration from India to the Gulf countries comes mostly from the state of Kerala (Percot and Rajan 2007) and to a lesser extent from the state of Andhra Pradesh and Goa, as well as other countries such as Sri Lanka, Bangladesh and the Philippines (al-Najjar 2002; Jureidini 2003). Jain (2007) pointed out that female migrants are fewer compared to male migrants and they have lesser job opportunities, e.g. as nurses, teachers and domestic servants. Although studies have shown that there has been a steady increase in the number of female migrants from Andhra Pradesh to the Gulf countries in recent times (see Rajan and Sukendran 2010: 184), we did not find sufficient female respondents for this study during the survey period. Securing work as a domestic labourer in the houses depends on networks, hence most migrants depend on their own family members or relatives to recommend such work. From the two districts (East Godavari and Cuddapah) it was found that the migrants were recruited to the Gulf through networks. Studies have shown that in many cases, female migrants who were engaged as housemaids, ayahs and cleaners were being exploited, cheated and abused (Jureidini 2003; Human

Rights Watch 2010). A few countries such as Nepal, Bangladesh and India restricted the out-migration of women to the Gulf countries (see Ahn 2005). Nevertheless, some women do travel via other countries illegally, for example, some Nepali women might travel via India and some Indian women via Sri Lanka (Ahmed 2010; Thimothy and Sasikumar 2012). After entering the host society, a heavy workload becomes a common problem for most of the women migrants; they work from early in the morning till midnight, and the work they engage in includes washing clothes, dishes, cleaning the house, cooking, cleaning vehicles, looking after the children and caring for elderly persons (Chammartin 2004). In recent times, women have been trafficked and cheated by unauthorised agents. A report in the *Times of India* revealed that:

> In 2008 a special team nabbed 13 women at the Hyderabad airport, for not complying with norms. The women in the age group of 20–30 years were on their way to the Gulf countries to work as domestic helpers. The women, all illiterate, are from East Godavari, West Godavari and Kadapa districts, they planned to visit Kuwait and Oman by flights ... but their passports did not carry Protector of Emigrants (POE) clearance, mandatory for those carrying an Emigration Check Required (ECR) stamp in their passport.
>
> (*Times of India*, 27 May 2008)

In terms of destination, 64 per cent of respondents migrated to UAE, 19 per cent to Kuwait, 5 per cent each to Saudi Arabia and Bahrain, 4 per cent to Qatar, and 2 per cent to Oman. Age is an important criterion for Gulf migration as most of the migrants engage in the construction and service sectors. Since these jobs are risky, only physically fit candidates are preferred and for that reason, most young people migrate to the Gulf countries. As Arnold and Shah noted, because of 'long hours and often harsh working and living conditions, the majority of workers are young' (1984: 298). Out of the respondents in the present study, 68 per cent belonged to the age group of 18–40 years, with the rest (32 per cent) above the age of 41. Zachariah and Rajan's (2012) study showed that 90 per cent of the male migrants and 66 per cent of the female migrants belonged to the age group of 19–39 years. It is therefore clear that age is the dominant criteria for Gulf migration in the present time. Since these migrants have returned to their places of origin after a few years of work in the host country, many of the respondents in this study opined that if opportunities were given, they would still prefer to travel again to the Gulf countries.

The dynamics of Gulf migration

There are several reasons for migration; these may be political, social, economic, cultural and/or geographical. India is one of the major players among the Asian countries in the economic game of exporting large numbers of skilled, semi-skilled and unskilled workers to the Middle East (Nair 1998). The major areas of Andhra Pradesh where significant migration to the Gulf countries took place include the northern Telangana regions of Nizamabad and Karimnagar, East Godavari from Coastal Andhra, and Kadapa from the Rayalaseema region beside Hyderabad. One of the important factors that led to this migration was the development of communication and transport facilities. For example, the Andhra Pradesh State Road Transportation Corporation (APSRTC) started direct bus services from Karimnagar and Nizamabad towns to Hyderabad Airport (Rajiv Gandhi International Airport). This service was initiated after feedback, especially from the Gulf passengers, was received.

Factors motivating migration include both push and pull factors. Pull factors are those that attract individual to migrate, i.e. better employment opportunities, good wages, or rising aspirations for a better life in other countries. On the other hand, there are push factors like poverty, indebtedness, or unemployment that compel people to move out (Cherunilam 1987). In the present study, 79 per cent of the respondents stated that the poor economic condition of their family was the main reason for migration, while 15 per cent said that a lack of job opportunities and a shortage of agricultural land for cultivation were the main reasons for migration. Some 6 per cent of the respondents did not reveal the reasons for their migration. Although studies (Osella and Osella 2000; Vora 2008) have shown that those from the middle and upper middle classes have also migrated to the Gulf countries, we were not able to find respondents belonging to the middle and upper middle classes[3] for this study.

Manga, a 26-year-old unmarried female respondent from Antervedi (East Godavari district) who migrated to Kuwait in the year 2007 to work as a housemaid explained:

> poor economic conditions of the family and lack of job opportunities are the reasons for my migration. After my elder sister got married I had to look after my parents. I worked as a housemaid in Kuwait and used to send INR4,000 per month to my parents. I returned to India because my visa term expired. I am planning to go again if I get the visa and work permit. In Kuwait I worked as a housemaid in an Arab house and they paid my salary regularly, but the work was very hard and I had to work the whole day with no time limit. I feel that the visa should be for more years because I have to spend a lot of money on the visa every time.

Thatha Rao, 55, is a returnee from Qatar who earlier migrated to the UAE and has now returned to his hometown in Cuddapah district. Thatha Rao has two sons who are currently working in Kuwait; his elder son's wife is also working as a housemaid in Kuwait. He recounted:

> migration to the Gulf changed my family status and we are in a good position now; without the Gulf migration we would be nothing. Because of the Gulf migration many people in my village are in a good position, although some have not benefitted. I did not have any work (employment) to do here so I planned to migrate to the Gulf countries. It started many years ago. I am

> one of the earliest migrants from this village. Migration to the Gulf in the present time is not as helpful as the situation has changed; there are more workers than work in the Gulf countries.

This study observed that there were other factors that influenced migration, apart from the basic economic factor. For example, in Karimnagar district, the Naxalite movement was a significant albeit indirect factor influencing migration. Naxalism influenced the northern Telangana region of Andhra Pradesh, mainly agricultural labourers' associations in the 1970s and early 1980s. Naxalism influenced the youth and educated male persons – the student and youth fronts were the instruments for the spread of Maoism (Naxalism) as an ideology and political practice (Balagopal 2006). As a result, most of the youth migrated to the urban areas to avoid entering the Naxalite movement. Coincidentally, during the same time, the Gulf migration was picking up and gaining popularity in the regions. Some youths started migrating to urban areas and even to the Gulf countries in order to avoid police harassment[4] after retiring from the Naxalite movement. Gardner reported that political and structural violence in the home countries influenced migration:

> the recent ethnic conflict in Sri Lanka, for example, pushed many Tamil men and women out of Sri Lanka to the Gulf, and the ongoing strife in Nepal is often a central factor in the decisions that led Nepalese men from their homes to the Gulf.
>
> (2011b: 5)

Economics of Gulf migration

As compared to the initial periods of migration, the economic aspect of migration to the Gulf countries has changed significantly in recent times. The demand for labour in the Gulf in the last two to three decades has resulted in a system called 'visa trading', which became a 'multi-million dollar industry' (Shah 2008). Migrants generally incur expenses from their travel abroad, mainly on various items such as passports, visa fees, medical check-ups and flight-fares. These charges often include middlemen and unauthorised agents' commissions. The migrants incur these costs before their migration. Hence, the financial costs for migration pose as a burden for migrants, since most of the migrants depend on moneylenders to pay the interest amount arising from their recruitment process.

A majority of respondents (87 per cent) in this study opined that they depended on others' (moneylenders, friends and/or relatives) support for their travel and visa costs, while a minority of the respondents (13 per cent) said that they had their own savings. Anisur Rahman's (2001) study in Bihar found that a quarter of the migrants relied on their savings. Another study by A.C. Nambiar (1995) in Kerala showed that 36.73 per cent of the respondents mobilised their funds by asset disposal and subsequent bank loans, rather than depending on moneylenders. In dealing with the Asian labour migration to the Gulf, Mizanur Rahman (2013: 2) mentions that 'many potential Gulf migrants pay the higher economic costs of migration by borrowing from moneylenders with higher rates of interests and risking the economic base of the family'. Supported by the opinions of respondents in this study, it is argued that since the majority of respondents did not have enough savings or assets to use for their migration, they depended completely on borrowing from the moneylenders. The moneylenders made huge profits in the process by lending money through the 'gold interest system'.[5] In Karimnagar district, for example, we found that most of the moneylenders extend their financial support to the Gulf migrants readily because they think that the migrants will repay their debts with money earned in the Gulf. Similarly, the migrants take huge amounts of loans while assuming that they will earn good money in the Gulf, out of which they will be able to easily repay their debts.

Gulf countries have recently introduced the *kafala*[6] or sponsorship system for the recruitment of labour (Thimothy and Sasikumar 2012). Since obtaining the visa is the crucial starting point for Gulf migration, most migrants spend large amounts in order to secure it. Getting the visa is a difficult task for the poor and illiterate migrants. They therefore have to enlist the help of agents by paying commissions. Rahman's (2011) study of the Bangladeshi community in the Gulf countries discusses the role of recruiting agencies and migrant networks in the recruitment process. He points out that:

> Due to the great supply of foreign workers and the intense competition between recruiting agencies, recruiting agents and migrant brokers need to pay *kafeel* to procure work visas for migrant workers. This development of visa-trade has transformed the modality and scale of transactions for intermediaries of both migrant networks and recruiting agencies alike. Forced by market pressures, actors of migrant networks are now required to charge fees for Gulf visas, leading to the commercialisation of network-assisted recruitment.
>
> (Rahman 2011: 4)

Migrants have to follow different rules and regulations before migration. They should possess all valid documents such as a passport with the required emigration clearance endorsement, an employment contract, a visa, a medical fitness certificate and a police clearance certificate. Before migration, the migrants must secure an appointment in the host country. This can be done through any of the following channels:

> Friends and relatives already in employment in the host country (informal networks); authorized private recruiting agencies; government recruiting institutions; contractors or companies in India who have construction projects in the host county, and direct application to employer.
>
> (Nair 1998)

The majority of the respondents (93 per cent) in this study mentioned that they depended on private recruiting agencies for obtaining the visa. These private recruiting agencies have emerged in the late 1970s as a result of the growing demand for overseas labour (Rahman 2012a: 221). Only 7 per cent of the respondents in this study said that they sought help from their family members or friends who were already in the Gulf countries in order to obtain the visa, defined in the literature as 'networks' or 'everyday interpersonal connections' (Rahman 2010). The authorised private recruiting agencies generally recruit subagents in the village level. These subagents deal with the migrants directly. They help migrants with recruitment, as well as in securing documents such as passports, emigration clearance, visa or work permits, medical certificates, and police clearance certificates. The present study revealed several reasons contributing to the success of these agents, and why the migrants depend on them.

First, most of the migrants recruited by these agents belong to the semi-skilled and unskilled categories and do not have any previous migration experience. Second, these agents are available round the clock in the village as they reside in the same locality. Last, since most of the agents belong to the same region or village, mutual understanding between migrants and agents is easily established.

The agent system's popularity encouraged educated, unemployed youths to start working as agents. It is, today, a competitive and profitable business. However, with huge competition for migration to the Gulf countries, local subagents have resorted to cheating the migrants. The poor and illiterate rural migrants easily fall prey to the fraudulent practices of such agents. Sometimes unauthorised agents also perform these activities for migrants in the absence of authorised agents in the villages, although in practice these unauthorised agents do not have any licence to perform these activities. According to the rules outlined for implementation of the Emigration Act 1983, the recruiting agent is entitled to only receive INR1,500 (per person recruited) as service charge. However, since the visas are mostly sold through subagents, the migrants have to pay four to eight times the amount as agent charges, i.e. INR6,000 to INR12,000. Illiterate migrants are less familiar with the rules, regulations and information regarding migration, and hence, depend on their agents completely. The work of an agent is to successfully send the migrant to the Gulf countries. However, for the sake of business, the agents only tell the good stories about the companies and salary structures in the Gulf countries. Falling prey to this falsely rosy picture, the less well-off migrants are persuaded to migrate. Breeding's (2011) study also painted a similar picture of the role of agents and subagents.

Remunerations, savings, and remittances

The working hours vary from company to company, as does the salary of the migrants, depending on the work they engage in. The basic expenditure for migrants in the Gulf is food and accommodation. Recent years have seen an increase in the number of return migrations coupled with declining remittances.

This is a result of crisis in the Gulf economy[7] (Rajan and Narayana 2011). This economic crisis resulted in raised rents for migrant workers in the Gulf. Pushed by a surge in the demand for housing for instance, this was 'an unprecedented 50 per cent in Dubai and 30 per cent in Riyadh, Jeddah, Manama, Abu Dhabi, Sharjah and Doha. This has raised the cost of living by about 15 per cent' (MFA 2008). Some migrants who work with big companies get free food and accommodation, while smaller companies do not provide these benefits. It is clear that the problem of food and accommodation only affect the semi-skilled, unskilled, and daily wage labourers, as accommodation and food are very expensive in the Gulf. However, despite these problems, many of the respondents highlighted that they tried hard to save money to remit to their families back home. Therefore, remittance is the most important criteria for Gulf migration.[8] Since migration to the Gulf countries is purely on a contract basis, the migrants generally do not purchase any house or related immovable property. As Arnold and Shah pointed out,

> the average Asian worker in the Middle East is able to remit over 50 per cent of total earnings (and often between 70 and 90 per cent of earnings). They tend to live quite frugally and their expenditures on entertainment and recreation are minimal.
>
> (1984: 301)

The majority of the respondents in this study agreed that they send remittances to their family members back home on a regular basis. Rahman and Fee point out the reason for this: 'since temporary migrants typically leave their families behind, they have a strong bond with the countries of origin and maintain regular contact through remittances' (2012: 689). Also, sending remittances is often necessary for these migrants because they belong to the lower income groups and their family members depend on their remittances. Moreover, since most of the migrants incur high amounts of debt for their migration by taking loans from moneylenders, they are compelled to repay the loan amounts on time. The amount of cash remittances received by migrant families back home varies from one month to another depending on the work their family members engage in (see Table 8.2).

Most of the remittances received by the families are spent on everyday consumptions: 83 per cent of respondents said that they use their remittances to first pay off the loans incurred for migration and for their children's education; a minority of the respondents (17 per cent) opined that they use it for savings,

Table 8.2 Remittances sent by respondents

Remittances sent home (in INR)	*Frequency* (n = *198)*	*Percentage (%)*
Not sent	19	9.59
1,000 to 3,000	85	42.92
3,001 to 6,000	44	22.22
>6,000	50	25.25

renovation of old houses or construction of new houses; 76 per cent of respondents said that the amount of remittances received by their families back home is insufficient for maintaining a decent life, let alone to pay for their children's education, marriage or house construction.

There are two types of funds transfer channels used by migrants globally, i.e. formal and informal channels: 'formal systems include banks, postal services, MTOs and other wire transfer services and card-based money transfers (credit and debit cards) … among informal fund transfers, *hundi* is a popular informal funds transfer system' (Rahman 2012b: 10). In this study, we found that migrants often transfer their remittances through private money transfer agencies or through banks. Although the money transfer agencies take commission through exchange charges, all the respondents in this study said that they did not encounter any difficulty as every village in the scope of this study had a money transfer agency.

Life in the Gulf

The working and living conditions of migrants completely depends on the host society. Indians in the Gulf countries face discrimination in terms of salaries and are sometimes ill-treated by their employers. Salaries paid to Arab migrants and non-Arab migrants are different (Kapiszewski 2006). Migrants have to live in labourers' camps, which in some cases are located near to their work places, and in others, located in isolated places far away. The majority of respondents in this study said that the labourers' camps are mostly temporary in nature and that the living conditions are poor, with no proper sanitation being maintained.[9] More than ten people live together in a single room. If a migrant decides to live outside the labourers' camps, he may have to bear the extra costs; this is beyond the ability of unskilled and semi-skilled workers.

The rationale behind living in such densely populated houses is to save money. As Khalaf and Alkobaisi point out,

> over-crowded housing patterns are not only confined to the large cities, but are also found in camel and agricultural farms, though to a lesser degree. Overcrowding results from strategies directed to securing savings from low salaries. The greater the number of people sharing a room the lesser cost to each individual.
>
> (1999: 292)

In Bahrain, for example, out of four labour camps the Human Rights Watch (2012) visited,

> three were extremely cramped and dilapidated … up to 20 men slept in a room that typically had only a small aisle separating 10 bunk beds. At one camp, workers slept on plywood cots, and in another camp on thin mats on the floor.

Similarly, food was another issue that the Human Rights Watch (2012) found problematic: 'almost all domestic workers in Bahrain live in their employers' homes. With limited opportunities to leave the house, they are completely dependent on their employers for food and housing'. Auwal reported similar facts:

> Migrant workers in the Gulf are provided free, though overcrowded, accommodations; they have no freedom to move around or change jobs; and they do not have the option to live with their families or visit them on a regular basis. They are given short-term one-to-three-year contracts. Even though these contracts are frequently renewed, in most cases the workers have to actually pay for their extension, leaving them with barely enough money to buy food and clothes for themselves, much less to send money home to the families they left behind.
>
> (2010: 94)

The processes of recruitment, wages, and terms and conditions of work were the critical factors that affected the living conditions of migrants in the Gulf countries (see Jureidini 2003). According to Rahman (2012a), several institutions play an important role in labour migration, such as employers, public employment services, migrant networks, private and for-profit recruitment agencies. Together they form a 'recruitment structure which facilitates the recruitment of migrant workers in the Gulf' (Rahman 2012a: 216). Although some companies provide medical and housing facilities to the workers, this again depends on the rules of the company. Some small companies prefer to recruit workers illegally because they cannot afford to pay for medical and housing facilities for legal migrants, which as a result burdens the migrant workers further. The poor health of migrant workers in the Gulf is also recognised, where

> laborers often suffer accidents, such as getting pieces of cement and steel chips in their eyes, sustaining hand injuries from grinders or power tools, and falls.... Only the most serious injuries receive medical care; the employer pays for transportation to the hospital and for medical expenses, which laborers must repay upon recovery – thereby increasing their debt.
>
> (Sönmez *et al.* 2011: 5)

Many of the respondents in this study said that they were considered 'illegal' (*kalli valli* in local language) in the host country because they arrived with tourist visas. On this note, tourist visas also create major problems for migrants, as they have to live illegally in the host country after the visa terms expire.

The construction and service sectors serve as the major workforce for Indian migrants in the Gulf. As Nambiar's (1995) study reveals, the migrant workers employed in the Middle East countries range from poorly educated ABCD workers (ayahs, bearers, cooks, drivers) to highly educated professionals. However, by and large, a majority belong to the category of less educated workers engaged in manual jobs. The problems of migrants are further compounded if one looks at the working hours of unskilled professions. Gardner points out that the 'migrants are often forced to work longer hours than those indicated in the contract they signed in the sending country, and many report not receiving additional wages for these additional (overtime) hours' (2011a: 10). The working hours vary from company to company, and sometimes migrants have to work until they finish a task that particular day, regardless of the time taken. Most of the respondents (78 per cent) in this study opined that they work more than ten hours a day, while a minority of respondents (22 per cent) said that they work less than eight hours a day.

The difficulties in accommodation, food, and salary are just a part of the migrants' woes. Migrants carrying a tourist visa in the Gulf countries face severe hardships compared to other migrants, as they are seen as illegal workers once their visa period expires. This may result in severe punishments, deportation, or even a jail term. Many respondents in this study were able to recall instances where Indians were sent to jail. Apart from this, migrants also face physical and psychological abuse during their period of stay in the Gulf. For example, in Bahrain,

> of the 62 workers Human Rights Watch interviewed, 12 said that their employers, supervisors, or recruiting agents had physically abused them. Physically abused workers reported being beaten, kicked, violently pushed, and slapped. Physical abuse was often accompanied by psychological and verbal abuse, such as insults or threats of further violence.
>
> (Human Rights Watch 2012)

In many cases, 'the victims have little recourse as government officials often ignore complaints or engage in even further physical abuse themselves' (Auwal 2010: 96). Another problem is that of fake trade certificates; migrants with good technical skills can achieve good salaries in the Gulf and for that reason many migrants make fake certificates. However, employers in the Gulf countries sometimes find that certificates are fakes, and migrants with such fake certificates are not offered professional jobs. They are often deported and sometimes even forced to engage in manual labour.

Conclusion

Gmelch (1980) has defined return migration as the movement of emigrants back to their homelands with the intention to resettle. Like international migration, return migration also has positive and negative impacts on the country of origin. While on the one hand, 'returnees return with the intention to use the material, human, and social capital, which they accumulated during the time they spend abroad to bring positive (socio-economic) change to their home countries' (Jonkers 2008), on the other, 'migrants returning home would mean more workers in an economy which is already overburdened with shrinking jobs due to the crisis' (Rajan and Narayana 2011: 7). Hence, migration not only facilitates development, it also yields underdevelopment and development challenges at the family level.

For migrants in the Gulf countries, returning to their homeland is compulsory as they are recruited on a contract basis. They cannot get permanent citizenship or own any property even if they stay for more than ten years.[10] The time of their return is determined mostly by the objective they set out to achieve at the time of migration. Migrants always think that they will earn good money and become successful if they migrate to another country. However, in this study, we found more failures than successes among the respondents. Several respondents opined that they had returned because of various reasons such as fake visas, job failures, harsh working conditions and deportation. In recent times, it was also observed that the recruiting companies in collaboration with the Government have reduced the salaries and wages for semi-skilled and unskilled workers due to the increasing number of foreign workers in the Gulf.

The manufacturing and construction sectors that employed the majority of Indian migrant workers in the Gulf have been severely affected by this financial crisis, which has resulted in large scale return migration as these workers were unable to find alternative employment (see Rajan and Narayana 2011). Several respondents in this study stressed that they actually wanted to return to India much earlier, but could not afford the airfare due to a lack of savings. In August 2008, the Indian consulate in Dubai arranged for the return of large number of impoverished workers through a special scheme.

Some 84 per cent of respondents in this study said that they were now the 'Gulf victims', having been burdened with huge debts, and were unemployed after returning from the Gulf. One of the unfortunate consequences was their being driven to suicide. An article on an Internet blog revealed that

> within the state of Andhra Pradesh, Karimnagar district has recorded the highest number of suicides, with 1,363 persons ending their lives in 2008, and 840 till September 2009 … the problem that the Gulf migrants face could account for the large number of suicides in Karimnagar.
>
> (Reddy 2009)

According to Rajan and Narayana, 'migrant workers are often the sole breadwinners of their families; any retrenchment is likely to push these families into poverty once again. The crisis may force some changes in the spending and investment habits of the migrant workers' (2011: 8).

Return is compulsory for all Gulf migrants. The policies of the Gulf countries do not allow the migrants to become permanent citizens despite them working for several years. In recent times, the Gulf countries have also started restricting the inflows of foreign workers despite the fact that the 'foreign workers have helped in the rapid transformation of the infrastructure as well as institutional development in the Gulf' (Shah 2008: 3). This chapter argues that failing at work in the Gulf has caused most of the migrants to return to their homeland.

A majority of respondents depended on personal loans for their international migration that chalked up significant amounts of interest, and the amount earned in the Gulf was so meagre that all their savings and remittances were used to merely pay off the interest, leaving them unable to clear their debts.

The study revealed that the social and economic lives of these returnees were not at all satisfactory during their stay in the Gulf countries, and their family life became worse after they returned to their places of origin. It may be concluded that a short duration of stay contributed as one of the factors for their failure as they could not earn a sufficient amount within the limited time of their stay in the Gulf. Because of their failure at work in the Gulf countries, the returnees were now labelled as 'Gulf victims' in the villages. They pose a serious and urgent need for government intervention, especially to help migrant families who are in debt and have members committing suicide.

Another factor is the lack of awareness among the migrants. Since many of the migrants are illiterate and unclear of the visa application process, they completely depend on the private recruiting agents. Because of fierce competition among the agents, these agents are more concerned about their commissions and therefore intentionally cheat migrants. Although in recent times the government of Andhra Pradesh has started special departments in the district, called 'NRI Cell' and 'OMCAP', in addition to starting several other special programmes (see MFA 2012) to help orientate the Gulf migrants, the migrants still lack an awareness of these programmes. This chapter therefore suggests that the government take further steps to popularise these programmes in the districts where migration to the Gulf is significant. More research on the lives of Gulf returnees in Andhra Pradesh should be undertaken to arrive at more conclusive and holistic findings.

Acknowledgements

This is a revised version of the paper presented at the International Workshop on 'Diaspora and Development: South Asian Diaspora Engagement in South Asia', organised by the Institute of South Asian Studies, National University of Singapore, 27–28 September 2012. I acknowledge with gratitude the cooperation and support received from the organisers (especially Dr Md Mizanur Rahman) for my participation in the workshop. I thank the University Grants Commission (UGC), New Delhi for funding this study under the Major Research Project (2008–2011). My thanks also go to the respondents who have given their valuable time and information. I thank Mr. Trilok Chandan Goud for collecting the information from the field and analysing the data.

Notes

1 Return migrants here mainly refer to the first generation migrants. Tsuda (2009: 5) differentiated between 'return migrants' and 'ethnic return migrants' in the sense that while 'return migrants are going back to their *natal* homeland (i.e. place of birth), the ethnic return migrants are later generation diasporic descendants returning to their *ethnic* homeland, where their ethnic group originated'.

2 Andhra Pradesh has three distinct regions known as Telangana, Rayalaseema and Andhra. The Andhra region is also called as Coastal Andhra. Telangana consists of ten districts, coastal Andhra consists of nine districts and Rayalaseema consists of four districts.

3 There is no official definition of the middle class in India, however,

> in comparison with lower-income households, the middle class in India has a greater amount of discretionary income (i.e. income available after taxes and essentials such as food and shelter are taken care of) to use and is more diversified in its consumption choices.
>
> (Saxena, 2010: 3)

4 It was observed that, 'in the Telangana villages of Andhra Pradesh, detention and questioning of suspected Naxalite sympathisers has become a routine feature of police action' (cited in Ahuja and Ganguly 2007: 268).

5 This system is common in the Karimnagar and Nizamabad districts, moneylenders calculate the total amount of loan on par with the gold cost, if the loan amount is equal to 10 g of gold then the migrants have to pay 15 g of gold for one year. Since the gold rate increases day by day, the interest also increases the loan amount. In this way, the moneylenders gain huge benefits.

6 In a *kafala* system, a migrant is sponsored by an employer who is a GCC citizen and assumes full economic and legal responsibility for the employee during the contract period. Kafeel may be an individual, a placement agency, or a company/institution (Rahman 2011: 8).

7 According to Rajan and Narayana (2011: 10) 'the global crisis has affected the Middle East through a large fall in the price of oil, deterioration of external financing conditions, reversal of capital inflows, depressed property and equity markets, and losses suffered by Sovereign Wealth Funds'.

8 The overseas Indian workers' remittances into India are estimated at US$12–15 billion annually. While the UAE, Saudi Arabia and Kuwait are the top destination countries for Overseas Indian workers, Kerala, Tamil Nadu and Andhra Pradesh are among the top sourcing States (MOIA 2007: 3).

9 As Truslé (2009–2010: 4) points out, the conditions of labourers' camps 'greatly depend on the willingness of their employer to provide them with proper conditions. If the employer is not a large company, workers share rooms in some derelict buildings in the centre of the town'.

10 Although in many cases it was found that the migrants continued to stay in the Gulf and make their families prosper over generations (see Ali 2011; Gardner 2011a; Vora 2011).

References

Ahmed, A. 2010. Migrant Domestic Workers in Kuwait: the Role of State Institutions. In *Viewpoints: Migration and the Gulf.* Washington, DC: The Middle East Institute, pp. 27–29.

Ahn, P.-S. 2005. Prospects and Challenges of Out-Migration from South Asia and its Neighboring Countries. *Labour and Development* 11(1): 1–33.

Ahuja, P. and R. Ganguly. 2007. The Fire Within: Naxalite Insurgency Violence in India. *Small Wars and Insurgencies* 18(2): 249–274.

Ali, A. 2011. Going and Coming and Going Again: Second-generation Migrants in Dubai. *Mobilities* 6(4): 553–568.

al-Najjar, S. 2002. Women Migrant Domestic Workers in Bahrain. International Migration Papers 47, International Labour Office, Geneva.

Arnold, F. and N.M. Shah. 1984. Asian Labour Migration to the Middle East. *International Migration Review* 18(2): 294–318.

Auwal, M.A. 2010. Ending the Exploitation of Migrant Workers in the Gulf. *Fletcher Forum of World Affairs* 34(2): 87–108.

Azeez, A. and M. Begum. 2009. Gulf Migration, Remittances and Economic Impact. *Journal of Social Sciences* 20(1): 55–60.

Balagopal, K. 2006. Maoist Movement in Andhra Pradesh. *Economic and Political Weekly* XLI (29): 3183–3187.

Bhachu, P. 1985. *Twice Migrants: East African Sikh Settlers in Britain.* London: Tavistock.

Breeding, M. 2011. India–Gulf Migration: Corruption and Capacity in Regulating Recruitment Agencies. In *Migrant Labour in the Gulf: Working Group Summary Report No. 2*, Center for International and Regional Studies, Georgetown University School of Foreign Service in Qatar.

Puslé, T. 2009–2010. Who's in a Labor Camp? A Socio-economic Analysis of Nepalese Migrants in Qatar. *European Bulletin of Himalayan Research* 35–36: 154–170.

Chammartin, G.M.-F. 2004. Women Migrant Workers' Protection in Arab League States. In S. Esim and M. Smith (eds), *Gender and Migration in Arab States: The Case of Domestic Workers*. Beirut: Regional Office for Arab States, pp. 7–23.

Cherunilam, F. 1987. *Migration: Causes, Correlates, Consequences, Trends and Policies.* Bombay: Himalaya Publishing.

Gardner, A. 2011a. Gulf Migration and the Family. *Journal of Arabian Studies: Arabia, the Gulf, and the Red Sea* 1(1): 3–25.

Gardner, A. 2011b. Why Do They Keep Coming? Labour Migrants in the Gulf States. *Migrant Labour in the Gulf: Working Group Summary Report No 2*, Centre for International and Regional Studies, Georgetown University School of Foreign Service in Qatar.

Gmelch, G. 1980. Return Migration. *Annual Review of Anthropology* 9: 135–159.

Gold, S.J. 2005. Migrant Networks: A Summary and Critique of Relational Approaches to International Migration. In M. Romero and E. Margolis (eds), *The Blackwell Companion to Social Inequalities*. London: Blackwell, pp. 257–285.

Human Rights Watch. 2010. *Slow Reform: Protection of Migrant Domestic Workers in Asia and the Middle East.* New York: Human Rights Watch.

Human Rights Watch. 2012. *For a Better Life: Migrant Worker Abuse in Bahrain and the Government Reform Agenda.* New York: Human Rights Watch.

Jain, P.C. 2007. *Indian Diaspora in West Asia: A Reader.* New Delhi: Manohar Publications.

Jonkers, K. 2008. A Comparative Study of Return Migration Policies Targeting the Highly Skilled in China, India, Mexico, and Argentina. MIREM Analytical Report, AR2008–05, RSCAS/EUI, Florence.

Jureidini, R. 2003. Migrant Workers and Xenophobia in the Middle East. *Identities, Conflict and Cohesion Programme Paper Number 2*, United Nations Research Institute for Social Development, Geneva.

Kapiszewski, A. 2006. Arab versus Asian Migrant Workers in the GCC Countries. UN Expert Group Meeting on International Migration and Development in the Arab Region, Beirut, 15–17 May 2006 (UN/POP/EGM/2006/02).

Khadria, B. 2006. *India: Skilled Migration to Developed Countries, Labour Migration to the Gulf.* Asia Research Institute, National University of Singapore.

Khadria, B. 2010. Paradigm Shifts in India's Migration Policy toward the Gulf. *Middle East Institute Viewpoints*, February 2010, pp. 67–69. Online, available at: www.voltairenet.org/IMG/pdf/Migration_and_the_Gulf.pdf.

Khalaf, S. and S. Alkobaisi. 1999. Migrants' Strategies of Coping and Patterns of Accommodation in the Oil-Rich Gulf Societies: Evidence from the UAE. *British Journal of Middle Eastern Studies* 26(2): 271–298.

Migrant Forum in Asia (MFA). 2008. The Plight of Migrant Workers in UAE, 19 April 2008: Philippines: Migrant Forum in Asia.

Migrant Forum in Asia (MFA). 2012. *Programs and Services for Migrant Workers and Members of their Families in Three Indian States: Kerala, Andhra Pradesh, and Tamil Nadu*, Philippines: Migrant Forum in Asia.

MOIA. 2007. *Issues Relating To Overseas Indians: Fourteenth Report Standing Committee on External Affairs.* New Delhi: Lok Sabha Secretariat.

Nair, P.R.G. 1998. The Process of Migration. In B.A. Prakash (ed.), *Indian Migration to the Middle East: Trends, Patterns and Socio-Economic Impacts.* Rohtak: Spellbound.

Nambiar, A.C.K. 1995. *The Socio-Economic Conditions of Gulf Migrants.* New Delhi: Commonwealth.

Osella, F. and C. Osella. 2000. Migration, Money and Masculinity in Kerala. *Journal of Royal Anthropological Institute* 6: 117–133.

Percot, M. and S.I. Rajan. 2007. Female Emigration from India: Case Study of Nurses. *Economic and Political Weekly* 42(4): 318–325.

Pradhan, S. 2010. India and the Gulf Cooperation Council (GCC): an Economic and Political Perspective. *Strategic Analysis* 34(1): 93–103.

Rahman, A. 2001. *Indian Labour Migration to the Gulf.* New Delhi: Rajat Publications.

Rahman, M.M. 2010. Remittance as a Social Process: the Singapore–Bangladesh Remittance Corridor. *Asia and Pacific Migration Journal* 19(2): 265–294.

Rahman, M.M. 2011. Recruitment of Labour Migrants for the Gulf States: the Bangladeshi Case. ISAS Working Paper No. 132. Institute of South Asian Studies, National University of Singapore.

Rahman, M.M. 2012a. Bangladeshi Labor Migration to the Gulf States: Patterns of Recruitment and Processes. *Canadian Journal of Development Studies* 33(2): 214–230.

Rahman, M.M. 2012b Gendering Migrant Remittances: Evidence from Bangladesh and the United Arab Emirates. *International Migration.*

Rahman, M.M. 2013. Migrant Indebtedness: Bangladeshis in the GCC Countries. *International Migration.*

Rahman, M.M. and L.K. Fee. 2012. Towards a Sociology of Migrant Remittances in Asia: Conceptual and Methodological Challenges. *Journal of Ethnic and Migration Studies* 38(4): 689–706.

Rajan, S.I. and S. Sukendran. 2010. Understanding Female Emigration: Experience of Housemaids. In S.I. Rajan (ed.), *Governance and Labor Migration: India Migration Report 2010.* New Delhi: Routledge, pp. 182–195.

Rajan S.I. and D. Narayana. 2011. The Financial Crisis in the Gulf and its Impact on South Asian Migrant Workers. SANEI Working Paper Series No. 11–13, South Asia Network of Economic Research Institutes, Dhaka.

Reddy, S.U. 2009. In Andhra Pradesh 39 Persons Commit Suicide a Day. Online, available at: http://udumulasudhakarreddy.blogspot.com/2009/11/in-andhra-pradesh-39-persons-commit.html (accessed 10 August 2011).

Sampath, R.P. 2006. Impact of Migration on Rural Power Structure: A Case Study of Karimnagar district in Andhra Pradesh, South India. Unpublished thesis, Jawaharlal Nehru University.

Saxena, R. 2010. *The Middle Class in India: Issues and Opportunities.* Frankfurt: Deutsche Bank Research.

Shah, N.M. 2008. Recent Labour Immigration Policies in the Oil-Rich Gulf: How Effective Are They Likely To Be? *International Publications Paper 52*, Cornell University ILR School.

Sönmez, S., Y. Apostopoulos, D. Tran and S. Rentrope. 2011. Human Rights and Health Disparities for Migrant Workers in the UAE. *Journal of Health and Human Rights: An International Journal* 13(2): 1–19.

Thimothy, R. and S.K. Sasikumar. 2012. *Migration of Women Workers from South Asia to the Gulf.* Noida: V.V. Giri National Labour Institute.

Tsuda, T. 2009. *Diasporic Homecoming: Ethnic Return Migration in Comparative Perspective*. Stanford: Stanford University Press.

Vertovec, S. 2002. Transnational Networks and Skilled Labour Migration. Working Paper 02, Transnational Communities Program, Oxford University.

Vora, N. 2008. Producing Diasporas and Globalization: Indian Middle-Class Migrants in Dubai. *Anthropological Quarterly* 81(2): 377–406.

Vora, N. 2011. From Golden Frontier to Global City: Shifting Forms of Belonging, 'Freedom', and Governance among Indian Businessmen in Dubai. *American Anthropologist* 113(2): 306–318.

Zachariah, K.C. and S.I. Rajan. 2012. *Kerala's Gulf Connection, 1998–2011: Economic and Social Impact of Migration*. Hyderabad: Orient Black Swan.

9 International migration and economic changes in South Asia

The emergence of the middle class

Shahid Javed Burki

> The idea of the future being different from the present is so repugnant to our conventional modes of thought and behaviour that we, most of us, offer a great deal of resistance to acting on it in practice.
>
> (John Maynard Keynes 1937: 13)

There is one unifying theme that runs through this chapter: the rise of the middle class as an important economic, political, and social player in both places – where the diaspora groups live and where they came from. The long bifurcated socio-politico-economic populations now view the middle class as a middle ground. This class is asserting itself in a number of different ways. Of equal importance – but a largely overlooked fact – is that while the middle class in several Western societies – in particular in the United States – is shrinking and losing economic ground to the rich in terms of their share in national income, the South Asian middle class have improved their situation. Their circumstances have improved in terms of their position in the host populations as well as within the diaspora community itself. From this perspective, the diaspora groups can play an even greater role in their original homeland. They will also exert considerable influence on the global market place.

In its Global Trend 2030 Report, the fifth in the series, the United States' National Council regards the growth of the global middle class as a tectonic shift between now and 2030, and mentions that middle classes everywhere in the developing world are poised to expand substantially in terms of both absolute numbers and the percentage of the population that can claim middle-class status during the next 15–20 years (United States National Intelligence Council 2012: v).

The middle class has increased in size in all South Asian countries. There is no consensus among scholars about how many people fall into this economic and social category. The scholars and the institutions that have researched in this area have used a number of different methodologies to define this group. Lopez-Calva *et al.* (2012) provide a comprehensive review of the recent literature on the middle class in Asia. India's National Council of Applied Economic Research (NCAER) has been at the forefront of shaping this debate.

The NCAER's current definition identifies the middle class as comprising two sub-groups: 'seekers' with annual household income of between Rs.200,000 and Rs.500,000, and 'strivers' with annual household income of between Rs.500,000 and Rs.1,000,000 at 2001/2002 prices. Assuming an average household size of five people and converting into constant 2005 purchasing power parity (PPP) dollars, these numbers would be about US$8 to US$20 per capita per day for 'seekers', and US$20 to US$40 per capita per day for 'strivers'. These income lines are much higher than those used by the World Bank in the extensive work that the institution has completed in studying the impact on the economies of the countries as a consequence of the rise of the middle class. Other researchers have also followed this approach. The most-often employed measure is the definition of 'income lines', one to estimate the number of poor, and the other to count the rich. All those that fall in between these two lines are counted as the middle class.

Several scholars have used levels of consumption as a measure of the size of the middle class. In the extensive work done by the McKinsey Global Initiative, a considerable amount of which used India as the case study, the focus was placed on the levels of consumption. Some have used even more comprehensive criteria, such as weighting the numbers by different attributes that distinguish the middle class from the poor.

While most estimates of the size of the middle class range between 500 million to 950 million people in South Asia's three largest countries – India, Pakistan and Bangladesh – some researchers such as Christian Meyer and Nancy Birdsall of the Center for Global Development have come up with much smaller numbers (Meyer and Birdsall 2012). They estimate the middle class to be at an implausibly low level of only 70 million for India or less than 100 million for all of South Asia.

In this chapter, we will work with the range of 500–950 million for the size of the middle class in South Asia (Table 9.2). The lower figure suggests that 25 per cent of the South Asian populations can be regarded as belonging to the middle class; the larger number is over twice that proportion, or 60 per cent of the total population. The larger figure includes what economists call the near poor. While these people are no longer living in absolute poverty, they remain exceptionally vulnerable to the changes in their economic environment. A significant number of them have migrated from poverty to the lower middle class status because of

Table 9.1 Class distribution of South Asian population: share in income (percentage)

	Poor (bottom 30%)	*Lower middle class*	*Upper middle class*	*Rich (top 10%)*
Bangladesh	15	25	33	27
India	15	24	32	29
Pakistan	17	23	34	26
Sri Lanka	16	28	26	30

Source: author's estimates based on the World Bank's income distribution data.

Table 9.2 Class incomes in South Asia

	India	*Pakistan*	*Bangladesh*	*Total*
Poor				
Number (millions)	371	54	47	472
Total income (US$ billions)	276	39	17	332
Per capita income (US$)	743	722	377	705
Lower middle class				
Number (millions)	371	54	46	471
Total income (US$ billions)	442	53	29	524
Per capita income (US$)	1,192	985	630	1,113
Upper middle class				
Number (millions)	371	54	46	471
Total income (US$ billions)	589	79	33	701
Per capita income (US$)	1,589	1,454	829	1,516
Rich				
Number (millions)	124	18	15	157
Total income (US$ billions)	534	60	31	625
Per capita income (US$)	4,308	3,333	2,066	3,981

Source: author's estimates based on the World Bank's income distribution data.

the remittances they have received from the members of their families living and working abroad. The number of people in South Asia that have moved out of poverty and joined the lower middle class as a result of the remittances these countries have received should be an area of considerable academic and policy interest. However, relatively little work has been done in this policy field. By making some estimates, this chapter attempts to fill the existing analytical gaps. Since they are based on a series of assumptions however, they should be treated with some caution.

As shown in Table 9.3, remittances, when measured in terms of flows per capita of the population living in poverty, were the highest for Bangladesh – US$106 per year in the five-year period between 2007 and 2011. This was a significant amount when viewed in the context of the yearly income of this group. However, not all the poor received remittances. Using Pakistan as an example to carry forward this line of thinking, we can roughly gauge the impact that remittances received by the poor have on them. Pakistan has about three million people working in the Middle East. Most of them are in the construction sector or in basic services. If we assume that two-thirds of them are from lower income groups and that they send money back to these people, there would be some two million households – or 10–12 million people – receiving incomes from abroad. Since approximately two-fifths of the total flow (about US$5 billion) that Pakistan receives from abroad by way of remittances go to the poor, the amount received works out to about US$500 a year per capita for poor households. This amount is enough to graduate four million people a year into the ranks of the lower-middle class. Without remittances, the size of the Pakistani middle class

Table 9.3 Worker remittances into four South Asian nations, 2007–2011

	Total (US$ million)	*Yearly average (US$ billion)*	*Per head poor (US$)*	*Per head of poor and lower middle class (US$)*
Bangladesh	48,897	9,779	92	106
India	253,696	50,739	742	68
Pakistan	43,707	8,741	108	81
Sri Lanka	18,045	3,609	–	–
Total	364,345	72,868		

Source: author's estimates based on the World Bank's income data.

would have been 40 per cent smaller than it is today. In other words, the migration to the Middle East of a sizeable number of low-income people has already profoundly affected the size of the middle class in the country. The same is true for other large South Asian countries – even more so for Bangladesh, although somewhat less for India. These estimates throw new light on how the South Asian diaspora groups in the Middle East are impacting their countries of origin.

Any large change in the levels of remittances can move this group up and down the income distribution scale. While the countries that receive large amounts of remittances can only marginally affect the quantum of flow, they must be prepared to intervene meaningfully to protect those who would be hurt if the flow suddenly declines. This can happen if the price of oil falls or if the labour-importing countries change their preferences about the places from which the workers would be allowed to come for work. The much-needed safety net will be an entirely new area of state activity for the governments in South Asia. This should be one of the subjects of concern in public policy that arises out of the phenomenon of diaspora creation.

The upper-middle class – an estimated 471 million people – has also benefitted from having some family and friends working abroad, but their help has been and will continue to be of a different nature. In the new age of rapid, almost instantaneous flow of information, ideas are transmitted fast. One particular area where the upper-middle class in the South Asian expatriate communities will profoundly influence those who live and work in the home countries is the appropriate role of the state. This subject has acquired considerable importance because of the recent developments in the economies of South Asia.

For more than four decades, South Asian countries adopted a home-grown model of economic management and development. This model was influenced by India's first prime minister, Jawaharlal Nehru. Several countries in the neighbourhood also adopted what India developed as the economic model. The result was the opposite of what was expected to be achieved. The state weighed the economy down with its dominating presence instead of lifting it. It also did little to reduce the incidence of poverty.

The break in this model came in the early 1990s. Half a dozen members of the Indian diaspora, having learnt their trade living and working abroad, picked up a great deal of what was incorporated in the Washington Consensus set of policies. This advocated the state's withdrawal and its replacement by private enterprise. Accordingly, the state was brought down from the Nehruvian heights, and private enterprise was allowed to climb up the economic hill to take its place. Now, a quarter of a century later, a new generation of expatriates is providing the intellectual capital to apply another twist to the structure of the Indian economy. The same kind of transformation is under way in neighbouring Pakistan.

When the first South Asian Diaspora Convention was held under the auspices of the Institute of South Asian Studies (ISAS) in Singapore, the South Asian economy had come out of the global slowdown almost unscathed. India, the sub-continent's premier economy, saw some slowdown, but it was not as significant as was the case for its partners in the BRICS (Brazil, Russia, India, China and South Africa) club. The situation is very different just over two years later. There is a loss of momentum that was built up over a period of a couple of decades. In the two-year period between 2011 and 2014, the South Asian rate of GDP growth declined by as much as three percentage points a year. This slowdown has little to do with the world outside the sub-continent's borders. It is the result of solely internal factors. It was India that led the way up; it is India that is leading the way down. To reverse the new trend, South Asians will have to rethink the growth model that has guided their policy makers for more than two decades. At the centre of this model were 'three emphases': a greater role for the private sector; greater integration of the sub-continent's economies with the industrial world; and rapid industrialisation as the driver of growth. All these need to be rethought and possibly reversed. Members of the diaspora groups can potentially play active roles in all three areas.

As already indicated, by pushing the state off the commanding heights of the economy, the South Asians, starting with both India and Pakistan in 1991, and followed soon after by Bangladesh, gave private enterprise a freer hand than it ever had in their economies. Expectedly, this change in the orientation of public policy quickened the pace of development. In the words of Gurucharan Das, the most articulate advocate of 'new India', the series of reforms aimed at doing away with what was called the 'licence raj' – an excessive control of the state in most economic matters – awakened India. The rate of growth of the Indian economy jumped from 3 to 3.5 per cent – the rate the Indian economist K.N. Raj had labelled the Hindu rate of growth – to 9 to 9.5 per cent. This almost three-fold increase in the rate of economic expansion placed India in an entirely different class of nations. In terms of the increase in GDP, India began to resemble China. In the famous words of president Barack Obama during his visit to India in November 2010, India was no longer a rising power, it had already risen.

This euphoria lasted for about a decade before the Indian economy began to stumble. While a great deal will be written to investigate the circumstances that led to India's sudden loss of economic momentum by 2012–2014 in the future, some things already seem clear. The Indian expansion was fuelled by the extraordinary growth of a few sectors of the economy and of a few locations in the country. Indian economic expansion was not what the 'economic left' had begun to call 'inclusive growth'. By allowing private enterprise to lead the way, the Indian leadership lost sight of the main objective of economic development: to relieve human misery and alleviate mass poverty. As a result of the model adopted by the Indian government in the early 1990s, income disparities have widened. Some people have benefitted a great deal, while many others have fallen way behind. The same is true of the Indian states, and the same situation can be seen in other countries of South Asia. In an important book, *Red Tape*, anthropologist Akhil Gupta, who teaches at the University of California, Los Angeles, offered an insightful diagnosis of the problem that India and the rest of South Asia face. He assigns the rigid and hide-bound bureaucracy the blame for keeping millions of Indians in poverty while the country was making important economic strides.

Pakistan, South Asia's other large economy, suffered from an entirely different set of problems. The country's economic performance hit a number of new lows during this five-year period. At this time the economy was in deep recession. For the last six years, the rate of GDP growth averaged 3 per cent. This is not high enough to provide productive employment to the workforce that is also growing at 3 per cent a year. The IMF has estimated that the economy must expand by at least 7 per cent a year to fully absorb the new entrants into the workforce who number about two million. The inability to accommodate the newcomers to the labour force will result in more stresses in an already fragile society. The tax-to-GDP ratio has fallen to a record low – at less than 9 per cent of GDP. It is one of the lowest among emerging nations. With such a low rate, the government is unable to invest in creating the needed infrastructure and improving the state of human development. Most worrying is the sharp decline in both public and private investment. At about 11 per cent of GDP and with the incremental capital output ratio of about four – the proportion of GDP that needs to be invested to produce a one percentage point increase in national output – Pakistan cannot make its GDP rise by more than 2.5 to 3 per cent a year. Also troubling is the continuous decline in the country's share in international trade. In other words, Pakistan faces a grim economic future unless the makers of public policy address the many structural problems the country faces with some much-needed seriousness.

What is clear is that the political establishment in South Asia cannot continue with 'business as usual'. It needs a new development paradigm that would bring the state back into economic management – not to climb the commanding heights as it did under the influence of Jawaharlal Nehru, but to provide for the less advantaged segments of the population. In designing the new paradigm, several influential voices from the South Asian diaspora groups have begun to be heard. Of many of these is Amartya Sen, the Nobel Prize winning economist, originally from India, who advocated for an increased role for the Indian state at all levels – at the central as well as at the state and local levels. His book, '*An Uncertain Glory*', co-authored with Jean Dreze, argues that there have been major failures in India to foster participatory growth and to make good use of public resources generated by economic growth to enhance living conditions.

The new paradigm would be one that provides care for the poor, the dispossessed, and the vulnerable. Attempts are being made in many parts of South Asia to use the state for that purpose. But the schemes that are being funded with generous amounts are borrowed from colonial times when a highly rule-bound bureaucracy was meant to aid the poor without involving the intended beneficiaries in the process. Other approaches that produce greater success have been developed, and some of these were the outcome of the work of South Asians working in several multilateral and bilateral development agencies and think tanks. One example of this is the income support fund that provides cash to the needy, rather than items of food. The programmes that do the latter are subject to enormous graft. According to some assessments, as much as 80 per cent of the amount spent by the government does not reach the intended beneficiaries. The income support programmes, developed by the World Bank and tried with some success in Latin America and the Middle East, identify the deserving by mapping poverty and selecting from censuses and surveys the attributes that make so many people vulnerable to the circumstances over which they have no control. With this information at hand, the state makes direct deposits in the bank accounts maintained by the poor. In most cases, these happen to be poor women. The state functionaries who would be involved in the traditional food distribution programmes would be kept out. The Benazir Income Support Programme (BISP) in Pakistan is an example of this type of effort. It has advanced significantly the proportion of leakage.

In other words, the South Asian diaspora community, by working abroad in various development organisations, has gained good understanding of the process of broad-based economic progress. By bringing this experience and knowledge to their homeland, the diaspora members can introduce new development paradigms to their homelands.

South Asian diaspora

South Asian diaspora groups spread all over the globe have been studied in some detail by academia as well as policy makers. Formed over several centuries, these communities have a total of between 35 million and 50 million people. The smaller number is for those that have retained some formal links with their former homelands, while the larger number includes people who have lived outside South Asia for generations. In other words, between 2.2 per cent and 3.1 per cent of the people of South Asian live outside their countries of origin. This proportion is much higher for Bangladesh and Pakistan as compared with India. Some of these South Asian diaspora groups are very old; they have seen several generations from the time they emerged as distinct communities. The largest number is in the Middle East, but there are sizable communities in Europe, North America, East Africa and Southeast Asia. Of late, Australia has become the favoured destination for South Asians with higher skill levels.

The socio-economic composition of these communities has changed significantly over the last couple of centuries. While most of the academic and policy work done on the subject of diaspora groups has focused on the flow of remittances and how this has augmented domestic savings and increased the rate of economic expansion in the labour-exporting countries, this chapter adds three dimensions to the unfolding story. These cover the enlargement of the middle class in the South Asian sub-continent; provision of various kinds of management skills by the members of the South Asian diaspora groups who are returning home; and the impact on the evolution of the political orders in the countries of origin.

The capital flows associated with the people of South Asian origin living abroad is large, averaging US$73 billion a year over the last five years, or more than 5 per cent of the combined gross national incomes (GNIs) in the sub-continent. That said, what is of considerable significance is the impact of this flow of money on the socio-economic structures of the societies receiving them. Remittances sent by the workers living abroad have created a large middle class in the South Asian sub-continent. Now estimated at 950 million people in the three large countries of the sub-continent – India, Pakistan and Bangladesh – the money that has come in has added 350 million to the middle class population. The number of people graduating from poverty and entering the ranks of the middle class is about ten million a year. At this time (2013), the number is evenly balanced between the lower and the upper classes – 471 million in each case. By the end of the decade – by the year 2020 – the lower middle class will have 550 million people while the number in the upper middle class will remain about the same. This skewed distribution within the middle class will have enormous economic and political consequences. Most of the new entrants into this class are those who have graduated from the ranks of the poor. The South Asian diaspora groups have, by impacting significantly on the size of the middle class in the sub-continent, substantially reduced the incidence of poverty and changed the economic structures of these societies. This trend will continue in the future as remittances continue to flow into these countries from the members of the diaspora groups.

The South Asian diaspora groups have skills and experiences not readily available in their home countries. These relate to several activities, including economic planning and management. The sudden economic downturn in South Asia and the loss of dynamism in the area demand new ways of thinking about the old development paradigm. The model that delivered high rates of economic growth in several South Asian countries, particularly in India, has to be re-examined. For instance, the role of the state has to be redefined in order to regenerate growth and to move towards what economists call an 'inclusive' development. Several South Asian diaspora economists and members with economic management skills have been brought back to their countries of origin to help re-ignite growth and develop plans for delivering rewards more equitably. Some of the expertise the South Asians have acquired through their work abroad may help to create a new development paradigm in which the state will have a different role to play. This will be consequential for the future of the emerging world, as was the development experience of what were once called the miracle economies of East Asia. The sector of finance – in particular banking – is another area where returning migrants are playing important roles in what were once their homelands.

What is of equal importance is the interaction between the middle classes of the South Asian diaspora groups and those in their countries of origin. Facilitated by the information revolution, this interaction has created a bigger political space for the South Asian middle classes. They are now introducing new social values and political thinking in the sub-continent. As a result, new borders are being visualised, beyond which the emerging middle classes will not allow the domestic political systems to go. The impact on the evolution of the political order will be more pronounced in the relatively newer and still-evolving domestic orders in Bangladesh and Pakistan; India, with a well-established political system in the area, may also be affected. For the first two, middle class activism is likely to foster resistance to any significant departure from democratic norms. The middle class may also use the street and the public square to ensure that this does not happen. Also – and this has relevance for India as well – the middle class is not likely to allow religious extremism, or extremism of any kind, to take deep roots in South Asian political soil. The growing economic power of the middle class and its increasing number will keep the South Asian political orders relatively open and liberal. This will remain the case even after a Hindu nationalist party, the BJP, won a landslide victory in India's 2014 elections.

Overview of the South Asian economic circumstances

To place the discussion that follows in its proper context – in particular the discussion on the impact South Asian diaspora groups are having in expanding the size of the lower middle class – it would be appropriate to begin with a short description of some features of the South Asian economy, especially those concerning the incidence of poverty and the distribution of incomes. As shown in Table 9.4, the combined size of the populations of South Asia's four large countries – India, Pakistan, Bangladesh and Sri Lanka – is a little under 1.6 billion people (Table 9.4). This is growing at an annual rate of 1.5 per cent, which means that the sub-continent is adding 24 million people a year to its already large population. India, with 1.24 billion people, accounts for 77.5 per cent of South Asia's

Table 9.4 South Asia: basic economic indicators

	Bangladesh	*India*	*Pakistan*	*Sri Lanka*	*Total*
Population (million)	155	1,237	179	20	1,591
GNI (US$ billion)	116	1,824	231	59	2,230
GNI (per capita US$)	748	1,489	1,291	2,950	–
Gini coefficient	32	34	30	36	–
Poverty incidence (% of population)	31.5	29.8	22.3	8.9	–

Source: World Bank, *World Development Indicators*, 2013.

total population. The country's share in the total GNI of the area is even higher at 81.1 per cent. Such a prominent space occupied in the regional economy means that the country would determine the future of the sub-continent in several different ways. This is the case even when South Asia is the least economically integrated region in the world. Once the economies in the region become more open to one another, the impact on the rest of the sub-continent will be profound. The move towards regional integration may pick up speed with the assumption of power by two business-oriented leaders. Mian Nawaz Sharif in Pakistan and Narendra Modi in India have shown interest in casting off the burdens of history and using economic integration as a way to improve their citizens' welfare.

There is a fairly significant difference in the levels of incomes per head of the population in the region, with Sri Lanka having achieved a level that is almost four times that of Bangladesh. In spite of a fairly high rate of GNI growth in the last several years, Bangladesh remains the poorest economy among South Asia's large economies. The incidence of poverty in the country is high compared to that in other countries – three and a half times that of Sri Lanka. Income distribution, when measured in terms of Gini coefficient, is less than that of Sri Lanka as well as India. According to the World Bank's estimates, Pakistan has the best income distribution in the sub-continent.

These numbers provide a useful background against which we can view the analysis that follows in the chapter. One of the main points is that the remittances sent by the workers – in particular those who have gone to the Middle East, since most of them are from low-income groups – are contributing to the alleviation of poverty in South Asia. These capital flows have made a sizeable contribution to increasing the size of the lower middle class by helping a large number of people to climb out of poverty. Since Bangladesh is a large contributor to the workforce around the world, the contribution made by their remittances will make a great deal of difference to the level of poverty in the country. Trade also helps to close both personal and locational income gaps. Greater trade among the South Asians should help the region's less-developed areas.

Rise of the South Asian diaspora groups

The South Asian diaspora groups were formed by several waves of migration. Initially, the outward flow from the sub-continent consisted of people from the countryside with low levels of skills. They were taken as plantation workers to several parts of the British Empire as indentured labour. Some historians have equated the export of this labour from India as slavery.[1] Over time, this group of South Asians became fully integrated into the cultures of the societies into which they were placed. In several islands in the Caribbean, the cultures developed by the South Asian migrant communities have become the dominant ones. There was some out-migration to Britain while India was a part of the British Empire; but in terms of numbers, this was relatively insignificant.[2] That changed after the end of the colonial period when there was a sizeable movement of people from the various economic classes, mostly to Britain and North America.

Those migrating to Britain had low skill levels. They were brought in to revive the industries hurt by the Second World War. Putting them back into operation required some skills. According to the 2011 census, there were 4.214 million Asians in England and Wales. Of these, 2.33 million were South Asians. In Britain, Indians accounted for 2.5 per cent of the total population, Pakistanis 2 per cent, and Bangladeshis 0.75 per cent. Scotland has another 90,000 South Asian residents. Most of these are located in the city of Glasgow. Even after passing through several generations, the migrants to Britain have yet to fully integrate into the host-country culture. This has caused considerable apprehension in Britain; especially after some of the South Asian youths opted for extremist politics and committed several acts of violence that took dozens of lives.

In the 1970s and 1980s, millions of low-skill workers from South Asia headed to the Middle East to work on hundreds of construction sites set up to build infrastructure, office parks, and housing estates in the area during the first oil boom. This group was largely made up of temporary workers recruited on fixed-term contracts. They were separated from host populations by the requirement that they live in isolated worker-camps. The 1990s and 2000s brought another wave of professional migration, with countries such as Australia being added to the list of favoured nations. This group is in the process of becoming well integrated into the host populations. Several of its members are now occupying important public positions in Britain, Canada and the United States.

The development of the South Asian communities in a number of countries outside the sub-continent's borders has been a subject of much interest for many years for both scholars and policy makers alike. Although, as indicated, migration from South Asia has gone on for centuries, interest in this subject has increased following the movement of millions of construction workers to the oil-exporting countries of the Middle East. As shown in Tables 9.5 and 9.6, surges in terms of the number of people leaving South Asia every year for foreign lands continue, even after the end of the first oil boom in the mid-1970s.

While the large annual increases in the number of migrants from Bangladesh and Sri Lanka (14.3 per cent a year for the former and 20.1 per cent a year for the latter) suggest that the reason for this significant outflow may be domestic insecurity, the large rate for India (9.3 per cent a year), South Asia's most stable country, indicates that other factors must also be at play (see Table 9.5 for

Table 9.5 Number of people migrated in recent years, net (thousands)

Country name	*2005*	*2010*	*Growth rate*
Bangladesh	1,493	2,908	14.3
India	1,923	3,000	9.3
Pakistan	1,750	2,000	2.7
Sri Lanka	100	250	20.1

Source: World Bank, *World Development Indicators*, 2013.

Table 9.6 Worker remittances to South Asia (current US$ millions)

	2007	*2008*	*2009*	*2010*	*2011*	*Growth rate*
Bangladesh	6,553	8,925	10,521	10,850	12,068	16.5
(% of GDP)	9.6	11.2	11.8	10.8	10.8	
India	37,217	49,977	49,204	53,480	63,818	14.4
(% of GDP)	3.0	4.1	3.6	3.1	3.4	
Pakistan	5,998	7,039	8,717	9,690	12,263	19.6
(% of GDP)	4.2	4.3	5.4	5.5	5.8	
Sri Lanka	2,507	2,925	3,337	4,123	5,153	19.7
(% of GDP)	7.8	7.2	7.9	8.3	8.7	

Source: World Bank, *World Development Indicators*, 2013.

migration statistics). It was mostly the 'push' factor in the case of the two former countries, while the 'pull' – the demand for Indian skills in a number of modern sectors – also contributed to the continuing outflow. Consequently, remittances have continued to remain a significant source of foreign capital for these Asian states. In 2011, the total amount received by the four countries mentioned in Table 9.6 was estimated at US$93 billion, a little more than 3.5 per cent of their combined GDP. Putting it another way, about 1 per cent of the increase in the GDP of these countries can be attributed to the inflow of remittances. For Bangladesh, the contribution is almost three times as large. One half of the rate of economic growth in that country was the result of the remittances received from the citizens living and working outside the country.

While the subject of the contribution that remittances have made to the South Asian economies has been studied, cross-border migration receives much less attention in the existing literature. Cross-border migration is important because it includes the other forms of influence that diaspora groups have had on their countries of origin. This chapter looks at one of them: The impact of the diaspora groups on the size of one socio-economic class – the middle class. By remitting large amounts of money to their countries of origin, the diaspora groups have made a significant contribution to poverty alleviation. Millions of people have graduated from poverty to the status of lower middle class as a result of the support they have received from the members of their families who have left their homes to work abroad.

Rise of the South Asian middle class: a new dynamic

The South Asian diaspora has begun to influence their countries of origin in several important ways. The impact on the area's economies is not the only contribution overseas South Asians are making to the sub-continent. The diaspora groups have contributed significantly to increasing the size of the middle class. They have also brought new political thinking and social values to the region's large and growing middle class. It can be argued – as the sociologist

Riaz Hassan has done in his work – that diaspora groups' influence on their homelands have created two types of middle classes. He calls them the 'vernacular' and the 'cosmopolitan', with the former under the influence of those communities that were formed in the Middle East, and the latter under the influence of those living in the West.[3] In both cases, the middle class has expanded its political presence. This was done by forcing the old establishment to surrender a bit of the area it traditionally occupied. With the lower middle class now asserting itself in politics with greater energy, there is a noticeable decline in old clientele-based politics. This was clearly evident in the May 2013 elections in Pakistan.

As a result of the rise of the middle class, the political systems of South Asia are now less vulnerable to non-democratic moves – contrary to what had happened in both Bangladesh and Pakistan on several occasions – and also to extremism. The latter conclusions are difficult to argue for, particularly in the case of Pakistan, which continues to experience considerable violence perpetrated by several extremist elements. Some of these have received financial support from the residents of the more conservative Arab states that are now home to millions of Pakistani workers. One example of the damage they are doing is the bombing of a Christian church in Peshawar on 22 September 2013 that resulted in the death of more than 80 people. That notwithstanding, it is unlikely that the extremists will expand their influence, let alone capture the institutions of the state as some have begun to fear. In June 2014, Pakistan launched a long awaited anti-terror military operation that was previously postponed several times – Zarb-e-Azb. Riaz Hassan has reached the same conclusion based on extensive field research (Hassan 2002: 234).

In fact, the middle class in Muslim South Asia will emulate the behaviour of those in large Muslim countries such as Egypt and Turkey. In the case of the former, it was the middle class youth that first drove an autocratic government from power, and then rebelled against a government that used what it saw as its democratic mandate to institute a system that would have advanced the role of Islam in politics. The Muslim Brotherhood government went well beyond what the middle class was prepared to accept. Likewise, the middle class youth in Turkey was successful in exercising the same moderating influence on the expressed preferences of that country's ruling party that had deep Islamic roots. The same moderating presence can be expected from the middle class in South Asia's Muslim countries; and this will be the result, to some considerable extent, of the influence of the diaspora groups.

'More generally, values shift and demand for socio-political change rises as more individuals move up into the middle class', write the authors of the Global Trends, 2013 (US National Intelligence Council 2012: 10).

> Historically the rise of a middle class has led to populism and dictatorships as well as pressures for democracy. The value of US$12,000 GDP per capita income is sometimes considered the level above which democracies do not revert to authoritarian systems.

Also, 'with the expansion of the middle class, income inequalities – which have been a striking characteristic of the rising developing states – may begin to lessen in the developing world' (US National Intelligence Council 2012: 11).

Will the South Asian diaspora continue to contribute to the sub-continent's economic, political, and social development? The answer is yes, even if no additional large-scale migration takes place. The current South Asian diaspora groups, even with no addition to their numbers through migration, will continue to increase at the rate of 1.5 per cent a year – the rate of natural increase corresponding to those in what were once their homelands. Their economic base will also continue to expand, as will their per capita income. The latter will happen as the members of the diaspora move up the economic scale in their adopted countries.

In so far as new migration is concerned, there are two contributing factors working in opposite directions. For much of today's rich world, there will be significant decline in the rate of fertility resulting in reductions in the size of its population. On the other hand, most developing nations in Asia and Africa will continue to see large increases in their populations. Some global demographic balancing would be of advantage to both groups of countries. The poor will benefit from an increase in the size of their diaspora groups; the rich will be rewarded, despite a slowdown in the aging of their populations, with the infusion of young people by way of immigration. However, there exists an opposing factor: the growing anti-immigration sentiment in many rich countries. In his new book *Exodus*, the economist Paul Collier addresses the question: How much new migration is beneficial and for whom?

He answers the question from three perspectives: that of the migrants, the countries of their origin, and the countries to which they move. The migrants clearly benefit. If they do not, they would go back home. After they move, the migrants' 'productivity rockets upwards', because they are 'escaping from countries with dysfunctional social models' (Collier 2013, cited in *The Economist* 2013a). Workers from the developing world, using not very different skills but by operating in a very different environment, are able to see an increase in their productivity, and hence in their incomes. However, Collier believes that continued mass immigration threatens the cultural cohesion of rich countries. 'A large unabsorbed Diaspora may cling to the cultural norms that made its country of origin dysfunctional and spread them to the host country' (Collier 2013, cited in *The Economist* 2013b). Collier, writing from Britain, must have had in mind the perverse behaviour of some of the Muslim youths who settled with their families in his country. They failed to assimilate even after generations spent in the host country. Some of them resent the culture of the adopted land so much that they have used violence as a form of expression. According to a review of the Collier book by the magazine, *The Economist*, 'furthermore when a society becomes too heterogeneous, its people may be unwilling to pay for a generous welfare state. Support for redistribution dwindles if tax payers think the benefits will be for people unlike them' (Collier 2013, cited in *The Economist* 2013a). For a good example of a response of this kind, we may look no further than at the shutdown of the US government on 1 October 2013, the start of that country's new fiscal year.

The shutdown lasted for 16 days and did some serious damage to the US economy. The American political right is obsessed with what it sees as the cost to society resulting from the welfare demands of the segments of society they find undeserving of any state support that uses tax dollars. These segments of people include the new class of migrants. This is the class that will benefit from the Affordable Care Act, also known as Obamacare. The right sees it as a giant welfare programme for the poor who can't afford health insurance unless it is subsidised by the state. In light of developments such as these, it may no longer be possible for the worker-surplus countries to send many more people to today's rich world.

Conclusion

This chapter shifts the focus of attention to the interplay between two sets of middle classes. One set belongs to the diaspora groups, and the other to their original homelands. The influence of the former on the latter will increase as the middle classes in the labour-exporting countries expand, as the contacts between those in South Asia and those in the diaspora groups grow, and as the political and economic systems mature. Much of the increase in the size of the middle class is occurring at the lower end of the income distribution scale. Liberated from the need to produce most of what they themselves need to consume, the new entrants to the ranks of the middle class are creating new demands that the business community has not fully understood as yet. This requires a major shift in the pattern of domestic production and distribution, as well as in the development of the infrastructure needed to bring about this change. The middle-class rise is already changing the business landscape in South Asia. In a story about the evolving Indian economy, *The Economist* wrote: 'India's villages and towns, far from the gaze of foreigners and urban elite, have been on a tear' (2013b: 34).

> It means people can turn their energy to starting businesses and escaping subsistence farming. Poultry production is booming, as it has become easier to get chickens to market. Villagers eat more processed food – India's artery-clogging pudding *gulab jamun*, now comes in packets, made in small factories in nearby towns.
>
> (*The Economist* 2013b: 34)

This is also the conclusion reached by the McKinsey Global Institute in its work on the rise of the Indian middle class. Three-quarters of India's (projected) consumer market in 2025 does not exist today – about 52.6 trillion rupees a year in future purchases will be up for grabs. Also, India's rapid upward mobility means that many of India's households will be new consumers, enjoying significant discretionary consumption in the organised economy for the first time in their lives. The rise of the middle class will transform the world of business in India.

> Incumbent (companies) and challengers alike face a sea change. India's incumbents, mostly domestic companies, will start with many advantages: Existing relationships with customers, an understanding of their needs, and recognised brands. The incumbents also have established distributional channels – very important in a country of vast geography and limited infrastructure.
>
> (Beinhocker *et al.* 2007: 59–60)

One major conclusion that emerges from the analysis offered here is that in looking at the impact of the South Asian diaspora groups, it is important to go beyond the flow of finance. The impact should be understood in terms of how these groups are helping to reshape the societies from which they originally hail. This chapter examines in some detail how the resources that are flowing back from the diaspora groups have resulted in vastly expanding the size of the middle class. This is particularly the case for those who are at the lower end of the income distribution scale within the middle class. The increase in the size of this group and the increase in its aggregate income are changing the structure of demand, which, in turn, is creating new opportunities for the businesses operating in the sub-continent.

Notes

1 The historian Hugh Tinker chronicled the use of the indentured Indian labour on the sugar and other plantations in various parts of the British Empire in the nineteenth century. See his *A New System of Slavery: Export of Indian Labor Overseas*, New Delhi: Hansib Publications, 2nd edition, 1993; and *Banyan Tree: Overseas Emigrants from India, Pakistan and Bangladesh*, London: Oxford University Press, 1977.

2 There is rich literature on the subject of migration from India to Britain during the colonial period. See Michael H. Fischer, *Counterflows to Colonialism: Indian Traveller and Settler in Britain 1600–1857*, London: Orient Black Swan, 2006. See the same author's Excluding and Including 'Natives of India': Early Nineteenth Century Race Relations in Britain, *Comparative Studies of South Asia, Africa, and the Middle East* 27(127): 303–314, 2007.

3 Professor Riaz Hassan's conversation with the author.

References

Akhtar, A. 2013. *Disgraced: A Play*. New York: Back Bay Books.

Beinhocker, E.D., D. Farrell and A.S. Zainulbhai. 2007. Tracking the Growth of the Indian Middle Class. *McKinsey Quarterly* 3: 59–60.

Burki, S.J. 2011a. South Asian Diasporas: Agents of Change in a Poorly Integrated Region. ISAS Special Report 03, 19 July 2011.

Burki, S.J. 2011b. *South Asia and New World Order*. London: Routledge.

Burki, S.J. 2014. Pakistan's Anti-Terror Offensive: The Zarb-e-Azb Operation. *ISAS Insight* 255, 20 June 2014.

Chun, N. 2010. Middle Class Size in the Past, Present and Future: a Descriptive Analysis of Distributional Trends, and Projections. Asian Development Bank Working Paper, Manila.

Chun, N. 2011. Estimating the Middle Class in Pakistan. Working Paper 2011–77, Pakistan Institute of Development Economics, Islamabad.

Collier, P. 2013. *Exodus: Migration, New Migration is Changing Our World*. London: Oxford University Press.

Das, G. 2002. *India Unbound: the Social and Economic Revolution from Independence to the Global Age*. New York: Anchor.

Economist, The. 2013a. Migration: the Mobile Masses: the Costs and Benefits of Mass Immigration. 28 September 2013. Online, available at: www.economist.com/news/books-and-arts/21586813-costs-and-benefits-mass-immigration-mobile-masses (accessed 8 August 2014).

Economist, The. 2013b. India's Informal Economy: Hidden Value. 28 September, 2013, p. 34.

Feingold, M. 2012. The New Jews: LCT3 Hosts Ayad Akhtar's Disgraced Dinner Party. In *Village Voice*, 24 October 2012. Online, available at: www.villagevoice.com/2012-10-24/theater/the-new-jews-lct3-hosts-ayad-akhtar-s-disgraced-dinner-party/full/ (accessed 8 August 2014).

Fischer, M.H. 2006. *Counterflows to Colonialism: India Traveller and Settler in Britain 1600–1857*. London: Orient Black Swan.

Fischer, M.H. 2007. Excluding and Including 'Natives of India': Early Nineteenth Century Race Relations in Britain. *Comparative Studies of South Asia, Africa, and the Middle East* 27(127): 303–314.

Global Voices. 2007. South Asia, 'Slaving in the Middle East'.

Gupta, A. 2012. *Red Tape: Bureaucracy, Structural Violence and Poverty in India*. London: Duke University Book.

Hassan, R. 2002. *Faithlines: Muslim Conceptions of Islam and Society*. London: Oxford University Press.

Her Majesty's Government. 2011. *Ethnicity and National Identity in England and Wales*, London.

Keynes, J.M. 1937. Some Economic Consequences of a Declining Population. *Eugenics Review* 29(1): 13–17.

Meyer, C. and N. Birdsall. 2012. New Estimates of India's Middle Class. Technical Note, Center for Global Development.

Lahiri, J. 2010. *Interpreter of Maladies*. New York: Houghton Mifflin Harcourt.

Lopez-Calva, L.F., J. Rigolini and F. Torche. 2012. Is There Something Such a Thing as Middle Class Values? Working Paper 286, Center for Global Development, Washington, DC.

National Council of Applied Economic Research (NCAER). 2010. Rich Indian Households Outnumber Low Income Families. *Hindustan Times*, 1 August 2010, p. 9.

Ratha, D. and S. Plaza. 2011. Harnessing Diasporas. *Finance and Development* 48(3).

Sen, A. and J. Dreze. 2013. *An Uncertain Glory*. Princeton, New Jersey: Princeton University Press.

Tinker, H. 1977. *Banyan Tree: Overseas Emigrants from India, Pakistan and Bangladesh*. London: Routledge.

Tinker, H. 1993. *A New System of Slavery: Export of Indian Labor Overseas*. New Delhi: Hansib Publications.

United States National Intelligence Council. 2012. *Global Trends 2030: Alternative Worlds*. Washington, DC.

10 Punjabi immigrants and rural development in the Doaba region of Indian Punjab

Jaswinder Singh Brar

The contribution of overseas Indians (Punjabis), especially that of Sikh emigrants, in the transformation of the socio-economic life of rural Punjab is significant and multifarious. With close to a century's worth of migration experience, the Sikh emigrants have not only maintained, but also become more proactive by playing the role of a catalyst in the improvement of their ancestral lands. Through adopting multiple renewed channels of economic interventions, contemporary rural Punjab has consequently been greatly impacted by the continuous involvement of the overseas emigrants. The impact was visible and discernible in the rural areas of the state of India in terms of the general lifestyle of the populace and the organisation of social, economic, agricultural, business and even political activities (Brar and Gill 2001). Over the decades, the developmental role of emigrant connection has been constantly shaped by the changing nature of emigration.

The amount of private remittances received by India increased substantially over a short period from US$15.8 billion in 2001–2002 to US$55.9 billion in 2010–2011 (MOIA 2010/2011). The government of India gradually accorded higher priority to the overseas community in terms of policies, programmes and various development initiatives. The state government adopted various ways and means to promote contribution efforts after recognising the actual potential contributions of the diasporic factor in the process of rural development. A policy framework consisting of various rules and regulations to facilitate the movement of persons, investable funds, goods, services and technology was implemented.

That being said, the emigrants-oriented development intensity in the state varied across the regions, sub-regions and clusters of villages. It also varied according to the duration, nature and destination of emigration, and the class and caste basis at the native villages. Consequently, the region witnessed higher levels of varied private investments by the emigrants, either directly or in collaboration with their family members from their ancestral villages in agricultural and allied activities, etc. Private remittances from abroad had thus contributed considerably to the income and consumption standards of the households (Kaur *et al.* 2011).

Evidently, the villages connected with members abroad had presented different lifestyles and cultures, unlike those that did not have these connections.

It is important to note that the scope of this study will also be dealing with the aspects of NRI involvement that fell into the exclusive category of philanthropy. The central focus of this study is to develop an understanding of emigrant contributions in the rural development within a concentrated area of emigrants. The analysis will take into account the background of the state's experiences of rural transformation, so that a coherent understanding can be generated based on both the actual and the ideal lines of intervention according to the requirements of a rural society. The chapter is divided into six sections.

The first section has briefly introduced the benefits accrued from overseas Punjabis that can be mapped back to the local, rural Punjabis. The second section will provide information about the specific profile of the process of rural transformation in the state under the cumulative impact of state intervention and market forces. The third section specifies the overall approach of the study, issues related to the generation of data and its sources and some constraints. The fourth section will illustrate the various modes of emigrant engagements and contributions. Section five discusses the various intricacies, nuances and other issues associated with emigration as a factor of development. Lastly, section six sums up the findings in the overall context of the state, rural requirements, and emerging policy issues.

Trajectory of rural transformation

The rural transformation of the state was quite problematic, beginning with a positive start that failed to endure the requirements of contemporary times. It started off as being projected and modelled as the story of great success, and was considered worthy of emulation by other states of the country. However, later on, particularly during the last two decades, certain contradictions surfaced together with problems that drew the attention of the media, policy makers, academicians and other people concerned with the well-being of the state and its inhabitants. The rural development of the state in fact kick-started, revolved around, and remained concentrated on the arising green revolution that began during the 1960s under the joint efforts of the state and national government in response to the national crisis of food shortage.

The green revolution in the state was a result of massive state intervention in the form of institutional and technological methods. Governmental interventions included the introduction of high yielding varieties of hybrid seeds, reasonable land reforms, consolidation of land holdings, application of chemical fertilisers and massive investment in the irrigation systems, abolition of intermediaries in that land tenure system, conferment of proprietary rights to the large number of land holders, etc. These types of reforms were combined with the assured purchase system that was tied to pre-announced prices for the principal crops of the region, particularly wheat and rice. For example, a large network of crop produce purchase systems was introduced by establishing the organised grain markets for almost all the villages. These steps resulted in the quantum jump in crop productivity, hence generating large marketable surpluses, which were dependent upon the size of holdings at the level of the individual farmer producers. The green revolution technology received widespread acceptance by the farmers as it readily resulted in higher levels of profitability for the producers, and many farmers experienced an increase in their households' disposable incomes. In 2010/2011, the cropping intensity in the state reached 190 per cent (GOP 2011: 4). Presently, the state is at its most agriculturally advanced, with almost complete mechanisation and commercialisation of all sorts of agricultural operations contributing substantially to national food stock.

The government became more involved in the rural scene of the state as a strong network of government schools was established in all the villages during the early phase of the green revolution. With the gradual establishment of cooperative societies, the supply of credit and other agricultural inputs to the farmers were facilitated, greatly improving the agricultural system and the adoption of new technology. The process also witnessed the construction of rural roads, opening up of village dispensaries, electrification of all villages on a priority basis, provision of safe drinking water, and sanitation programmes.

The long-term sustained growth in the agriculture sector paved the way for structural changes in the state's economy. Sectorial shares started shifting from the dominance of agriculture in the early phases of the green revolution to that of the other sectors, including the growth of industry and service based activities. From 2010/2011, the maximum income in the state originated from the tertiary sector with its share of 44.85 per cent, followed by the secondary sector (29.72 per cent), and the primary sector at 25.43 per cent (GOP 2011: 63). At current prices, the per capita net state domestic product was equivalent to Rs.68,998 as compared to the national level of Rs.53,331 (GOP 2011: 67) during 2010/2011. Thus, the state acquired the status of the most developed state of the country and was continuously ranked among the higher per capita income states during the last four decades.

However, due to the long absence of democratic governments, the state passed through a spell of militancy-related violence from the early 1980s to mid-1990s. The priorities of the state administration turned from being development-oriented to a focus on maintaining law and order instead. Public spending was also diverted to non-developmental areas within the budget and spending on public welfare-related activities was reduced. In 1992, the process of democratic restoration eventually started by holding popular elections for state assembly. Since then, four successive governments have indulged in populism instead of making difficult decisions that were urgently required for the restoration of the state's economy. Moreover, the state economy was developed and nurtured under the framework of maximum state intervention up to 1991. This was under the national protectionist regime that could not keep up with the changing national economic regime. The new national policy based on privatisation, liberalisation and globalisation, along with minimalist state intervention, altogether changed the dynamics of development. Subsequently, the state started slipping from its rapid development growth path. Rural distress began to emerge in many forms, including farmers' suicides, deterioration of health and education, and an ecological crisis related to ground water depletion, salinity and waterlogging. The lack of employment opportunities also clashed with the aspirations of the educated, thus generating a mass of educated unemployed who fell prey to social vices such as drugs.

Consequently, the state experienced a large number of problems following its high level of development. Initially as per the 2001census, the proportion of the scheduled castes population was 28.85 per cent out of the total population of the state. From 2004/2005, exactly 5.20 per cent of the population of the state dropped to below the officially defined national poverty line (GOP 2008/2009a: 202). The total number of below poverty line (BPL) families in the state was 5.23 lakh, which was up to 12.42 per cent of the total number of families. According to the *Atta-Dal* scheme (i.e. provision of subsidies on wheat and pulses) initiated by the state government on 15 August 2007, the number of poor families in the state was 13.47 lakh (GOP 2008/2009: 38). This meant that 30.98 per cent of the total number of families/households (43.48 lakh) fell within the category of poor families. The families that were included under this scheme had incomes of less than Rs.30,000 per annum (GOP 2008/2009a: 100). Within the rural areas in six districts, the proportion of the population that fell below the poverty line from 2004/2005 was reported as follows: Moga (25.2 per cent), Firozepur (17.9 per cent), Mukatsar (28.3 per cent), Faridkot (23.9 per cent), Bathinda (23.1 per cent), and Mansa (16.6 per cent). These six districts constituted 26.40 per cent of the total rural population of the state (Chaudhuri and Gupta 2009). Various studies have examined the extreme income inequality in the country (see for example UNDP 2007: 283). Eventually, the extreme income inequality fuelled people's desperation, urging them to compete with others by embarking on the route of overseas migration in order to increase their income.

Delving deeper into the problem of poverty, the majority of the people whose livelihoods depended on the primary sector were poor – from 1999 to 2000, 53.23 per cent of the workforce was engaged in this sector (Gill *et al.* 2010). The proportion of cultivators and agricultural labourers to total number of main workers was 22.63 per cent and 16.33 per cent respectively (GOP 2008/2009a). In 2005/2006, the average monthly per capita expenditure (MPCE) of the state was Rs.1,520 in urban areas, and Rs.1,010 in rural areas according to NSSO Round-62, which translated to Rs.18,240 and Rs.12,120 on an annual basis (GOP 2008/2009: 549). The marginal, small and semi-medium class of farmers, which constituted 62.60 per cent of the total farmers of the state, possessed low incomes that were insufficient for a decent living. The average farmer's household debt was Rs.41,576 in the state, the highest in the country during 2004/2005 (GOP 2008–2009: 12). As per the 2001 census, out of the total 50,362 sq. km area of the state, the rural area consisted of 48,265 sq. km, i.e. 95.84 per cent (GOP 2011: 3). Moreover, as per the 2011 census, the total population of the state was equivalent to 277.04 lakh, out of which the share of rural population was 62.51 per cent (173.2 lakh) (GOP 2011: 3).

Still, neither the state nor the market throughout the course of economic development have seriously addressed the various inadequacies experienced by the rural inhabitants. Instead, entrusted with the task of rural development were the village-level elected bodies, created under the seventy-third constitutional amendment. The state government, however, did not delegate the required powers to these bodies due to the much-touted programme of decentralising decision-making. Hence, these village-level elected bodies were unable to foster any significant social and economic development in the situation due to the deficiency of funds, functionaries and functions. Gradually, a large majority of these bodies were involved in a rural power structure that was based on political formations with loyal alliances to political parties. The development process thus started bypassing the marginal, needy populace to become exclusionary (Gill *et al.* 2010).

The aforementioned problems faced by rural Punjabis have contributed to the high proportion of Punjabis in the overall emigration from the country. During the period of six years spanning 2006 to 2011, the portion of Punjabis stood at 5.65 per cent among the total number of workers who were granted emigration by India, This was about 2.38 lakh workers, working out to be 39,642 workers annually (MOIA 2010/2011), reflected against the proportion of Punjabis constituting 2.37 per cent of the total population of the country (GOP 2011). The emigrants' efforts and involvement in the rural development of the state have persisted over a considerable span of time and modified according to both the general pattern and problems of the rural society, as well as the priorities of the emigrants. The diasporic involvement got its expression, space and relevance within the context of unattended or under-attended tasks by the principal developmental actors such as the state, market, and constitutional bodies of village governance. Thus, there prevailed considerable space in the rural setup of the state that needed to be filled up by the state and non-state agencies' conscious efforts. This space has been hitherto widening, due to the backlog of problems and tasks that were never attended to, the unbridled operation of market forces, rising state apathy, and undesirable development consequences in the form of the growing stock of environmental, health and societal problems.

Methodology: approaches, data and constraints

Against the abovementioned background of rural transformation, the present study has been modelled and focused upon the Doaba region of the state. Out of the 22 districts of the state, the Doaba region presently consists of four districts (Jalandhar, Nawan Shahar/Shaheed Bhagat Singh Nagar, Hoshiarpur and Kapurthala). Situated between the Sutlej and Beas rivers of Indian Punjab, it is the hub of Sikh emigration, with every third household having at least one member settled abroad, mainly in Western or Middle Eastern countries.

Of the 12,283 inhabited villages (i.e. 27.77 per cent of the total villages of the state), the Doaba region consisted of 3,411 villages (i.e. 17.85 per cent of the total area of the state). As per the 2001 census, the share of workers in the total population of the state varied between 35.3 per cent and 46.2 per cent among the various districts of the region. Agricultural workers constituted between 32 and 42.1 per cent of the total workers. The region also had a relatively equal sex ratio ranging between 912 and 962 females per 1,000 of males for its four districts in 2011. As a result of a high population density due to the heavy demographic pressure and limited land space, a high incidence of out-migration was observed. In 2011, the total population of the region was equivalent to 5,218,332 persons, i.e. 18.71 per cent of the total population of the state (GOP 2011: 36). The region had attained a comparatively higher level of literacy earlier than the rest of the state; as of 2011 the literacy for the various districts of the region was as follows: Jalandhar (82.40 per cent), Nawan Shahar/Shaheed Bhagat Singh Nagar (80.30 per cent), Hoshiarpur (85.40 per cent) and Kapurthala (69.40 per cent).

The emigrants' involvement in the development of the region received the vast attention of policy makers, academicians and various types of organisations, media and associations. The NRI Sabha Punjab then conducted a large-scale survey during 2002 and 2007 (Chana 2009). According to the 2002 survey based on 477 villages, the total amount of investments in religious and other development projects was more than Rs.200 crore. A re-survey in December 2007 was conducted on 28 villages among the previously surveyed 477 villages. These findings presented an increase in the pace of philanthropy, manifested from the rise in the amount of contribution equivalent to Rs.4,000,000 per village from 2002 to 2007 (Chana 2009: 115–116).

Within the Doaba region, the maximum incidence of migration occurring in the Nakodar area resulted in it being chosen as the locale of the study. Due to the administrative set up of the state, it formed the base of resource for the various types of officially available data. Hence, the Nakodar development block was selected to represent the Nakodar area, which belonged to one of the 11 development blocks of the Jalandhar district. Presently, the state has 145 development blocks in total. It is important to note that the development block was officially created by the state to pursue and implement the various developmental schemes and programmes for the rural areas. The development block was headed by the block development officer (BDO), who was the most important official overseeing the villages. In any case, no data was collected at the level of government for the nature and extent of emigrants' involvement in the villages.

Some information about the extent of emigration was made available for the Nakodar block. For example, with the aid of the state government, data showed that there were 1,417 families who had a family member living abroad in 2010/2011 – about 5 per cent of the total number of families in the block. The village-level number of the families having a member in a foreign country presented interesting results; there were 13 villages (9.29 per cent) with not even a single family that had a member abroad. However, the number of families with a member abroad varied significantly across the villages. On average, as many as 42 villages (30 per cent) had between 3.1 and five of such families. Another group of 24 villages (17.14 per cent) had an average of between 5.1 and 7 of such families. Comparatively, there were some villages that had a higher proportion of such families. Interestingly, in the case of a few villages, the proportion of such families was as high as between one-third to one-half of the total number of families in the respective villages (ESO 2010/2011).

The attainment of literacy was the most important indicator of the development of any region. On this front, the Nakodar block was relatively better positioned as compared to the other rural areas of the country; where the average family size worked out to be 5.64 persons per family, the average literacy rate of the block stood at 60.46 per cent. The proportion of the scheduled castes population was 41.20 per cent in 2001. It was noted that the Doaba region in the state consisted of a very large proportion of the SC population. In terms of economics, out of the total population of the block, the proportion of the active workers stood at 36.40 per cent in total, the proportion of agricultural workers was 16.16 per cent, and that of the non-agricultural workers was 20.24 per cent. This indicated the diversification of the rural economy of the block (ESO 2010/2011).

The Nakodar development block consisted of 140 villages, with a population of 160,380 persons. Huge variation in the population size of villages prevailed, with the smallest village having a population of just four and the largest having 5,937 persons. Keeping in mind the objectives of the study, an attempt was made to select a fairly representative sample of the villages situated in the block. The method of stratified random sampling was used to select the villages. Accordingly, as per statistical wisdom related to sampling methodology, the extreme cases in size were excluded. For example, the four villages with populations of 4–30 persons were excluded. Similarly, the placing of villages' populations in ascending order further showed that village populations above the size of 2,500 led to uneven distribution and did not fit into any specific order of size, therefore seven villages were excluded. Eventually, 129 villages of the Nakodar development block that fell into proper size categories with an orderly distribution were selected (ESO 2010/2011). The population distribution of all of 129 villages, in descending order, with the number of villages shown in brackets, stood as follows: 501–1,000 (43 villages); 1,001–1,500 (31 villages); 100–500 (29 villages); 1,501–2000 (13 villages); and 2,001–2,500 (13 villages). The proportionate sections of the various size categories were 33.33 per cent, 24.03 per cent, 22.48 per cent, 10.08 per cent and 10.08 per cent respectively. Among these five strata of villages, 12 villages were selected randomly; one village was selected in every group of ten villages. The selection of villages was also guided by factors such as the occurrence of emigration, convenience of data collection, and population sizes within the size-category itself. The sample size constituted 9.3 per cent of the universal sample population, which was regarded as an objectively high sample size.

The data was collected through a pre-tested questionnaire using a pilot survey. The information was collected from the village representatives, village-level officials, people associated with the important projects initiated with philanthropic involvement, the local trusts and associations constituted for this purpose, and important persons who remained involved with such activities. It was important to bear in mind that the level of information varied significantly from village to village. In some villages, a fairly good record of spending was available, while the situation was less straightforward in others. Moreover, the information level varied from project to project. For example, more information was available for large projects. The information for the projects that were successfully completed in a single round of investment was also accessible. However, the projects that witnessed slow completion or had gone through multiple stages with significant gaps of time in-between were difficult to ascertain. Lastly, the collected information was crosschecked, verified, and refined accordingly.

Engagement modes and magnitude

The analysis of the generated data raised some interesting and crucial dimensions of philanthropy within a particular rural hub of the state. The total number of emigrants from the sampled villages had been reported to be 257 persons (Table 10.1) who had settled in Asia, Europe and North America (United Kingdom, Canada, United States, Australia, Dubai (UAE), Kuwait, Bahrain, Saudi Arabia, Germany, Italy, Philippines, Malaysia and Hong Kong). The largest number resided in the United Kingdom, viz. 114 persons (44.36 per cent). This was followed by Canada and the United States with a corresponding share of 23.35 per cent and 13.23 per cent respectively. These three countries constituted 80.94 per cent of the total number of emigrants from the sampled countries. The collective share of the remainder of the ten countries was equal to 19.06 per cent, whereas the share of Middle Eastern countries was as follows: Dubai (UAE) (4.67 per cent), Kuwait (2.72 per cent), Bahrain (1.95 per cent), and Saudi Arabia (1.95 per cent).

The sampled villages witnessed a total investment of Rs.456 lakh for various projects with a philanthropic nature as of December 2011 (Table 10.2), which was equivalent to Rs.38 lakh per village. Overall, the amount of money invested according to the 11 types of socio-economic projects, with level of investment

Table 10.1 The country distribution of NRIs of sampled villages (in descending order)

Country	*Number*	*Per cent*
United Kingdom	114	44.36
Canada	60	23.35
United States	34	13.23
Dubai (UAE)	12	4.67
Australia	7	2.72
Kuwait	7	2.72
Bahrain	5	1.95
Saudi Arabia	5	1.95
Germany	3	1.17
Italy	3	1.17
Philippines	3	1.17
Malaysia	2	0.78
Hong Kong	2	0.78
Total	257	100.00

Source: primary survey.

Table 10.2 Expenditure by emigrants in sampled villages in Nakodar block (in descending order) (as of December 2011)

Nature of activity	*Amount (Rs. Lakh)*	*Per cent*
1 Religious	174.75	38.32
2 Education	95.99	21.05
3 Hospitals	39.50	8.66
4 Village streets	30.34	6.65
5 Water supply	26.77	5.87
6 Social ceremonies	24.53	5.38
7 Cultural events	19.74	4.33
8 Sports events	17.07	3.74
9 Sanitation	10.91	2.39
10 Old age care	10.59	2.32
11 Eye camps	5.79	1.27
Total	456.00	100.00

Source: primary survey.

and proportions in descending order given in brackets, were as follows: religious (174.5 lakh, 38.32 per cent); education (95.99 lakh, 21.05 per cent); hospitals (39.50 lakh, 8.66 per cent); village streets (30.34 lakh, 6.65 per cent); water supply (26.77 lakh, 5.87 per cent); social ceremonies (24.53 lakh, 5.38 per cent); cultural events (19.74 lakh, 4.33 per cent); sports events (17.07 lakh, 3.74 per cent); sanitation(10.91lakh, 2.39 per cent); old age care (10.59 lakh, 2.32 per cent); and eye camps (5.79 lakh, 1.27 per cent). In particular, most of the investments allocated to the domain of education were directed to the ethos and teachings of the Sikh religion. This was because an overwhelmingly high proportion of rural emigrants from Punjab are Sikh. It was estimated that there were between 1.5 and two million overseas Punjabis, with an overwhelming majority professing the Sikh faith (Tatla 2008: 462). Originally, the educational infrastructure in major parts of the country was not up to mark due to the constraint of public resources and the lack of effective decentralisation of rural governance structures (Acharya 2002). The emigrants' involvement in the education sector had been considered as the means to fulfil the gap created by the deficiency of both the state and the market.

The analysis of the diasporic philanthropy over different time durations highlighted some interesting facts at two levels, viz. the inter-temporal allocation of money, and changes in spending priorities (Table 10.3). Out of a total spending of Rs.456 lakh, as much as Rs.165 lakh was spent as of 1990 (first time-duration); Rs.135 lakh during the period of ten years from 1991 to 2000 (second time-duration); and Rs.156 lakh during the last 11 years from 2001 to 2011 (third time-duration). It indicated that philanthropic interest had increased over the years, which could be a result of the improved financial positions of the emigrants in their adopted countries. Furthermore, though religious activities continuously attracted the highest level of funds in absolute terms, the proportionate spending declined

Table 10.3 Expenditure by emigrants in sampled villages in Nakodar block (Rs. Lakh)

Nature of activity	*Up to 1990*	*1991–2000*	*2001–2011*
1 Religious	72.91 (44.19)	54.49 (40.36)	47.46 (30.42)
2 Education	30.51 (18.49)	26.06 (19.30)	39.56 (25.60)
3 Hospitals	10.68 (6.47)	12.31 (9.12)	16.22 (10.40)
4 Village streets	10.81 (6.55)	11.48 (8.50)	7.66 (4.91)
5 Water supply	6.96 (4.22)	8.42 (6.24)	11.15 (7.15)
6 Social ceremonies	14.55 (8.82)	3.78 (2.80)	7.05 (4.52)
7 Cultural events	5.40 (3.27)	5.41 (4.01)	8.91 (5.71)
8 Sports events	4.22 (2.56)	4.75 (3.52)	8.03 (5.15)
9 Sanitation	2.62 (1.59)	4.54 (3.36)	3.48 (2.23)
10 Old age care	4.27 (2.59)	1.66 (1.23)	4.91 (3.15)
11 Eye camps	2.06 (1.25)	2.11 (1.56)	1.56 (1.00)
Total	165.00 (100)	135.00 (100)	156.00 (100)

Source: primary survey.

Note
Figures in brackets indicate percentage shares.

over the various time intervals. From 44.19 per cent during the first time-duration, spending for religion declined marginally to 40.36 per cent during the second time-duration, and much more significantly during the third time-duration to 30.42 per cent – a decline of more than 10 per cent from the first time-duration. Significantly, the proportionate spending on education, health and other areas of vital human needs increased consistently. The share of education went up from 18.49 per cent during the first time-duration to 19.30 per cent during the second time duration and 25.60 per cent during the third time duration. The expenditure on hospitals also witnessed a consistent rise, increasing from 6.47 per cent to 9.12 per cent, and reaching 10.40 per cent in the final time period. Other areas that experienced a continuous rise in their shares in overall spending included sports, water supply, and cultural and sports events. The remaining areas witnessed varied levels of expenditure during various periods.

Referring to Table 10.4, there were a variety of activities in the ancestral villages within the broad spending categories that received the attention of emigrants. Noticeably, it was the physical infrastructure of varied natures that received a sizeable level of funds. The deficiency of disposable funds of the village communities and their formal and informal bodies led to a lack of basic amenities in the villages, which the emigrants made up for with their contributions. All in all, the composition of spending within every activity depended upon the basic requirements for the performance of that activity.

Emigrants' priorities and local requirements

Emigrants' interest and therefore involvement in the development of ancestral villages was simultaneously complex and simplistic when it came to selecting

Table 10.4 Expenditure across various sub categories in sampled villages in Nakodar block

Category	*Sub categories*
1 Religious	Buildings, electricity, air conditioning, holdings of community kitchens, religious congregations
2 Education	Class rooms, girls' toilets, furniture, drinking water, training centre for girls, village library, computers
3 Hospitals	Opening of dispensaries, medicines, ambulances, portable mortuary, funeral vans, crematoriums
4 Village streets	Concrete pavements, street lights, small bridges, levelling, earth filling
5 Water supply	RO systems, deep tube wells, water coolers
6 Social ceremonies	Marriage of poor girls, marriage halls, accommodation and meals for pilgrimages, celebration of days, rest houses
7 Cultural events	Folk festivals, seasonal festivals, folk dances, competitions
8 Sports	Tournaments, equipment, awards, stadiums, sports kits
9 Sanitation	Sewerage, drainage, garbage removal, pond cleaning, septic tank
10 Old age care	Buildings, shelters, cooling/heating systems, food, clothes
11 Health check-up	Eye camps, polio camps, medical check-up, medicines

Source: primary survey.

the types of projects for development. The majority of the projects that ultimately were selected resulted from the government's failure to provide due to the general neglect of social well-being. The development vacuum of basic necessities could easily be understood by examining the nature and various types of sub activities involved in any project. Through its initial conception to final execution, the process of completing any project revealed aspects of complexity. A majority of the projects had witnessed and undergone numerous modes of social-political changes embedded in the rural power structure. This was based on class and social prestige associated with the unremitting dominance of a few families and the competing nature of divided clans. Well-off individuals belonging to the core families of original settlers within village communities settled abroad played crucial roles in the philanthropic activity in the rural areas (Dhesi 2009: 227).

Due to the emigrants' exposure and interaction with their comparatively more egalitarian adopted societies, they valued individual liberties and human values. This was evident in the prioritisation of many projects where the emigrants spent large amounts on religious projects involving the construction of religious buildings and the provision of amenities and accessories. Similarly, in the sampled villages, the amount spent on such activities in absolute terms increased considerably. One main reason behind the large spending on religious activities was the sense of fulfilling the spiritual duty duly incorporated in religious texts. Apart from this consideration, such spending also enhanced one's social and political prestige in both the village and among neighbouring villages, social networks and political surroundings. It also effectively established the fact that the individual had made a fortune in the adopted country.

These religious buildings were also used for purposes such as social gatherings to discuss community affairs involving social, developmental and political issues. The conducting of various death and marriage related ceremonies were also facilitated with the availability of religious buildings with modern fittings, particularly for people who could not afford to pay for commercial venues. Thus, the spending on such activities improved the receptiveness towards emigrants in the village, and also generated goodwill for the rest of their family members residing in these villages. Therefore, the influencing factors ranged from the exclusive domain of the individual to the general social, cultural and dominant way of life of the village societies.

It was highlighted from the discussions with the residents of the sampled villages that the interaction between the residents and emigrants played a significant role in deciding the priorities of the various non-religious projects. The modes of engagement and actual practices involved varied across the villages and projects. Over the years, the emigrants have learnt from their experiences of carrying out development works. In some cases, reliable groups that sprouted up in the ancestral villages have managed to bring in huge earnings from performing such work.

The local handlers of money have essentially been the informal groups of people keeping proper records of such money in order to ensure public accountability. Comparatively, emigrants provided more money when they were convinced of cautious utilisation. In some cases, the villages that failed to ensure proper and transparent utilisation of emigrants' money experienced a decline in money flow. Yet, the decision to use the funds ultimately fell into the hands of the people involved in the village affairs who represented the interests of the village communities. Several formal institutions played crucial roles in the determination of the priorities and attempted to convince donors to spend on activities for the larger interests of the village population; money spent on these activities included health, education, old age care, eye camps, sanitation and the improvement of village streets.

It has also been reported that in some cases, a specific culture of emigrant activity evolved particularly in villages not affected by local antagonism and conflicts. In such villages, the local residents approached people with known philanthropic behaviour for the provision of money as and when they required. The sponsoring of cultural and sports events primarily emerged out of such interaction of the emigrants with their ancestral lands and growing social concern about the channelling of the energies of the rural youth towards productive activities. Due to the serious problem of large scale substance abuse by the rural youth, the idea of involving them in the various cultural and sports activities was suggested as a way to encourage them to spend their time meaningfully. Hence, the emergence of village welfare associations played a catalytic role in the mobilisation of community finances from abroad for the pursuit of various types of similar development goals (Thandi 2008).

Generally, the emigrants' involvement coincided with the requirements of the local society and the village requirements. Many public-spirited persons, local intelligentsia, state government agencies, emigrant associations abroad and local agencies also channel philanthropic money into producing large positive externalities. Having said this, there have been cases of ostentatious spending, such as the construction of memorial gates at village entrances roads. It was not until the later stages of construction that the futility of such spending was realised. However, there have also been cases reported from the sampled villages where the local community resisted the efforts of the emigrants – this was the case when emigrants wanted to build liquor shops on the village periphery. The resistance to such activities is evidence that village communities expect only responsible engagements from emigrants.

Conclusion: summing up and policy concerns

The analysis and discussion of emigrants' engagement in the rural development of the state have established that emigrants have made sincere efforts to improve the well-being of the inhabitants of their ancestral villages. On the whole, the nature and extent of interventions were decided by a mutual interplay of reaching an understanding of the local requirements, emigrants' perceptions about the nature of existent problems, and possible solutions. Other influential factors also included prompt solutions and hasty decisions guided by social prestige and status. Many of the projects were carried out independently and were crucially dependent upon the continuous supply of funds by emigrants. This raised concerns about sustainability in the long run, as emigrant funds were ultimately individually motivated initiatives. Several projects had not been designed to be self-sustainable and hence, had not generated sufficient operation and maintenance funds. Moreover, there have been reports that village leaders ultimately held control of the projects, further complicating their progress. Evidently, the overseas Punjabis' contributions to rural development, though significant, have been infrequent and inconsistent (Dhesi 2008: 427).

People-centric rural transformations of the state are therefore becoming increasingly problematic as the process of development is fundamentally constrained. Commercialisation, privatisation and a lack of transparency in governance have become prevalent, together with the rising level of income, consumption, wealth and educational inequalities, which have disturbed the general equilibrium in society. Hence, the prevailing scenario does not match up to the rising aspirations of the younger generations, who experience a variety of exposures, one of which is that to other countries. Instead, the rural scene is dominated by small and marginal farmers, agricultural labourers, petty traders, and tiny repair units and workshops, which have been experiencing dwindling incomes and marginalisation. Those who were relatively better off struggled to emigrate and inevitably contributed to emigration businesses. Rural areas also experienced migration to the urban areas for livelihood and readily available urban amenities, while the huge rural population continued to be unable to make effective demands due to lower incomes. In fact, the diasporic projects and activities only marginally improved the existing provision of numerous varieties of public goods and services.

Although emigrant involvement continues to be critically important, it is essentially clearly insufficient in eradicating the large number of problems confronting the rural societies. It has generated localised impacts with fairly weak linkages with the larger economy. With the near absence of infrastructural planning and non-responsive formal institutions at the state level, the overseas communities find it difficult to be sufficiently persuaded to transfer the funds for the projects that would bring economic improvement for the cluster of villages. Also, with inadequate staffing and political will, the massive deficit of public resources has crippled the public infrastructure related to education, health, sanitation, water supply, community assets, etc.

That being said, emigrants' initiatives do have the potential to become more meaningful in the process of rural transformation if overseas providers and recipients stay connected with each other beyond individual efforts. Be it in the form of credible and innovative associations, or institutions being mediated by proactive state planning agencies, the combining of the diasporic resources along with public and local community resources is the only way to correct the distortions created by the persistent neglect of the rural sector.

References

Acharya, P. 2002. Education: Panchayats and Decentralization – Myth and Reality. *Economic and Political Weekly* 37(8): 788–796.

Brar, J.S., and S.S. Gill. 2001. Tenancy Reversal and Operational Enclosures: a Study of Doaba Region. In Sucha Singh Gill (ed.), *Land Reforms in India: Intervention for Agrarian Capitalist Transformation in Punjab and Haryana*', Vol. VI. New Delhi: Sage Publications, pp. 215–237.

Chaudhuri, S. and N. Gupta. 2009. Levels of Living and Poverty Patterns – a District Wise Analysis for India. *Economic and Political Weekly* (44)9: 94–110.

Chana, S. 2009. NRI Investment in Social Development Projects: Findings from Two Sample Surveys in Doaba, Punjab. In V.A. Dusenbery and D.S. Tatla (eds), *Sikh Diaspora Philanthropy in Punjab*. New Delhi: Oxford University Press, pp. 107–119.

Dhesi, A.S. 2008. Overseas Punjabis and Rural Development. In A.S. Dhesi and Gurmail Singh (eds), *Rural Development in Punjab: a Success Story Going Astray*. New Delhi: Routledge, pp. 427–445.

Dhesi, A.S. 2009. Diasporic Intervention in Rural Development; Boon or Bane? In V.A. Dusenbery and D.S. Tatla (eds), *Sikh Diaspora Philanthropy in Punjab*. New Delhi: Oxford University Press, pp. 219–235.

ESO. 2010/2011. *Village Directory, Population and Loan Details*, Jalandhar District, Economic and Statistical Organization, Government of Punjab, Chandigarh.

Gill, S.S., S. Singh and J.S. Brar. 2010. *Globalization and Indian State: Education, Health and Agricultural Extension Services in Punjab*. New Delhi: Aakar Publisher.

GOP. 2008/2009. *Annual Plan*, Vol. 1. Department of Planning, Government of Punjab (GOP), Chandigarh.

GOP. 2008/2009a. *Economic Survey of Punjab*. Economic and Statistical Organization, Government of Punjab (GOP), Chandigarh.

GOP. 2011. *Statistical Abstract of Punjab 2011*. Economic and Statistical Organization, Government of Punjab (GOP), Chandigarh.

Kaur, B, J.M. Singh, J Singh and B.R. Garg. 2011. Out Migration; Causes and Impact on Rural Households in Punjab. In H.S. Shergill, Sucha Singh Gill and Gurmail Singh (eds), *Economy of North-West India*. New Delhi: Serial Publications, pp. 389–399.

MOIA. 2010/2011. *Annual Report*, Government of India, New Delhi.

MOIA. 2011/2012. *Annual Report*, Government of India, New Delhi.

Tatla, D. 2008. The Punjabi Diaspora's Impact on Punjab's Economy and Society: an Assessment. In A.S. Dhesi and Gurmail Singh (eds), *Rural Development in Punjab: a Success Story Going Astray*. New Delhi: Routledge, pp. 460–481.

Thandi, S.S. 2008. Evaluating the Potential Contribution of the Punjabi Diaspora to Rural development. In A.S. Dhesi and Gurmail Singh (eds), *Rural Development in Punjab: a Success Story Going Astray*. New Delhi: Routledge, pp. 446–459.

UNDP. 2007. *Human Development Report 2007–08*, United Nations Development Programme. New York: Palgrave-Macmillan.

11 International migration and development

Prospects and challenges for Nepal

Thakur Subedi

It is widely agreed that diasporas play an immense role in the development of their home countries. Colombia's Caldas network shows how a developing nation's linking with its diaspora abroad can play a significant role in home country development projects (Meyer *et al.* 1997). Not only do diasporas support their homeland by 'injecting new ideas and resources that can catalyse progress in otherwise stagnant economies', they also facilitate the opening up of home countries to the global economy (Johnson and Sedaca 2004: 63). They contribute through remittances, and are the major source of FDI, technology transfer, philanthropy, and political powers, and influence the source of foreign aid. Recently, India and China have shown how a country can benefit from their overseas populations (see Kapur 2001; Zweig *et al.* 2008). By creating linkages with the diaspora, many developing countries inspire their overseas populations to engage, invest and run businesses in their country of origin (Meyer *et al.* 1997).

Today, most states recognise their expatriates and acknowledge their potentiality. A reliance on migrant capitals such as remittances and knowledge and technology has prompted many home countries to incorporate their populations abroad (Guarnizo 1998). A good diaspora approach involves an organised and clear policy that manages and cultivates the relationships with a country's population abroad (Kitchin and Boyle 2011). Countries such as Israel, Mexico and Macedonia use their diaspora as a tool for 'lobbies' and an instrument of foreign policy (Shain 1989). Similarly, countries like Croatia, Italy and Armenia provide their expatriates with the right to vote, while others deny political participation and representation (Bauböck 2005).

Countries have different strategies in approaching their diaspora populations. Mexico, China, India and the Philippines have multiple organisations to facilitate their diaspora both at 'home' and 'abroad'. In Bangladesh, there is a Ministry of Expatriates' Welfare and Overseas Employment. China has a State Council, Overseas Chinese Affairs Office of the State Council (OCAOSC) and Overseas Chinese Affairs Committee (OCAC) for its people living abroad. Likewise, India's Ministry of Overseas Indian Affairs (MOIA) looks after Indians abroad (World Bank 2008). India's MOIA deals with the state policy coordination on migration with numerous packages for overseas Indians. Similarly, the Ministry of Foreign Employment in Sri Lanka and the Ministry of Expatriates' Welfare and Overseas Employment in Bangladesh focus on the welfare of their expat workers. They provide their citizens overseas with protection and various training to support them in finding jobs. It is through these establishments that home country governments are able to engage their overseas populations to better realise the target of acquiring remittances, fetching investment and gaining access to diaspora skills.

Additionally, countries such as Israel, Mexico and Macedonia use their diaspora as a tool for 'lobbies' and an instrument of foreign policy (Shain 1989). Similarly, Croatia, Italy and Armenia provide their expatriates with the right to vote (Bauböck 2005). In contrast, Nepalese populations living abroad are not governed by state policies even in the post-democratic era. This is especially so for return migrants, in terms of their investments and immigrant rights (Ojha 2012). The country monitors its overseas population of two million through limited embassies and consulates. It would suffice to say that Nepal's policies, which are mainly related to migrant prevention and promotion, are more focused on 'extracting material resources' from its people abroad in the form of remittances (Barry 2006: 28).

Although the Nepali government started to send its people to work overseas with the enactment of the Foreign Employment Act in 1985, the country does not have any concrete plans to mobilise their resources in the home country's development projects. Since existing policies are mostly related to labour migration, they do not cover the entire diaspora population. Despite the structural changes in Nepalese politics, only minor deviations have taken place in its diaspora policy. Moreover, scholars in Nepal not only view the country's poor growth from a socio-economic perspective, they also ignore the importance of its diaspora in the development of the home country (Tamot 2008). Taking into account the country's dependency on remittances, ignoring the role of migration in the development of Nepal would be costly, especially when the Nepali diaspora in the United States and Canada alone possess a combined 'annual personal earning' of about US$12 billion (Adhikari 2011).

An overview of emigration from Nepal

Nepal is one of the poorest and least developed countries in the world. Central Bureau of Statistics (2008) report shows that about 24.7 per cent of the country's population falls below the poverty line, with per capita GDP standing at US$470. Agriculture is the backbone of the Nepalese economy, providing a livelihood for three-quarters of the population and accounting for about one-third of the GDP. More than 76 per cent of the population depend on agriculture. While 6 per cent of people are engaged in industry-related occupations, 18 per cent are surviving by means of the service sectors. A lack of industries and service sectors in the country, continuous political instability and the displacements during the Maoist-led civil war in Nepal have pushed the unemployment rate from 42 per cent in

2004 to over 46 per cent in 2008 (CBS 2008). There is therefore no denying the fact that poverty and the absence of opportunity at home have forced many Nepalese to go abroad to look for jobs.

Economic, social and political forces push people out of one country and pull them towards another country (Stalker 2001). Harris and Todaro (1970) consider an excess of labour, scarce capital, population compression and unemployment in the sending countries as push factors, while labour scarcity, surplus capital, high income and social facilities in the destination countries serve as pull factors. Individuals make a rational decision to maximise these opportunities (Massey *et al.* 1993). Nepalese people's exit can be categorised as economic,[1] political[2] and socio-cultural.[3] Both push and pull factors are significant in the context of Nepal. While the push factors in Nepal are associated with the marginal or labour migrants, the pull factors are linked to professional or skilled immigrants (Upreti 2002).

Political migration from Nepal during the Rana regime was common as many political leaders left the country for India to escape persecution. However, it was the perpetual political instability in post-democratic Nepal that stirred the en masse movement of people across the border. Emigration from Nepal spiked during the Maoist insurgency, and after the declaration of a 'state of emergency' in 2001, the country witnessed a massive exodus. Today, the demand for labour force in industrialised countries has worked as a 'pull factor', enticing many Nepalese to go abroad for work. The movement of Nepali people seems to be the result of a way of surviving amidst market imperfections, where people go abroad to diversify their labour portfolios and receive incomes (Massey 1999). For Nepal, the DV[4] lottery is another 'pull factor' as thousands of Nepalese try their luck for this visa annually, and a large number of them are selected to migrate to America each year.

Nepal is among the top ten countries with the highest rate of emigration (World Bank 2011). Almost half a million Nepalese leave for abroad annually (*Dainik Nepal* 2014). Due to an open border with India, it is difficult to determine the real number of people moving out of the country. Labour migration to banned countries like Afghanistan and Iraq, and Middle East countries for women, are under-reported, as many people emigrate through job brokers and via India. Most of them go to India and the Gulf countries as the former does not require any visa while the latter is easier and cheaper. On the other hand, the educated and skilled professionals prefer developed countries – mainly the United States and the United Kingdom. In the absence of reliable information on the number of Nepalese leaving and returning to the country, Nepal considers its 'absentee'[5] population as 'emigrants'. Figure 11.1 shows the number of emigrants from Nepal during the last four decades.

Figure 11.1 shows a sharp rise in the number of emigrants from Nepal as the total absentee in 2011 reached 1.92 million, more than double the number ten years previously. This sudden spike in the post-democratic era is due to the escalation of Maoist conflict and the growing impact of globalisation, especially between 2001 and 2011. Due to the growing features of migration, we find three

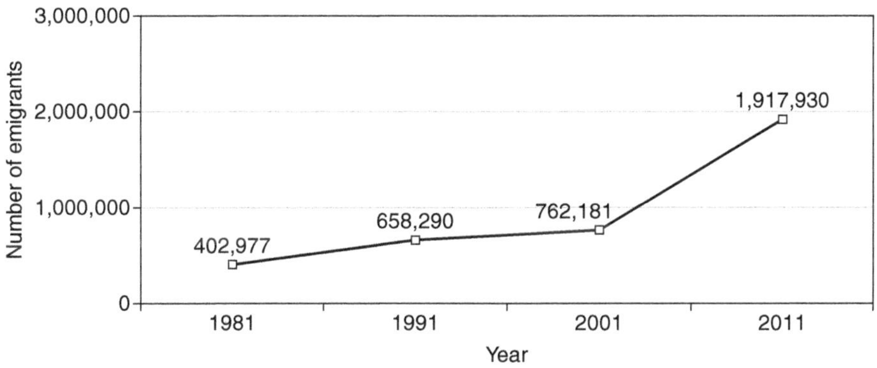

Figure 11.1 Emigrants from Nepal, 1981–2011 (source: Central Bureau of Statistics Nepal, 2012).

types of Nepalese emigrants: unskilled, students and highly skilled professionals. The majority of Nepalese emigrants are unskilled, with skilled emigrants making up 20 to 30 per cent, and the remaining 3 to 4 per cent being made up of highly skilled emigrants (UNDP 2010).

Making of Nepali diaspora

Although the early wave of Nepali people's movement started with the settlement across Nepal towards the eastern region, then into Sikkim and Bhutan, the first Nepalese diaspora is considered to be the group of soldiers and workers who went to work for British-India during the mid-nineteenth century. The second wave started with the recruitment of the Nepali population as British soldiers who settled in the British Isles and Southeast Asia, for example, in Myanmar (Nath 2009), after their retirement. Since they were well paid, many people of Nepali origin hopped on the bandwagon, accompanied by their families. They stayed there permanently, thus creating the first set of Nepali diaspora (Lal 2003). The third wave began during the 1970s, when job-related migration to India, the Middle East, Europe and North America took place. Many of the immigrants eventually settled in the developed countries and adopted a transnational lifestyle, as most of them maintained strong connections with their home country. The current number of Nepali diaspora living abroad is estimated to be in the millions. Table 11.1 shows the number of Nepali diaspora members in various regions of the world.

According to Table 11.1, the majority of Nepalese are located in the Middle East, and Asian countries closely follow this. In truth however, the largest number of Nepali diaspora reside in India, due to the country's historical links. It is believed that temporary migrant workers residing mainly in the Gulf countries and in Asia constitute some 80 per cent of the Nepali diaspora. Some of them

Table 11.1 Nepali diaspora abroad

Region	*Numbers*	*Percentage*
Middle East	860,755	44.3
Asia	824,200	42.4
North America	150,000	7.7
Europe	76,050	3.9
Oceania	32,700	1.7
South America	1,100	–
Africa	195	–
1,945,000 Nepalese in 55 countries and more than 5,000,000 in South Asia		

Source: *Nepal Migration Year Book*, 2009.

reside there for a long time and are involved in businesses and entrepreneurships. Interestingly, Nepalese living in South Asian countries are not considered as diaspora by the government of Nepal.

Contribution to the homeland

Diasporas are observed as the major actors in home country development through various means, such as economic, political, socio-cultural, and knowledge and technology transfer (Kapur 2001). They influence the home country's affairs even without being physically present. In this regard, diaspora not only contribute through remittances, they are also the major source of FDI, technology transfer, philanthropy and political influences (Newland and Patrick 2004). Diaspora also influence the source of foreign aid. For example, a large percentage of aid from Germany goes to Turkey. A similar observation can be made for the United Kingdom's aid to India and the aid from the United States to Israel (Beine and Sekkat 2013).

Although diaspora facilitate cultural, political and social changes in the home countries, remittance is considered to be the most important contribution to a developing country. This is why citizens working abroad are often referred to as heroes and heroines in Mexico and the Philippines (Stalker 2001). On a similar note, Nepal receives substantial remittances and other support packages from its people who are migrating en masse every year. The major contributions made by Nepali diaspora to their country of origin can be assessed as follows.

Remittances and diaspora bonds

Today, the volume of remittances is larger than FDI in many low-income countries, and is much 'better targeted and effective' in the development of the home countries (Lapper 2004: 2). Remittances help increase capital formation, reduce poverty in certain households, and bring changes in the pattern of disparity in certain regions (Yang 2008). In Nepal, remittances through the formal sector alone make 22.3 per cent of the country's GDP (World Bank 2012). The largest share (27.4 per cent) of remittances comes from Qatar, followed by Saudi Arabia and India. Considering the fact that many migrants send money through informal routes, this figure might very well be greater in reality. Sometimes, developing countries issue diaspora bonds, targeting their overseas people for economic development in the home country (Ketkar and Ratha 2009). Nepal tried to raise funds thorough diaspora bonds in 2009; however, it could only collect NPR4.5 million (US$60,000) in the first round (4.5 per cent of the revised target) and NPR3.38 million (US$47,000) in the second round, accounting for only 0.68 per cent of the target value (Probst 2012).

Trades and investments

In the absence of a reliable source, it is difficult to figure out the exact volume of investment by Nepali people in their country of origin. However, a study estimates that NRN (Non Resident Nepali) investment in the country is approximately US$350 million, accumulated mostly in the banking, telecom, health, education and hydropower sectors. The Total Business Institute Group[6] and Sanima Group have invested in airways and hydropower projects. Other major NRN investments in Nepal include United Breweries, Kantipur TV, Karobar Daily, Kantipur Engineering College, Acme Engineering College, etc. (Subedi 2011). NRNs have also built a Kriyaputri Bhawan (US$100,000), NRN Devghat Bridhhasharam (US$222,000) and five trade schools. They have financially supported (US$10,000) the Arya Tara Nuns School, established a contact office for Nepali people in Lebanon, assisted the Dolma Sherpa (US$25,000), constructed Phulkumari Mahato Secondary high school (US$10,000), and donated around US$175,000 to Sunsari flood victims in 2009 (NRNA 2013). In addition, there are several co-opted and ongoing projects like 'One village one Product' and 'Trade School', and the Nepal Public Library, Open University Initiative Nepal, Nepal Investment Fund, and the 75 Home District Project respectively.

Moreover, many Nepali diaspora communities have contributed to Nepal through private and shared activities. Contributions for electricity, education and health development made by the Myagdi Bim UK Society – a diaspora organisation in the United Kingdom representing Bim VDC of Myagdi district in Nepal – in their village is one example. Gulmi Sewa Samaj[7] have contributed more than US$1.3 million for their townships, including four ambulances. They also run a power plant in addition to several training and income generating activities for handicapped people in their locality. The organisation has more than 1,200 members, who routinely support activities at 'home' through membership fees (OnlineKhabar 2012).

Knowledge and technology transfer

Diaspora encourage prolific growth through the transfer of skills and implementation of information and technology in the country of origin (Lodigiani 2009).

There are a few projects that Nepalese, mainly from the United States and the United Kingdom, run to link back to their home country. The major projects include the Nepalese Diaspora Volunteering Programme, the Centre for Nepal Studies (CNS), the Centre for Nepal Studies UK (CNSUK), the Nepal Study Centre (NSC), Nyaya Health, and Youth for Nepal (YFN). Nyaya Health provides free community-based healthcare services to poor and deprived people in the rural areas of Nepal. It trains, funds and employs 20 medical staff and about 30 community health workers, serving around 3,000 patients every month. Similarly, while CNSUK has carried out a large scale survey of Nepalese ethnic minorities living in the United Kingdom in 2008, the Nepal Study Centre has developed a Himalayan Research Papers Archive for the research done on the issues related to the Himalayan region. Likewise, YFN funds local development projects and social awareness-raising programmes, and has raised US$22,000 worth of funds in 2010 to support school rebuilding, first-aid training and reproductive health education projects in Nepal (Thapa 2011).

Likewise, US-based Computer Association of Nepal-United States of America has supported the establishment of an 8.0-magnitude earthquake-resistant cross band repeater, and has also contributed nine handheld amateur radio sets to five organisations in Kathmandu. Some Nepali youths in the United States have also contributed to the Doko Dai Mobile Library project. Additionally, websites like 'Thamel.com' and 'Nepalisite.com' in the United States have been promoting e-commerce back in Nepal endorsing Nepal's expertise in the US market. The Non Resident Nepali Association (NRNA) has also established a Skills Knowledge and Innovation Task Force to support science and technology education through a programme called Knowledge Investment in Nepal to promote Science and Technology. The 'Open University' initiative and Science Fellowships through the NRN Science Foundation are some of the good examples by the NRNA in this field (Adhikari 2013).

Nepali diaspora abroad often raise funds and advice and lobby for political parties and candidates back home. They have successfully organised rallies, protests, produced press releases, and campaigned a signature drive to overthrow the monarchy in Nepal (Adhikari 2011). It was their activism that overthrew the Rana Regime, ousted the monarchy, and established Nepal as a democratic republic in 2007. Leading political parties such as the Nepali Congress and the Communist Party of Nepal were founded and nurtured by Nepali diaspora members in India. In 2009, they also established the Constitution Recommendation Committee to carry out surveys of all the National Coordination Councils of the NRNA around the world, collating suggestions for the formation of a Constitution Assembly.

Promoting national image

Nepali diaspora promote Nepal's image through Nepali arts, music, films, books, food, crafts and other cultural relics (Nath 2009). They actively participate in major Nepali national and cultural celebrations to endorse Nepal and Nepali culture. Such exposure of culture through the diaspora helps in developing a broad interest about their native land, including the economic and political state of affairs in a foreign land (Newland 2010). To promote the national image, many websites and publications in the diaspora emphasise national symbols such as flags, emblems and maps (Lyons 2004). Introducing Nepal as the birthplace of Lord Buddha and Nepal as the Himalaya Kingdom have also helped improve the image of Nepal as well as that of the Nepali community abroad.

For instance, a statue of Buddha with inscription 'Buddha was born in Nepal' was recently placed at the International Criminal Court in The Hague. Many Nepalese in the diaspora have also successfully campaigned for Anuradha Koirala and Pushpa Basnet to become CNN Hero of the year in 2010 and 2012 respectively, and Prashant Tamang as Indian Idol in 2007. Their contribution through festivals, Republic day parades, etc. has promoted a better image of Nepal both in the home and the host countries. Georgia Osborne, a British national once stated, 'The people of Nepali origin here are role models for the other immigrant groups from across the world. Their friendly, non-violent nature and tolerant behaviour are a matter of pride in the local community' (CNSUK 2010).

The challenges

As observed, most investments by Nepali diaspora in the home country are limited to hydropower projects, telecom industries and banking sectors. NRNs have already established the Global Capital Investment Company for collective investment in Nepal as a commitment (*Himalayan Times* 2012). They have also organised six global conferences and five regional conferences. However, several factors have dented their efforts. As a result, with the exception of a few personal investments and altruistic actions, no large-scale investments have taken place in Nepal. Some of the major socio-cultural and political challenges that might have undermined the nexus between migration and devolvement in Nepal are summarised below.

Weak diaspora incorporation strategy

Home country policies play a significant role in attracting diaspora for development practices at home (Hunger 2002). In this regard, home countries must protect, promote and facilitate their populations abroad and enable them to compete globally. A good diaspora approach involves managing an organised and clear policy, as well as the cultivation of relationships with its diaspora abroad (Kitchin and Boyle 2011). Unfortunately, Nepal's diaspora incorporation strategy is weak and sluggish. Apart from a few foreign labour related policies, the country has only promulgated the 'Non Resident Nepali Act 2064' in 2008 and the 'Non Resident Nepali Regulation Act 2066' in 2009 allowing any NRNs or their family members to register as an NRN. The Act offers them an NRN card, which permits them to invest in Nepal while safeguarding the return of capital, and the right to run businesses and to purchase land for residential purposes. However, programmes to facilitate and promote diaspora networks or to seek expertise from expat specialists hardly exist. Besides, there is no established reward system that encourages the Nepali diaspora to make a contribution to their homeland. Conversely, the domestic political impacts and conflicts sometimes see officials working in Nepalese missions abroad resigning, citing a poor working environment and political differences as their reasons (DC Nepal 2012).

Poor remittance management

Remittances have worked as a safety valve for Nepal's dwindling economy for a long time – they have worked as a social protection mechanism for more than 58 per cent of the migrant households. Despite most of the remittances being used to build houses and pay tuition fees and healthcare costs, they have also helped to reduce poverty in Nepal – from 42 per cent in 1996 to 31 per cent in 2004 (Tiwari 2007). Sadly, they have also caused inflation in the Nepalese economy (World Bank 2011).

Despite receiving a huge volume of remittances, Nepal has failed to capitalise this resource in the absence of an effective remittance management. As a result, only 2.9 per cent of remittances are used in capital formation, while a large chunk goes into unproductive sectors (CBS 2011). From this perspective, instead of helping development through investment, remittances in Nepal seem to have caused more dependency on remittance. The growing trend of re-emigration can be the result of such negative impacts of remittances. Similarly, Nepal's failure to enhance its diaspora bond was the result of poor strategy. Nepalese settlers in India and those living in the OECD countries were excluded from the scheme despite the fact that the former holds the largest number while the latter enjoys higher incomes compared to those working in the Gulf and the Middle East.

Bad governance practices

Nepal remains in a state of perpetual political transition, uncertainty and chaos, as more than two dozen regimes have taken over since democracy was restored in 1990. Due to political instability, most governmental decisions are subject to political connection, bribery, and temptation, resulting in slow decision-making (Dangal 2005). Upon assuming office, senior level officials hired by the outgoing administrations are swapped with those officials perceived to be loyal, and they are assigned key responsibilities regardless of their expertise and commitment (Tamot 2008). This has resulted in the country witnessing many incompetent and corrupt leaders in the post-democracy era (Kantipur 2011). In addition, ethnicity has often been used for political gain since the early 1990s as many politicians in Nepal tend to divide the general public along the lines of caste and ethnicity. The concept of federal states proposed by the Maoists in 2009 became a prime agenda for almost all political parties. Similarly, the Federal Democratic Alliance (FDA) drive for socio-economic reform in Nepal was also a strategy to attract people to form allies to protest against the sit-in government (Basnet 2012).

Due to the increasing obstacles that political strikes and slow bureaucracy presented, promoting trade and investments in Nepal became a challenging feat. For instance, obstructions against hydropower projects and labour unrest in industrial sectors have deterred many potential investors from investing in Nepal (Humahgain and Khanal 2011). This was the reason why Nepal failed to witness an increase in FDI despite the fact that FDI was increased in majority of the less developed countries between 1990 and 2008 (UNCTAD 2012). Investors like Rana,[8] are often frustrated and discouraged due to the lengthy legal and bureaucratic procedures (Giri 2012). The deceptive laws related to foreign investment in Nepal have resulted in entrepreneurs and even NRNs turning to African nations for investment instead (OnlineKhabar 2013).

The issue of ethnicity and diaspora demands

The Nepali diaspora community is cracked due to lines being drawn along caste and ethnicity. Globally, hundreds of Nepali diaspora associations exist, struggling for their respective representation within the social groups based on caste and ethnicity. For instance, more than 400 Nepali communities-based organisations are operating in the United Kingdom alone (Paudyal 2010). Even a small country like Qatar has 115 Nepali organisations. Being at the centre of political and academic debate, the issue of ethnicity has significantly shaped diasporic decisions. Party affiliation and ethnic politics play a central role in claims for representation and legitimacy among the Nepalese communities abroad. Their diversity has not only affected their homeland orientations, it has also created some disarray within the diaspora communities abroad (see Subedi 2013).

Collectively, the NRNA lobbies for economic and political concessions at home, often tying the issue of investment with dual citizenship. Recently, Jiba Lamichhane, the previous NRN president, openly expressed concern that

> The government is trying to disconnect us from this land and expects our investment here. What motivates us to come here if we are not the citizen of this country? No matter how much the government tries to help us in policy related matters for bringing our investment here, we must be provided with the dual citizenships.
>
> (NRN Update 2012)

Unfortunately, because of their weak leverages, diaspora demands often go unheard by the home country government.

Case study: Nepali immigrants in South Korea

South Korea is thought to be a lucrative destination among the Nepalese for its high paying jobs. Korea's amazing economic growth and extensive demands for foreign labour during the late 1980s welcomed many foreign workers into the country. Although the actual date of Nepalese arrival in Korea cannot be pinpointed, it is believed that the tide began after the Seoul Olympics in 1988, when Korea formally opened its doors to foreign workers. The country's initiative to assist small- and medium-sized industries suffering from labour shortages for the 3D (dirty, dangerous and difficult) jobs created an environment that allowed many Nepali workers to visit Korea. Many of them are thought to have entered Korea as temporary visitors who eventually stayed longer than the expected period. However, after the Asian crisis in 1997, the Korean government started to regulate the influx of immigrants. For example, to regulate illegal migration and to fill the blue-collar jobs market, the country introduced the Industrial Trainee System in 1994. Later, it adopted the Employment Permit System (EPS) in 2003, and once Korea signed the MoU with Nepal in 2007, the gate for many Nepalese workers was opened (see Subedi and Jung 2010).

In numbers

At present, there are 22,687 Nepalese immigrants living in Korea, including the undocumented population who make up a little over 2,200 in numbers. The demography is dominated by the male population (20,043), with most (18,800) of them being unskilled workers employed in the manufacturing industries, while 2,267 of them work in the agricultural, fisheries and livestock sectors. The second largest group is made up of married immigrants, which accounts for 946 people, mainly dominated by the female population (825). Additionally, there are 488 Nepali students currently pursuing higher education in the country, with 251 enrolled in a Master's programme and 153 in a PhD programme. The majority (about 8,600) of these Nepalese immigrants reside in Gyeonggi province (MOJ Korea 2014).

Networks: heterogeneous

Diaspora networks in Korea can be categorised into four major groups: migrant workers, married immigrants, entrepreneurs and academia. The first group constitutes the numerical majority. While majority of the entrepreneurs represent NRN, the students and professionals are associated with the Society of Nepalese Students in Korea (SONSIK), which is limited to students, scholars and professionals. Most networks are independent and are managed by an executive committee or council. Some organisations like the NRNA and SONSIK demand its allied members to pay a registration fee. These communities mobilise their membership through these linkages among the network members and related associations and members back home. To facilitate interaction, many of them have their own web portals where they share information about the ongoing issues in both their home and host country.

Nepali migrants in Korea are also divided along the lines of caste, ethnicity and religion. As a result, there appears to exist several parallel community organisations in the diaspora. Currently, more than 70 Nepali organisations are operating in Korea. However, only about 50 per cent of them are very active (Basnet 2014). Almost all the major ethnic groups from Nepal have their own associations. Many of them serve the communal and ethnic needs of their members and bring hundreds of members together to cooperate and contribute to wider society. To meet their goals, they engage in diverse sociocultural and educational events, such as meetings, conferences, workshops, discussions and social events like gatherings or picnics. Some associations also have their own online newsgroups or newsletters to facilitate communication. Due to the diversity in the diaspora, many diaspora groups – such as Kirat sangha, Gurung sangha, Manang samaj, Myagdi samaj, Sudur pashchim samaj, Thakuri sewa samaj, Kaski samaj, Gulmi samaj, etc. – often organise sport or cultural festivals limited to their own ethnicity and region.

Cultural practices and feelings of belonging

Diaspora groups maintain linkages, form organisations, sustain communications, and influence the events in their home countries (Schiller *et al.* 1995). Their activities range from the exchanging of belongings to the association of the homeland orientation. Although the migration of Nepalese people to Korea is a new phenomenon, they are very transnational as they maintain a firm link between their home country and the country of their residence. It is important to note, however, that their transnational linkages are highly asymmetrical. Their social-cultural, economic and political engagements operate more at individual and specific levels than at the collective level. In general, the aspects of transnationalism in the Nepali diaspora are structured around Nepali political parties, ethnicity, regionalism and various diaspora organisations in the host countries.

The celebrations of major Nepali festivals like Dashain and Tihar in Korea is one way of maintaining strong feelings about 'home' in the diaspora. Despite the workload, Nepalese in Korea participate in several socio-cultural activities. They congregate during the time of festivals that aim to promote their traditions. In this way, they keep alive the social-ethnic identifications of their homeland. Similarly, buying objects related to Nepal, communicating with the homeland, eating home country foods, and sharing music and songs from Nepal are very common activities they engage in. For them, Nepal is a 'home' around which many events are structured. The growing demand and presence of Nepali films and concerts in Korea has also shaped Nepali settlers' cultural cultivation. In the same breath, reading news related to Nepal and sending money back regularly have helped preserve their attachment to their 'home'.

Gatherings usually take place on Saturday evenings, Sundays, or on holidays, in nearby restaurants and stores run by natives, mostly in the Dongdaemoon,

Yeongdeungpo, Wuijeongbu, Suwon, Ansan, Daegu and Busan areas. During their visit, they buy Nepali foods and phone cards and send money to Nepal through 'Hundi'.[9] They also often visit their friends to celebrate national and ethnic festivals. While the majority of Nepalese enjoy get-together sessions with friends during their free time, a small handful people prefer to stay at home to prepare for the next day's work. However, coming from a strong Hindu tradition and living in a country where the majority of the population is non-religious seems to have affected the daily pattern of religious practices among the Nepalese immigrants in Korea (see Subedi and Jung 2010).

Homeland orientation

In spite of internal divisions and a weak leverage, Nepali migrants in Korea have built a strong transnational network through which they transmit their resources as a commitment to Nepal. The Nepalese embassy in Seoul has a hard time serving its 22,000 people with a measly manpower of nine staff and limited resources. Apart from consular work and labour-related issues, the embassy also promotes cultural and economic activities that include trade, investment and tourism, with the objectives of enhancing image of Nepal in Korea. It has been collaborating with several Korean NGOs and universities for the benefit of Nepal (Bartaula 2014). However, despite everyone's active participation in multi-disciplinary fields, not much has been achieved to date. Although the NRNA's motto claims to 'represent the interests, concerns and commitment of all NRNs' and to enable their participation in the socioeconomic aspects of Nepal (NRN Update 2013), it has failed to make any impact in Korea despite having a strong presence. The major contributions made by Nepali people living in Korea are summarised below.

Tangible contributions

Remittance is the most tangible benefit Nepal receives from its people living abroad. Nepal received a hefty US$40 million in remittances from Korea in 2013. The actual figure is estimated to be much higher (almost four times), considering the fact that many immigrants send money through informal routes – such as Hundi – because it is cheaper and more convenient than the banks (*Karobar Daily* 2014). Although major investments in Nepal by Nepalese immigrants from Korea are lacking, they have successfully pursued many Korean firms and organisations to operate several projects in Nepal. Additionally, it is important to note that many individual aids and investments go unnoticed. In 2013 alone, the Nepalese diaspora living in Korea contributed about NPR260,708,795 (approx. US$2,756,734) to Nepal. The majority of this input was channelled towards the health sector (67.4 per cent), followed by the education sector (19.6 per cent), social welfare (8.9 per cent), and relief works (4.1 per cent) (Basnet 2014).

Korea is also one of the top five investors in Nepal. Since 1991, Korea has been providing various equipment and project aids in the areas of agriculture, hydropower, infrastructure, communication, health, education, culture, volunteer services and FDI, etc. As of July 2012, 171 projects under South Korean investment have come into operation, with an investment of Rs.6,422 million, helping to create 6,820 jobs (MOFA Nepal 2014). Some of the major projects include solar light projects in the villages of Makawanpur, Nuwakot and Kavre districts, micro power generation project in Makawanpur, and building libraries in the Gorkha district of Nepal. Additionally, Chameliya, Upper Trishuli and Modikhola hydropower projects are being handled by Korean companies. In the same breath, the establishment of the Tikapur Medical Centre, the feasibility study of the Kathmandu metro, Nizgadh International Airport, and the Greater Lumbini development plan are also worthy of mention (Bartaula 2014). Moreover, with support from Korean professors and universities, some SONSIK members have also implemented projects related to hydropower, health, and education in Nepal.

Intangible contributions

Despite being unable to promote knowledge, trade and investments in Nepal, both the NRNA and SONSIK were instrumental in the 'Save Dolma' fund collection project and the 'Buddha was born in Nepal not in India' campaign in Korea. Presently, NRN Korea is running a 'Nepal House' in Seoul. The house provides shelter for needy people, where occasional gatherings and a free health check camp takes place twice a month. Philanthropic campaigning for 'Nepal' from Korea has also been quite remarkable. For instance, Nepalese living in Korea raised about US$20,000 through the 'Save Anish Campaign' last year as blood money to save the life of Anish Khaling Rai, a Nepali migrant worker who faced a death sentence in the UAE (Kantipur 2011). Similarly, by organising 'Resunga cultural Jhalak' during the lunar new year, Gulmi Samparka Samiti raised approximately US$11,000 to donate to the 'Rudrabeni Elderly House'. In addition to all of these, Nepali immigrants in Korea have been engaging in endless fundraising efforts for the Help Nepal Network project to establish an e-library in a school in the remote districts of Nepal.

Nepali immigrants often launch campaigns in Korea to support needy Nepalese people around the world who are fighting against death or disease, to bring a dead body back home, or to provide economic support to the deceased's family members. Once the funds are raised, these organisations send money to the individuals concerned through organisations in Nepal. In the event where they run out of money for their own welfare activities in Korea, Nepali immigrants turn to social networking sites like Facebook to raise funds. Apart from sending money, some organisations such as Women for Women also run shelters to provide accommodation for fellow immigrants without jobs. These organisations sometimes target Korean donors and make a pledge to support them through their web portals.

Nepalese living in Korea are also active in promoting their national image. In 2011, Nepal's then ambassador to Korea wrote a letter to the then Korean president, requesting him to change the flawed information in South Korean textbooks regarding the birth of Lord Buddha. Factually, Lord Buddha was born in

Lumbini, Nepal, and not in India (*Korea Times* 2011). This act was campaigned and supported by the Nepalese communities throughout Korea. To upgrade Nepal's image, these immigrant groups also sometimes donate to local charity organisations and participate in Korean celebrations such as International Day and other multicultural events. Through the organisation and promotion of various home country cultural festivals and events, the Nepalese population in Korea has successfully upgraded the image of Nepal.

Final reflections and policy implications

The lack of opportunity at home and better prospects of life abroad have pushed many Nepalese out of the country. Despite having strong diaspora populations, Nepal has yet to fully capitalise her diaspora resources. Nepalese diaspora living abroad have been contributing much-needed social services to their homeland. Almost all of their homeland orientations are confined at the grass roots level, and are philanthropic in nature. In this way, we see a bottom-up approach without any collaboration from the state. Taking the potentiality of these activities into consideration, the eventual impact it has on the home country's development is very miserable, even in the case of Korea. Nepal's weak and sluggish strategy to mobilise its people abroad is the main reason for this outcome. Nepal's perpetual political instability has made it difficult to set a common agenda. Moreover, the democratic leaders in Nepal have, for a long time, ignored the importance of the Nepalese diaspora.

Bad governance practices at home have created an insecure domestic environment, dissuading many Nepali diaspora from investing in Nepal since the risks appear to be too high. Moreover, the country's inability to respond to diaspora demands has also limited their engagement in Nepal. Similarly, the division based on caste and ethnicity in the diaspora have resulted in splitting acts that have achieved little in terms of Nepal's needs. Regardless of a citizen's willingness to serve, no individual would like to 'return' or 'engage' in such a risky environment as Nepal poses now, especially when they are having a relatively affluent life abroad. However, the potentiality of diaspora contributions makes Nepal a strong case for diaspora-led development practices at home.

First, Nepal would need to identify its people abroad and facilitate their initiatives through policy changes, such as through the creation of a separate diaspora ministry. The country must focus on economic growth, as this may help solve some political agendas. The political parties need to maintain rule of law, order, peace and security. To utilise the huge remittances and diaspora skills, Nepal needs an effective cash management system so that several micro-level projects can be created. Since the NRNA represents all Nepali communities abroad, the country must respond to its concerns. Similarly, diaspora populations should unite by abandoning issues related to caste and ethnicity. They must work together as a driving force of the knowledge economy and promote local industries abroad. Contributing their capital, leadership and managerial skills, Nepali diaspora can become an agent of change in the development of Nepal.

Notes

1 Poor job market and low pay.
2 Political instability, corrupt bureaucracy, privileged nepotism, etc.
3 Education, security, family ties, neighbourhood impact, social status, etc.
4 The Diversity Visa is a lottery programme mandated by the US Congress that awards approximately 55,000 visas annually to people of countries with low rates of immigration in the United States.
5 People who are absent in households for more than six months.
6 Total Business Institute is an investment company established by an NRN in Japan. The company runs restaurant management, real estate, advertising agency, travel, trade and apparel business.
7 Gulmi (a district in Nepal) Service Society – in English.
8 A US graduated Nepali citizen who tried to initiate a venture capital industry in Nepal.
9 An informal way to send money from one country to another.

References

Adhikari, A. 2011. How NRNs Can Chip In. *Republica.* Online, available at: http://archives.myrepublica.com/portal/index.php?action=news_details&news_id=26908 (accessed 5 November 2013).

Adhikari, R. 2013. Nepal's Prosperity: the Missing Link. Online, available at: www.nepalnews.com/archive/2013/others/guestcolumn/feb/guest_columns_10.php (accessed 28 September 2013).

Barry, K. 2006. Home and Away: the Construction of Citizenship in an Emigration Context. *New York University Law Review* 81, 11. Online, available at: http://papers.ssrn.com/sol3/papers.cfm?abstract_id=907674 (accessed 23 September 2013).

Bartaula, R.R. 2014. Regarding Information. Email (26 May 2014).

Basnet, B. 2012. Divide and Rule. *Republica.* Online, available at: www.myrepublica.com/~myrepub/portal/index.php?action=news_details&news_id=44098 (accessed 6 October 2013).

Basnet, D.B. 2014. Answers on Migration. Email (31 May 2014).

Bauböck, R. 2005. Expansive Citizenship Voting beyond Territory and Membership. *Political Science and Politics* 38(4): 683–687.

Beine, M. and K. Sekkat. 2013. Skilled Migration and the Transfer of Institutional Norms. *Journal of Migration* 2(1): 1–19.

CBS, Nepal. 2008. Nepal Standard Living Survey. Central Bureau of Statistics. Online, available at: www.cbs.gov.np/statis_2008_content.html (accessed 12 October 2013).

CBS, Nepal. 2011. Nepal Standard Living Survey. Central Bureau of Statistics, Nepal.

CNSUK. 2011. Centre for Nepal Studies UK. Online, available at: www.cnsuk.org.uk/index.php (accessed 14 November 2013).

Dainik Nepal. 2014. Half Million Youths go Abroad Yearly. Online, available at: http://dainiknepal.com/2014/05/2153.html (accessed 27 May 2014).

Dangal, R. 2005. Administrative Culture in Nepal: Does it Reflect the Dominant Sociocultural Values of Nepal? Master's Thesis, University of Bergen. Online, available at: www.ub.uib.no/elpub/2005/h/701002/Masteroppgave.pdf (accessed 9 June 2013).

DC Nepal. 2012. Resignation by an Embassy Official in Korea Citing the Bad Environment for Work. Online, available at: www.dcnepal.me/news_nepali_archive.php?nid=16378 (accessed 9 October 2013).

Giri, S. 2012. Returning Nepalese Students Assist New Entrepreneurs. *Khabar South Asia.* Online, available at: http://khabarsouthasia.com/en_GB/articles/apwi/articles/features/2012/06/01/feature-01?change_locale=true (accessed 5 November 2013).

Guarnizo, L.E. 1998. The Rise of Transnational Social Formations: Mexican and Dominican State Response to Transnational Migration. *Political Power and Social Theory* 12: 45–95.

Harris, J.R. and M.P. Todaro. 1970. Migration, Unemployment and Development: a Two-sector Analysis. *American Economic Review* 60: 126–142.

Himalayan Times. 2012. NRNs Allowed to Invest in Capital Market. Online, available at: http://thehimalayantimes.com/fullNews.php?headline=NRNs+allowed+to+invest+in+capital+market&NewsID=336854 (accessed 28 September 2013).

Humahgain, M. and R. Khanal. 2011. Nepal Ranks 134th on FDI Inflow Index. *Kathmandu Post.* Online, available at: www.ekantipur.com/the-kathmandupost/2011/07/27/money/nepal-ranks-134th-on-fdi-inflowindex/224519.html (accessed 22 September 2013).

Hunger, U. 2002. The 'Brain Gain' Hypothesis: Third World Elites in Industrialized Countries and Socioeconomic Development in their Home Country. Online, available at: http://escholarship.org/uc/item/9jh5k800 (accessed 27 May 2014).

Johnson, B. and S. Sedaca. 2004. Diasporas, Émigrés and Development, Economic Linkages and Programmatic Responses. *CARANA–United States Agency for International Development.*

Kantipur. 2011. Parties 'Most Corrupt Institution' in Nepal. Online, available at: www.ekantipur.com/2011/12/23/editors-pick/parties-mostcorrupt-institution-in-nepal/345992.html (accessed 22 October 2013).

Kapur, D. 2001. Diasporas and Technology Transfer. *Journal of Human Development* 2(2): 265–286.

Karobar Daily. 2014. Four Times More Remittance through Hawala. Online, available at: www.karobardaily.com/news/2014/01/four-times-more-remittance-through-hawala (accessed 25 May 2014).

Ketkar, S.L. and D. Ratha. 2009. Development Finance via Diaspora Bonds. *Innovative Financing for Development*, 59–78.

Kitchin, R. and M. Boyle. 2011. Diaspora Strategies in Transition States: Prospects and Opportunities for Armenia. Online, available at: http://eprints.nuim.ie/2929/ (accessed 28 May 2014).

Korea Times. 2011. Nepal Asks President Lee to Correct Buddha's Birthplace. Online, available at: www.koreatimes.co.kr/www/news/include/print.asp?newsIdx=101619 (accessed 23 April 2014).

Lal, C.K. 2003. Homecoming. *Nepali Times*, 165.

Lapper, R. 2004. Study Finds More Migrants Sending More Money Home. *Financial Times*, 2.

Lodigiani, E. 2009. Diaspora Externalities and Technology Diffusion. *Economie Internationale* (3): 43–64.

Lyons, T. 2004. Engaging Diasporas to Promote Conflict Resolution: Transforming Hawks into Doves. Working Paper, Washington, DC: Institute of Conflict Analysis and Resolution, George Mason University.

Massey, D.S. 1999. International Migration at the Dawn of the Twenty-first Century: the Role of the State. *Population and Development Review* 25(2): 303–322.

Massey, D.S., J. Arango, G. Hugo, A. Kouaouci, A. Pellegrino and J.E. Taylor. 1993. Theories of International Migration: a Review and Appraisal. *Population and Development Review* 19(3): 431–466.

Meyer, J.B., J. Charum, D. Bernal, J. Gaillard, J. Granés, J. Leon and B. Schlemmer. 1997. Turning Brain Drain into Brain Gain: the Colombian Experience of the Diaspora Option. *Science Technology and Society* 2(2): 285–315.

MOFA. 2014. Ministry of Foreign Affairs Nepal. Online, available at: www.mofa.gov.np/en/bilateral-relations-nepal-south-korea-95.html (accessed 26 May 2014).

MOJ. 2014. Short-and Long-term Alien Status. Ministry of Justice Korea. Online, available at: www.moj.go.kr/HP/COM/bbs_03/ (accessed 28 May 2014).

Nath, L. 2009. A Little of Nepal: Nepali Diaspora in the US in an Age of Globalization. *Bodhi: An Interdisciplinary Journal* 3(1): 106–119.

Newland, K. 2010. Voice after Exit: Diaspora Advocacy. *Migration Policy Institute*. Online, available at: www.mekendeshter.org/upload/diaspora/diasporas-advocacy.pdf (accessed 18 March 2014).

Newland, K. and E. Patrick. 2004. Beyond Remittances: The Role of Diaspora in Poverty Reduction in their Countries of Origin, a Scoping Study by the Migration Policy Institute for the Department of International Development. *Migration Policy Institute*. Online, available at: www.migrationinformation.org/sites/default/files/publications/Beyond_Remittances_0704.pdf (accessed 24 May 2014).

NRNA. 2013. Online, available at: www.nrn.org.np/#sthash.VZp0Pqsh.dpbs (accessed 19 February 2014).

NRN Update. 2011. We'll Lobby Strongly for Dual Citizenship. Online, available at: www.nrn.org.np (accessed 21 May 2014).

Ojha, P. 2012. Tapping Nepalis Abroad. *Republica*. Online, available at: www.myrepublica.com/portal/index.php?action=news_details&news_id=34761 (accessed 16 November 2013).

Onlinekhabar. 2012. Pravasi Le Gare Gaubikasko Lagi 23lac Sahayog. Online, available at: http://onlinekhabar.com/2012/02/130369.html (accessed 19 October 2013).

Onlinekhabar. 2013. Nepali Investments going to Africa. Online, available at: www.onlinekhabar.com/2013/02/38392/ (accessed 9 September 2013).

Paudyal, C. 2010. Multiculturalism Flourishes with Nepali Community. CNSUK. Online, available at: www.cnsuk.org.uk/index.php?option=articles&id=10 (accessed 14 February 2014).

Probst, T. 2012. Learning from Nepal's First Diaspora Bond Issuances. Online, available at: www.nadel.ethz.ch/Essays/MAS_2010_Probst_Thomas.pdf (accessed 24 September 2013).

Schiller, N.G., L. Basch and C.S. Blanc. 1995. From Immigrant to Transmigrant: Theorizing Transnational Migration. *Anthropological Quarterly* 48–63.

Shain, Y. 1989. The War of Governments against Their Opposition in Exile. *Government and Opposition* 24(3): 341–356.

Stalker, P. 2001. *The No-nonsense Guide to International Migration*. London: Verso.

Subedi, B. 2011. Giving it back to their Homeland. *Kathmandu Post*. Online, available at: www.ekantipur.com/the-kathmandupost/2011/10/11/money/giving-it-back-to-their-homeland/227109.html (accessed 28 November 2013).

Subedi, T.P. 2013. Turning 'Brain Drain' into 'Brain Gain': Nepal's Diaspora Option from the Perspective of State–Diaspora Responses. Unpublished thesis, Inha University.

Subedi, T.P. and Y.T. Jung. 2010. Impact of Working Environment and Lack of Religious Facilities on Migrant Workers' Religious Sustainability: A Case Study of Nepalese Migrant workers in Korea. *Inha Journal of Social Science* 26: 229–251.

Subedi, T.P. and Y.T. Jung. 2011. International Marriage: Factors Causing Marital Disruption: A Case Study of Nepalese Brides in Korea. *Inha Journal of Social Science* 27: 95–118.

Tamot, R. 2008. *Marginal Professionals, Predatory Nepalese Elites, and Emigration to the 'Dreamland'*. Michigan: ProQuest.

Thapa, S.R. 2011. How young Nepalis abroad are serving their country. *Republica.* Online, available at: http://archives.myrepublica.com/portal/index.php?action=news_details&news_id=29340 (accessed 12 November 2013).

Tiwari, B.N. 2007. Assessment of Causes of Conflict in Nepal. Online, available at: http://repository.unm.edu/handle/1928/3294 (accessed 22 March 2012).

UNCTAD. 2012. World Investment Report 2012 – Towards a New Generation of Investment Policies: United Nations Conference on Trade and Development.

UNDP. 2010. HIV and Mobility in South Asia. Online, available at: http://asiapacific.undp.org/practices/hivaids/documents/HIV_and_Mobility_in_South_Asia_web_Nepal.pdf (accessed 29 March 2014).

Upreti, B.C. 2002. *The Marginal Migrants: a Study of Nepali Emigrants in India*: New Delhi: Kalinga Publications.

World Bank. 2008. *Migration and Remittances Factbook.* Washington, DC: World Bank.

World Bank. 2011. *Migration and Remittances Factbook.* Second edition. Washington, DC: World Bank.

World Bank. 2012. *Migration and Remittances Factbook.* Second edition. Washington, DC: World Bank.

Yang, D. 2008. International Migration, Remittances and Household Investment: Evidence from Philippine Migrants. *Economic Journal* 118(528): 591–630.

Zweig, D., C.S. Fung and D. Han. 2008. Redefining the Brain Drain: China's Diaspora Option. *Science Technology and Society* 13(1): 1–33.

12 Pakistani migration to the Gulf and development in the Miranzai valley in Pakistan

Syed Minhaj ul Hassan

Pakhtun tribesmen have been nomads for centuries, before permanently settling in the sixteenth century. One very important land settlement during this period was that of Shaikh Mali, who is still venerated for his extraordinary land distribution system amongst the Pakhtun tribesmen. However, apart from the Peshawar valley, which was vast and more productive, the rest of the Pakhtun areas and the southern districts of Khyber-Pakhtunkhwa province were barren and mountainous, unable to produce enough sustenance for its inhabitants. Pakhtun menfolk have therefore always been in search of better opportunities elsewhere. Under British colonial rule, many Pakhtuns, especially those from the southern districts, worked in the main cities of India such as Calcutta (now Kolkata) and Bombay (now known as Mumbai). As part of this larger labour emigration movement, the Pakhtuns of the Miranzai valley also started going to the Gulf Cooperation Council (GCC) countries because their own land's production was not enough to feed their families and there were no industries in the valley where they could earn their livelihoods.

With the creation of Pakistan, Pakhtuns in search of jobs started migrating to Karachi, Pakistan's first capital industrial city and only port city for a long time. It was only in the early 1970s, after the oil boom, that they started immigrating to the GCC countries. It was also during this period of time when the government of Pakistan encouraged its citizens to immigrate to the GCC countries in order to bring home much needed foreign remittances – the country sustained enormous economic losses due to the East Pakistan crisis and a war with India from 1970–1971.

The Miranzai valley is a beautiful but narrow valley located in the southern part of the Khyber-Pakhtunkhwa province of Pakistan. The valley is sandwiched between Kohat and Thall towns, and is home to the Bangash tribe of Pakhtuns/Afghans. It is also bounded on its north-western sides by the tribal area of Orakzai, and its political administration headquarters is in the town of Hangu. The Orakzai tribesmen have added an extra demographic burden on the valley by migrating and settling in the valley to seek better living conditions as compared to their own homeland.

Traditionally, uneducated tribesmen of the valley would join defence forces and law enforcing agencies. However, after the Gulf oil boom, a large number of them moved to the GCC countries – Saudi Arabia and UAE in particular. Economically, these emigrants earned a lot of money. However, this brought new challenges to the socio-cultural and socio-economic traditions of the valley that were centuries old.

There was a blend of positive and negative impacts on the traditions of the tribesmen of the valley that influenced their daily lives. These brought changes to the demographic situation, tribal structure, social behaviour, political and religious outlook, and attitude towards women and education. Ultimately, these changes disturbed the tribal structure of the valley – traditional elite families who once had influence and control over the tribesmen were now challenged by the neo-rich of the society who previously had no say in tribal affairs.

This study set out to analyse the changes in the valley, and to investigate why such changes did not take place earlier in the area though migration had remained part and parcel of the tribesmen's lives. Another objective was to analyse the changes in the tribal structure and organisation of the tribes, and the resulting impacts that ensued. This study also focused on the new phenomena of religious fanaticism, which was non-existent a few decades earlier.

This chapter has been divided into different sections and sub-sections in order to detail the impacts and changes that have been witnessed. The study was subdivided into the following areas: Pakistani emigration to the GCC countries and remittances inflow: patterns and volume; reconfiguration of social hierarchy or changes in social sphere of the community; changes in the economic sphere of the community; changes in the educational sphere; changes in healthcare; changes in the political sphere; changes in dressing, arts and culture. This chapter also discusses the negative impacts of emigration that have created issues concerning law and order in the valley. This chapter concludes by highlighting the government's apathy towards the emigrants and their families, in hopes that the relevant authorities will be able to come forth with practical and beneficial policies for the stakeholders.

The data for this study were primarily collected from field trips to the Miranzai valley of Khyber-Pakhtunkhwa and the primary educational institution of the province viz. the University of Peshawar where personal interviews were conducted. Interviews were conducted mainly in 2011 and 2012, in person, on the phone, and through written requests. In terms of secondary research, relevant Internet sources and published materials were consulted. Both qualitative and quantitative methods were employed for research, and the confirmatory approach, together with data mining and data integration, were the methods employed for analysis.

Theoretical orientation

Migration of human beings both within and beyond boundaries has been going on for centuries, resulting in changes in both the sending and receiving areas (Castles 2010: 1567). Different scholars have come up with different theories for the study of migration related issues. These have been summarised by Alejandro

Portes as the following: First, the neoclassical approach, based on an individualistic calculus of benefits and costs among would-be migrants. Second, the 'new economics' approach, based on the concept of relative deprivation and an emphasis on family strategies to overcome capitalist market imperfections in sending regions. Third, the world-system perspective, grounded on the concepts of structural penetration and 'imbalancing' of peripheral areas creating the conditions for mass displacements out of them. Fourth and finally, the social networks approach, based on the concepts of 'path depending' and 'diminishing costs of migration' (Portes 2010: 1544).

Messey and his colleagues believed that all theories were relevant in the study of migration (Messey *et al.* 1994). What was crucial was how they were applied to the different processes of migration, as the explanations carry different meanings for different regions according to their history, politics, and geography. It is reported that 'world system theory is best for explaining emigration from developing countries, while bits of world system theory, segmented labour market theory and neo-classical macro-economics can [be] cobbled together to explain the forces attracting migration to developed destination countries' (Castles 2010: 1575). Stephen Castles believed that migration was a complex phenomenon and could not be studied through one single theory as it required a cross-discipline approach. However, in spite of his early pessimism, Castles eventually came up with the idea that a middle-range theory would be useful in the 'analysis of the regularities and variations in specific types of migration that share some important common characteristics: for instance flows of different types (e.g. labour migration and asylum migration)' (2010: 1574).

The changes occurring from migration vary in scope and level – some scholars have studied the individuals and families, some communities and regions, while others nation-states and the global economy. In the same manner, the resultant changes that have occurred because of migration also vary.

> Effects may simply scratch the surface of society, affecting some economic organisations, role expectations, or norms. On the other hand, they may go deep into the culture, transforming the value system, or into the social structure, transforming the distribution of power.
>
> (Portes 2010: 1544)

Though changes are brought by migration, the extent of these changes mainly depend on three factors: How many people were involved in the process? For how long did the movement continue? What was the class composition of the movement? (Portes 2010: 1544).

Alejandro Portes, while discussing the cyclical movements or circular flows of short duration, argued that it would produce less durable change than permanent displacement; but while studying the temporary or cyclical migration of the Pakhtuns of the Miranzai valley I discovered that although these migrations were circular in nature, they have brought profound changes to society. Portes' contention that such migrations in sending regions strengthen the existing socio-political order also differs with the findings of this chapter. In fact, these cyclical/circular migrations have brought about all the changes discussed in this chapter (Portes 2010: 1554).

Pakistani emigration to the GCC countries and remittances inflows

Together with other Pakistanis, the inhabitants of the Miranzai valley started migrating to the GCC countries in the 1970s after the oil boom as it provided new economic opportunities for them (Hashmatullah and Rafiullah 2005–2007: 48). According to the 2012 estimate of the Ministry of Overseas Pakistanis, the total Pakistani emigrant population was 5.5 million, amongst which 47 per cent were working in the Middle East. Out of the GCC countries, the largest numbers were working in Saudi Arabia and the UAE – 1,200,000 and 737,000 respectively. Amongst the emigrant population of Pakistan, the Pakhtun diaspora made up 35 per cent (Hashmatullah and Rafiullah), far higher than the Pakhtun population percentage in the Pakistani population (15.42 per cent) (Population Census Organization of Pakistan 1998). Emigrants from the Miranzai valley form a larger number than other areas of Pakhtuns in the GCC countries, especially from District Hangu, which figures very high in the emigrant population of the GCC. In villages like Doaba, Naryab, and Thall of District Hangu, almost every household had an emigrant in the GCC (Janan 2012).

At the start of the migration wave, a majority of these emigrants were semi or unskilled labourers who migrated to the Gulf countries through both legal and illegal means. There were scores of people who emigrated via boats and were commonly referred to as *Jatha*. Migrating through *Jatha* was a very risky affair as people were prone to drowning, losing their way in the deserts and dying of thirst and hunger, and even at risk of police arrest in the GCC countries. However, many accepted these risks/challenges in hopes of better economic opportunities. While there were many people who lost their lives this way, those who were able to make it to the GCC countries were eventually able to settle, adjust, and earn huge amounts of money (Badshah, K. 2012).

After realising the importance of emigrant workers, the federal government of Pakistan established the Bureau of Emigration and Overseas Employment by amalgamating the National Manpower Council, Protectorate of Emigrants and Directorate of Seamen's Welfare in October 1971. Only then did emigrants start going to the GCC countries through legal means. Initially, the bureau worked under the Emigration Act of 1922. In 1979 however, the federal government promulgated the Emigration Ordinance that framed the rules for the export of manpower to other countries. The objectives and functions of the bureau, as defined in the Emigration Ordinance 1979 and rules made thereunder, are to control, regulate, facilitate and monitor the emigration besides looking after the interests of such emigrants (Hashmatuallah and Rafiullah 2005).

Though the federal government's involvement streamlined the migration of workers, emigrants still faced a lot of problems. In spite of these problems however, they still managed to earn a good amount of foreign exchange for their home country and families. According to a report by the state bank of Pakistan, they remitted US$7.44 billion in the first seven months of Financial Year 2012 and were expected to cross the US$14 billion mark by the end of the year. In the first seven months, the remittances from Saudi Arabia, UAE, and other GCC countries including Qatar, Kuwait, Bahrain, Oman were US$2,008.47 million, US$1,644.34 million, and US$845.47 million respectively (Voice of Overseas Pakistanis 2012).

Impact of Gulf emigration on the Miranzai valley

Reconfiguration of social hierarchy

Though the diaspora of the valley earned a lot of money abroad, they hardly spent on themselves, as they would rather remit their earnings back home regularly. With the regular inflow of remittances, the families of emigrants in the valley experienced new conditions that also affected the overall environment of the valley. The most important and visible change due to the inflow of diaspora remittances was the demographic structure of the valley. Initially the home of the Bangash tribe, the valley saw its neighbouring Orakzai tribesmen purchasing agricultural and non-agricultural lands in the valley after earning money in the GCC countries. These purchases caused the value of the land to increase, particularly in the main towns of Hangu, Thall, Doaba and Kohat. Besides the Orakzai tribesmen, the poor classes of the Miranzai valley who had migrated to the GCC countries also started purchasing lands from the landowners of the valley. This affected the tribal structure of the Miranzai valley in the long run as the original landowners such as the Khans, Maliks and Syeds who were the traditional chiefs in the valley started losing their power over the tribesmen. This outcome was made ever more significant when the traditional chiefs failed to clamp down on religious militant activities as they had lost their control of the tribes (Khan, A. 2012).

This new wealthy class of diaspora and their families also started showing off their newly acquired wealth by constructing large brick/cemented houses with modern facilities. This negatively affected the landed class of the valley, who started selling more and more of their lands to the diaspora and their families in order to compete with the new wealthy class. The diaspora and their families consequently became more and more influential as they exerted their influence on the tribal set up of the society. Lawlessness ensued, because many amongst these newly rich belonged to the lower classes of the Pakhtuns and were not accepted as leaders of the tribe (Khan, S. 2012).

The *hujra*, a common guest house of the tribe, *mohallah* or village, is an important pillar of Pakhtun society. Joint *hujras* are normally used as guest rooms/houses, as well as meeting places for the discussion of important issues and as training places for the young. Young Pakhtuns would listen to stories from their elders and learn about etiquette, thus enabling the inheritance of traditions. When an individual behaved in a socially unacceptable manner, it was commonly remarked that the person had not seen a *hujra* or mosque. However, with the inflow of the diaspora's newfound wealth, families began constructing brick houses as their own individual guest rooms/houses, eroding a basic cultural characteristic of the Pakhtuns. Resultantly, the culture of *hujra* and all that it brought with it started to disappear (Ghulam 2011).

Diaspora remittances also have a great influence on the economic life of the tribesmen. Since the families of the diaspora acquired purchasing power, trading businesses flourished in the main towns of the Miranzai valley. Besides traditional businesses, people also started new businesses that better catered to customers' demands. For example, in order to facilitate the travelling of the diaspora, travel agencies not only dealt with the purchase of air tickets, they also facilitated the preparation of other documents necessary for foreign travel. The business of letter-writing also flourished, since the majority of the early diaspora and their family members were illiterate and modern telecommunication facilities were not yet available (Zulfiqar 2012).

Changes to the once simple lifestyle of the tribesmen of the valley was also visible. Houses in the valley that were generally made of mud with a few large rooms mostly shared by the family members were replaced by large brick houses equipped with modern facilities. The early houses did not have washrooms and lavatories, so male members of the tribes would go to the natural springs or other fresh water sources to take baths, while the females would go to their own specified areas, known as *Gudar*. There, they would wash clothes, take baths, and also bring water for drinking back home. *Gudar* areas were traditionally out of bounds for male members of the tribe.

With the large amount of money from their expatriate family members, the people in the villages and towns started constructing brick houses with medium or small rooms so that each individual (or at least the male members), gets a separate room with attached bathing and lavatory facilities. Resultantly, the tradition of bath places and other related necessities started disappearing. The traditional *Gudar*s were also abandoned due to the availability of piped or well-water in homes. The vanishing of which has been sung about by the well-known Pashto singer Haroon Badshah in the following words:

> *Khalq Badal shu ka Badal shwaloo wakhtoona*
> *Jeenakai na razee Gudar ta jeenakai na razee Gudar ta* (Pashto).
> (Badshah 2006)
>
> Translation:
> People have changed or the times have changed
> Girls are no more coming to *Gudar*, Girls are no more coming to *Gudar*.

Central fireplaces in traditional Pakhtun houses gave way to modern kitchens with the construction of new houses. This affected the family system as it removed an important socialisation space in the house; previously, family members would sit around the fireplace in a large room where the women would cook and the rest of the family members would eat. During long winter nights the older women and men would also share stories of their past life experiences with the younger generation (Badshah, K. 2012).

Changes in economic sphere of the community

The diaspora demand for the purchase of land also gave rise to property businesses. While some established property dealing offices, many others dealt through informal means by using their personal contacts and information. Diaspora remittances also helped in the construction of new brick and cemented shopping markets in the main towns that replaced traditional mud shops. The diaspora also purchased properties outside the valley in areas like Peshawar and Islamabad for both residential and investment purposes (Khan, S.Y. 2012).

An important development of the Miranzai valley diaspora in GCC countries was the start of *Doaba Mela* for foreign products. Doaba was a small town in District Hangu, where an informal bazaar for foreign goods was established every Thursday for people to trade imported products. It started when the diaspora brought different kinds of household products, electronic gadgets, and other personal use items when they returned to the valley. When the diaspora or their families were in need of money or wanted to get rid of these items, they would bring them to *Doaba Mela*, where items would be sold below the market price. Over a period of time, *Doaba Mela* flourished and became very popular, and non-diaspora businessmen also started trading foreign products there (Bangash 2012).

The diaspora and their families also got involved in the transportation and hotel businesses. Many ex-diasporas and their family members purchase their own vehicles, and even name their transport companies after well-known places in the GCC countries – the Mazdalfa Transport Company is an example (Hassan 2012). The hotel businesses were mainly established by the diaspora or their families in the major towns of Khyber-Pakhtunkhwa like Peshawar and Kohat. In Peshawar, many hotels owned by the diaspora are named after well-known places and personalities, such as the Dubai Hotel, Peshawar; Gulf Hotel, Peshawar; Qazafi Hotel, Peshawar; and Amin Hotel, Peshawar (Jan 2012).

Another agricultural tradition of the valley that has vanished due to the inflow of diaspora remittances are the water-mills. In the pre-Gulf migration period, traditional water-mills were used for grinding grains. The operator of the water-mill, known as the *Zhrandeegarai*, used to visit the *mohallahs* to either collect the grain for grinding or to deliver the flour (ground grain). With the availability of modern agricultural equipment however, these water-mills and *Zhrandeegarai* have largely disappeared (Raza 2012).

The tribesmen in the valley owned goats, sheep, cows and buffalo a few decades back. Shepherds, known as *Gadba/Shpoon/Shpoonkai*, used to take them to the pastures for grazing. All the animals of a *mohallah* or a small village were driven to a common place every morning. From there, they were taken by the shepherds to the pastures. This arrangement made the residents of the valley self-sufficient in dairy products. When the economic migrations started, the shepherds left for greener pastures. The residents of the valley eventually stopped breeding the animals as it required hard labour. They therefore mostly depend on commercial dairy products for consumption, changing the lifestyle of the tribesmen in the valley (Hussain 2011).

Changes in the educational sphere

Diaspora remittances have a positive impact on the literacy rate of the valley as well. As reported in the Population Census Organization of Pakistan's 1998 census (it was the last official census conducted in Pakistan), the literacy rate was very low. According to this census the literacy ratio of the Hangu district, which is located wholly in the Miranzai valley, was as follows: total: 30.5 per cent; male: 53.48 per cent and female: 9.84 per cent. Though there is currently no official data available, observers believe that literacy rate has definitely increased as it is noticeable from the spread of education institutions as well as the behavioural patterns of people. Earlier on, there were few educational facilities available and the poor tribesmen could ill afford education for their children. However, with the improvement of economic conditions, they started sending their children to educational institutions. This compelled the government to increase the number of educational institutions in the valley and to open up some colleges as well. The new demand for education also encouraged some educated persons in the valley to establish private educational institutions, as people were looking for quality education. We can therefore see hundreds of private educational institutions in the valley that were non-existent before the Gulf migration.

A well-known educational academy that the diaspora have contributed generously to is the Al-Asar Academy, Usterzai Payan, which provides education to a large number of children in the valley. Responding to people's demand for quality education, the Overseas Pakistanis Foundation established a school and college in the main town of the Miranzai valley, namely, the Hangu, for the benefit of the children of diaspora (Khan, S.Y. 2012).

With increased literacy and economic prosperity the lives of women folk also saw change and improvement. Previously engaged in hard physical labour along with their men folk, their standard of living has improved with the availability of economic resources. For example, they used to get up at dawn and go to the mountains to collect firewood, but now, due to resources being made available, the use of natural gas has replaced firewood. This change not only lessens their hardship, it also has a positive impact on the environment. The forests that provided wood to be used for cooking and for keeping warm in winters are now spared, increasing the forested areas in the valley.

Female education has also taken a turn for the better. Previously a non-priority, the availability of money has seen families sending girls to schools and even institutes of higher education. We now see many females from the valley in professional fields, like doctors, engineers, psychologists, geologists and social scientists who work in public as well as private sectors (Bano 2012).

Changes in healthcare

Diaspora influence has also brought about changes in the health sector. With money and education, people have become increasingly health conscious, demanding better health facilities for themselves and their families. To cope with the demand, many doctors and businessmen turned to establishing private clinics and hospitals where ordinary treatment and surgeries are carried out. Al-Zahra Hospital, constructed by a group of rich Arab businessmen, was recently inaugurated in the town of Hangu. The hospital provides treatment to many patients on nominal charges (Hassnain 2012).

Changes in the political sphere

Other than at the individual level, society has also been collectively affected due to the diaspora remittances and influence. One such major change can be seen in the politics of the valley. Traditionally the local chiefs or *Mullahs* used to contest elections for assemblies, both provincial and national, but with the large earnings of the diaspora, they themselves or their family members have started contesting and even winning the elections. A few such prominent names that can be pointed out are Shams ul Haq (ex-member of the National Assembly, Abdul Nabi Bangash (Senator), Syed Haider Ali Shah (member of the National Assembly), Farid Mufakir (former member of the Provincial Assembly), Dr Nadeem, a candidate for the provincial assembly seat, etc. (Orakzai 2012).

Changes in dressing, arts and culture

With the increase of diaspora remittances came the spread of individualism. The popularity of modern audio-visual equipment like tape-recorders, television, VCRs and CD players replaced the storytelling culture. Rarely do we find the older people telling stories today (Badshah 2012).The dressing, language and folk songs of the tribes of the valley also underwent changes when the diaspora of the Gulf States and Saudi Arabia brought such influences back to their ancestral villages. For example, the traditional dress of the tribes in the valley were often of dark colours, as they were mostly involved in physical labour. Living in the Gulf States where the Arabs mostly wear white dresses has however influenced the diaspora to adopt white dresses. The use of slippers by the diaspora instead of traditional shoes was another facet of change. The tribesmen also started using *Qatra* – a special small piece of cloth used by the Arabs for headgear – on their shoulders and on their heads against the scorching sun. In the same manner, people in the valley have also started naming their male children after well-known Arabs, such as Shah Faisal, Fahad, Saud, Yasser Arafat, Saddam Hussain, Osama, etc. Arabic words are also used to refer to modern household appliances, for example for fridge, *Salaja*; for resident card or visa, *Iqama*; for long Arabic shirt, *Qandoora*; for visa sponsor, *Kafeel*, etc. From these examples, it is evident that the diaspora in Arab countries have even influenced the language of the tribes in the valley (Jan 2012).

Like Pashto language, Pashto poetry and songs have also been influenced in the Miranzai valley by the diaspora. A famous singer of the valley, Musharaf Bangash, passionately expresses the feelings of an expatriate worker in the following song (2010):

> *Dher raata yadegi kor na rana heraigi mor*
> *Ya malgaro owayai kali ta ba kala zoo* (Pashto).
>
> Translation:
> I recall my home quite often and cannot forget my mother
> O friends tell me when we'll go home.

Similarly, a well-known *tappa*, a kind of Pashto folksong, goes:

> *Khwdaya da, dee Qatar Badshah Mar kai*
> *Sa shta meero kai Khazai Kwandai Naastai Deena* (Pashto).
> (Bint-i 2012)
>
> Translation:
> God may put to death the ruler of Qatar
> as in spite of being married the women are sitting like widows.

Before the inflow of diaspora remittances, the valley was primarily agricultural and had many traditions that were closely associated with the agricultural lifestyle. For example, during the corn growing season, young tribesmen would go to the corn fields, pluck the corn-sticks, cook them on a fire in the fields, and eat them on the spot. This was known as *Daaza* (which literally means the sound of corn popping). However, with the decrease in agricultural products from many of the valley areas – due either to non-availability of farmers or people who prefer purchasing corn sticks instead of going to the field and cooking it by themselves – this tradition has vanished.

Another tradition associated with the agricultural economy that has vanished is barter-trading. The landed classes of the valley used to have stores of grain in their houses. When the children asked for money to buy something from the *mohallah* shop, they would be given some grain to exchange for whatever they desired. With the abundance of money, barter-trading has disappeared (Ayub 2012).

A positive change that has taken place is the replacement of the traditional cooking style that women of the valley adopted. Women used to cook their food with firewood, and would light the bonfire for heating during winters. The firewood was either collected from the nearby mountains by the women themselves (Siegmann 2010: 354) or by their men folk. With the increase in income, most families use liquefied petroleum gas (LPG). In large towns, natural gas is supplied through pipe connections, and the women use it for cooking instead of the traditional firewood. The same happens when heating is required during the winters. Electricity is used as a substitute when LPG or natural gas is not available. This change has improved the living standards of Pakhtun women who used to labour under and live in harsher conditions (Ghulam 2010).

The other side of emigration-induced changes in society: drawbacks

While the women have benefited from diaspora remittances on one hand, they have also suffered from the immoral activities of some expatriates in the Gulf areas like the UAE on the other. Since UAE (Dubai in particular) has become very liberal in terms of sexual relations, some individuals have found themselves infected with HIV/AIDS. As extramarital sex is a taboo in Pakhtun society, such men do not reveal their infection out of fear or shame. As a result, they transmit the virus to their partners when they return home and spend normal conjugal lives with them. Such relationships even lead to babies being born with the virus. Many such cases occur, but are kept under wraps by the families involved (Khan, S. 2012).

Migration has also affected other aspects of social relations in the Miranzai valley. Since these emigrants are all young male members of the society, their wives and children are emotionally, psychologically and socially affected. The young children feel insecure in the absence of the fathers. In the worst cases, children end up participating in immoral activities. Some of the children also drop out of schools and aspire to go abroad like their fathers and uncles. Young wives are also emotionally and psychologically affected. There have been cases where expatriates get married and leave for their jobs in the foreign countries the very next day, not returning home for months or years. Their wives are consequently put under stress and sometimes even develop diseases. In extreme cases, these wives develop illicit sexual relations, including incest. These incidents have led to the killing of the individuals involved by the expatriates after their return (Hashmatullah and Rafiullah 2007: 26–27; Farid 2003–2004: 88).

The religious lives and thinking of the tribesmen in the valley have also been affected and influenced. The diaspora in GCC countries like Saudi Arabia has brought in its wake religious bigotry and extremism. Some who work and live in Saudi Arabia and the other GCC countries have been influenced by the extremist Arabs. Those living in Saudi Arabia are particularly prone to influence by the extremist *Salafi* ideas. They are the ones sponsoring religious *madrassas*, extremist groups, and other religious activities. These people also get the support of rich Arabs and are mostly responsible for religious extremism in their home countries (Taj 2010).

Such religious extremism was unknown to the tribesmen in their traditional Pakhtun society. Pakhtuns and non-Muslims have been living for centuries in most parts of the Pakhtun territory, but of special significance were their concentrations in the Orakzai Agency, Khyber-Agency, Swat, Buner, etc. (Spain 1985: 60) These non-Muslims were generally engaged in businesses and were used to travelling in Khyber-Pakhtunkhwa without fear or intimidation. They also had special relationships with the host Pakhtuns who were responsible for their protection. The protector of the non-Muslims for them was known as the *Naik*, which literally means the boss. The tolerance for non-Muslims was high. There is a famous folklore that goes like this: A Hindu sweet-maker developed some problem with the *Mullah* (the Priest of Pakhtuns), making the latter angry at the sweet-maker. The angry *Mullah* announced from the pulpit of the mosque that the Hindu had converted to *Wahabism* (a sect of Islam). As a result, the villagers stopped buying sweets from the Hindu. When the Hindu realised the reason, he went to the *Mullah* and apologised, appeasing him by giving him some gifts. After that, the *Mullah* again announced from the pulpit that the Hindu sweet-maker had rescinded his decision and converted back to Hinduism. With this announcement, the villagers once again started purchasing sweets from him (Khattak 1992, 2011). However, with the import of religious bigotry from the Gulf States like Saudi Arabia, non-Muslims no longer consider themselves safe in the traditional Pakhtun culture.

Another very dangerous and damaging impact of diaspora remittances is the introduction and spread of the Kalashnikov culture in the Miranzai valley. Pakhtuns are known for keeping and loving weapons. However, only rich people could afford sophisticated and lethal weapons capable of causing large and widespread damage; common Pakhtuns had few weapons of lethal effect. However, with the inflow of diaspora earnings, Pakhtuns started purchasing modern, more lethal weapons, especially Kalashnikov rifles. The inter-tribal, inter-sectarian, and inter-family rivalries and tensions proliferated with the introduction of heavy weapons, including small- and medium-sized missiles, rocket-launchers, grenades, anti-aircraft guns, etc. This trend militarised and equipped the tribes in the valley for more deadly fighting. This phenomenon was, however, not the sole result of diaspora remittances, but also the result of the Afghan crisis. The Afghan crisis caused Pakhtun territories to be flooded with modern and sophisticated weapons. Pakhtuns' increased purchasing power, coupled with their love for weapons and the influence of the Afghan crisis, therefore caused the spread of the Kalashnikov culture in the Pakhtun territories and the valley (Bangash 2012).

Conclusion

Though the Miranzai valley diaspora in GCC countries created an overall positive impact on the socio-economic life of the Miranzai valley, it also brought with it some negative influences, such as the breakdown of the traditional tribal structure, degeneration of moral values, and the introduction of heroin and the Kalashnikov culture.

The diaspora in the GCC countries is a major source of foreign exchange earnings for the government of Pakistan. However, the government has failed to fulfil its responsibilities to provide a better environment for these expatriates where they can fully utilise their potential. Nothing is done for them or for their families' welfare on the part of the government. The diaspora take care of their own needs, and have in fact replaced the government's broken and inefficient social safety net. We can see that their remittances pay for rents, medicines, grocery bills, marriage expenses, and other similar needs of low-income households who are unlikely to receive any meaningful support from the government. Similarly, remittances pay for the tuition fees of children who would otherwise not be educated because of inadequate public schools. The remittances therefore plug the gap in social spending in Pakistan.

It is the duty of the government to come up with some form of social security system for these expatriates who are remitting billions of dollars every year. The government should also provide some facilities to the diaspora to facilitate remittance transfers, as well as to provide safe and reliable investment opportunities for them.

One major drawback in the official policy towards emigrants is the absence of guidance for uneducated emigrants. Since most of these emigrants are uneducated, they fail to spend their hard-earned money carefully. When they return, they find themselves in poverty, placing a lot of stress on them as well as their families. To avoid such situations, the government should come forth with economic schemes that serve to channel their hard-earned money into profitable schemes. Such schemes would have a positive impact on the emigrants, as well as the whole of society.

Another important step that the government should take for the betterment of emigrants and their families is to establish an Overseas Pakistanis Foundation branch office in the valley. This office would be useful in providing information to would-be emigrants and their families about the schemes that the government has launched or plans to launch for them.

Last but not the least, the government should establish vocational institutions in different towns of the valley, which would serve to impart technical skills to the would-be emigrants. Most of these emigrants currently migrate without any practical skills, putting them in a very disadvantageous position in the GCC countries' job market. They either spend a lot of time learning skills, or continue to languish as day labourers. If they are given vocational training before leaving the country it will put them in good stead to increase their own income as well as to earn precious foreign exchange for the country.

References

Ayub, M. 2012. Assistant Professor in History, Government Degree College, Charsadda, Khyber-Pakhtunkhwa. Interview conducted by author, 9 March.

Badshah, H. 2006. Pashto Song on YouTube, Online, available at: www.youtube.com/watch?v=XAlqVyBQZwE&list=PL5A693E0025754856&index=6&feature=plpp_video (accessed 16 May 2012).

Badshah, H. 2012. Education Officer, Department of Education, Hangu, Khyber-Pakhtunkhwa. Interview conducted by author, 10 February.

Badshah, K. 2012. Resident of Naryab Distt. Hangu, Khyber-Pakhtunkhwa, an ex-Diaspora of Abu-Dhabi, Interview conducted by author, 20 June.

Bangash, M. 2010. Pashto Song on YouTube. Online, available at: www.youtube.com/watch?v=GeH1CcIEA_o&list=PLF9D21730E4A7D383&index=3&feature=plpp_video (accessed 16 May 2012).

Bangash, N.A. 2012. Local Businessman in Main Bazar Hangu, Khyber-Pakhtunkhwa. Interview conducted by author, 19 June.

Bano, A, 2012. Chief Psychologist, Khyber-Pakhtunkhwa Public Service Commission, Peshawar. Interview conducted by author, 18 July.

Bint-i, A. 2012. Resident of Mohallah Paskalai, Hangu. Interview conducted by author, 29 July.

Castles, S. 2010. Understanding Global Migration: A Social Transformation Perspective. *Journal of Ethnic and Migration Studies* 36(10): 1565–1586.

Farid, S. 2003–2004. Labour Export to the Middle East and its Impacts on their Family Life (A Case Study of Village Adhami Piran, Tehsil and Distt. Bannu. Unpublished Master of Arts thesis submitted to the Department of Social Work, University of Peshawar.

Ghulam, S. 2011. Mohallah Paskalai, Hangu, Khyber-Pakhtunkhwa. Interview conducted by author, 25 October.

Ghulam, Z. 2010. Resident of Mohallah Paskalai, Hangu, Khyber-Pakhtunkhwa, an ex-Farmer and a Current Diaspora. Interview conducted by author, 2 January.

Hashmatullah, S. and A.Q. Rafiullah. 2005–2007. Impact of Emigrant's Children in District Dir (Lower): A Case Study of Village Rabat. Unpublished Master of Arts in Sociology thesis submitted to the Department of Sociology and Social Anthropology, University of Peshawar.

Hassan, S.A. 2012. An ex-Diaspora and Owner of Transport Business, Resident of Railway Station Road, Hangu, Khyber-Pakhtunkhwa. Interview conducted by author, 26 June.

Hassnain, S.K. 2012. Mohallah Paskalai, Hangu, Khyber-Pakhtunkhwa. Interview conducted by author, 25 July.

Hussain, S.G. 2011. Liaison Officer, Iran Cultural Centre, Peshawar Cantt, Khyber-Pakhtunkhwa. Interview conducted by author, 20 December.

Jan, S.Q. 2012. A Diaspora in Abu-Dhabi from Hangu, Khyber-Pakhtunkhwa. Interview conducted by author, 15 March.

Janan, G. 2012. Resident of Doaba Dist. Hangu, Khyber-Pakhtunkhwa, an ex-Diaspora of Abu-Dhabi. Interview conducted by author, 25 June.

Khan, A. 2012. Teacher in the Public School, Hangu, Khyber-Pakhtunkhwa. Interview conducted by author, 30 June.

Khan, S. 2012. An Informal Property Dealer in Hangu, Khyber-Pakhtunkhwa. Interview conducted by author, 27 June.

Khan, S.Y. 2012. Executive Director, Roshan Development Society, Hangu, Khyber-Pakhtunkhwa. Interview conducted by author, 24 July.

Khattak, N.J. 2011. Vice Chancellor, Kohat University of Science and Technology, Kohat, Khyber-Pakhtunkhwa. Interview conducted by author, 20 December.

Khattak, R.W.S. 1992. Former Director, Pashto Academy and Dean, Faculty of Islamic and Oriental Studies, University of Peshawar, Pakistan. Interview conducted by author, 15 May.

Massey, D.S., J. Arango, G. Hugo, A. Kouaouci, A. Pellegrino and J.E. Taylor. 1994. An Evaluation of International Migration Theory: The North American Case. *Population and Development Review* 20(4): 699–751.

Orakzai, H. 2012. Resident of Wrasta Road, Hangu, Khyber-Pakhtunkhwa. Interview conducted by author, 18 June.

Population Census Organization of Pakistan, Government of Pakistan. 1998. Population by Mother Tongue, Online, available at: www.census.gov.pk/MotherTongue.html (accessed 2 September 2012).

Population Census Organization, Pakistan. 1998. Census 1998 Data. Online, available at: www.census.gov.pk/NWFP/HANGU.htmL (accessed 16 September 2012).

Portes, A. 2010. Migration and Social Change: Some Conceptual Reflections. *Journal of Ethnic and Migration Studies* 36(10): 1537–1563.

Raza, S.W. 2012. Resident of Railway Station Road, Hangu, Khyber-Pakhtunkhwa. Interview conducted by author, 3 July.

Siegmann, K.A. 2010. Strengthening Whom? The Role of International Migration for Women and Men in Northwest Pakistan. *Progress in Development Studies* 10(4): 345–361.

Spain, J.W. 1985. *The Pathan Borderland.* Karachi: Indus Publications.

Taj, F. 2010. Analysis: Pakhtun Diaspora Irresponsible and Insensitive. *Daily Times*, 9 January. Online, available: at: www.dailytimes.com.pk/default.asp?page=2010/01/09/story_9-1-2010_pg3_5 (accessed 9 March 2012).

Voice of Overseas Pakistanis. 2012. Online, available at: www.oversaeaspakistanis.net (accessed 20 March 2012).

13 The other side of the migration and development nexus

Human trafficking in Sri Lanka

Kopalapillai Amirthalingam, Danesh Jayatilaka and Rajith W.D. Lakshman

People use various forms of international migration as a pathway to secure income. This inherent goal of international migration lies at the heart of the debate for migration and development. We often identify successful migrants to study the broader implications migration has on them and their families. However, migration is not a smooth, linear process for individual migrants. This chapter argues that there is a need to investigate the experiences of those migrants who are not fortunate enough to accumulate wealth in the migration process, and to include them in the debate as well. This chapter discusses the risks certain migrants are exposed to when seeking prosperity overseas. The research was conducted in the backdrop of Sri Lanka's post-war situation in 2010, and focused on four districts in the coastal belt in Sri Lanka.

De Haas (2009) postulates that international migration occurs under a continuum of low to high constraints, and that the poorest and most vulnerable groups experience the most of these constraints. As a result, these groups take extreme risks, and quite a large number of them end up being trafficked (Salt and Stein 1997). Using data from Sri Lanka, this chapter studies the often-overlooked section of international migrants from the global South whose dream to be successful was stolen in the migration process. In the year 2000, the United Nations adopted the Protocol to Prevent, Suppress, and Punish Trafficking in Persons, Especially Women and Children, also known as the Palermo Protocol. Sri Lanka has ratified this protocol along with several other international and regional instruments that seek, among other things, to address the human trafficking problem.[1] In spite of years of commitment against human trafficking in Sri Lanka, reports suggest that the issue has not yet been controlled. For instance, the most recent Trafficking in Persons (TIP) report of the US Department of State (2013) places Sri Lanka at the 'Tier 2 watch list', which is just one level above the worst category, 'Tier 3'. The country was downgraded to 'Tier 2' in 2007 and has been at that level since then.

Previous studies have contributed to the appreciation and understanding of human trafficking realities and challenges in Sri Lanka, particularly in relation to the trafficking of women and children: (i) people are in situations of modern slavery in Sri Lanka; (ii) trafficking is a fluid phenomenon responding to market demands, weakness in laws, and economic and development disparities;

(iii) trafficking is less often about the flat-out duping and kidnapping of naïve victims, than it is about the coercion and exploitation of people who initially entered a particular form of service voluntarily or migrated willingly; (iv) traffickers often use sexual violence as a weapon against women to keep them in compelled service, whether in a field, a factory, a brothel, or a home; and (v) child sex trafficking is on the decline in the country (Coomaraswamy and Satkunanathan 2006; Frederick 2010; Samaranayake 2010; Squire and Wijeratne 2008).

Foreign employment is a vital support element to keep the Sri Lankan economy afloat. According to the Sri Lanka Bureau of Foreign Employment – SLBFE – (2009) foreign employment increased from 7.32 per cent in 1992 to 23.83 per cent as a percentage of the total labour force in 2010. It is estimated that as a percentage of total exports, private remittances increased from 20.95 per cent in 1990 to 48.74 per cent in 2011. According to the Central Bank of Sri Lanka (2013), this amount is equivalent to 8.7 per cent of the GDP in 2011. At the macro level, these numbers explain the government's rationale of promoting the foreign employment of Sri Lankans. At a micro level, they explain why people brave so many risks, including trafficking, to find work abroad.

The highest number of labour migrants left to the kingdom of Saudi Arabia (26.1 per cent), Kuwait (19.26 per cent), Qatar (19.99 per cent) and UAE (14.96 per cent) in the Middle East (SLBFE 2011). It is also evident that while females made up the bulk of people departing to these destinations during the 1990s, their numbers presently come close to that of the males. These migrants left for occupations at the various levels – these are professionals (1.46 per cent), middle level (2.32 per cent), clerical and related (3.76 per cent), skilled (25.75 per cent), semi-skilled (1.59 per cent), unskilled (24.13 per cent), and housemaids (41.0 per cent) in 2011 (SLBFE 2011).

In 2011, of the total of 9,994 complaints lodged with the conciliation division of the SLFBE, 81 per cent were made by females (SLBFE 2011: 85). When the total number of complaints were separated into specific issues in the data, it revealed that most trafficking-related issues of migrant workers impacted females (physical and sexual harassment, female 96 per cent; not sent back after completion of contract, female 92 per cent; non-payment of agreed wages, female 76 per cent; breach of employment contract, female 58 per cent) (SLBFE 2011: 87). The higher number of female complaints may be a reflection of more women migrating as temporary labour in the past two decades. Since the 1980s, men have dominated international migration in Sri Lanka – 76 per cent of migrants in 1986 were males. However this figure declined to nearly 29 per cent in 1997, but increased again to 50.9 per cent in 2012, making an almost even division between males and females at present.

Table 13.1 shows the close link between these locations of absorption and the violations taking place. Saudi Arabia ranks first in both the lists. The case of Ariyawathi, where a female migrant worker was reportedly brutally tortured by her Saudi employer in 2010, presents us with a case in point for the issues at hand.

Table 13.1 Complaints by country of origin

Country	*2007*			*2009*			*2011*		
	M	*F*	*Total*	*M*	*F*	*Total*	*M*	*F*	*Total*
KSA	424	3,343	3,767	1,232	4,565	5,797	862	3,915	4,777
Kuwait	70	1,486	1,556	259	2,096	2,355	199	1,769	1,968
Jordan	12	833	845	38	1,190	1,228	30	1,000	1,030
UAE	193	510	703	374	598	972	154	437	591
Qatar	338	114	452	440	208	648	349	244	593
Lebanon	5	617	622	6	312	318	11	171	182
Bahrain	6	149	155	21	172	193	6	192	198
Oman	12	57	69	38	136	174	12	139	151

Source: Sri Lanka Bureau of Foreign Employment (SLBFE), 2011.

Research methods

The methodology of this study includes a comprehensive literature review, a set of key informant interviews at the central and field levels, and a survey of affected communities using face-to-face interviews and focus group discussions. At the onset, we conducted a set of elite interviews with senior officials in Colombo in areas covering academia, justice, law enforcement, protection and monitoring. In total, 21 interviews were held in Colombo and 26 in the field. The fieldwork for this study was conducted during the period of 15 July 2010 to 15 October 2010 along the coastal belt of Sri Lanka in three districts: Puttalam, Galle, and Trincomalee.

Agencies in the study districts that work with the target groups helped with the logistics and selection of participants for the interviews. These purposive selections included trafficked/potential migrant workers and sex workers. Both females and males were included in the sample, and key informant discussions were conducted to gather corroborating information. One caveat being that the migration-related trafficking victims interviewed consisted mostly of migrants to the Middle East.[2] A semi-structured questionnaire was used for interviewing key informants directly involved in, or indirectly connected to human trafficking. The group included government officials, NGO workers and international agency staff. Besides verbal information, feedback was at times received with the assistance of a site visit or field interviews, and the provision of statistics/data.

A structured questionnaire was employed for interviewing former victims of trafficking and potential traffickees. These tools were developed by the researchers to gather information on victim profile, motivation, case process details, and behavioural data that was useful in identifying the causes and processes of trafficking. Three separate methods for the sourcing of participants was arranged to maximise interview numbers and to affect the in-sample breadth of victims/participants. The researchers noticed that there seemed to be reluctance on the part of respondents to share personal encounters of sexual harassment while abroad. All respondents, with the exception of prostitutes, referred to the stories as something that happened to 'their friend', to a 'known person', or as a 'common occurrence'. This may be due to the rapid nature of the research or cultural inhibitions, and may be something that requires more time and in-depth probing.

The research findings are organised under themes based on two main exploitative situations that render men and women in Sri Lanka vulnerable to trafficking: labour migration and commercial sex exploitation.

Trafficking of labour migrants

Many migrants from Sri Lanka leave home in search of a better life, often seeking new horizons in oil-rich Gulf countries. The study discovers ways in which this quest for a brighter future could in fact lead to misery at a destination where deceit and exploitation await. A significant number of Sri Lankan migrant workers, mostly from the female domestic labour category, suffered exploitative conditions that made them victims of trafficking. There are no formal statistics on the break down, but according to the Rural Development Foundation (RDF), an NGO in Puttalam, about 40 per cent of migrant workers do not face difficulties abroad (based on the experience of RDF). Of the remaining 60 per cent, a third find themselves directly at the mercy of traffickers, and the balance face problems not related to trafficking in the formal sense.[3]

Several parties are involved in connecting foreign employers in the Middle East with potential migrant workers in Sri Lanka. Who gets involved depends on the migrant's choice of channels, which usually include state agencies such as SLBFE, licensed recruitment agencies, as well as individuals and unlicensed agencies. For example, if a licensed agency is used, it would involve a foreign agent (for example in the Middle East) who would seek out or receive job orders from the employee, and a local agent who, through subagents, would recruit workers for the vacancy. This process can be pictorialised as follows.

It is clear that the worker is the most vulnerable party, which is why the overseeing function of the SLBFE and the embassies are important (Figure 13.1). The bureau, established under the SLBFE Act of 1985, is the main government arm to regulate the industry. The Sri Lankan embassies in the Middle East also play a part in compiling and vetting employer information and job requests in the foreign country. Last but not least, the Bandaranaike International Airport (BIA) performs the role of the final point of control and monitoring for the individuals at their time of departure. If any of the links above involve a fraud

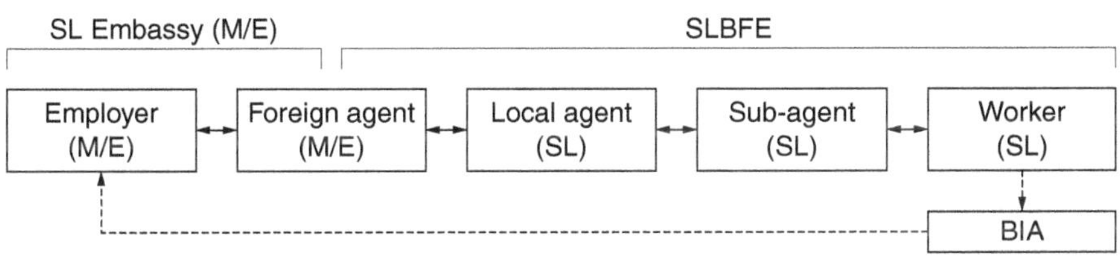

Figure 13.1 Connecting foreign employers.

leading to the breaking of contract, the vulnerability of workers, especially the females, will increase. This is because they have no political, financial, or human capital to protect them. Such vulnerabilities expose them to trafficking.

Most common frauds involve subagents who either break their contract with the worker, or their informal agreements with the local agent. However, it is not uncommon for the employer or the foreign agent to break their contracts as well. For example, the focus group with eight female workers in Puttalam underscored some of these issues: non-payment or delayed payment of salary, having to beg to be paid, payment of lower salaries than was contracted for, long working hours (e.g. 5.30 a.m. to midnight), mobility restrictions by withholding passports and communication restrictions by curtailing telephone use, inadequate food, threats and dangerous work (cleaning high windows). Similar information was obtained from in-depth interviews with three migrant workers in Galle. Therefore, the implementation of contractual work terms is a major issue that needs attention.

For its part, SLBFE made efforts to minimise the harm to, and to strengthen the position of, the overseas labour migrants by setting up various regulations. For instance, SLBFE inspects and approves all the job contracts that come through them. There are hotlines for workers to check on the legitimacy of the agents and the job, and the charge and commission rates. Workers have to come to Colombo or go to a district SLBFE office to sign the contract in the presence of an officer.

However, even if a person goes through the channels that SLBFE prescribes, there is no guarantee that he or she will be free of danger. For example, SLBFE reported incidences where workers were stranded after using its channels, which include the registered agencies (40 in Riyadh, and 11 in India).

There is also the case of victims being 'trapped' in the contract for three months. This is a three-month salary deduction to cover the agency commission, subagents' fee, costs of travel and a small advance to the worker. This is why the workers have to work for three months without salary. If they should leave their jobs during that period, they would need to return using personal funds. Agreements are also (sometimes) known to be in Arabic, while several governmental and non-governmental agencies have attempted to remedy the situation.

Causes

Primarily, it is a mix of economic factors that motivate men and women to seek employment outside Sri Lanka. These include a lack of suitable employment opportunities, economic necessity, poverty, and the search for a good life. Trincomalee in particular exhibited high levels of unemployment and poverty in the rural areas of the district. For instance, the 11 trafficked labour migrants that were interviewed had monthly incomes in the range of Rs.4,500 to Rs.10,000 before they decided to go abroad; four of them were unemployed. However, this study is more interested in why they were trafficked in the process of migration.

The primary and most obvious reason as to why labour trafficking occurs is that there is a great deal of money in it for the traffickers, and it is a fairly simple occupation requiring little financial and infrastructural inputs. Traffickers use legal foreign employment gaps to exploit the existing system. The benefits for the traffickers come in various forms, depending on which point they position themselves in the chain of transactions between employee and worker. If the trafficker is posing as an agent, then he or she will benefit from legal or illegal commissions and other monetary or in-kind benefits. If, on the other hand, the employer is the trafficker, then he or she will benefit by exploiting the worker (salary cuts, workload and poor work conditions).

The trafficking risk of migrant workers can be reduced if they have timely access to accurate information. However, they are known to rely mostly on informal sources of information (Transparency International Sri Lanka 2009). In the study sample, all informants relied on friends, relatives and return migrants, or subagents for their information. Interviews in Trincomalee also highlight another risky behaviour on the part of migrants: haste. Migrants are hasty in preparing for foreign jobs and, as a result, are ill-prepared for the venture due to the lack of crucial information. Those in Trincomalee have even less access to information than those in Puttalam and Galle. This is probably because they decide to look for overseas work when all else fails, leaving their household financial situation in poor shape. Often, they sell or mortgage their assets (such as land and jewellery) to finance their trip, increasing their vulnerability. It goes without saying that a significant portion of those who encountered problems had little knowledge of the legitimate labour-related migration process with its various safeguards and steps prior to their departure.

It was noted earlier that trafficking could befall a migrant worker without him or her ever leaving the country. These involve victims who are cheated and misled by any of the Sri Lanka-based parties involved. However, the fingers are usually pointed at the subagents. It is easy for a subagent to mislead migrants as they completely rely on the subagents for all aspects of their migration. Subagents are also known to employ strategies that strengthen this advantage. For example, in Puttalam and Trincomalee, the subagents recruit only a few from each village. This prevents communication and exchange of information between migrants. They will 'catch' the subjects in a web of psychological and financial pressure. The errant subagents always operate with mobile telephones that can be changed easily, or with wrong land telephone numbers.

A subagent would usually be a good talker, be very mobile, and would know the area well. This profile makes it very hard for the local agency to sufficiently monitor the subagents. There are cases where subagents cheat the local agency. Even with an SLBFE-approved legitimate job order, the subagent can cheat the main agent. The method includes pilfering the monies given to provide services to the migrant, charging illegal amounts from the migrant, etc. The flip side of this argument, according to interviews, is that the local agencies in fact use the subagents as a scapegoat and decidedly do not want the latter to be regulated.

According to the SLBFE, the hardest problem relating to trafficking is the breaking of contracts after the worker leaves Sri Lanka. The caveat is that trafficking occurs when subagents, registered agents, or employees break contracts, but not when the worker breaks them. The latter is not uncommon with Sri Lankan migrants. For instance, SLBFE reports that there are about 40,000 Sri Lankans working in Afghanistan and Iraq – both banned countries. Men in the South reach these countries by first going to Dubai, and then to Afghanistan and Iraq. Charges for these banned work opportunists are in the range of Rs.250,000 to Rs.300,000 per job. It is not clear whether these men consented or were exploited in these countries. What is clear from this example, however, is that there is only a very thin line between trafficking and a breach of contract by a worker.

As previously discussed, there is a system in the Middle East where the staff is 'owned' by the employer after signing the documents, meaning that the labourer is completely under the control of the employer. This is strengthened by the fact that the employer already paid US$2,000 as deposit, and the workers are expected to work with no salary for three months till the deposit is paid off. It is said that until this period lapses, there is very little that Sri Lankan embassies can or will do to protect the worker. If or when problems arise, the foreign agent will try to switch workers so that the employer has a worker and the worker a master. If this fails completely, then the migrant is put in a safe house and gets sent back to Sri Lanka. The agent is not liable to compensate the worker.

Some of the victim migrants interviewed hold the opinion that Sri Lankan embassies in the Middle East intervene in migrant problems in a weak manner that opens up opportunities for trafficking. For instance, Sri Lankan embassy officials, along with foreign agencies, will put the troubled worker to various other places and not follow up on his or her condition. Victims interviewed compared this with strong and forceful action on the part of embassies of the Philippines or Nepal, to bring redress to their citizens facing trafficking-related issues. Here, the capabilities of Sri Lankan embassies to manage the task are highly questionable, either because of the volume of cases, or the skills and commitment of the staff.

In addition to migrant labour trafficking, domestic labour trafficking is also common in Sri Lanka (internal labour trafficking). It is common to see 'servants' being employed at the household level in Sri Lanka. They are usually in exploitative work situations that are socially accepted and widely practised throughout the island and in Southeast Asia. There is usually no contract between the two parties; there are no specific laws for their protection (no minimum wages or guidelines) and they often face verbal, even physical abuse, low wages and long working hours. One of the interviewees from the National Workers Congress (NWC), an NGO, pointed out that human trafficking only brings this household-level practice out into the open, and raises its operational level of intensity. With a culture of servants taking place, the bridge to domestic trafficking is much shorter and convenient for the would-be trafficker.

The following cases examine victim experiences to highlight the causes of labour trafficking as outlined above. The reader can note the diversity of their experiences and the difficult circumstances faced by these victims. The reported ambiguities and challenges with regards to the trafficking definition (where incidents require the act, means, and purpose conditionality) from an operational approach are also evident.

Case study 1

Sanjeewa was a shopkeeper in Galle who earned about Rs.15,000 a month. In 2006, he was approached by a friend and a subagent about a job in Italy. The cleaning job on contract for a company would pay Rs.150,000 per month for two years and the agent would provide the visa and ticket. In return, he would pay Rs.550,000 in two equal instalments. When he paid the first advance, he was taken to an agency office in Dehiwala where he enlisted in a short training programme. Sanjeewa arrived at the BIA with five similar members in his group. They were stopped by customs in Italy for possessing false visas and were sent back. Upon return, he found out that the agency in Dehiwala had closed up. He managed to track the subagent down and recover his money. Sanjeewa lodged a complaint at the BIA but did not report it to the police in Galle. He still works as a shopkeeper and earns around Rs.20,000 a month. He would still like to go abroad to increase his income, but will be more careful in the next instance.

Case study 2

Piyawathi made a living out of preparing rice packets, earning an income of Rs.7,000 to Rs.10,000 a month. She had made inquiries about jobs abroad and was approached by a subagent who offered employment in Saudi. The housework job for a small family would pay Rs.13,000 for a period of two years. In return, the agent would provide the visa, ticket and passport. Once she made a small advance payment, she was taken to an agency office in Dehiwala for a briefing. She was not given a contract. She ended up working for three families and two other persons in Saudi. She was allowed to leave after three months due to her complaints, and the employer provided her the return ticket. However, she received no salary for this period. She did not lodge a complaint or search for the agent and feels it is better to do something in Sri Lanka. She currently earns about Rs.18,000 from her food parcelling business.

Case study 3

Dayawathi did not have much work and sold peanuts occasionally. She wanted to go abroad to earn some money as she was building a small house. Her brother in Colombo informed her about an actress who was managing a reputed agency providing jobs. She was impressed by the big office in Colombo and immediately agreed to be a housemaid for a family of ten in Bahrain. She did not ask about the salary or the length of the employment. There was also no contract. The agency supplied her ticket and visa and provided some self-defence and other training. In Bahrain, Dayawathi had to look after an extended family of more than 30 people. She ran away after a month when they refused to increase her salary. Representatives of the agency brought her back to Colombo. The company then sent her to Singapore where she had to care of a sick and mentally unstable man. She was not comfortable with the job and returned after three weeks. She received no salary and did not lodge any complaints. Dayawathi is not interested in going abroad again and currently makes paper bags for packing, earning Rs.3,000 a month.

Trafficking for commercial sex work

Generally, victims being trafficked for commercial sex work is less prevalent in Sri Lanka as compared to labour trafficking. However, the violations of human rights and freedoms that result from it are often different and more horrific. Female, male and child sex trafficking is prevalent in the country. This section of the study focuses on the first two categories.

It might be important to revisit the definition of trafficking here, because quite a number of sex workers in the country are consensual workers. UNAIDS for instance, believes that only about 20 per cent of those in the sex trade are trafficked, and the rest have not been tricked into it. For example, officers at the Women and Children's desk in Puttalam confirmed that the police usually looks at consent in a trafficking case and takes the victim to a hospital for an examination and compilation of medical evidence. In the case of consensual sex workers who are rounded up, after producing them to the courts, the prison authorities (not the hospital) do the medical examination, and they are then released after a small fine (Rs.100 up to Rs.3,000; the latter is rare). Such a fine fails to pose as a deterrent for sex workers as it could be covered in one day's work. If they are unable to pay the fine, they are remanded for three months.

There are, however, extreme sex trafficking issues or cases in Sri Lanka: Anuradhapura has figured as a high-risk locality as there are a significant number of war widows who are vulnerable to trafficking because of poverty. Also, the high incidence of consensual sex in the form of (i) commercial sex (about 35,000 workers) with clear transactions in terms of the services provided and moneys exchanged, and (ii) undocumented numbers of transactional sex for non-monetary considerations, which are troubling. It is worrying because the case histories of some who were interviewed suggest that transgression from consensual sex to trafficking and vice versa are not uncommon in Sri Lanka. For this reason, this study also looked at some of these consensual sex workers to better understand the motives, networks, and finances. Moreover, many of them had undergone incidents when they were young (incest, molestation and rape by family and outsiders), making them victims of circumstantial trafficking.

Many sex-related offences, including trafficking, go unreported because of cultural and religious factors. The desire to avoid community and family problems and social stigma are also reasons. For instance, Galle police only reported two cases of sex trafficking for the whole of 2010, while our interviews revealed that there is a significant level of sex trade activity in the area. A similar state of affairs was reported by Puttalam police in relation to the internally displaced persons camps in the district. Rarely do the police get complaints from the residents of the IDP camps, though many sex-related offences are known to take place. Because the victims are scared to express themselves, attempts are made to resolve the issues internally, and they therefore do not surface.

The prominent sex worker outlets include brothels, hotels, lodges, massage parlours, karaoke bars, homes, and even vehicles. Apart from instances where underage girls are employed in these, most of these locations, according to second-hand information, are not likely to traffic women for sex work. The employees themselves know exactly what they are getting into. For instance, there are advertisements for massage parlours and karaoke bars in newspapers.

Male sex workers are a much more hidden group as compared to females, and their numbers are low. Galle is known for MSM (men who have sex with men)[4] activity and its services of male guides and beach boys. Though they suffer human rights violations, they are not known to make complaints against such practices (Police, Galle). Male guides and beach boys provide services such as tours, hotel bookings, business, girls, boys, drugs, and even themselves, mostly to foreigners. They do it for money (including commissions from purchases made by the foreigner), for gifts, or to get a chance to go to Europe. There are demarcated territories for guides (some operate in the Galle railway station, in the Galle fort, on the beach, etc.) and there are local networks and groups. There are unwritten agreements that UNAIDS described as part of a subculture. Hotel waiters can also be bought; when that happens there are conflicts between the waiters and beach boys. The client usually buys the waiter in subtle ways (room delivery, body language, informal offer and acceptance, lucrative financial transactions in dollars).

There were nine sex workers (eight females and one male) interviewed at length for this research; five of them in Puttalam, and four in Galle. Their responses with regard to how they entered sex work are summarised in Table 13.2. Their reasons for entering the sex trade include high levels of poverty, lack of support from family (either parents, or husband), social marginalisation, sexual abuse and drug addiction. Though these were cases of the individual's own drug addiction, a separate incident was mentioned to us where an addicted mother forced her daughters into sex work to find money for drugs (Police, Puttalam). The reverse, where addicted children push reluctant mothers into sex work, is also occurring. The 'How' column in Table 13.2 suggests that three out of the nine cases were clear cases of trafficking: a 30-year-old male, a 32-year-old female, and a 28-year-old female. Others indicate elements of consent under trying circumstances. The cases also show the operation of a diverse network of friends and acquaintances that introduced these persons to the trade.

Family disputes, even domestic violence, make females vulnerable to sex trafficking. The researchers were told of an incident where a woman confided in the driver of a three-wheel taxi after an argument with her husband. The driver raped her and sold her to a brothel where she was kept for a few months. After

Table 13.2 Sex worker experiences

Age now (sex)	*Age first incident*	*Why*	*Who initiated first experience*	*How*	*Where*	*Finances*
40 (F)	20	Needed drugs	Navy person	Offered money for sex	Hotel in Unawatuna	Rs.1,000/short time
31 (F)	18	No family/poor	3-wheel driver	I offered sex	Small lodge	Rs.1,000/short time
22 (F)	21	Addicted to drugs/poor	Navy person	Sex for money	Victim's house	Rs.2,500/short time
30 (M)	28	Was initially raped, then later mental comfort and livelihood security provided in exchange for sex	Known person	Was tricked into staying the night	In perpetrator's house	No payments
30 (F)	20	No husband/poor	Women in village	Offered me job	Brothel	Rs.5,000 per month with food/room
49 (F)	17	No parents/raped by stepfather at 16	Another female patient at hospital	Offered a job with food/lodging	Brothel	Rs.2,000/less than 1 hour
29 (F)	18	Husband ill-treating/drunkard	Friend introduced me to man	Sex for money	Victim's house	Rs.500/short time
32 (F)	22	No husband/poor	Boyfriend's friend	Was locked in room	Hotel	Rs.300/short time
28 (F)	26	Husband left/no job/poor	Girlfriend	Forcibly kept	Guest house	Rs.200 with tip

being rescued, she was given counselling, but attempted suicide later and her marriage broke up. Discussions with UNFPA officials revealed an interesting insight when it came to examining the case histories of sex workers. According to them, an allowance must be made to 'the stage' the individual is in in their sex work occupation (recently joined industry – accepting their circumstance – happy and lucrative stage – slowing down/marriage/children – in retirement). This is because the distance to events and their memories would influence the person's responses as to whether or not he or she was trafficked. Conscious about this, we crosschecked most information provided by victims. However, it is difficult to gather wholly accurate information from these individuals unless a substantial amount of time is spent earning their trust and confidence. This was a challenge we encountered due to the rapid nature of the research.

Female-headed families in the country have reached epic proportions in recent times. Quoting the social services minister, the *Daily Mirror* (16/10/2010) reported that 23 per cent of the families in Sri Lanka are single-parent families. These are a particularly vulnerable group prone to trafficking. The reasons for single parenthood in the country include war widowing, divorce and separation. The report added that the worst affected province is the North.

Another important cause of sex trafficking involves labour migration. For instance, the interviews in Puttalam revealed that sex traffickers use foreign employment as bait, where women who had been promised foreign jobs were later forced into prostitution (RDF, Puttalam). Rural women who are brought to Colombo in the guise of various migration-related official matters (obtaining a passport, leaving the country, etc.) are given various excuses and put up in lodges. Once separated from their homes and villages, these women are extremely vulnerable to molestation and rape. Victims of such abuse are often subjected to forced prostitution. There is some evidence that the practice has been stepped up with 'easy victims' in the newly opened up North and East.

There is another group of migration-related sex trafficking victims who, instead of being exploited locally, are being pushed to prostitution abroad. This happens primarily in East Asian destinations such as Singapore. However, our sample did not have such victims. Causes of this form of international sex trafficking may be similar to the causes previously outlined in relation to labour trafficking.

As victims of sex trafficking and consensual sex workers share commonalities, we believe that studying either would help us understand the other. The proliferation of sex work seems to be gathering momentum in Puttalam and Galle. At least in these two districts, a higher level of promiscuity and social acceptance of the practice are the alleged reasons for this trend. For example, there are known cases where husbands or boyfriends, parents and children support, or even force these individuals into the sex trade. Having extramarital affairs when working abroad, having multiple affairs as teenagers and young adults, and greater sexual activity between young lovers reveal this trend. The lower social stigma is supported by the upward trend in sex worker incomes in recent times.

In contrast, these trends are not visible in Trincomalee. Triangulated interviews suggest that sex at a commercial level is currently an infant industry (there are a few street prostitutes in Trincomalee town). Currently, no beach boys, brothels and massage parlours are found there. UNICEF, however, had information that tourism-related prostitution is emerging in the Nilawali and Kutchiwali areas of Trincomalee. It was interesting to note that the conservative community in Trincomalee, in comparison to areas such as Galle and Puttalam, saw promiscuity as a form of prostitution. This was a case in point where widows and women who had returned from the Middle East were having sexual relations with multiple partners, including members of the security forces. If this is a case of subtle trafficking by way of coercion by individuals, it has yet to be discovered.

The following case studies are useful in illustrating the intricate ways that various causes impact the lives of sex workers.

Case study 1

X is a 22-year-old girl from Galle. Her girlfriend who worked for an NGO introduced her to drugs two years ago. She then got addicted and required about Rs.1,000 worth of drugs a day. Her husband's income supported her addiction, but when the army arrested him for desertion, she had no other means for living or drugs. A known prostitute brought a man from the navy to her place and he paid Rs.2,500 for sex. She then continued the occupation and earned up to Rs.10,000 a day or Rs.200,000 a month from numerous clients from all over. As her husband has returned home, she is no longer able to sell sex due to his disapproval. They now sell fruit outside the Galle fort for a living. X does not want to return to the sex trade but is willing to go with other men if her husband becomes absent to finance her drug problem.

Case study 2

X is a young man from Panadura who now resides in Galle. Two years ago while staying at another male friend's house in Kadawatha, his friend raped him at night. He stayed with the man for one year, as the person offered him lodging and other comforts in exchange for regular sex. He later came to Galle to work as a clerk in a hotel school. Since then, he has been involved with men and sleeps with them for money. He earns up to Rs.10,000 a month from prostitution as a second occupation. He keeps his affairs private and his clients are mostly from outside towns such as Matara, Nuwara Eliya, Badulla and Kandy. He saves a little money every month and would like to build a house one day to get married and settle down. X feels if he gets a better paying job and has self-control, he will be able to give up his current practice.

Case study 3

X is a 30-year-old woman from Kurunegala now living in Puttalam. Her first husband with whom she had two children died, and the second left her. While in desperation, a woman in the village offered her a job in a garment factory. She was taken by bus and then by a three-wheeler to a hotel. There, she was sold to various men and paid Rs.5,000 a month with food and lodging. She worked at the hotel for four years, and eventually left freely, as the hotel had by then earned a substantial amount by selling her. She then commenced the occupation independently, earning up to Rs.30,000 a month. However, now that her children are grown up and they disapprove of it, she has reduced her business, earning a quarter of the previous amount. X would like to have decent work and have a happy marriage and family, and is presently making plans to leave for Saudi to work as a domestic servant.

Conclusions

Migration has been beneficial for migrants as well as Sri Lanka's economy. However, due to trafficking, many migrants and aspiring migrants are unable to get the full benefit of migration, as revealed in the analysis. This study looked at the causes and consequences of trafficking among labour migrants and commercial sex workers. The overall findings from the study indicate a strong correlation between poverty and a lack of opportunity, and some of the main types of human trafficking in Sri Lanka. Victims fall into trafficking through a series of occurrences over a period of time, chiefly related to a lack of economic opportunities and awareness. Trafficked individuals transit to their helpless status over a prolonged period of time, undergoing a rash of distressing situations. The benefits they secure are also highly complex when considering the sacrifices made, opportunities that were forgone, and dangers encountered. Victims usually get trafficked due to reasons that include a lack of suitable employment opportunities, poverty, economic necessity, and even the search for a good life. Migrants and aspiring migrants can get trafficked during any point of the migration process, such as at the point of recruitment, while en route, or at destinations. The hasty behaviour of migrants to earn lucrative incomes, without sufficiently verifying the costs, benefits and risks, is an impediment to control trafficking. Due to these conducts, they fall further into debt and financial problems, making their situation even more vulnerable. The separation between consent and exploitation is also grey, and victims normally give their consent without knowing they are going to be trafficked. These are compounded by structural weaknesses that see the state and agencies unable to facilitate and provide safe and legal passages.

Those trafficked for sex work are smaller in number than those trafficked for labour in Sri Lanka. Certain locations are known to be more prone to sex trafficking than others due to various reasons, such as war and tourism. This study found that factors such as family disputes, domestic violence, and single parenthood make women vulnerable to sex trafficking. Further, foreign and/or local employment has been used as bait for labour trafficking, and subsequently sex trafficking. Tourism is known to bring about trafficking risks, spreading from the south to the former war zones. Studying sex workers is also not easy due to the complex nature of the occupation, and the transgressions that take place between consensual sex and trafficking and vice versa.

The relevant authorities involved with labour migration should bring in regulations to monitor subagents and their activities. Similar to registered agencies, they should penalise these agents or the agencies that are affiliated with them. A comprehensive information management system is worth installing, connecting all the nodes in the migrant's departure, with a blacklist of offending recruiters and employers. Further, a multi-medium awareness and information campaign on the migratory process, benefits and potential risks will be beneficial in educating the masses. On the commercial sex trafficking front, care-giving, law enforcement, health, and legal apparatuses must all be strengthened to support these individuals and to raise their confidence. Poverty and disempowerment remain at the core of the problem, so it is imperative that vulnerable groups are identified, and income-generating programmes launched for them. On a similar note, vocational training and employment opportunities should be expanded for middle-class and lower middle-class youth to enhance the choices available to them.

Acknowledgements

The research was funded by the International Labour Organization (ILO) office in Sri Lanka. The researchers are thankful to Ms. Chandrika Karunaratne for supporting the study and Ms. Nishadi Liyanage for research assistance.

Notes

1 *International:* UN Slavery Convention (1926), Forced Labour Convention of the International Labour Organization (1930), UN Convention for the Suppression of the Traffic in Persons and of the Exploitation of the Prostitution of Others (1949), UN Supplementary Convention of the Abolition of Slavery, the Slave Trade and Institutions of Practices Similar to Slavery (1956), International Covenant on Civil and Political Rights (1966), UN Convention on Elimination of All Forms of Discrimination Against Women (1979), UN Convention on the Protection of the Rights of All Migrant Workers and Members of Thiers Families (1991).
Regional: Bangkok Accord and Plan of Action (1998), SAARC Convention of Protecting and Combating Trafficking in woman and Children for Prostitution (2002)

2 This was not purposely done but was a result of the fact that only a smaller population of migrants was trafficked to other destinations.

3 Trafficking in Persons (TIP) (2010) citing an NGO says

> a survey in mid-2009 found that 48 per cent of returned Sri Lankan domestic workers were assaulted by a member of their employers' household, 52 per cent were not paid the salary promised to them, and 84 per cent were not paid for their overtime work, abuses that may indicate forced labor.

4 MSM includes social identities of gay and bisexual men.

References

Blitz, B.K. and M. Lynch. 2011. *Statelessness and Citizenship: A Comparative Study on the Benefits of Nationality*. London: Edward Elgar Publishing.

Carling, J.R. 2002. Migration in the Age of Involuntary Immobility: Theoretical Reflections and Cape Verdean Experiences. *Journal of Ethnic and Migration Studies* 28(1): 5–42.

Central Bank of Sri Lanka. 2013. *Annual Report 2012*, Colombo: Central Bank of Sri Lanka.

Chawla, R. 2009. *Study of Most-at-Risk Populations in Sri Lanka*, UNFPA.

Coomaraswamy, R. and A. Satkunanathan. 2006. *Anti-Child Trafficking Legislation in Asia: a Six-Country Review (Bangladesh, Nepal, Pakistan, Sri Lanka, Thailand and Indonesia)*. Bangkok, Thailand: International Labour Office.

Das, D.K. 2009. *Two Faces of Globalization: Munificent and Malevolent*. Cheltenham and Camberley: Edward Elgar Publishing.

De Haas, H. 2005. International Migration, Remittances and Development: Myths and Facts. *Third World Quarterly* 26(8): 1269–1284.

De Haas, H. 2009. Mobility and Human Development. IMI Working Paper 14.

Frederick, J. 2010. Sexual Abuse and Exploitation of Boys in South Asia a Review of Research Findings, Legislation, Policy and Programme Responses. UNICEF, Innocenti Working Paper IWP-2010–02.

Human Development Report. 2010. *The Real Wealth of Nations: Pathways to Human Development*. New York: United Nations Development Programme.

International Labour Organization. 2005. *Tools for Prevention: Participatory Monitoring – Guidelines for Practitioners in the Fight against Human Trafficking.*

International Labour Organization and EC. 2009. *Operational Indicators of Trafficking in Human Beings, Results from the Delphi Survey.*

International Labour Organization and US Department of State. 2010. *Trafficking in Persons, Smuggling, and Forced Labour – an Introduction to the Legal and Normative Framework.*

Jayatilaka, D. 2010. *Research Study on Human Smuggling in Sri Lanka: Windows for Intervention by the International Organization for Migration (IOM).*

Kapiszewski, A. 2006. Arab versus Asian Migrant Workers in the GCC Countries, United Nations Expert Group Meeting on International Migration and Development in the Arab Region. United Nations Population Division, Department of Economic and Social Affairs, United Nations Secretariat, Beirut, 15–17 May 2006. Document number UN/POP/EGM/2006/02, published 22 May 2006.

Karunaratne, C. 2010a. Existing Legislation on Trafficking in Persons in Sri Lanka, Presentation, International Labour Organization, 31 March.

Karunaratne, C. 2010b. Stakeholder Consultation on the Existing Legislation on Trafficking in Persons. Ministry of Justice and Law Reforms and International Labour Organization.

Pearson, E., S. Punpuing, A. Jampaklay, S. Kittisuksathit and A. Prohmmo. 2006. *The Mekong Challenge: Underpaid, Overworked, and Overlooked: The Realities of Young Migrant Workers in Thailand*, International Labour Organization.

Penal Code Amendment Act No. 16. 2006.

Perera, M. and M. Gunatilaka. 2004. *Study of Female Trafficking in Sri Lanka*, Colombo: Marga.

Ranaraja, S. 2010. *Review of National Legislation and Regulations on Migration for Foreign Employment and Their Implementation*, Colombo: International Labour Organization.

Salt, J. and J. Stein. 1997. Migration as a Business: the Case of Trafficking. *International Migration* 35(4): 467–494.

Samaranayake, S. 2010. *Sri Lanka and Human Trafficking: Professional's Handbook* [Working Draft].

SLBFE. 2009. Annual Statistical Report for Foreign Employment.

South Asia Partnership International. 2003. A Situational Analysis of Child Sex Tourism in Sri Lanka (Negombo, Colombo, Mt. Lavinia, Hikkaduwa, Galle, Anuradhapura and Trincomalee). Online, available at: www.childtrafficking.com/Docs/ecpat_south_asia_partnershi.pdf (accessed 10 October 2010).

Sriskandarajah, D. 2005. Migration and Development, Global Commission on International Migration (GCIM). Online, available at: http://iom.ch/jahia/webdav/site/myjahiasite/shared/shared/mainsite/policy_and_research/gcim/tp/TP4.pdf (accessed 30 August 2013).

Squire, J. and S. Wijeratne. 2008. The Sexual Abuse, Commercial Sexual Exploitation and Trafficking of Children in Sri Lanka, Colombo: SAPSRI and Swiss Solidarity.

Transparency International Sri Lanka. 2009. *Integrity in Foreign Employment: An Analysis of Corruption Risks in Recruitment.*

United Nations, Department of Economic and Social Affairs, Population Division. 2009. *Trends in International Migrant Stock: the 2008 Revision* (United Nations database, POP/DB/MIG/Stock/Rev.2008).

UNDP. 2008. *HIV Vulnerabilities of Migrant Women: From Asia to the Arab States.* Colombo, Sri Lanka: UNDP Regional Centre in Colombo.

UNDP. 2010. Multidimensional Poverty Index. Online, available at: http://hdr.undp.org/en/reports/global/hdr2010/mpi/ (accessed 10 October 2010).

US Department of State. 2010. Trafficking in Persons Report 2010. Online, available at: www.state.gov/g/tip/rls/tiprpt/2010/ (accessed 10 October 2010).

US Department of State. 2010. Trafficking in Persons Report 2013. Online, available at: www.state.gov/j/tip/rls/tiprpt/2013/210551.htm (accessed 29 August 2013)

World Bank. 2011. *Migration and Remittances Factbook 2011*, Washington, DC: World Bank, pp. 31–32. Online, available at: http://siteresources.worldbank.org/INTLAC/Resources/Factbook2011-Ebook.pdf.

Index

Page numbers in *italics* denote tables, those in **bold** denote figures.

For Product Safety Concerns and Information please contact our EU representative GPSR@taylorandfrancis.com
Taylor & Francis Verlag GmbH, Kaufingerstraße 24, 80331 München, Germany

www.ingramcontent.com/pod-product-compliance
Ingram Content Group UK Ltd.
Pitfield, Milton Keynes, MK11 3LW, UK
UKHW010959180926
475701UK00004B/455
* 9 7 8 0 8 1 5 3 6 8 0 1 4 *